Regions of Memory

Uncollected Prose, 1949–82

W. S. Merwin

Edited and with
an Introduction by
Ed Folsom and Cary Nelson

T0123916

University of Illinois Press

URBANA AND CHICAGO

LIBRARY OF CONGRESS CATALOGING-IN-PUBLICATION DATA

Merwin, W. S. (William Stanley), 1927–
Regions of memory.

I. Folsom, Ed, 1947–   II. Nelson, Cary.
III. Title.
PS3563.E75R4 1987 818'.5408 86-1358
ISBN 0-252-01241-0 (alk. paper)

Contents

Preface

W. S. Merwin falls into a tradition of American writers who, while they are thought of and called "poets," are active in several genres and whose prose works rival their poetry for quality of achievement. For that reason, we have not merely assembled a typical volume of poet's prose—interviews and statements on poetics—though we do include such work, but have rather emphasized uncollected works of intrinsic quality that did not fit appropriately into Merwin's other volumes of prose. In addition to selections from Merwin's previously published but uncollected prose, we have published two pieces for the first time, "A Recollection of Stones," events from which are told in a different way in Merwin's "Foie Gras" (1984), and "Milton: A Revisitation," both identified from the W. S. Merwin archive at the University of Illinois. A complete list of Merwin's uncollected prose is included in Cary Nelson and Ed Folsom, eds., *W. S. Merwin: Essays on the Poetry,* also published by the University of Illinois Press.

Introduction

by Cary Nelson and Ed Folsom

In the later hours of the day the morning is hard to recall. That first age of daylight, moving in its own time, cool, dewy, spacious, new, and already ancient like all beginnings—no sooner has it left than it seems improbable that it was ever there, that it happened once, that it was not only present but was the present and was everything. Trying to summon it again, to lay claim to it, we recognize how far from it we have come and how we have changed. We look at the surviving representations of it that were made, supposedly, from the life, when it was alive, and we find ourselves studying cracked carvings in stone, rags of tapestries, words in idioms no longer spoken and in conventions remote from ours. Between us and that fresh moment we encounter relics, fragments, shards of fact perpetuating distance, dust, and dust under it, and among all those we catch glimpses occasionally that appear to be revelations of ourselves, as we are now, in our only time.

Merwin's subject above is ostensibly the translations collected in *From the Spanish Morning,* but his language, as often happens with his critical prose, echoes throughout the rest of his work. His metaphors are those of simultaneous proximity and distance, presence and absence, the eerie irresolution of historical knowledge. "The subject of history," he writes in the foreword to *Four French Plays,* published at the same time, "is always out of reach, or seems to be. Apparently that is a condition of history." The uneasy relations between presence and absence, some would argue, are the dialectical conditions of Western metaphor. If so, then Merwin's project can be said to be that of bringing these figures so close together as to make them reversible or inseparable, so that we find the very "shards of fact perpetuating distance."

Consider, as a model of Merwin's sense of specified absence, the photograph of an old house with a distant, bearded figure on the porch that appears on the cover of *Unframed Originals.* The image hovers like a palpable presence through all these autobiographical reminiscences, but it is never directly discussed or even mentioned in *Unframed Originals.* Later, though, in a book of poems, *Opening the Hand,* the photograph appears in words, the bearded figure on the porch becoming explicitly the "Unknown Forbear." This unknown ancestor in a faded photograph is a manifest image of visualized silence, of clearly present absence, that is at the heart of Merwin's poetry and prose: the specified absence that his words move toward, the silence that all myth and story eventually come to and talk around.

Passages evoking this collision of objects with emptiness, presence with absence, abound in this collection. Consider the image of "the depths of that forest of black light" from "Campbell," the expectation "that the wintry sun would fill all the slopes with a colorless windless shining until night" in "Return to the Mountains," this passage from "The Museum"—"I went downstairs and out onto the platform. It was as though the trains had never been there. I could hear the rust forming on the rails and the grass beginning to grow up among them"—or Merwin's observation about one of the monks he meets on Athos in "Aspects of a Mountain": "His attention was mine, but almost all of his life was elsewhere." Moments like these will be pleasurable but not perhaps surprising to Merwin's readers. Consider, however, the stunning conclusion to "A Recollection of Stones," which hints of a more devastating presence—the memories of a mass slaughter of innocents, and which implicitly asks what it would mean to take possession of, to claim as one's own, a building which was once the site of terrible cruelty. The question may remain unanswered because we take possession of this structure, calling it history, every day.

Other effects of a diverse collection like this one will also be unexpected. Among the first discoveries here is how the pervasiveness of such moments undermines the generic stability of Merwin's prose. In the following passages, the first from a story and the second from an essay, the line between fiction and autobiography is impossible to fix:

> We began to go around a bend, and as we did, the mountain directly across from us came into sight. It was a view of it such as I had never had before, and none of the glimpses of it from the valley or from other slopes would have led me to suspect what the whole of it was like.

Then, without warning, a sudden presence, off to the right, across a great empty space: the first view of the mountain. Once it has been seen, the sense of it remains wherever one goes on the promontory, whether or not the peak itself is visible.

Such generic instability becomes pervasive here. Thus a story like "Return to the Mountains" is fascinating in part because it combines the haunting and distant quality of many of the pieces in *The Miner's Pale Children* and *Houses and Travellers* with the more discursive, autobiographical qualities of *Unframed Originals*. The story in fact reads as if it were autobiographical right up through the strange fog-immersed night in the mountains when the narrator emerges at a house of death. On the other hand, there are very few decisively autobiographical markers in "A Recollection of Stones," a travel essay as haunting and uncanny as any of Merwin's fiction. In the end, it is not only generic distinctions that are undermined here but also our whole construction of the relation between the self and writing, a construction that generic distinctions are partly designed to maintain.

What is also evident, both here and elsewhere, is how closely vertiginous experience in Merwin's extended prose is linked to the most meticulous physical observation and description. "Aspects of a Mountain," the longest essay in the book and one of Merwin's most elegant and accomplished pieces of writing, begins with an improbable comparison between Venice and the Greek mountain of Athos: "Neither of them belongs to our century, yet both provide the transient with that sense that is clearly shared by all periods but that seems characteristic of our time and its furnishings: a vertiginous touch, the feeling of stepping-stones sinking under the feet they help to cross." The exact registering of each step in a journey is a repeated technique here, both in the fiction and the essays. "The Academy," in fact, opens with a journey over crumbling bridges, invoking a physical world whose unsteady surfaces mask consuming depths.

In "Aspects of a Mountain" the journey proceeds by a regular rhythm. Highly accurate descriptions of nature—"Flurries of cyclamens, jays diving through the trees with light folded in their wings"—alternate with descriptions of the monasteries Merwin visits and the people he meets there. The natural detail, often offered in sentence fragments, is both crafted and minimalist. All the while, Merwin himself is ironically observant and unobtrusively self-aware. Even when his subject is not himself, the arrangement of objects, scenes, people, and time evokes a sensibility that defines the self and its memories, its commitments and ironies: "There is a rule against riding down the main street, and the monks dismount and lead their horses and mules over the big, worn cobbles. The rule does not seem to apply to the Greek police jeeps—no doubt a jeep is harder to lead. That vehicle had roared past me as I climbed down from the sea, driven by a young man ostentatiously in tune with his uniform, his face, and the station in life to which he had risen: the James Bond of Daphne." But this is near the opening of the essay. As it proceeds, the narrative movement draws us away from the contemporary world—through centuries-old monasteries toward equally old meditative practices. We seem to be moving not only into the past but also into timeless and eternal versions of consciousness. Fascinated with distance and with meditative knowledge, often himself choosing to live far from the metropolitan centers that include most of his readers, Merwin is nonetheless never far at all from an awareness of history. Indeed, near the mountain's heights and near the end of the essay one of the monks tries to get the BBC news on the radio. A war is in progress in the Middle East, and the monk indulges in an anti-Semitic lecture. At the outer reaches of metaphysics, history at its worst returns again.

Of course history as ruin and loss, especially since *The Lice,* has been widely recognized as one of Merwin's central preoccupations. Some readers will also be aware that Merwin has regularly written political and historical essays over the years, but few will know all the essays gathered here. Moreover, this book highlights the consistency of Merwin's commitments. He has been writing about ecology, for example, since the 1950s, and from the start he linked human and natural survival, seeing the potential nuclear destruction of the planet as spiritually of a piece with our elimination of natural habitats and animal species. Indeed, the same political sensibilities—a sensitivity to intellectual arrogance, a rejection of our generalized cultural imperialism, and a concern for the survival of life in all its diversity—enter into his comments on translation. Thus, in the selection from "A Sight of the Bright Life" that opens the section on translation, he writes that translations from Third World literatures should be read uneasily, for they offer us "representations in languages brought from Europe by the same conquest that overran the American natives." As the revised and expanded version of our interview with Merwin shows, these commitments are coming together with special intensity in the political, historical, and ecological prose he is now writing about Hawaii.

Merwin has also regularly felt it necessary to mark his distance from institutional occasions designed to hide their political and historical specificity. He has not sought to be visibly associated with public institutions, but when he has been asked to participate in ceremonial events he has done so on his own terms. In so doing, he has sometimes earned the anger of his peers, but his acts, to our minds, show both his sense of individual responsibility and his deeper understanding of how a culture's different institutions are mutually implicated in their historical moment. The first time he took such a stand may, in fact, have been at his 1947 Princeton graduation where, as "Senior Poet," he felt it essential to speak, not of the bright promise for the graduates, but of those who had died in the war. The most notorious of his public stands is, no doubt, his statement on receiving the Pulitzer Prize for poetry in 1971. We have reprinted it, along with W. H. Auden's letter to the *New York Review of Books* and Merwin's reply. We have also reprinted his longer statement, "On Being Loyal," which explains why he refused to sign a loyalty oath before giving a reading in 1970.

Merwin's two most accomplished political essays, "Letter from Aldermaston" and "Act of Conscience," are less well known. Both involve us again at once in Merwin's political commitments and in his skill at effective description and ironic commentary. Now nearly twenty-five years old, "Act of Conscience" will seem hardly dated at all, not only because concern about nuclear weapons is once again heightened but also because the rhetorical struggles over nonviolent civil disobedience in America reproduce themselves with uncanny precision decade after decade. In effect, twenty-five years of accumulated stories of civil disobedience, war protests, and nuclear disarmament debate have energized rather than deadened Merwin's telling of the *Everyman* story, a story that questions whether, in human history, "It's too late for an act of conscience, any act of conscience, to be effective any longer." Part of what has kept this essay vital, moreover, is Merwin's skill at describing the diverse courage and folly of the people involved in the different sides of this drama. Yet sometimes his irony, while evocative and concise, acquires an aggressive edge, as when he describes those who scorn the protestors: "Ladies in crisp hats and men with ventilated shoes and little identities in their lapels picked their way past to collect mail." At other points, he struggles for a precise morality of description, working to distinguish between the very different government representatives.

In a curious way, "Act of Conscience" blends a deep concern for historical specificity with a sense of the recurring, mythic qualities in daily events. Merwin's very sensitivity toward signs and images—from his account of the naming of the boat to his version of the semiotics of the peace sign—leads him to read the whole series of events as a dark historical reenactment of the morality play, *Everyman,* as death comes to claim us all. At the same time, he makes the artifice of these self-consciously *literary* connections apparent, so that we are left uneasily to ourselves to decide how seriously to take his evocations of demonic recurrence. Indeed, the special power of the element of mythological parable in "Act of Conscience" is dependent precisely on Merwin's willingness to veer close to a style of simple reportage, so that we see the visible world transform itself as we read.

Some of Merwin's skill at description probably comes from the fact that he has often chosen to be a distant observer of his own country, a vantage point evoked most pointedly in "Flight Home." It is also worth noting that, like "Aspects of a Mountain," "Act of Conscience" is clearly carefully researched, but, interestingly, both pieces wear their learning lightly, handling it rhetorically almost as if it were visual observation. The range of voices in these essays—reverent, ironic, critical, self-aware—makes for an extremely subtle and complex textual surface. In Merwin's other books, all much more unified than this one, it is easier for the reader to suppress awareness of these tonal differences. Here the play of similarity and difference in Merwin's writing is inevitably in the foreground.

The first piece of prose in the book, "John," a story Merwin regards as juvenilia and one that will be unfamiliar to virtually all of Merwin's readers, at first seems unlike anything else Merwin has written. Yet before one has completed the first section of this book, unexpected connections and parallels with Merwin's other work begin to surface. In many ways, the thoroughly unstable, compromised first-person narrator in "John" is the predecessor of the obsessive narrators in "The Church of Sounds" and "The Flyover" and of the more delicately undermined first-person voice in many of Merwin's other stories. The narrative voice in "John" is clearly an early stage in the development of the same voice that would emerge with such confidence in some of the pieces in *The Miner's Pale Children;* compare, for example, "The Trembler," where the narrator is obsessed with a double and takes on a Poe-like rational control as he works toward that double's secret. Thus it is instructive to listen to the first-person voice in "John" and hear a version of it, again, in the beginning of "The Hawk and the Mules" over twenty years later, a story that in turn is ultimately indistinguishable in tone and substance from Merwin's autobiographical pieces. These connections may then lead us to examine more closely the ways in which the first person is qualified and brought into question in the essays. Similarly, the Poe-like rational voice in "John," a voice that tries just too hard to convince us it is not mad, reaches its prime in "A New Right Arm," an essay in the Swiftian mode written in the same year as "Act of Conscience."

"A New Right Arm" in fact deals with the same apocalyptic issues as "Act of Conscience," but in a satiric mode. It is a modest proposal to make use of the inevitable population explosion of mutants resulting from radiation exposure. In a voice every bit as calm and reasoned as that of Swift's narrator's proposal for eating the Irish, Merwin mimics the bureaucratic thinking that produces actual government position papers proposing schemes like postal change-of-address forms for post-holocaust living arrangements, or shovels and doors for quick nuclear bomb shelters. Merwin's narrator simply advocates using the genetic defectives for military service.

Throughout a diverse collection like this one, one feels a tug across time and genre to other moments in Merwin's career. Once we begin to trace any one path, the intersections compound, and the associations and echoes are endlessly useful:

—Merwin's current project about Hawaii concerns, in part, the nuclear-free Pacific movement. As he talks about this project in the interview, we hear echoes over decades; his voice circles back to "Act of Conscience" to move forward, the contemporary Hawaiian movement to stop the bombing of a small island resonating with the effort of a small boat twenty-some years ago to stop the bombing of another small Pacific island.

—Pieces like "A New Right Arm" and "Act of Conscience" gain additional power when seen in the context of the poems Merwin was working on at the same time, poems that would come to form the haunting postapocalyptic voice of *The Lice*, where the head has become ash, where we realize "we were born not to survive / Only to live." Similarly, the statements on ecology collected here will also resonate with and help illuminate the dark poems of *The Lice*.

—A story like "Air," at once humorous, fanciful, and allusive (or allegorical—building the boat here echoes the story of Noah, Merwin's boat becoming the ark of his own past, his writing peopled now by those he has known), resonates with much of Merwin's recent work. Compare, for example, this version of a boy's fanciful musing in a church with the version of Merwin's own past in *Unframed Originals,* where, in "The Skyline," Merwin muses on the growing stains on the walls in his father's church. Or consider the passage in *Unframed Originals* when he dreams of taking a boat, filled with friends, and sailing away from the destructive impulses of Western progress.

—For a destabilizing but mutually reinforcing picture of Merwin's view of education, compare the story "The Academy" with "Affable Irregular," Merwin's recollections of R. P. Blackmur and his own days at Princeton.

—Consider how the fiction often offers narrativized versions of kinds of imagery familiar from the more gnomic context of the poetry. In "The Church of Sounds," for example, as the protagonist weaves through a crowd searching for an elusive woman, he is described in a simile that echoes through Merwin's poetry of the 1960s and 1970s: "he went on as cautiously and as quickly as he could, like a comb with one tooth." And in the same paragraph, as the sun sets, the narrator bows down to its yellow disk "as a beetle . . . his eyes dazzled by it and by the pallor of the bare landscape," images that later form the opening movement of *Writings to an Unfinished Accompaniment.*

—Compare "Aspects of a Mountain" with the final section of *Unframed Originals,* in which Merwin recalls wandering Athos at the time his mother died. Merwin is haunted by a line from Dante's *Purgatorio* —"And you have rested from the long way," the long way signifying life, the rest death. His mother's death refocuses the entire journey, imposing a pattern of imagery that deepens his understanding of his relationship with her. Uncannily, in "Aspects," which recounts an earlier journey, the line is there as well, for it is what the monks say to him when he enters a monastery: "I had come a long way, he told me, and what I should do was rest."

At times, as with the two readings of Athos, a bond is forged between two texts that deepens and reinforces both of them. At other moments, the similarities and differences, as with the mutually contaminating undermining of the first-person voice, produces not only illumination but also stress. For unlike, say, Ezra Pound and William Carlos Williams, Merwin does not move seamlessly between genres, breaking down boundaries between poetry and prose and absorbing one into the other. Merwin has in fact retained rather traditional distinctions between different forms of writing, as his statements on poetry and politics here will suggest. Williams used prose passages in his poetry; Pound moved his political harangue from poetry to prose. Merwin, however, works to maintain these distinctions, though this collection will demonstrate how his unified sensibility suffuses all his work.

This book also substantially undermines the existing view of Merwin's development as a prose writer. His first prose volume, *The Miner's Pale Children*, appeared in 1970, followed by *Houses and Travellers* (1977) and *Unframed Originals* (1982). These volumes seem to trace a clear progression in Merwin's prose writing, from the very short fables and parables of *Miner's*—regularly described as "visionary fictions" and "sharp, disturbing little narratives" that never neatly translate to meaning but rather pull the reader continually to the edges of understanding—to a development of this form in *Houses*, where many of the brief, tightly constructed parables begin to relax into allegorical stories with more developed characters and dialogue than any of the pieces in *Miner's* contain. Toward the end of *Houses*, though, a new and very different voice begins to emerge, an autobiographical voice that recalls scenes from the poet's childhood, still cryptic but clearly a voice more intricately attached to Merwin's direct experience. This voice comes to fruition in *Unframed Originals*, where the fleeting autobiographical memories relax into extended reminiscences of family figures who hover around and define Merwin's early memories; these reminiscences still contain the mythical elements of the earlier prose—*Unframed Originals* opens by evoking a garden that alludes to Eden while stubbornly remaining the very real vegetable garden of his grandfather—but they are much more accessible, firmly rooted in Merwin's experience. If tone and idea and fabulation were the primary concerns of the earlier work, characterization, memory, and experience become the focus of the later work. A similar shift can be traced in Merwin's poetry from the 1950s to the present. But such a scheme works well only if we look solely at Merwin's books. Merwin's uncollected work, conversely, both published and unpublished, from as early as the 1940s, reveals that he has long worked in all these tones and genres, that his unique brand of autobiography was very much developed in the 1950s, nearly thirty years before it appeared in one of his books. This collection of previously uncollected and unpublished prose will allow readers to explore the real development of Merwin's prose—not an unbroken line from brief parables to lengthy reminiscences, but rather many lines: political prose that anticipates some of his allegorical prose as well as some of his most powerful poetry; book reviews that give trenchant expression to concerns that would be developed in later poetry and prose; stories that seem inseparable from later autobiographical prose; even statements about his own poetry that echo some of his dark fictional narratives. This volume, then, does offer a region of memory—the array of remembering that defines the self; it pulls together unfamiliar work from various genres and periods which in turn help regionalize all of Merwin's work; that work is crossed by many paths, and every intersection offers the reader multiple choices.

I

Other Worlds, Other Selves:
Fiction

JOHN

(1949)

Once upon a time John said (the birds were bright meantime among the trees, water went in the usual streams, and the leaves let wind through), "If Clare was a piece of red paper she'd be a kite." He meant, I suppose, that, being an angel, she'd fly. John was mad; his head hurt him. When he had asked the doctor, whose own sanity I have at times doubted, what was the matter with the hurting head, the doctor had explained in detail, at length, that the seams of John's head were parting (this later led to an obvious joke about heaven, a place which was a particular obsession of John's) and that John's poor thin brains would soon leak out and soup down all over his face, mussing his hair and blurring his eyes on the way. John had worn his head in huge turban bandages which smelled ever since. He sat mildly on the street corner under an awning and people gave him things to live on; nobody knew where he slept. In spite of all this for some time I paid him as little attention as I could. He was a stranger, you might say, to most of us. But he remembered that my wife was dead and the thing bothered him. I could tell this from the way he continually spoke to me about her whenever he could get me to stop and listen to him for a moment. He did not forget her and the fact that she was dead as he seemed to forget everything else, sometimes even his head.

He had forgotten, for example, my father, who was a judge, who had died on a Christmas Eve, and my married sister who had moved away the following spring. John remarked to me as I passed one day that the water was moving out of the roof gutters where they came down the sides of the buildings, that it was leaving over the sidewalk, taking things with it "like someone." He said he had been down in the fields watching the children and that the water there (this in astonishment)

Juvenilia reprinted from *Perspective,* 2 (Spring 1949).

was going. Soon, he feared, he would be left high and dry, yet not so high, he feared, as heaven, nor as dry, perhaps, as a righteous man. But he forgot my father and sister almost as soon as they left, and Clare stuck fast in his head, an angel.

Personally, I am tired of madmen: everybody solicits sympathy for them because they have been thought, and by perfectly intelligent, responsible people, not only unfortunate but profound. I find this a double mistake. Madmen have a shallowness of their own, and like the rest of us they toss and cough until they manage to drown in it. But Clare, a perfect bitch in most things, liked, nevertheless, John. In the summer when the birds banked and the water was wet they would stand together watching how the children laughed and played marbles in the dirt. And then John would tell her all about heaven. The pearly gates at that season were great horseshoes of marbles shining all by themselves. It was conventional at the basis, this heaven of John's. Some days the pair of them would take long walks together down through the fields, and when John stopped behind a bush to watch the children playing Clare would stop with him to watch the children playing. That was what she said she was doing; although people have wagged and complained I have never questioned Clare's faithfulness.

Sunday afternoons especially they two cavorted and talked. She would come home from church expanding upon apocalyptical visions with a wide smile on her face. Sometimes I worried when I thought she must be coming actually to believe the things John told her. Really, I do not care for apocalypses; I prefer stories. An apocalypse is the end of all stories. But the terrible thing was that after a month or so things about the house began to move to John's way of thinking, or at least as I watched Clare I thought they did, and the thought worried me. Clare actually began to talk like John, and I could not always persuade myself that she was joking. She used his strange expressions so often that I myself began to begin my stories, which grew stranger and stranger, with absurd "Once upon a time" 's. She talked so much about angels it gave me gooseflesh.

John had the habit of moving only his lips when he talked and of keeping the corners of his mouth rigid so that all one saw was his lips moving open and out, in and closing. I used to watch him from behind windows where I could not hear what he was saying; he would talk to himself; I drank my coffee or watched from the barber's chair although he disgusted me so much that once or twice I had to leave my coffee, hot and half-drunk, on the table, and at least twice that I can remember I shuddered so when I was being shaved that I received really painful cuts. Then my wife began to talk in the same way.

On Sunday evenings Clare would converse with the minister. Sometimes she went to his house, sometimes he came to ours. I do not like ministers; I especially did not like this one, but at least he argued with Clare. When he was there she did not even talk about angels. She said there were no angels no god no heaven. The fool of a minister did not believe her but I tolerated him because he kept her away from her usual side of the subject. All he talked about was Sunday school.

With ordinary people, you might say, there is a disparity between what they see and what they think they see. Sometimes they realize that the gap is there, sometimes not. They can seldom do much about this separation even if they want to. This is one of my cleverest thoughts; I wish all my readers to note it down or at least to underline it. The trouble with John was that there was no disparity at all: he thought what he saw, or else he took the things he saw as though they had already been thought. If he could see it that would do by way of thinking about it. Some people, I suppose, would still think this interesting. It is appalling. It makes me want to believe in god, not in angels.

John came to love Clare; I hope I am right in saying that he loved her as a dog loves his mistress. A dog could have all kinds of feelings. But everyone noticed this attraction Clare and John had for each other, and though they could see that John was different from the rest of us they could not think of John as a dog. Nevertheless they made things so miserable for John and Clare that they stopped seeing each other on Sunday afternoons. Clare would stop for a moment on John's street corner to hear what he had to say about the weather (I will say this for the fellow, he could talk more interestingly about the weather than anyone else in town) but then she walked on by herself. John did not seem to notice much that she did not go walking with him anymore. Maybe he imagined that she still did and that was enough.

I must be pardoned for mentioning it; I recall it with extreme regret, but it is true that people began to find the idiot abusing himself. He did it in corners of people's yards, sitting on garbage cans. Sometimes he did not even have the decency to get off his box on the street corner and would have the joy of the worm right there in public until someone with a kind but disgusted face pushed him into a doorway or a yard or anywhere that would do for the moment. After a year of this kind of public nuisance it was noted that John behaved like this almost always after he had been talking with Clare. I had found him repulsive for a long time; everyone in town felt the same way by now. The only person who still liked him was Clare.

After she stopped seeing him she would sit at home rocking her chair in the bay window, smoking cigarettes and telling me about angels. I could not endure it. I was almost disgusted at the thought of going home. I remember thinking how glad I was that Clare and I had no children. She had never been an attractive woman; she was perpetually indignant about something. She would stand and harangue until many a poor person was willing to admit anything merely to escape. After she began to hold her mouth when she talked as John held his she became really terrible, not only to listen to but to watch. Almost in a frenzy of wavering rage, the thread of which only she could follow, as only she enjoyed it, she would wag, not her head, as some people do, but her whole body from the hips up, showering her wordy anger, her sense of outrage, shaking her purse and parcels until her unfortunate victim began to look about him for a safe hidey-hole. I did it myself sometimes, I wagged my shoulders; you know how traits like that can graft themselves upon you however much you dislike them. But I was stupefied when I saw John doing it. He never, of course, had the justification of being indignant. The more angry I got about the whole run of affairs the more I gestured and stammered like John and Clare—it was like a nightmare. I never cared for most of the people in town, but I got to buttonholing them on the streets until they paled with (I imagine) fear; I told them all about the whole nasty situation. I acted as Clare did; she always told people about something irritating that somebody else had done, acting as though the person she was shouting at were to blame. Everybody runs around with a guilty conscience anyway; all you have to do is pretend to blame something on someone and he half believes the fault is his. People began to look, when I was talking to them, the same way they looked when Clare talked to them. I did not like this state of affairs at all; I could not bear it; it made me more angry whenever I thought about it.

Clare, however, left all the shouting to me at last and shut herself up in the house. She kept the place very clean and cooked well; she said she "thought" in her spare time while I was working the drugstore, but sometimes in my cynical moments I accused her to myself of thinking of John, even of thinking of him with more than just her mind. I have never known to what extent women do things like that. And of course I shall never know now: one day she shot herself through the head when autumn was coming in. How should I know; maybe she really had been "thinking" all the time. It was really very upsetting, especially when some particularly vicious people began to hint that I was responsible for it, that I had helped to drive her to it. I should like to know how. I cannot imagine myself ever driving Clare to anything. People began to cater to John when they remembered he had been a favorite of hers. For a few days everyone gave him fruit, nuts, presents of all sorts. They even let him sleep for a few nights in the jail. They threw him out of there shortly: nobody could ignore the fact that he had dirty habits.

I bought Clare an inexpensive casket; that was the way she would have wanted it. I put her in the front room with the flowers people had sent. A few bunches were from the hothouse but most of them were the last remnants of the summer crop from people's gardens. They didn't brighten the place up much. The front room is always dark because of the high bushes that have been let grow very high between the house and the road. One summer they even began to grow in at the front bedroom window on the second story. There was little I could do to make things comfortably visible in the room. At one time we had used it for a dining room; there was a beautiful lamp with mottled stained leaded glass still hanging from the ceiling. The edge of the shade was hung with a dark red fringe; I lowered the thing and left it turned on day and night. Clare did not look as though she were sleeping. There was a pout on her face; I even thought I could notice that that stupid undertaker had left her with her neck twisted so that her head was at an angle from her body. Certainly he had done a dreadful job with her hands: they were almost fists and hanging right at her sides.

She had always said that she did not want a clergyman or a religious funeral, which surprised people when they heard it, because they remembered how faithful a churchgoer she had been. And she left instructions that she wanted to be cremated which surprised people too. Still, at the last moment she had left a note requesting the minister she had argued with on Sunday evenings, but she had still wanted to be cremated. I made the arrangements as she wished, in spite of the cost of cremation and the fact that the only crematory around was a good distance from town. I had never considered that the event would touch John, that he would understand that Clare was dead even if someone told him. I certainly never even suspected that John would consider himself as a natural guest at the funeral. Imagine my astonishment when I saw him all tricked out in a brown suit which no one had ever seen before, making his way through the leaves and shadows of the front yard as though they belonged to him, neither smiling nor looking at anyone.

The minister, as I have noted to myself many times, is a person of no sense whatever. On that day he outdid my expectations. Aside from the depressing air natural to obsequies, aside from the expected sentimental eruptions, apart from the funeral entirely, he made the afternoon positively painful, embarrassing. I swear Clare's death, thanks to him, was more painful to me than to her; people making fools of themselves always pain me, especially when I am forced to watch, and watch. And this time I was forced practically to participate, at least to approve: I was sponsoring the beast.

With a "let's be brave-and-yet-tender about all this, conducting everything as adults, in good taste, yet with due consciousness of our really only temporary bereavement" air, he stood up and grinned at the assemblage of long-faced people like a little boy caught in a jam jar. I agreed roughly with the sentiments of such an air; I thought a little good taste would have spared a lot of us our discomforts, but I was revolted by the way he shone with the attitude. And he shined up to things quickly; he stood for a moment with his head bowed (I forget what effect he seemed to be trying to provoke) and then in a quavering voice playing at trying to be brave, playing at manfully trying to conceal its own effort (I noticed all that carefully) he broke into

> *I'm a pilgrim*
> *And I'm a stranger;*
> *I can tarry* (long pause; sigh)
> *I can tarry* (shorter pause)
> *But a night.*
> *Do not detain me*
> *For I must hurry—*

And so on in the same vein, not paying any attention to how long it took. John meanwhile sat with his lips moving in and out, up and down; he was profoundly moved by the whole thing. The people, I noticed, couldn't see Clare very well; the glare of the light was in the way. I was happy about this in a way; it helped keep them under control.

I'm still not sure how he got there—which car he went in—but someone must have felt that "poor John who was a favorite of hers" deserved as a special privilege to be taken to the cemetery. Things seemed to happen beyond my reach; I had no desire for it to be my show but I would have liked to have had some say in things. The crematory, as might have been expected, had the same air as that repulsive minister: an organ was advertising that "Somewhere the Sun Is Shining" while the yellow dust of Indian summer drifted during and afterwards about the brick building. Yellow and green wallpaper meant to be soothing presented white frisky lambs with ecstatic saintly faces. I do not mean to sound critical but it was really dreadful. We saw Clare's coffin into the wall and that was all. After everyone was out, I remember, some fool noticed that John was not with us (was he ever?). He was found back in the crematory chapel staring at the hole in the wall, sitting with his lips crinkling and spreading, his torso waving above the seat. He was led to a car. At least his antics took the moaners' minds off the funeral; you might say he stole the show.

He kept on as he always had, making queer remarks in his strange language, often telling me what Clare would do if she were something or other. If she were a star she would be up and see: she would not be as up as she was now as an angel, but John would be better able to keep tabs on her—nonsense like that. I could have killed him for the trick he had of stopping me as I came from the barber's, of whiffing delightedly and saying, "I can smell you like a funeral." I spoke as little as possible because I hated the speech habits I had formed: they were strong and I didn't talk with anyone enough to break them. Once I was so enraged when he told me he smelled me like a funeral that I stopped in front of him, my legs spread, uncertain of just what it was I wanted to do to him—shout, beat, strangle . . . That someone like that should be allowed to go on in such a way on people's sensitive subjects! (It was a sensitive subject, too, Clare's funeral. I hadn't got about with people enough for the impressions to wear off much and it did disturb me when I thought of her death. I loved her, really; at least I was well used to her.) At any rate all I did that one time was to roll my lips and sway from the waist out of sheer fury. I must have been a sight. John was a little frightened at first—I guess my face was red—but then he grinned, showing his gums, and started rolling his lips and swaying from the waist himself. I have never been so embarrassed in my life. As I walked away, fuming, someone said he was glad to see that John and I got on so well; after all, he said, John in a manner of speaking "survived" Clare too, didn't he? It was enough to drive a man out of his senses.

I have always liked summer when the greens glow and windows are open. I am a sentimental man at heart in spite of everything. I was particularly happy the summer after the spring when John died. I did not realize until that summer how I had come to hate him, how his absence relieved me. I was glad to find so sore a spot no longer irritating me without having come to a bursting point. At the same time it had been rather unpleasant, John's death, the people in town seemed to regard me as somehow responsible for the fellow. They came to tell me first as soon as he was found dead; they wanted to throw the corpse off on my hands; they even expected me to have the funeral in my house; in the front room, I suppose. I was so furious I shouted to them that they could roll him out and toss him in the dump for all of me; I slammed the door shut, leaving them astonished on my porch. They seem to have disliked me, to have avoided me, ever since; they pretend not to notice when I am present among them; they do not speak when I walk down the street. One day I tried a somersault on the sidewalk in front of the church just as Sunday morning service was letting out and nobody so much as looked.

They buried John, I gather, in potter's field. In spite of the fact that nobody pays any attention to me now, that they act as though I did not exist, I do not miss John. I am still lighthearted suddenly as I pass the emptiness of his street corner. The wind has walked off with his box; they can sweep where he sat. I walk right on top of the place where he used to sit; I congratulate myself; I smile—without having to pay any attention to my lips. I hope he is rotten and fallen apart by now. I hope there is very little left and that going fast. I do not care at all about his angels, nor does he. If he were a piece of red paper he could burn, like hell.

RETURN TO
THE MOUNTAINS

(1963)

Once, nearly ten years before, I had spent a winter and part of a spring in that bit of high country far away from any cities, and this short return visit was touched with a happiness like the sunlight of the first days of summer: a feeling that was part recollection, part fulfilment.

I had not been married when I had lived in those mountains. I had known a girl in a little town near the top of the valley. She came from a mountain family which owned a small business in the town. They themselves still lived on their farms high up in the cold ridges. The firm was a kind of shipping agency. It had come into being a few generations earlier when her family had felt the need of having some-one of their own established in what was then still a village, in order to take care of sending the family products to the markets in the cities. Over the years the fact that the family kept a permanent representative in the town had led other mountain farmers to make use of them, and in time the family had expanded the practice somewhat, and had employed a manager and bought a building in the town. When I knew the establishment it also employed a sallow young spinster who kept the files, and a clean, thin, silent old man who helped with some of the loading and unloading, and with the storing of bags of nuts, wool, piles of hides, and stacks of baskets, who wore a cap with a long visor which dropped nearly to his collarbone when he dozed in his chair, and who spent a great deal of time sweeping, as it seemed to me, in the dark. The manager I remember only as a tall man in very correct clothes: they were black, long, and out of fashion, and the unshiny parts had a greenish cast. It was said that he was very good, but the meaning of the

Reprinted from *Evergreen Review*, 7 (Oct.–Nov. 1963).

phrase was never explained, and I never saw much of him because he was seldom around at the hours when I was there. But the family had never allowed the firm to develop a separate existence: there had always been some descendant of the original founders living in town in order to keep charge of it. The business had no official name, no stationery, and no sign. It was a small brown-shuttered stone house on a narrow, curving side street; apart from the fact that the windows on the ground floor had been enlarged during the last century and held the desk at which the spinster sat with her papers, it looked like the other houses on the street.

And the girl I had known had in fact lived upstairs over the office and the storerooms. Later when I recalled visits to the building I remembered at the same time the winter evenings settling into the mountain town which seemed at that hour to be trying to retreat and be a village again: the feeble amber glimmer of the one naked light bulb in the street at the corner, the smell of woodsmoke, the fog that besets those mountains in winter beginning to dilute the few remaining colors, the skirts of broad-bottomed women brushing windows as they turned in their kitchens. Evening is too soft a word: there is no such thing in those regions at that time of year. It was the first part of the night, usually, when I got to the building. And yet often the spinster was still there, and at the beginning she would get up to hurry into her coat as I was shutting the door, and if she was alone in the office she would be torn, as she hurried past me, between a desire to warn me to keep the door locked, and confusion at referring to the situation. Almost always the old man would still be around and would emerge into activity from somewhere in the storerooms. I never understood his hours, and I wondered whether he did not sleep, at least some nights, back among the piled hides and wool, though his red, clean-shaven chicken-neck and his boiled and ironed shirts, and the fact that there were only the most rudimentary sanitary facilities on that floor, made it seem unlikely.

I would not have inquired about such things of the girl I came to visit, though she had answered all the questions I had ever put to her about the business and about her family. Her replies had always been made with a calm and matter-of-fact directness which seemed perfectly candid and I believe was meant to be so, but I was always left with the feeling that she had answered some question which was quite different from the one I had asked, and that it would be unfair to her seriousness

for a mile or more, with the cement poles rushing past closer and closer together at different angles, and then it suddenly tilted and started a climb at an angle so steep that it seemed impossible that it could continue. But everything had been calculated long before: the car slowed indeed, and at one moment it seemed that it must stop and begin to slide back down the fearful slope in front of us, but just then the angle became gentler and the car ground on. After a time the tracks leveled off and the car stopped again. From there on, she told me, the car climbed very gradually. But it was always there that we got off.

Those slopes must have been pasture for centuries. Even in the spring the earth showed through the sparse, close-bitten, brilliant green grass when one bent down to look. I remember only one afternoon in which the sky was settled, and it was plain that the wintry sun would fill all the slopes with a colorless windless shining until night. That day the passengers had spoken in even quieter voices than usual as they had got down from the car. Perhaps we had done the same. We had started up the slope to the south of the car, away from the passengers who had got off at the same place. She never suggested which way we should go, but waited for me to lead, as though she were in those mountains for the first time. On those days we walked for long stretches in silence, crossing the tilted pastures, winding up into the scree and the snow-filled clefts and into the bases of the crags at the top of the ridge, but it was a silence filled with an unnameable exhilaration and with a tenderness for her such as I felt nowhere else. Even when we lay down, as we did every time, in little grass declivities high up in the scree, with snow drifts and stone rising around us like fragments of something that had gone, we would not kiss or touch, but lie on our backs and talk in low voices, looking upside down at the corvines and swifts and, from time to time, the kites, flying in and out of the spurs of ice and stone far above us. It was on the cloudless day, lying together in one of those green bowls, that she told me about a brother of hers, about my age, who had been killed in the war. She told me the details as she knew them, the barbed wire, the bombing, the death in a hospital. The story led back into their childhood. He had been the member of her family whom she had loved most intensely. It was he who had taught her to see the animals. Not only the ones whose cheeses and wool and hides they sent to the valley, and the others who guarded them, though he had given those too a sharpness and a depth of existence in her mind which they would never lose. The others too: the ones that the mountain people shot or trapped for their meat or their furs or plumage or their predatory ways or simply because they enjoyed it. And the others, she said; all of them. He showed her what had never been owned, and the tracks. I was surprised, because the people from those mountains, even the women, seem to be born with the senses and knowledge of hunters as well as of farmers, and they take no more interest in the animals than is usual among country people who are their own butchers and tanners. I imagined that what she was telling me revealed more about what she had felt for her brother than it did about what she felt for the animals. I was surprised too because I realized that although I could easily imagine her as a child there were many things that I could not imagine her having learned; I took it for granted that she had always known them. On our first night together I had been aware—as I might have been before that if I had thought about it—that she had never known a man before me. And yet the fact was a fact and nothing more. There was nothing diffident or startled in her desire, nor in the rush of feeling that came with it and was never spoken of except with her body and her eyes. The first time had been like every other, and the anticipation of her eyes in the room, or of her arms late at night, would have been enough to account for the quickening with which I entered that street on my way to see her, though it was the thought of her whole elusive presence that tightened my throat every time I set out to go to her, and dissolved time and other circumstances, for me at least, when we were together. On the day I have been referring to she went on telling me of her dead brother, while we lay in the high patch of grass, and she mentioned him again—one of the rare times that I saw her laugh—in the streetcar on the way down to the valley, as the feeble lights began to appear far below us and the iron trolley tipped forward at its awesome angle and started to grind slowly down the steep place. It was something he had said about the trolley that had made her laugh, but the noise of the car itself prevented my hearing all of it. When she mentioned him again—and that was seldom—it was with the same grave, measured, and yet undeliberate distance with which she spoke of anything else— the news, the small affairs of the town, books, history, the cities.

We never spoke of the future. She seemed to remember everything I ever told her, but when she asked me anything about myself it was done with an air of formality and a sense of the exceptional which endowed my answers with a dignity I could never have claimed for them. At the same time this reserve of hers did not prompt me to tell her much about myself apart from the main facts. What we did know about each other we knew without details but also without doubt. And yet when, in the spring, not more than a few weeks after the trip on which she had talked about her brother, she was suddenly summoned to the city, neither of us had any illusion that we would see each other again. She was needed in a household of a relative in the city where a child was about to be born, and there was also some question of her being married into another family whose history resembled that of hers. I heard from her once; a message that said she was well. I spent my last few weeks there, between her departure and my own, walking in the mountains above the town, watching the spring come into the pastures and the ice melt, darkening the cliffs, and one last snowfall with large furred flakes. My landlord tried to interest me in carving in horn, which he did very intricately—it is a traditional occupation in that part of the country. He had carved elaborate buttons, portraits, and religious figures, a few favorite saints, over and over. I left, as I had planned to do, before the spring was in full flower. He too sent me one card, a few years later, saying that he had heard she was well and had married.

And when I returned to the mountains I was married myself, and had been for several years. My wife and I stayed in another town a little farther down the valley. It was in fact late July but the early summer had been rainy and cold, and when we arrived the light and the colors of the slopes were such as they must have been in May, in other years: bright, lucent, and soft, at least in the valley itself. It was much broader there than in the town where I had spent so much time before. The stream widens out into a shallow lake with rich farms around its shores. The sun shone day after day on the lake and the humid farms and the peach orchards. The colors, even in the weeks we were there, began to turn dusty and tawny. We walked to other little towns and villages. We went up to the town that I had known so well in the winter, and we visited, as I had done then, the reliquary of the local saint: the great face in hammered silver that looks like a battered breastplate with two red glass nipples for eyes. We walked up into the slopes—there are mountains everywhere around there—and heard the cliffs, warmed by the sun, echo when we laughed. We even took the streetcar once and came back down as the long afternoon light was flooding the valley, turning all the stone to brass. And then we walked on down to where we were staying—another five or six miles—as the evening came on, taking the unpaved road that follows the stream and the lake, and stopped at an inn to have dinner out of doors under a vine, looking over the water where the terns were catching their last minnows before dark. Increasingly through those weeks I felt as though the valley had given me my wife, and as though, for all our love before and our years of marriage, I had come to know her only there. She had never been anywhere near that region and had wanted to see the mountains I had told her about. In those long summer days and the nights that followed them I came to see in her a capacity for happiness such as I had never seen in anyone. Of course we stayed too long there—longer than we had intended to stay. The heat of the delayed midsummer had turned the hay fields pale since we had come, and the farmers on the upper slopes were beginning to complain of drought, and her face had become more deeply tanned than I ever remembered it. We had stayed too long and still had not gone to half the places that, during our first few days, we had planned to visit. We decided to take one last trip into the mountains: another ancient streetcar that went up into a different range. I had never taken it when I had lived in the valley, and had always meant to. We seldom planned trips very far in advance, but this time, so that we should not let the chance slip past, we decided, at the beginning of our last week, what day we would save for the trip into the mountains. And the next morning there was a telegram for my wife. Her mother had fallen sick, and she was needed. We began to pack. But my wife stopped me after a moment to beg me to stay another day or so and take the trip as we had planned to do together. She wanted me to do it, she said, so that the end of our time in the valley should not be simply a rushed journey filled with anxiety. She said that there would probably not be much that I would be able to do to help her with her mother, or not much that could not wait for a few days. She wanted to be able to think of me in the mountains as she traveled toward her family. She said it would help her to be able to leave there what she most loved, for another day or two, and to be able to look forward to my following later, and describing it to her. Whatever shadow of desperation there was in it, the request was born of our happiness that summer, and I could not refuse it.

I saw her off on a train that left early in the morning. When it was gone I had another coffee and then went back to the place where we had been staying, and changed my clothes to go up into the mountains. It was a hot, airless morning but I deliberately dressed too warmly and threw a sweater and coat over my shoulder. The streetcar left shortly before noon. I walked down to the lake and took off my clothes in an

orchard and bathed in the brownish water and dried in the sun. Then I
dressed and walked to the station. I was early. I bought my ticket and got
on the car. It was pleasant in the shade of the iron roof. The echoes felt
cool. I was thinking of my wife and our summer together, and what she
would find in the different life of the city where we had been living,
and I paid no attention to the car filling up with peasant women in
black clothes, as usual, and I did not hear their voices any more than
I had heard the voices of people on the road beyond the orchard when I
had been swimming underwater in the lake, a few minutes before. The
car hissed and clanged and screeched and rolled slowly out into the
withering sunlight. It rocked through the back gardens of the town, past
the roses and hen coops and pig sheds, and around farms and a loop of
the lake, and began to climb. There was a long, winding ascent through
lemon groves and then through oak woods; then the tracks leveled off in
country that had evidently been much more carefully farmed at one
time than was now the case: there were overgrown orchards and little
meadows where the hay was full of weeds, and there were ruined stone
barns and stone houses. Even with all the windows open the heat was
terrible in the iron car. It stopped and a few women got off. No one was
waiting for them. They called back their good-byes and the raised voices
sounded startling. The car left them. And as the other streetcar had
done, this one suddenly began to gather speed and hurtle forward
through the remains of half-dead vineyards, and the fields of thistles
and brambles, lurching and swinging as though it was about to jump
the track, and all at once it tipped upward at a frightening angle and
began a climb which seemed even steeper than the one I knew, and even
more likely to stall the trolley and send it slithering and crashing back
down the slope. As in the other car we were all facing to the rear as we
rose from the valley; we were looking back and down. The cement poles
appeared from behind our shoulders less often and passed us more
slowly. We began to go around a bend, and as we did, the mountain
directly across from us came into sight. It was a view of it such as I had
never had before, and none of the glimpses of it from the valley or from
other slopes would have led me to suspect what the whole of it was like.
As the car turned slowly it turned too, huge and, as it seemed, a little
below us, rising from a turn of the valley on the other side of the lake,
and climbing in one even sweep to a long, curving crest. The whole
mountain, on the side that faced us, was the shape of an immense
mussel lying on its base, and the color was a shade of dark brownish

gray between that of iron and that of rust; its surface was crusty, shiny in places and stony in others, with a spongy look like a piece of coke. One could not have been sure, at that distance, but it did not look as though there was anything whatever growing on it, except at the very top, where there were some green stains. Then the car turned another bend; we saw the lake once more as we turned, before the tracks began to level out and the car started a more gradual climb. The country above the steep rise here was utterly empty. I got off at the next stop, a few miles farther up, and most of the other passengers did too. They made off through the brush, following the tracks for a few steps. I turned to look around and when I glanced back they were scarcely visible among the bushes.

It was already well into the afternoon. Ahead of me, in the direction to which I was naturally drawn, there was a stretch of wild upland, rolling and full of dry grass taller than a man, that waved as though the different clumps were responding to different winds. Through the grass I could see patches of bare ground and what looked like marsh and shallow ponds. Great outcroppings of rock the size of houses jutted up here and there. They were like smaller versions of the stone mountain face I had seen from the car: they were all shaped like mussels lying on the hinged side, and they were all pointing the same way. But some of them had tiny dwarfed thorn trees and oaks growing out of clefts in the tops, and ivy and old man's beard and lichens dripping down them and swaying. I walked into the country around them toward the line of dry gray cliffs beyond, which made the top of the ridge. The dry smells of the grass and the rocks were mixed with the smells of stagnant water. What I had seen had indeed been patches of shallow marsh and mud. The first one I came to was marked with the hooves of many animals, though I realized that I had seen none since I left the valley. It must have been an hour or more before I came to the next bit of marsh—it did not seem nearly that long, but judging by the change in the light it could not have been less. There too the ground for yards around the muddy water had been chewed by hooves. There seemed to be not only the prints of sheep and of cows there, but of others as well, and there were paw marks of different sizes. It was growing cooler. I put on one of the garments I was carrying. Ahead of me the light in the cliffs where they were broken into gorges, drew me like a window in the dark and I went on. But it was getting to be late in the afternoon; the midday stillness ended as the coolness began. I was aware all at once of the stirring of the animals. I heard them in the tall grass. I saw their shadows, immensely long and rapid, hurrying and changing shape, when I could not see them themselves. I stood near one of the large rocks and waited. The shadows slipped back and forth. The light fell from the cliffs. I began to see the animals themselves. Only at a distance at first, looking paler than the shadows, which in turn were no longer so definite. They were hooved, most of them, like elk; they moved in small groups, flitting through the clumps of grass at a rocking canter that I could not hear. The wind rose a little and I saw that dusk had fallen. But as I watched I saw more of them, closer. There were many sizes, some with long necks and horns that curved back over their shoulders. They ran between me and what was left of the light, and from where I stood they all looked to be different shades of gray. There were other animals too that walked, but whether they were large dogs, or what they were, I could not be sure. It began to grow dark. The moon would rise soon, but the fog that sometimes drifts over those uplands all night in the summer too had begun to gather and to shut out the cliffs and when it did rise the moon would be veiled. When I moved there was a flurry of animal shapes around me as far as I could see. I was moving to go back the way I had come, but I was still looking over my shoulder toward the animals, trying to make out their shapes in the dimness, and as I watched, one of the large doglike animals came out of the grass not far from me. There was something of a cat about him, and something high in the withers and long-necked, like the hooved animals. He lay down facing away from me, as a dog sometimes lies down when he wants you to throw a stick for him. All his attention was fixed toward a point beyond him. As I watched him I saw him wriggle his haunches to get into a position of even greater alertness. Beyond him in open spaces in the grass I could see other animals and groups of animals following his example, lying down, facing in the same direction. It was not the direction in which I had been going, but well to one side of it. Then as I stood there I too smelled it. Smoke. And not the smell of bush fires sweeping over the uplands, nor that of chestnut woods burning and writhing at a distance. It was the smell of wood fires in houses, the smell of evenings before dinnertime in villages. I began to walk toward it. The animals vanished, to reappear at a distance, lying down, showing me my direction. The moon set but I could still see just enough. I put on the last garment. I could no longer smell the smoke, but I had begun to feel a path under my feet.

The dampness got into my clothes. I was coldest just as the fog began to turn from dark gray to a paler color, and as it did the path led me onto a cart track and before long I saw that I was at the beginning of a village street.

It was light enough so that, when I got to the first building, a large gray mass on my left, I could make out the separate swirls of fog in the mud street. There seemed to be nothing on the other side of the thoroughfare—a vegetable garden, perhaps, or a few rows of potatoes, but no building. A sense whose accuracy is sometimes heightened by fatigue led me to believe that beyond the patch of tilled ground there would be nothing, a drop: the village was built on the brink of a ridge. When I went up to it I could see that the building on my left was an immense Renaissance structure, built in some stone that I was sure had not come from those mountains, but whether it was genuinely old—a palace built with a commanding view of the valley—or whether it was a recent imitation I could not even guess in the fog. The elaborately carved stone ornamentation looked recent, but perhaps it was part of a modern restoration. Certainly the building now had the appearance of an institution. I walked into a paved recess between two wings, wondering whether anyone was awake. At the end of the recess there was a large glass door, three panels of small panes, the middle one with the handle, and the other two, I supposed, for light. As I came closer I saw that there was an old woman sitting in the doorway behind the glass, blocking it so that the door could not open. She was dressed as a peasant but not in black: a red sweater, a faded print tied around her head. She was sewing something in her lap; the bulk of it flowed down from her knees and was partly hidden in her skirts, partly piled up on the floor. She was wearing thick black-rimmed glasses through which she was watching me, without any expression, while she continued her sewing. The needle and thimble never hesitated. I saw what she was sewing. It was the top of a plastic tablecloth wrapped like a caul around the fully clothed dead body of a middle-aged woman. The knees were drawn up, but loosely. The arms held them, but loosely. The head was tipped forward. It was smiling, but as though by chance; in the smile one could see that many of the teeth must be gone from inside. I looked around me. All the windows on the ground floor were glass doors of the same kind, and inside each of them there was an aging woman at the same kind of sewing. The fog was withdrawing, but slowly. There was absolute silence, and it was emphasized by an atmosphere of intense preparation, as though everyone would be too hurried to talk. In the eyes of the old woman there was a bitter reproach, but I could not divine whether it was directed specifically at me or at the whole world of which I was simply a convenient representative. I realized that I should know. Certainly I could not inquire, nor could I ask whether these victims were relatives of the old women who were stitching the cauls, or whether they were the fruit of some sudden disaster or were a continually recurring charge. The tensed grief that seemed to breathe out from the building, the quality of shock in the silence around it, seemed to indicate that the catastrophe that had brought so many dead suddenly to the feet of these women with their needles, in the first half-light, must be an exception, must be related to them in some exceptional way that could not be repeated day after day, but the profound bitterness in the old woman's face, and the monastic severity of the building would have led me to suspect that this kind of task was not strange to the place and its tenants.

While I was looking at the face in the caul, trying to catch some glimpse of how it had come to be there, the old woman put in the last stitches and stood up. She seized the plastic sack by the top, opened the door and stepped out, dragging it behind her. I nodded to her as I might have done at a funeral. She glared at me for an instant and then indicated with her head that I should come with her. Dragging the caul at her side, she led me out of the recess, past the other women at their doors, none of them so much as looking up, and around the corner to the left. Here there was a wider entrance to the building. The doors stood open, letting the fog in, but the hallway inside was well lit. The plastic bag squeaked as it slid along the polished yellow tiles of the floor. The sense of some appalling and unusual catastrophe was many times more powerful inside the building. Everything added to it: the doors open onto the fog, the silence of the doors along the hall. The old woman shoved the plastic sack into a place beside a large wardrobe standing against the wall. The first. As she took her hand away from it and straightened up I was certain that the caul contained a relative of hers. At the same moment a woman emerged from a door behind me: a head nurse of some kind. Her gaunt face was smiling. I could not tell whether she was part of some religious order, and I could not at once be sure whether her air of radiant cheerfulness was the heartiness of a gym teacher, or was an expression of genuine sweetness of nature. She smiled at me, showing several large silver teeth, and strode to the body, nudging it into a position where it took up less space, as a master mason might change the position of the first stone of a wall. She spoke to the old woman in a tone that implied confidence and satisfaction, as a teacher might speak to a good but discouraged student. It had not been decided yet, she said, how big the casket would be. The old woman's face showed no response, though it was apparent that her feeling for the other woman approached reverence. The head nurse caught my eye, as I stood watching her pushing the body into a more compact shape.

"They," she said to me with a smile which I was sure now was the result of sweetness, "they are nothing now."

THE MUSEUM

(1964)

I HAD had a wicker trunk made to hold all that I was keeping, because I did not expect to be coming back. When it was packed, a neighbor and I loaded it onto his cart, and we took it down to the valley to the station and shipped it to the frontier, where I intended to pick it up on my way out of the country. Then I went to the capital to make some final arrangements and say good-bye to friends there. A few days later, when these things had been done, I took the train to the frontier myself.

It is a full day's trip. I was traveling during a warm spell in late September. The completed summer was silent. One morning very soon it would suddenly be autumn, with the light appearing to come through shallow water, and overnight half of the gray dust would have disappeared from the tiny leaves of the mimosas. On the day I left, there was a fragrance like that of the mimosas in winter. In spite of the dust and heat, it hung in the air like a remembered chill, and it was there all the way from the capital, down on the plain, in the morning, to the frontier, on the high plateau, late in the afternoon. But there was no breeze except what was raised by the passage of the train, and I spent most of the day hanging out the windows of the nearly empty car, watching the flat country with its canals and meadows give way to farmed hills, vineyards, woods, and the first mountains, and the stations become smaller and closer to silence.

When I got to the frontier station, the trunk was not there. There was a long pause scheduled in any case before the other train, the night train, was to pull out and continue into the other country: time for the passengers to descend, go through customs, board the night train with their baggage, and wait until they wondered whether something had gone wrong. And time for things to go wrong. And obviously the officials were used to losses and delays, and the matter was passed from hand to hand like a photograph of a stranger which somebody had found on a beach. It seemed to belong to nobody, including me. It evoked indifference, irrelevant suspicion, and discourses on complexity mumbled around stained ends of dead cigarettes and delivered in low, impersonal voices to the upper corners of one small crammed dusty office after another.

The rest of the passengers had already vanished onto the night train by the time the pertinent documents had produced an old official who had never been surprised by anything. He began telephoning the freight handlers at all the junctions between the frontier and the village from which the trunk had been sent, and he located it at last, but he informed me that it would be another day before the trunk could reach the frontier. The handlers had sworn that it would be on the next day's train, and nothing could be done to make it come any faster. The train on which I had come was about to start back, and the night train with which it connected was ready to cross the frontier. If I wanted to see the trunk again I had no choice but to spend the night there and hope that it would arrive and that I could continue with it on the following evening. I could spend the night at the station itself, they told me. There were rooms upstairs, and they assured me that the food was very good.

I told them that I would stay, and immediately one of the uniformed officials turned into a guide and with an air of genuine pleasure and hospitality picked up my bag and led me down the hall and through the empty customs shed with its long trestles—an actor leading me through his dark auditorium. We made our way through a storeroom piled with crates and sealed tubs, some of which must have been there for months, and came to a door which led down into a great tiled kitchen. There he introduced me to a fat woman, who beamed up at me, drying her hands on her colorless apron, and announced that I would be so well taken care of that I would never want to go on. She turned and called to somebody, and my guide put the bag down, nudged me, told me I'd be fine, and left.

I heard bare feet on the tiles behind me. A girl or young woman had come in, red hands and feet, head in a kerchief. Chickens were running in and out the door behind her. She led me up a boxed-in flight of dusty stairs to a wide hall. A window at the end, hung with coarse lace, looked out onto the hills I had come through. There were four doors, two on each side. She showed me into a dark room where the shutters had not been opened for weeks, and she folded them back, revealing more of the same lace, and then the same bright, yellowish hills. I opened all the windows. It was a large room containing one immense bed covered with an ageless, darned spread of the same lace as the curtains, a washstand and a chair, and nothing else. The walls were whitewashed plaster, chipped here and there, and the board floors were bare and dusty. She told me that I had the whole floor to myself and might use the great round unpainted table that was the only piece of furniture out in the hall. I asked her why the rooms were so large and whether the building had originally been built for some other purpose and whether the huge bed had come from somewhere else, but she did not know. As she was turning back the bed I heard the train on which I had arrived pulling out of the station. I asked her when the night train would leave, and she said she thought it had already gone, probably while we were down in the kitchen.

I went downstairs and out onto the platform. It was as though the trains had never been there. I could hear the rust forming on the rails and the grass beginning to grow up among them. The light had begun to go out of the hills, but as the first coolness returned to the day I was aware that the smell of mimosas was gone. I could see a long way into the hills in every direction. There were few trees, no villages in sight. Somewhere in the bony uplands to the east, where range after range of dry shadows were beginning to grow, was the frontier. A long way off, through an opening in the hills, I saw a squat castle: half of a thumb with its shadow bleeding out of it. Everything was the same bleached straw color; even the station, which was made of brick that had once been red, was now nearly indistinguishable from the dust.

It had become a different building. The officials had vanished, and there were no sounds except from the hens at the kitchen door. The cook fanning her charcoal stove told me that the meal would have been better if she had known I was going to be there. When I asked her about the castle she said it was a long way off. It would take most of a day to get there even with a donkey cart. She seemed not to know much more about it. She shrugged and bent down to peer under the pots, and then she asked whether I'd seen the museum. She said I should certainly see the museum while I was there. It was the most interesting thing around, she informed me, and I'd have plenty of time. It was no distance. She pointed through the narrow window at the empty road.

I FOLLOWED her suggestion the next afternoon. There was no one else on the dust road until I got to the first bend. Then a long, straight stretch appeared in front of me, and at the end of it, as though the road were leading straight up to it, stood a large symmetrical stone house surrounded by evergreens and eucalyptus trees and a high parched wall. Even from a considerable distance it was plain that the house was closed. The double stone steps led up one flight to blank shutters, and all the windows were sealed in the same way. In that part of the world shutters were normally of wood and were inside the windows. These were on the outside and appeared to be made of metal. They had been painted green and had faded to a grayish olive; they added to the foreign look of the place, as did the slate roof in a country where normally the roofs were tiled. There was an oxcart ahead of me, almost at the house, with an old man walking in front of it. When I had gone a few steps along the straight stretch it seemed as though the road were sealed off at both ends and there were nothing else. Heat, dust, silence, and the road at the bottom of all of them, and all motion an illusion. Then I came to a dead snake lying across the road. It had just been killed, and the cart had run over it. As I looked up, the old man and the cart turned a corner that I could not yet see, and disappeared.

I knocked at the front gate, but nobody came. As I turned to follow the road along the wall the same old man emerged from a smaller gate and asked me whether I wanted something. His hearing was undependable, and it was a moment before I managed to convey to him that I would like to see the place. Then he began explaining to me that the owners were away. I supposed that an entrance fee was customary and offered him one which he took with a resigned air, barely interrupting his explanation. He led me in through the little gate and turned and said that obviously he would only be able to admit me to the grounds: he could not let me into the house in the owners' absence. By then, of course, I had to follow him as he led me around the quite ordinary, rather overgrown little park, among frayed topiary figures, with a long pause at the empty artificial spring while he explained to me how it worked and where the original, from which it had been copied, was to be found.

The owners, he told me, were in the capital. Whenever they came they brought at least a dozen house servants with them. At one time even when they were away there had been a staff to look after the house and the stables and the grounds. Now there was only he, and it had been a long time since they had been there. It was because of the daughter, he said, as though that explained everything. Eventually I understood that she was either dying or had just died, but he would say no more about her. And how long had it been, I asked, since the museum had actually been open. His face changed when he understood my question. This, he informed me, was not the museum. He led me back to the gate and pointed further along the road to a cluster of buildings.

"There," he said. "Ask the barber."

I WENT on to the group of whitewashed houses: a little hamlet built on an abrupt outcrop of reddish stone. The entrances, at the top of short dirt ramps, stood open and empty, as though there were no doors. The most prosperous building had a low brick wall around it. A tall man was standing in front of the doorway watching me approach. He was wearing the usual high leather boots and a long canvas coat that reached to his knees. He greeted me; we discussed the fact that it was Sunday. He said, with a laugh and some measure of irony, that it made no difference to him, but he did not explain. There was a pile of hair on the doorsill.

He was affable, but he was watching for an opening. He said it was a pity the station wasn't nearer because he'd have more customers. People came and went, he explained, and never even knew he was there. He asked me whether I had any idea why the station had been built so far away, and when I declared that I knew nothing about the matter, he said he would tell me. Very deliberately he turned and pointed back toward the house where I had just been. It was their doing, he said. The owners. He had found out the details himself. They had not wanted the station to be built too near their house, and they had used their influence, and their money.

"They must be very old," I said. "The station seems to have been built some time ago."

"The family, the family," he said impatiently, evoking an image of a presence in which individuals and generations came and went without changing its essentially malign nature.

"You don't know them?" he asked, dropping the question from a certain height but at the same time anxious to make sure. Perhaps he had seen me emerging from the little gate in the company of the old caretaker. I told him how I had gone up to the house thinking it was the museum, and he smiled and nodded, savoring some familiar bitterness in the situation.

"But it's the museum you want to see," he repeated, and paused to make sure that the significance of his sentence had been taken in by some invisible audience.

"I can show you the museum," he said.

The first room he led me into was the barbershop. The paneless window by the doorway was reflected dimly in a tarnished oval mirror fixed to one of the walls, and on the gray board floor between the window and the mirror stood an old armchair with a straw seat and more hair drifting around its legs. There was a murky shelf of bottles with a dozen yellowish postcards nailed above it. On another wall, in a place of pride above a row of straight-backed chairs, was a rough rack containing two guns. I saw it all in a cloud, after the glare of the sun on the whitewashed walls outside, and before I could make out anything clearly he announced to someone that I had come to see the museum.

"Get out new candles," he said.

In the arch that led into the next room someone stirred. A woman in a dress as colorless as the walls turned from where she must have been watching us, and behind her I could make out another person, much older, in black, slumped in a chair against a wall. He led me through the arch and explained to me that the first woman was his sister and the older one was his mother. We were standing in the kitchen, which I imagined was the main room of the house. Half of the floor was covered with a platform of the same gray boards I had seen in the barbershop. Then there was a step down, and the rest of the floor was stone or beaten earth, on which the fire was built in the corner. Some pots stood in the ashes. There was no chimney. The blackened walls and the sooty tiles in the roof showed where the smoke found its way out. The place smelled of beans burnt in oil and of grape mash. The barber was explaining to me that all the houses were built on the same rock and that the ancients had known what they were doing when they came there in the first place.

"Before history," he kept saying. "But they knew just the same."

It was the holes in the rock, he said. The cellars. The defenders above. The dead below, where it was hidden. They were wonderful cellars, he told me. Warm in the winter, cool in the summer. And no one would suspect they were there, he said. I wouldn't have suspected from outside, would I? I assured him that I would never have suspected anything, and it was with a gesture of great satisfaction that he took a new candle from his sister and lighted it with a cigarette lighter.

"Now," he said, and he turned and led me to a far corner of the room and lifted up a sloping cellar door. He leaned it back against the wall and raised the candle. I supposed that he was already lighting my way to what I had come to see, and I took a step forward, but as I did so he breathed deeply, half closed his eyes, and began to recite to me, in a monotonous tenor quite different from the voice he had been using. The text was evidently of his own composition, and it had to do with the Obliterated Ages.

Even in that unspeakably long ago time, he explained, the inhabitants had understood the rock and what it was for, and in it they had buried their dead—not all of the dead, of course, but the bodies of those on whom they had wished to confer immortality. Their kings and their great ones; their hunters. Their religion was not the same as the one now, but it was their own affair, and no one nowadays had ever mastered it entirely. Their heads were different from ours, as could be seen from the remains. Then they had been forgotten, and wine had been set to age in the rock, and it was not known that they were there. He took one step down the stairs, then he turned and said:

"It remained for my father to find them."

When the bones had drifted down through the dirt between the wine casks, he said, other people had declared that they were pig bones. And, indeed, was it not true that you could find chicken bones, dog bones, sheep bones in most people's cellars if you dug? It was reasonable. But his father had not been deceived. He had not come from those parts, the barber explained, but had moved there when he had married. The house had belonged to his wife who was an only daughter. When he had found the bones, he had not listened to the people from around there. He had dug behind the casks and uncovered the bodies at last. They had been lying with their heads all pointing the same way, and the wrappings around the bones in some places had turned to stone. Skins of stone with stone bones inside them. In other places you would be groping along a body and find that it had crumbled to nothing, bones and all. But once they had found the first bodies they had discovered others everywhere. They could not understand how they had been able to be unaware of the bodies all that time when they had been so near. They were in the rock on all sides and at all different levels. Some of them were scarcely covered, inside their tombs. The barber descended another step and held the candle to the face of the stone from which the irregular stairs had been hollowed. He showed me that it was full of holes, like an anthill, some much larger than others, and he explained that down below they were all much larger, though some of them were filled with earth. He struck the smooth stone with the palm of his hand, and a faint but long-drawn-out echo came back.

"You see?" he said.

Of course, he continued, as soon as the bodies had been discovered, there had been no lack of old people from those parts, in this village and others, who had declared that they had always known that the things were buried there but that they had had better ways to occupy their time than in attending to old bodies that belonged to nobody's family. The barber shrugged and climbed down another step and invited me to follow him.

THE stairs were steep and nowhere straight. He stood with his candle on the earth floor at the bottom, waiting for me beside a half dozen large wine barrels, several vats, piles of rags, beams, presses, pieces of wheels, broken tools, all covered with dust and cobwebs. Little points like eyes reflected the candle here and there in the darkness beyond.

"Here is where the first one was found," he said, leading me around a vat. The stone ceiling was too low for me to stand straight. Beyond him his candle had lit up a wide niche in the stone, extending to left and right into the shadows. In the middle of the niche, on a little table made of stone, a stuffed wolf stood staring through glass eyes over our shoulders into the darkness.

"Where is the body?" I said.

"That one I got myself," he said after a moment. "On the north side of the mountain we call the Roof. You know the Roof?"

"Did your father take out the body when he found it?" I asked.

He turned to me and laughed. "No," he said, "my father never moved it."

"What did he do when he found them?"

"Nothing."

He turned another corner and held his candle in front of the next niche. It was empty, as the first had been, except that it too was arranged like a chapel with a small stone platform on which a dead civet cat was standing in an unnatural posture.

"That one too I got," he said. "Near the frontier."

He led me from opening to opening in the natural catacombs. Some of them were high up in the wall, some at knee level; in many of them the darkness led on past the dimensions of a tomb and beyond the reach of the candlelight. In every tomb that he showed me, a stuffed animal was standing looking toward the entrance with eyes that must have been brought to it from some city and buttoned into its emptied sockets. In one of the graves an eagle, nearly black, waited with ill-folded wings.

"Some of them my sons got," the barber admitted as he started back toward the stairs. "I have two sons. One of them is a guard at the frontier." He laughed. "He gets things sometimes."

He paused and looked me over carefully. "My other son comes and goes. He's been everywhere. He gets things. All the time."

And from the way he said it I could imagine his other son as well as I could the border guard. A contrabandist, perpetually in overshoes and dirty gabardine, acquainted with the least fortunate quarters of a dozen towns along the frontier, and no doubt of a number of larger cities.

"But the bodies," I said again. "Where are they?"

He opened a rotting cupboard and brought out a candied-fruit box full of photographs. Most of them were very old and appeared to have been underexposed to start with, but with the aid of his fingernail I could make out the bodies lying in the holes, mummified and shrunken: narrow foreheads, large teeth. Even in the blackened snapshots they looked like stone. In some of the pictures, as he explained to me, he himself, rather younger, was standing pointing into the holes, smiling. One of these photographs had been made into a postcard. There was a bundle of these, and he told me the price and said they could be obtained nowhere else.

"And where are the bodies now? That's what you want to know, of course," he said. And a ring of anger, as long-practiced as his opening spiel about the ancients, came into his voice.

"A man like me," he said, "is not allowed to have rare things and things of value."

The bodies had come to no harm, he pointed out, for centuries and centuries in their places when nobody knew about them. They had come to no harm even after his father had found them. Nobody had paid much attention to them.

"It was I who brought their value to them," the barber announced, and he told how he had met a man at the station years before, a traveler, a man of learning from the capital, and how he had told this gentleman about the bones and ended by showing them to him. The man of learning had understood all about them and had explained about them to the barber. He had taken photographs and had even written about the bodies later, and his opinions were on record in a library. He was an exceptionally fine gentleman, and his goodwill was not to be doubted. But he had been very old and he had died.

The barber had realized that the bodies were of public interest, and he had had a sign printed and had had a photograph of himself pointing into a tomb put on the sign and had hung it in the station. His museum had become famous and had been put in the guidebooks, and people had come long distances simply to see the bodies. He had charged admission. He had sold postcards. But the living are full of envy.

Even, he said, when his wife turned out to be incurably sick, he had had enough money to buy medicine. He opened a drawer in the same cupboard and showed me the needle and the empty phials carefully lined up in rows.

"It was the owners," he said. "It was the owners who took the bodies away from me." He was referring to the owners of the empty house which I had seen on the way, but the phrase as he used it seemed to embrace a whole order of existence. The owners, he explained, wanted to have everything.

I could see that it had been some time since he had had a visitor and that his rancor against his powerful neighbors had not grown calmer as the golden days of his museum had receded from him, and it was plain that I would not have to prompt him in order to hear the story.

He told me that when the museum had been at its most successful, the owners had used their influence, and the government had requisitioned the bodies for the public good. They had been taken away to a museum in the capital, where, it had been claimed, they would be better cared for. Every bone had been removed; they had not missed one. What could he do to stop them? They had produced papers declaring that the earth more than so many meters below the surface was the property of the state, and other papers announcing over and over again in different ways that the state had the power to requisition objects of extreme antiquity or objects of unique historical importance, and finally they had produced papers showing that he was running, publicly proclaiming, and profiting from a museum without a license, and could be prosecuted. They had paid him nothing for the bodies because they had declared that the objects did not belong to him. They had paid him nothing for using his house to pass through because they said they were acting on orders and in the public interest. At the end they had even warned him that if any more bodies were uncovered in his cellar they would automatically become the property of the state. Some time after everything had been taken, someone who had visited the museum in former days had sent him some postcards showing how everything was displayed now in the capital. And a pamphlet about the bones in which the "owners" were honored for "indicating" them to the authorities. They had been found, it said, near the "owners' " country estate, and it had named the village. He himself had not even been mentioned, nor his father either.

And his obscurity had returned, and his wife had died. But none of it had done the "owners" any good, the barber insisted. Some people said they had done it in order to prove their power to the people who lived around there. Some said they had done it to gain distinction and to be received by the nobility—for three generations they had been trying to obtain an invitation to the castle which could be seen over near the frontier, but they had never succeeded. Some said they did it out of simple jealousy or even simple malevolence. But they had gained no respect in the country, the barber assured me, and no invitation had come from the castle. And nobody knew the name of the disease with which their daughter, an only child, had fallen sick, and of which she would surely die.

They had not managed to rob him of his distinction, either. The tombs themselves were still there, after all. And he had thought to honor them with new bones, as he told me. People could come and see them if they were interested. He did not need a license since he put up no sign and made no claims and charged no admission. He could stuff the dead animals himself. His second son, he explained, could always get him materials.

"Oh, yes," he said, passing the candle around for a last glance before he held it to light me up the stairs, "it will be a long time before this is forgotten."

At the top of the stairs he winked and opened a cupboard. The woman he had introduced as his sister set two glasses on the table as he drew out a bottle and set it down, and then he reached in his hand again and brought out a battered tin box, which he unfastened and held out smiling. It was full of glass eyes tied together with little bows.

THE CHURCH OF SOUNDS

(1964)

IT WAS always late when they were together. He started as soon as he could, in the same clothes in spite of the heat, but whenever he was crossing the dry upland the sun was already going down. The black inherited coat was of some use, he realized, saving his arms and shoulders from the needles of the juniper thickets while he went on as fast as he could over the thin red ground among white rocks. But in the afternoon heat the sleeves and what was left of the lining and the flaps of ironed serge were oppressive. If anything, the coat was too big for him, but at every movement it stuck to him for an instant like a thumb counting money, and it had its own breath. He would never be naked enough. At the thought of her lying with her head on his body, the dark hair drifting across him, the musky skin over her collarbone, the thighs within reach, and the softness of the palms of her hands just inside the base of her thumb, he was stricken as often before with the knowledge that no nudity would ever be enough when he was with her. His skin itself would be in the way, and no laying bare would ever entirely banish from between them the tragedy of garments. He would lie in the dusk watching her, and hear feathers in the shadows, and think that no way of touching her was complete enough, which was why time continued and would separate them again. There were no paths over the upland. If there were birds, they kept to the shade. Locusts shot up in front of him and whirred aside. In some places he ran. As he crossed a stream bed the sun was going down.

One time they had stood in the dusk by the stream, further along the bank where the trees were taller and there was grass. They were still naked. The warm night was ahead of them. As they watched the glassy water he described to her its devious journeys before it reached them—the underground pools, the connecting chambers in the limestone, the little ferns flickering up where a crevice let in the sunlight. When he had turned to look at her, she had vanished.

But on the upland itself it was hard to imagine the flowing of water, a season that was not summer, or a time of day that was not rocked with heat and lit by the descending sun. It was through colors of leather and bone that he went to find her, to be with her before dark and be able to see her.

He had even pled with her, he remembered, as they had stood by the stream. He had wanted her to understand the descent of the water. He had begged her to see that it had come to them from places that had nothing to do with them, and that it could not be otherwise. He had described them carefully. She never argued. She fell silent. And when he had turned to her, realizing that he had failed to persuade her and had raised a ghost between them, she had gone, and his eyes had been dazzled as though he had been staring at the sun, and what he had seen was a dark organ loft and the back of an organ at which a figure was seated with its head slumped forward into the keyboard but its hands still playing. Then already he had known what it would be like to come to the bank of the same stream, on his way to her, when the rains had begun.

He would have grown certain by then that she would be there every time and that nothing would change, and one afternoon as he crossed the upland the red would have gone from everything and it would be turning cold. When he came to the bank, the water would have risen to the foot of the yellow ledge, a sinewy gray current. He would jump down but find that it was already too deep, and that he had no choice but to snatch at a root and heave himself out again and beat his way further along the stream, looking for shallows, wondering whether she would really be there at such a season, and whether he would be able to explain to her. The banks would grow no gentler, and the stream would broaden as he went. The ledge, as he made his way along it, would become steeper and smoother, until it was as regular as the wall of a canal. And by then it would be too late to turn back.

HE SAT at the table on the sidewalk retracing in his mind the anguish on the bank, trying once again to isolate the exact moment at which he had lost hope, so that he could be sure whether he had had any choice. There was scarcely any traffic on the avenue. The few other marble tables were empty, as were the other chairs at his own. The bright table umbrellas were folded after a long warm day. The sun was going down.

In front of the closed real estate agency next door three or four little girls were practicing walking on stilts. He watched them out of the corner of his eye. They were showing off, and their voices were pitched high and shrill to attract attention. They took turns trying to outdo each other, teetering out into the brick avenue on their stilts, doing handstands and acrobatics. They did them well. Their bodies looked as light as the curtains blowing out of the upper windows. Behind him in the restaurant the meal was being served.

The black serge coat was good for sitting in at such times. It had its own history and reminded him silently of parts of it. He had never paid much attention to its fit, and it would not have occurred to him, once he had worn it a few times, that it might have been a bit narrower here or a bit more rounded there in order to comply with some general view of the way a coat should be shaped to a person. It fitted him in its own way, rather loosely, which was an advantage in many situations. It was somewhat longer than most coats you saw around, if you happened to notice, though the evening was too warm and there were too few passersby to provide much immediate comparison. Plainly, it had been made for someone taller. And its cut was rather more formal than his circumstances usually warranted, but it made up for occasional clumsiness with an overall copiousness and convenience. The lapels could be turned up high and buttoned across the front, and the pockets were deep and solidly made.

Two of the little girls were able to dance on their stilts. For a few seconds they could sway in time with some slow popular tune they kept humming, and when the rhythm broke and their weight caught them again, the others would prop themselves against a wall or a parked car to laugh. The building tops were brilliant, and the red flush was deepening in the avenue. In the restaurant behind him the lights were already on, phosphorescent at that hour.

He was on the point of leaving and had stood up to go when out of the door behind him came a woman whom he did not at first recognize, but who approached him and greeted him like a dear friend while he tried ineptly to remember where he had met her, at what gathering or on what conveyance, and whose wife she was. It seemed clear at once that she was foreign, and he was able to discover that she was French, but her English was unfailing and impeccable. A prettily got-up woman in early middle age, looking younger, but when she had been younger surely she would have looked utterly different. Her prettiness would have been of another variety. No doubt there would have been a hazy frailty to her then, however deceptive, whereas now she affected a casually ironic good sense to clothe her intelligent but overwrought ambitions. She referred continually to her years spent in this city as a student, and presumably she had acquired at that time not only her command of the language but also some of the brittle unease that marked the women of the place. And still she seemed to regard it from the viewpoint of an exploring foreigner, and was as proud of her acquaintance with the metropolis as though she were still at school. She was explaining. She had already eaten, she informed him, displaying her adjustment to the odd meal hours of this country. Her yellow coat with the fur collar was scarcely what would have been expected on that block at that hour, but she went on explaining. It was a favorite haunt of hers, she said. She had been there with some name he did not catch, but she had never managed to get her husband to eat there, and he was to have met her there this evening; they had planned to go on to some function or other after they had eaten. But her husband had telephoned the restaurant to say that he must fly to Paris for a week on government business and must catch the next plane. The children were in the country. She began to put forth alternating plans for the evening, asking his opinion of them.

The little girls on stilts were clattering against the tables. As he began to think of excuses she remembered that she had had no coffee and that she would like some, and she sat down and asked him to join her.

She was talking about her maid, who was Spanish and who would have left a large cold meal in the kitchen of the apartment, to which he was welcome. He wondered what she thought she wanted. He could not believe that she was moved by physical desire. He imagined that she was made of enamel, ranged forever on a clean shelf in the middle distance, talking. He was too shabby for her to want to be seen with, and surely she must have remarked that he was a poor listener. He wondered whether after all there were parts of her curiosity, her restlessness, or her vanity which she had managed to conceal. She wanted her coffee. He looked for a waiter. He turned and slowly sat down.

As he settled into the chair a gray coat brushed against him and a head of loose dark hair turned back to gaze at him with eyes full of confusion and distress. It was to that face that he had made his way over the uplands. And now it turned from him again and was going, and a thin figure was receding up the avenue. He pushed back the wire-legged chair, to get to his feet, to go after her. The girls on stilts were swaying among the tables and got in his way. He could not risk knocking them down and being delayed. And the cultivated woman who wanted coffee stood up and asked him why and went on talking and came with him a few steps as he made his way out among the chairs and tables. He had tried to keep the dark hair and gray coat in sight, but he had lost them among the stilts and the folded umbrellas. He thought he had seen the coat turn the corner, but when he reached the place, he could not recognize it in the straggling crowd on the cross street flooded with the light of the setting sun. He turned the way he thought he had seen her go, and hurried into the light. It was pointless to run. He would be more likely to miss her that way. He could not see clearly very far ahead with the sun in his eyes.

As he went on as cautiously and as quickly as he could, like a comb with one tooth, through the growing numbers of pedestrians, he was aware that what he was doing was familiar. For one thing, it resembled his flailing along the bank of the torrent. The thought made him sweat, but the anguish itself, as he realized, meant that the true despair was gone; it was over, or it had not yet begun. But he kept uncovering another familiarity as he went. He could not place it. It was no mere reminder of similar circumstances at some time in the past. And yet it was specific enough so that before he had taken many steps he could tell how they would lead him on and on through the same slow crowd, under the cinema marquees translucent with sunlight, and would bring him out, finally, on a ridge looking across an empty expanse, gray and white, marked with patches of rubble and glittering sheets of what appeared to be water in the distance, where the sun, no longer red, was going down. As a beetle, he would bow to its yellow disk, his eyes dazzled by it and by the pallor of the bare landscape. He could see how, as he bowed, his closed eyes would be filled again with the organ loft and the back of the organ at which two figures sat playing. He could see himself bowing like a beetle, and the pallid wastes in front of him, and the colorless plate going down out of the sky taking the light with it, and he could see himself twice at the organ, once as he was, and once smaller, in white, leaning over as though to turn the pages for the other whose long fingers continued to move in the empty keyboard. And when his eyes opened again, between him and the sun and him and the earth her face would rise, inquiring.

THE ACADEMY

(1969)

Gradually, as we went on, the green came back into the country, and in the latter part of the afternoon we passed into lush woods, dazzling here and there with summer sunlight and polished leaves, but surprisingly empty of birds. A marsh seemed to occupy most of the woodland. It was probably not deep and it was nowhere visible but its presence was betrayed by the broad leaves of the undergrowth, species that thrive only in dank soft ground and moist and filtered light, and by the high brakes of reeds in the little clearings. The road was raised on a low dike, with drier vegetation tangled along both sides. We came to a bridge built of wooden piles and dirt-covered planks, with a railing of splintery timbers, its floor barely clearing a slow stream as wide as a house, that moved with a sound like breathing in sleep, out of the overhanging darkness on one side and into it again on the other. After the bridge the woods were deeper, and a mile or so farther on we came to another bridge like the first, but in worse condition, over a second stream like the one we had just crossed, or another loop of the same one. And beyond the second bridge there were more, a series of them, across barely moving water, the structures becoming more dilapidated as we went, as though the urge to keep them safe grew weaker or rarer as the bridges drew closer together. On all of them there were piles that shook or sank as we passed, and even on the first one there were planks that gave and had let the dirt slip between them into the stream, while on those farther on there were boards that were not nailed down at all but had worked loose or had merely been laid across gaps, from which some of them were slipping askew. Finally there was a long bridge with numbers of planks missing from it altogether. The framed water inched along beneath, perfectly bare, and each gap raised the questions: whether the plank on

"The Academy" first appeared in *Quarterly Review of Literature.*

51

the other side of it was securely nailed or would slip when the wheel struck it, and whether the gap was too wide for the wheels and would stop them and wedge them, and whether it was safer to go faster on the swaying structure, so that the momentum might give us a better chance of not having the wheels caught and jammed in a gap, or more slowly, lest the thing should collapse altogether. There was one place where it seemed that we could not possibly manage to go farther: a broad gap with a loose plank beyond it. But obviously we could not go back, nor stay where we were, and in fact it was probably the loose plank that got us over: it had slewed around so that one end of it half-covered the gap beside it. At the very end there was another gap and a drop to the sloping bank. When we were finally there it was a relief to realize that the road was no longer laid on a dike but led gently uphill through deep woods.

They were silent, and as we went through them the road continued to climb gradually, so that the sunlight appeared to be coming back into the spaces between the tall trees, growing stronger and more direct than it had been a while before, at the bridges, as though it were actually becoming earlier, rather than later, in the afternoon. After a few miles the shadowed mossy ruins of walls appeared here and there, running and vanishing among them, and then in clearings not yet completely overgrown there were apple trees, still living, and some large cherries, most of them dead, rising through thorn and bramble thickets, among the oaks and beeches. But they did not look like a preparation for anything and it startled us when we came around a bend in the road and found ourselves in a large green, like an oblong shaded pasture, surrounded by buildings. Beyond them on each side the great trees began again.

The green itself was silent, echoing the slight stirrings of the woods. The stillness had contributed to our surprise: nothing had led us to suppose that we were coming to human habitation. But as we looked it was clear that the buildings, or at least most of them, were empty. Louvered shutters were closed on windows; several of them were broken and hanging loose. There were broken fanlights in the porches; one front door leaned, half-rotted, half-smashed, with nettles growing from its sill; the largest of the buildings had entirely collapsed. But there was enough of everything left to reveal a common architecture: no two of the buildings were alike, but they differed as members of a united family. A plain neoclassical style of red brick and white-painted wood, with pillared colonnades of wood or iron running along the fronts of some of the larger houses, and balconies above. The green common was well tended and had been cropped recently by cows. At the farther end of it, where the sunlight fell brightest, a large red dog got up slowly, keeping us in his eye, and trotted off behind one of the houses, in front of which a few flowers were growing, the ground was worn bare of grass, and a woman was looking at us. She stood half in shadow, half in bright sunlight, shading her eyes, while we walked slowly along the green looking at the houses and the ruin, and approached her. Her hair, caught up in a bun, was graying; her cotton print dress and worn cardigan were stained and faded; on her feet she had an old pair of boys' brown shoes. A thin face, lined, calm, and slightly amused—an expression that appeared to be natural to it. And her voice, when she answered our greeting, was low and pleasant, and carried the same suggestion of incurious amusement.

The place had been a school, she told us. The large building, the most beautiful of them, had been half-demolished when the fireplaces had been sold out of it some years back. After that the rest of the structure had fallen by itself. I left my wife talking to her about her rosebushes and walked back to examine the ruin. In the middle at least it had stood three and perhaps four stories tall. The walls had crashed only here and there, like something imperfectly remembered, so that the bits that were left stood in new relation to each other, with uses that now were entirely their own, and consequently indecipherable. Several fluted doorframes stood erect with their long-paneled doors shut, and nothing left of the partitions around them. One tall window was still standing, topless, but with most of its panes unbroken, dividing the open air; whole chimneys had survived, and there were pieces of staircase lying on their sides, and tiers and tiers of empty shelves. I climbed into the rubble and walked along an elegantly molded wooden beam from which the white paint was flaking. They may have been built in the same generation, that family of edifices, but when the big one had collapsed it had ceased at once to belong to the same calendar as its abandoned but unfallen neighbors, and had passed into a different time, which it shared with fossils and ripped bits of clothes in dust bins. From then on it would decay but it would no longer age. Draped across the spine of the heaped rubble and buried under it here and there were lengths of ironwork: a balcony railing, with medallions gathering it together at intervals, and faces on the medallions. I looked closer, expecting to see profiles of emperors or the conventional mythological features, and saw instead

that the bas-reliefs on the medallions were lifelike portraits of a man
and a woman, neither idealized nor young. The man's face was thin
and a shade abstracted, except for the full mouth, gentle and smiling.
The woman's face was plump and merry despite the prominent forehead
and sharply focused eyes. I might still, perhaps, have taken them for
illustrations of virtues, or for outmoded exemplars of some sort if it had
not been for a quality which the iron still revealed in each profile,
something unmistakably perishable in the features, which bespoke
individuality. Looking up I could see through the broken walls that the
building, on the back, had given onto a long apple orchard, now hardly
distinguishable from woodland again, and as I turned to climb out I
noticed across the green, between two buildings, the remains of another
orchard of the same age and shape.

At the house, where I had left my wife and the woman we had met, a
man had come to join the company. He stood a few feet away by a corner
of the building and did not enter the conversation except occasionally,
to agree with what the woman said. A small man in his sixties, benign
but closed, in rubber boots, an old rust-colored jacket, and a checked
cap. The dog came back and stood beside him. The woman replied to
everything in the same level quiet voice, with the same smile, looking
directly at us. At the beginning she volunteered nothing, she simply
answered our questions. It was only later that she began to tell us what
we could not have asked.

The faces on the medallions, she said, were those of the founders of
the school, a clergyman and his wife. In her mind they seemed to
inhabit the undefined epoch that depends on living memory but begins
just beyond it. She said she thought her grandfather had been to school
here when the couple were both still alive but were very old and were no
longer teaching. He may have seen them, at least. Her vagueness about
their dates was remarkable since she must have read them many times
on publications of the school, on plaques over doorways, in the chapel,
indeed on their tombstones which probably were not far away. But from
the manner in which she referred to the founders—a Rev. and Mrs.
Saylor—it appeared that their dates meant little to her and had doubtless been effaced in her mind by habit; very probably they had never
seemed to have anything to do with those two dim but inherited
presences, any more than if they had referred to members of her own
family. Her father, she said, had spoken of the Rev. and Mrs. Saylor with
reverence, but by the time her father had come there to school they had

been dead for years; and those who had come later (she referred to these always as "the young" as though she thought of them from the point of view of her father's generation) had known the founders only, it appeared, as tokens of a scene at which they had not assisted, yet for which they were held daily more responsible.

In due course her father had been a teacher there, she told us with pride. A professor, of Latin. He had taught elsewhere but not for long. Early in his career he had returned to the academy and had never left it again. When he had retired he had gone on living in the house in front of which we were standing, occupying his last years with a late-found passion for botany, and undertaking a massive work on the regional flora, in Latin and English, which he had never completed.

The academy had been open to both sexes, she said, and the note that had come into her voice, as she had talked of her father, went out of it again. As a child she had dreamed of only one thing, and that was to be old enough to attend the classes, to be a student "who was sent here." Everything she had wanted, she said with a laugh, was here. She began to describe the girls in long dark dresses and gloves, carrying books on the green; the soprano voices on the demolished porch, singing hymns in the dark, at vespers; the ribbons and veils in the carriages; she had loved a parasol, she said, like a doll, and she had stood and recited imaginary lessons to the front steps, these front steps. She had never wanted to go away, to see anywhere else; people from everywhere came here, and were pleased to stay, to be asked to stay. She had understood that, even when she was very small. Here, they used to say, things went on the same.

But the school had closed before she had been old enough to go to her first class. She had been sent away to be educated. She dismissed the subject with a wave.

"This is Mr. Akmiller," she said suddenly, introducing the man beside her, who raised his hat and shook hands, affable and shy, and never moved from where he was standing.

"I could scarcely manage without him," she said, with the same laugh. "Though my son helps. Whenever he's here."

I asked how much they had to take care of and Mr. Akmiller smiled and gestured, apparently indicating everything around us.

"All this," he said. And then nodding toward the back of the house he added, "With the animals."

"Enough for us," she said.

"They look after themselves, you might almost say, once you get onto it," Mr. Akmiller said, as though he were defending them. "Once you get onto it," he said again, "it's a pleasure."

He looked a few years older than the woman; I asked him whether he had known the school before it closed.

"Oh yes," he said, "I seen it."

But he said no more than that and I was beginning to feel that I had overindulged my curiosity, when he continued,

"My father seen to the grounds and buildings up to the end. The fires, the roofs. It was an education in itself. Afterwards I had no difficulty. That kind of experience is always in demand." After another of his pauses he said, "And then he always had his pension."

"But you came back, too," I said, hoping to hear what had brought him.

"I'd been to sea," he said, as though that were an explanation. "I'd worked in churches. I came back to see."

"I keep thinking perhaps my son will come back one day, to stay, I mean," the woman said. "You never know. He was educated here even if I wasn't."

She explained that after her husband's death she had returned to her father's house at the academy, with her son, who had not yet been to school. Her father had still been active, as she said, and many of the houses that were now windowless and overgrown with brambles and honeysuckle were at that time lived in by other professors in retirement, while yet others who had been associated with the school in its last days—young teachers or even students when it closed—had formed the habit of coming back there during the summers, most of them bringing their young families, and living in the spacious buildings as though they were cottages. Several of the farms had still been occupied, where now the brush was twice the height of a man. It had been summer when she had arrived, and her son had spent the first months running with the other estranged descendants of the place, haying, helping with the cows, and when the autumn had come and his friends had dispersed unwillingly to different schools and she had not wished to leave, the ring of retired professors had welcomed one last pupil. Without a word they had entered into a conspiracy to believe that nothing could be more natural than one small boy's presence, alone among the elders and receiving the whole of their teaching. It was as though they were afraid that if they countenanced the slightest doubt of the naturalness of the situation the boy would vanish. She had wondered about it a bit at the time, she said, watching them standing in the doors of their houses to receive their one student at the appointed hours and welcoming him gravely and ceremoniously. She had thought at first how odd it was the way they took it for granted, and then she had realized that they were not taking it for granted at all, but quite the opposite: they were treating it as an incredible stroke of fortune which at any moment they might learn was not theirs after all, or was not true. And their civility had become daily more courtly; they had seemed to her to grow gentler in their habits, and a gaiety, such as can come from the keeping of a secret, had gradually possessed them. She turned to Mr. Akmiller and placed her spread hand on her chest, and inclining her head, said, "Good morning, sir," with a mimic benevolence, to show us how they had welcomed the boy to their porches.

"He was never late," she said. "Never." He had never missed a lesson, except for a few days' illness, and it had never occurred to him not to complete the assignments they gave him to do at home. And they, the professors, appeared to bend all their efforts and their accumulated pedagogical skill and experience toward imparting cunningly, seductively, unforgettably, the whole of their different mysteries, if that had been possible. It had become a serious game for them. They had gone back one more time to the elements of their subjects and begun again, trying to cast them around the boy like spells and make them indispensable to him. From the beginning there was no question of his being too young for any subject; all of the teachers had something to commend to him, and he had lessons of a kind with the professors of history and Greek and Latin and philosophy while he was still learning to read. In a few days it had indeed seemed perfectly natural. She pointed out to us the itinerary she had watched him make, the first autumn, from house to house, some of which were now invisible behind the thick growth. In the late afternoon he had gone down to the farms and hung around the barns, or disappeared for long solitary expeditions in the woods. One surprising thing, almost from the start, was the laughter she heard coming from the professors' houses as he left one for the next. His demeanor toward them and theirs toward him had never lost any of its essential formality, and yet since there were no other children living in the place he seemed to be relatively unaware of age, and this coupled with his interest in everything, his quickness and application at his studies, and a precocious love of the incongruous, had led to the lessons being conducted, often, with humor. She had been able to catch glimpses of this in the boy's Latin and botany lessons with her father, there in the house. And on the other hand, in the summers when the other children came back, as they still did for a few years, he treated them with the same formal good humor he displayed toward his teachers.

"And he ran the place," she said.

She broke off. The image of that time appeared to be complete in her mind, so that she felt no need to continue.

Mr. Akmiller said, "There's the cemetery," pointing to the woods through which the sun was setting. I could see nothing but the trees and tall growth.

"That's where my father's buried," she said without looking.

"I keep it up as best I can," Mr. Akmiller said.

"He never did what I wanted him to, but he's a good son to me all the same," she said, and I had thought at first that she was speaking of her father, but I saw that the object of her thoughts had never changed. I asked how long the boy had been able to stay at school there and she looked startled, as though she did not understand the question, and then she went on.

The system had worked perfectly for several years, she said, until the first of the teachers died. When that happened it had struck like a possibility that had not been considered. The man who had died had taught a language, and his lessons were taken over by another of the professors, but it had not been the same. She tried to explain: a sense of inviolability had gone, it was as though they had all been caught at something, and might go on, but would not get away with it. She had forgotten dates. She groped for them, trying to fix them. Another professor had fallen sick and had been taken away. He had taught Greek, and her father had taken over his lessons. A third teacher had become partially paralysed and though he had refused to leave, and had looked after himself with silent tenacity, he had given up trying to give lessons months before he died. His branch of history had been taught, after that, by another of his colleagues. One after the other they had dropped out; the circle had drawn tight. Two of the farms had been abandoned, one after the other. Then her father had died and finally there had been only one of the ring of teachers left, originally the professor of philosophy, teaching the boy all the subjects in which he had a competence. He had done so for two years, and had come to her himself one morning at the end of the summer (only one family had come back that year, and they had already left) to tell her that now she should send the boy away. The old man had already made the arrangements. He had got the boy a scholarship at a university. He supervised the packing and the departure in the farm wagon, but he did not go to the station. He had died in the course of that winter. He had had no family living there.

And in the same winter the last of the farms had been abandoned. She had stayed. It had never occurred to her to leave. She had kept some of the animals, and the farmer had helped her install them in the stables that ran behind the house, and had supplied her with wood for the winter. She had been alone on the green. And in the spring Mr. Akmiller had come.

I asked what the boy had studied when he had gone to the university and instead of answering she turned and said, "I'll show you," and went up the unpainted steps and into the house, motioning us to follow. Mr. Akmiller did not come with us. She led us into the kitchen, a farm kitchen piled with boots and bins and unwashed dishes. On a shelf near the sink, by the clock, there was a photograph of a young man in a uniform.

"That's my son," she said. "I might have taken you for him. If you'd been in uniform." I did not see the resemblance. She fetched another, in a leather frame, from a bookshelf in the hall. He was older in that one, still in uniform. He was an engineer, she said.

"They keep them terribly busy."

He was in the army. He had been in the army ever since he was old enough. It had not pleased her. She had tried to dissuade him, to suggest something more suitable, as she said, but he had simply laughed. He went everywhere now, she told us, designing things for the army; new bases, buildings—for he was really more an architect than an engineer, she insisted, whatever they called it. He had been all over the world, working for them. It was why he never managed to get home and lend a hand as he kept saying he wanted to do. But that wasn't the worst, she said. The worst was when she had learned that they had used him, partly because of his having come from here, as the chief designer for The Building—that it was in fact based on his plans. They might at least have refrained from that, she considered, from tact, or decency, but then no doubt they would have supposed that the choice was something she would be proud of, just as they surely imagined, if they thought of it at all, that she must be pleased at the prospect of The Building and all it would mean.

I asked about The Building; it was clear that she assumed that everyone must know about it. Delight at being able to reveal it to someone new overtook her surprise and sweetened her indignation. She took a moment to make sure that we really did not know of the existence of the structure and then she led us, without a word, back out of the house, down the dilapidated steps, past the splinters of fence picket propping up flowers, and the rusty cans full of water, and toward the end of the green. Mr. Akmiller joined us and said he had come to say good-bye, he had to see to the animals.

"They've never seen The Building," she said to him, and he turned and came with us into the woods and up a little rise. There abruptly the woods stopped. The slope dropped away in front of us covered in nothing but low scrub, and led out onto an enormous barren plain, the color of dressed pigskin, in the light of the sunset. Not a tree was in sight anywhere on the expanse, not a single patch of green. It was perfectly level, as though it had been scraped and rolled, and a few miles away on its surface The Building, the one feature in the landscape, was being built. It was so huge that it was hard to judge its distance. An enormous tower, rising from the middle of the struc-ture, looked as though it alone must already be higher and more massive than any building I had ever seen. It rose from a series of immense arches like a piece of an aqueduct, that ran some distance from it on either side, into the plain, though what use they could be I could not guess, for they dwarfed the monstrous construction vehicles that were parked under them. At that distance it was hard to make out movement. A crane on the top of the tower was swinging, and another under one of the arches; a truck was rolling slowly, raising dust. There looked to be no road to The Building, and I could not see where the trucks came from and how they left. I asked, but both the woman and Mr. Akmiller shook their heads as though they did not know. I asked what The Building was for and the woman said, "The army," her voice betraying fright as well as contempt. It was not to be a base exactly, and its use was a secret. A kind of city, as far as she had been able to understand it. She was not sure. A kind of city the army was building.

"It goes down, too," Mr. Akmiller said. "Into the ground, just as far, maybe farther."

I could find out no more from them, and the light was going. I said we must leave, and I asked if there were not some other road than the one we had come by. Mr. Akmiller was astonished to hear that we had arrived over the swamp road. "Even the cows wouldn't use it," he said. "Not those bridges."

He showed us a track that came up to the side of the house where we had been standing, and led down to the abandoned farms that had once been worked for the academy. It took us to a highway, and several hours later to a sizable town and a hotel.

I asked the desk clerk about The Building and he knew of it, about as much as the woman and Mr. Akmiller. A city the army was building, for some secret purpose. He was acquainted with the academy too, "that old place." He knew who lived there; it was obviously common knowledge. "An old character whose father used to be the handyman up there." I asked about the woman. He said she had come from up there, and married away while she was off at school. Quite a looker, she'd been, he could still remember. The couple had lived in the city where her husband had been brought up. They had a mansion, he'd heard. He believed they'd traveled. Her husband had had money and lost it. But the clerk said he'd heard things about the marriage, and that it wasn't as big a blow to her as it might have been when the man had died. And then she'd gone back to that old place and been there ever since. But he was quite unshakable in his insistence that she had never had a child.

CAMPBELL

(1969)

He could not have been more than five when he saw Campbell—the only time. But he must have been five. His mother had already been a widow for a long time. Nearly three years: he had overheard conversations about how long it had been. They had said three years, and he had found it hard to remember when she had not worn mourning, in a past that seemed inexpressibly remote in other respects, a secret, the life around an overgrown garden that was still there beyond a frosted-glass door at the end of a long corridor, forgotten, for the most part, even by him. The corridor was sealed off from him and from everyone by some force there in the dark air that he had not seen arrive. And yet at times he would surprise patches of that age again, present for an instant in the world before him, or in his own mind—he could not be sure which— like bits of dazzling sunlight coming and going on the dark flowered carpet. Each time he watched they faded, and when they were gone he was not sure whether he had been remembering things he had actually seen, himself, or had been imagining things he had been told or had heard, or whether the overhearing, or the seeing, or both, were dreams.

Occasionally, when it seemed that the world was made of comprehension, he had started to talk about one of the things he remembered, or seemed to remember, from the other age, before the mourning. Almost every time it had been something that he was quite sure of, an event or appearance that he had never doubted at all. The large man in the brown suit, for example: heavy, glinting, remote but tentatively benevolent, redolent of calm and indeed cold administration, who had been present in some helpful capacity distinct from old family acquaintance —an acquaintance, however, not close enough to save the occasion from a constant ingredient of embarrassment. This figure had stood at the

"Campbell" first appeared in *Quarterly Review of Literature*.

bay window overlooking the front steps and had commented with distant kindness on the small painted flowerpot full of polished gravel through which the brown beak of a bulb was just emerging. He had agreed, vaguely but distinctly, that the pot and bulb, purchased on a shopping tour in a good department store, named as always, as though the name of the store were a credential, would be educational. But no one remembered this apparition, from the boy's descriptions. And it was the same each time, with revenants from that age. His mother, or the aunt who had lived with them for a year, or the friends who had come to call, had shown, perhaps without meaning to, that he was describing, or asking about, something which they did not recognize. He could see the puzzlement grow into their faces—a way of looking, as though they were listening to something else. They would question him, but from a growing height. Sometimes it was plain that they hoped to surprise something harmless that was hiding from them, perhaps only a step away; but it was also plain, from the questions, that they did not know what he was talking about. Once or twice they were stern and scolded him, remotely, like strangers, for telling things that were not true. But the worst was their pretending, as they sometimes did, to recall the same things he described, when it was plain that they believed his descriptions were either embroidery or pure fantasy, childish inventions, to be humored. On occasion he had even joined in the pretense himself, entering into their deceit, behaving as though his own account was something he was making up, and which was not, consequently, anything that he took seriously or would remember again. But in every case his references to that age left him with a smarting sensation in the chest, an ache and a burning in which, as he would not recognize for many years, anger had some discreet but growing part, as did bewilderment, but the principal component was shame. Each time there remained, along with a new uncertainty, a feeling not so much that he had been betrayed as that he had betrayed something. It was bitter. It taught him more about the pain of what was irrevocable than did the remembered things themselves. What puzzled him most was that he would sometimes hear his mother and her friends talking of people and things in that age and he was convinced that at moments what they were talking about corresponded closely, if not exactly, with things that he remembered. But he learned not to enter those conversations.

He understood something about all this, he thought, sitting beside the folds of his mother's black coat, one Sunday in church. He was pondering the black fur of the collar and wondering why it would be poisonous for him or for other children even to touch but was not poisonous for his mother to wear against her white neck, a question that he had asked, but never with any illuminating result. He was peering into the depths of that forest of black light when he heard the minister read from the Bible about the children of Israel walking in the fiery furnace. The scene was immediately sharp and present to him, and in no way either frightening or surprising. He could see the three children, much older than he was, walking on the stones and the water, both made of light, through the leaping yellow and orange flames. They moved slowly. Their faces were turned away but everything about them was calm. The fire reached up around them like trees on an afternoon in a wood, a place where they were glad to be. The king and the people watching saw only the other side of the fire and they had to stand back from its heat. And he himself, as he watched, was troubled by a dread that something would happen, a slight sound or shift in the light would break the seal, or they would turn and see the people staring, and then they would notice the heat, and instantly they would burst into flames like paper, and be caught up and vanish. The possibility troubled him, but he knew in a calm part of his anatomy that it would not come about. He could see that the children of Israel were like the things he remembered from the time before his mother had begun to wear mourning, and he knew that he himself would go away but that they would go on moving calmly in their furnace whether he was watching or not. He listened to the end of the Scripture story, and he was sure it must all be equally true, but there was one part of it that never became visible. He was not able to imagine the children of Israel coming out of the furnace again.

But he could not remember, either, that the sight of his mother wearing mourning had ever troubled him. On the contrary, although her appearance wrapped in black had become completely familiar to him long before the day they went to see Campbell, and by then had seemed to be part of a settled, if not immutable, order of things, whose authority lay outside anything in his memory, the fact itself of her wearing mourning was still a source of pleasure to him, almost as though it were a novelty. In the house much of the time she wore quite ordinary dresses, some of them black, it was true, but others merely dark, or faded to gray. Most of them, in fact, themselves came from the earlier and unapproachable time whose secrets were kept all around him, but if the garments had ever been luminous the light was dead now. The sight of her dressed in full mourning meant that she was going out, or that someone was coming, and provided that he was to be with her he looked forward to either, but there was more than that to his delight in the black, and if some time had passed without his having seen her in full mourning he would urge his mother to wear the dark formal clothes all the time. Both she and his aunt had told him in different ways that he must try to understand, as though if he understood he would care less about the black clothes. Each of them, having started, had paused and then said that the clothes showed respect, but he could not see how this was a reason for wearing them less often. His aunt, who sometimes wore black clothes too, but without the same effect as when his mother did, said that they were a sign that the angel of death had visited the person who wore them, and he could see at once how the clothes would be like a preservation of the angel's shadow, but it seemed to him that a person would be able to choose afterwards whether to wear such garments or not. And in fact his mother had said to him once, as though she were telling him a secret—not a deep one, but one that had been kept from him and from strangers—that she was wearing heavier mourning now than was strictly called for, but when he had asked her what she meant her eyes had filled up, and she had shaken her head, saying that she had her reasons. It had never occurred to him that he might have worn black himself. It seemed to him that mourning clothes were exclusive to women, and he had been surprised when his mother said to him one day, as though it were something which he already knew and she was simply repeating, that she had never wanted him to wear any tokens, as she called them, of mourning, because she did not hold with children being made to display the marks in public. The consideration of such a possibility, which had been snatched away as soon as it had been shown to him, left him faintly curious, but not for long.

He thought about it on the way to Campbell's, walking along the quiet street in the spring sunlight. The mourning made people look at the person who wore it. It always did. He had known it did, now, for a long time. It was right. It was part of growing up; it was something to be proud of. It surrounded his mother, and him too, with importance, even more than did the fact, which he had overheard more than once, that his mother was still a beautiful woman. He decided again that it was better to share the reflected glory of his mother's mourning, and the respect that came with it, than to wear mourning himself, which perhaps no one including himself would have been able to take seriously. But he could imagine how it would feel to wear mourning. Like having had a bath, a thing that began with reluctance and led to a feeling of superiority.

It was not usual for them to be out this early: the hour in the morning when schools and offices have just settled down to an industrious scarcely audible hum, concentrated inside their windows. The streets were nearly empty. Sunbeams hung in them. The sound of a huckster calling the names of vegetables, as though they were children lost beyond hope of recovery, carried from many streets away. He considered the expressions of the houses: the ones with asbestos shingles overlapping in different shapes; the ones covered in stucco jeweled with broken glass, that Italians liked; the yellow brick ones with iron fences. Whoever passed on that street, on the way to the butcher's at this hour, would greet them or at least look at them as persons of privilege, as though they were cleaner, or better, or taller than people around. The way was familiar—the beginning of it—though it was to lead them to somewhere that he had never been. The chief difference from other walks along that street, apart from the hour, was his mother's demeanor. She walked faster than usual, without looking pensively at the houses where people they knew lived. When she spoke her voice was different too: quicker and harder, as though she were talking to someone else. She did not look at him, except to pull the front of his jacket down and brush it off with her hand after they had gotten onto the streetcar. And what she said also seemed to be addressed to someone else, but someone else who was still him, as though to an older self who was already there but whom he could not see. She spoke as though he knew a great many things that she was fully aware he could not know. She referred to Campbell as though he knew him and had been there before. She did not talk long or in detail about anything, and he realized after a bit that questions from him were out of place and would not be answered except, after a pause, by more of those assumptions, that talk addressed to someone whom he was not, whom he wished he could be. He hoped that she would not suddenly remember what she knew: who he really was, and how little he understood of what she was saying.

The streetcar reached the place where the tracks swung out over a viaduct, where there was no rail and the car seemed to hang suspended in space, hundreds of feet above the warehouses and railroad yards of the port. It was always a breathless moment when they took that car. He turned as usual from the brief dizzying sight of the city sprawled far below like nets drying, to reassure himself by looking at his mother's face, but this day he was unable to meet her eye even when he looked at her for a long time, and her face suddenly looked like no one he knew.

It was a long way. They had to change to the ferry, then to two subways. Then they were walking in a street that was certainly not one that he had ever seen but that seemed to resemble another that they knew: cool, with brownstone fronts and low brownstone walls along the sidewalk. Once they had paid regular visits to a doctor on such a street, whom his mother and the doctor had agreed that he liked, and he had known that they must of course be right, but had been puzzled because he had felt that he hated the man. He asked his mother whether Campbell knew the doctor, but she answered him with the same incomprehension as when he had asked about the reappearances of remote memories. She seemed to get farther from him as they walked down this strange street. He could smell the harbor: stronger here, more penetrating than where they lived, full of an advanced implacable private knowledge, older and shared only by those who belonged here, the essence of a different country.

They passed the stone houses, and a few blocks with little grimy shops, and open garages with men welding inside, and an empty lot across which the marshes and the harbor water could be seen between buildings, and came to a large wooden warehouse or factory building, once painted red, but faded, blistered, and peeled, standing on a corner from which one street sloped down toward the water. The few windows in the upper stories were blank with dust. The entrance—a double house door with glass panels covered with frosted flowers—was up several stone steps and was flanked by large plate-glass window bays. There had once been a drugstore on the ground floor, as you could tell from the painting on the plate glass, and one great glass amphora half full of milky amber water was leaning in a corner, with its chains draped around it. An open truck and a closed moving van were standing on the street and several men in overalls were coming down the steps carrying a long bundle of swaying copper pipe. His mother paused at the corner, and then, with him by the hand, went up the steps and into the building.

What was wrong was in there everywhere. The smell of age violated and probed by a day like chlorine. Naked patches on the floor and walls, where furniture and frames had recently been. Rusted screws still groping out from joists and walls. Ends of wires clutching the air; piping lying everywhere. Plaster rubble and rags on the stairs. Broken glass, broken glass, clear, blue, and amber, under every step. His mother did not even urge him to step carefully, but whenever he kicked a piece of broken glass, in the bad light, her hand tightened on his. In the room to the right, which had been half of the drugstore, there were still two cabinets with sliding glass fronts, standing empty. She went up to one of them and laid her hand, in its glove, on the dust, and looked around the room as though there might be an angel hiding in the air. The workmen stomped back in and through the hall between the rooms and on toward the back of the building and when they had passed he and his mother went out and up the stairs where she seemed to have heard something. Upstairs the wreck was no less evident but the materials were different: papers, crockery, cardboard boxes, more pipe, more broken glass. Large metal bins still ensconced in the tin-paneled walls, both brown with paint and time. In a back room, with two windows open onto the harbor, long laboratory tables, and the walls lined with shelves, he was introduced to Campbell.

He had imagined, he could not have said why, someone like the apparition in the brown suit who had stood at the bay window and directed a vague and limited benevolence toward the flowerpot, in a time now immeasurably remote. He had also envisaged a personage resembling the doctor whom they used to come to visit. But these may have figured in his expectations largely for lack of enough variety of examples to fit to the tone of his mother's voice. He could not of course remember any reference to the man in the brown suit. When she had mentioned the doctor it had been with a note of initiated awe, as though he added to her safety, but not without contributing some small inoculatory dread of his own. But when she had spoken of Campbell it had been with a clearer pride and pleasure, scarcely worried, open to surprise: something like the way in which she spoke of her elder brother whom he had never met, who was dead.

Even to the eyes of a child Campbell was much younger than the doctor or the apparition in the brown suit. He realized that he had imagined Campbell to be older for another reason: the man was a relative of his mother's. The relationship was a complicated one that he had not understood. It meant remembering the relatives and marriages of other people whom he had never known. But his mother had very few living relatives and most of those were remote—cousins of cousins, and when they were identified it was with photographs brown with age, which showed them as starved-looking children or adults in clothes like wrinkled petals, always from long before he was born. Or when he met them, once or twice, they were older than his mother, older than his aunt, old. "This is your cousin Campbell," she said, and he was surprised at the word, and surprised to see that it applied to a slim young man, with a shining smooth-shaven face, in an elegant suit, who had been wearing a derby hat on the back of his head, until he had caught sight of the woman and child in the doorway. Campbell had been examining a blue bottle, and set it down to greet them, hanging his hat on it and stepping forward laughing.

The laugh seemed never to stop. It punctuated all of Campbell's talk, which began to flow in an easy, confidential, amused, varied, eventful current. Whatever had led to the wreckage now littering every room did not seem to trouble Campbell any more than if he were moving to a better address and the workmen were employed by him, but a cloud hanging in the rooms listening to all that was said had surely come from the tents of disaster.

While Campbell was talking he went and opened a drawer in the shelves and took out several small packages which he presented to the boy, as though it were a joke. Seeds. The boy recognized the packets, in the same brittle tan paper, with the same copper staples, colored and marked in the same way as the ones his mother had used and had given him and helped him to plant. They had planted a great many, it seemed to him, recently, and he did not know what to do with the new packages except to say thank you. But Campbell had already turned away and was laughing to his mother. And the child suddenly heard Campbell's voice as though it were his own, talking to her with the appearance of great assurance, laughing about himself, how lazy and foolish he was, how he had never found the place half as interesting as it was now, how if he had half the interest in it regularly that he had at this moment he would have spent his best hours of the past years here, whereas, as it was, he was still trying to find where some of the records were kept. Campbell went and stood at the door leading out to the stairs and listened for a moment. "They're off to lunch," he said, and laughed. And then he started the boy's mother on a tour of the wreckage, the equipment removed, the instruments broken or carted off, all as though it were deeply comic.

"And," he said, "it seems I'm in debt for thousands, besides, just for copper." It was nothing to run into that much in copper, he said, and there would have been no point in doing it out of a piggy bank. But it did seem unjust, he said, to have it removed and be in debt for it just the same. But that, he admitted, laughing, was in the wine part of the business, which she had never approved of anyway. It was, he said, striking his chest, a branch that he had added to the firm himself, and against other advice than hers. "But something will come of it yet," he said, and with a great air of secrecy he produced the blue bottle from under his hat, propped it at an angle on the laboratory table, drew an open bottle down from an upper shelf and commanded the child to watch while he tipped the one bottle, in a cradle, so that it ran into the other by itself. The boy watched, thinking of the two molded monkeys that he had seen on a mantelpiece during a visit, holding between them a glass tube through which a mindless section of red water passed back and forth, as he had been told, forever. Campbell pointed out to them both that the blue bottle was blown in the form of a large folded jackknife, and he said that it was the beginning of something. The same wine in curious bottles, and he already had enough laid by, which he was sure he would be able to get out with, for a start. He went into a farther room, looking for more bottles, and the child's mother went with him. Their voices came wandering back through the back rooms, his mother asking, her voice coming rarely, with a soft weight on it, frightened, in short questions, Campbell laughing and answering something else, at length. The boy went out and sat on the stairs, looking down and out through the open front door to the broken stone of the top step and the pocked iron hand rail until he heard them coming back. Then he got up and moved slowly back into the room. His mother was still in the other doorway of the room, looking at Campbell who was gazing out through the open window, over the water, with four blue bottles under his arm, saying that it made him think of his sister, living in the country not because she liked anything else about the country except waking up there in the mornings with a view of the sea, and how angry she would be with him when she heard, because she had had money in it too, of course. "But she can afford it," Campbell said, and turned as he laughed, and saw the boy, and bore down on him again.

"Look what I found," he said. More packets of seeds. "Look," Campbell said, bending down, pointing to the printing on them, the fading handwriting on some. The boy could not read what they said, and

Campbell's breath smelt unpleasant, like the purple piles steaming outside the back steps of the Italians' houses on autumn days before his birthday. "They're seeds from my uncle's incumbency, and my grandfather's, and his father's. It's a sound concern, steady as a rock, you see. These are what sent me to college." He laughed and one of the large packets in his hand burst and fine seeds began to trickle out onto the floor, and as he bent down to look, reddening, he bumped into the laboratory table and the two propped bottles rolled and crashed together and onto the floor, where the wine had already spilled over the edge of the table. "What I should have been was a minister," Campbell went on saying, "with my voice. I hear myself in the other rooms." And when the boy looked up from the wine and the seeds he saw tears for the first time running down his mother's face under the short veil.

And then he was Campbell, the voice, the smooth skin, the laugh, as he would be at ineradicable moments for the rest of his life. When he woke once, drunk, by a small culvert in a seaside town, in good and scarcely wrinkled clothes, staring up at the blue sky and knowing that catastrophe was about to arrive like the flood. Or when good news came, expected or unexpected. Or money from his mother. Or when he felt a hollow freedom after some death, as though nothing, suddenly, were any fault of his. Then he would be again, without warning, the soft stomach born, as his mother had told him, under Cancer (which was not his own real sign, as he knew, and insisted) and would see again the small boy dropping packets and leaping to pound him on the handsome waistcoat with its chain, shrieking, "Campbell, Campbell, Campbell, I've always hated you."

THE FLYOVER

(1969)

Do you know, I was never sure about why you went back to work. After the vacation, I mean. I had understood that you had planned not to, and this is not the moment or the place to go into it, of course, but those are always the moments and places when we do—have—aren't they? Gone into things. Money inevitably would have been given as a reason. But we'd managed, hadn't we, with less, and we could have managed, and it wouldn't have been important to us to have less, as you've said yourself, and it was true. I'd have wondered, and I wonder what money would have represented in such a conversation. Maybe you simply wanted to be dissuaded. And were doubtful about being there all day, in the heat at the bottom of the house, looking at the lucent patches of sun moving like moorings on the sooty flagstones and over the spindly plants in the square of garden deep among the uptown buildings, and wondering what to do next, and how next to navigate the recurrent resentments of having to decide, at not being alone, at being alone. This should help to explain, when it arrives. I finished earlier than I had expected to, and you know how you laugh when I say that's always fatal. The heat downtown and the presence of traffic and of all that was urging it on were oppressive, and everyone appeared to be moving through them as though these things were inevitable and right. I set out to do the same, but they were all going somewhere where they meant to be by a certain time, with no particular intervals to spare, in spite of the heat, and I had some time left whether I went uptown to meet you after work, or went straight on back. Not enough time to accomplish anything, start on anything. Just enough to walk out and look at the lucent patches of sun and wonder whether to go out again where at least there was some air, or to wait, or to telephone. As usual I decided to walk, while I was

"The Flyover" first appeared in *Quarterly Review of Literature*.

deciding about the rest, at least, and headed north toward the park. By the time I was there I thought I would take the new flyover, though certainly it had not been conceived as a footwalk (as they say), and cross town that way, which would doubtless be quicker than the old threading through others on their way to behind one, and so I might be able to walk all the way back and arrive just about at the same time you did unless you had made some sort of other plans. Oh well. You know the usual sign about No Motorcycles, No Bicycles, No Picnics, etc., but it didn't say Nobody on Foot, perhaps only because of the sheer unlikeliness, and you know there's that foot of ledge at the bottom of the railings that will be one of the classic features of our age. It's there on the big skyways that were made before we were born. I've hitchhiked, walking along one (not a place I had chosen, because who would stop there, but because I was getting out of town however I could at the time). The same ledge has been incorporated in the new structure, whether to give stability to the railings or walls, whichever they happen to be at that place, or to repel cars and prevent them from crashing into the balustrade itself at the least misjudgment or swerve, or to provide a shelf for pedestrians in emergencies: officials, attendants, mechanics, helpless drivers, although in some places it looked to me as though the ledge (I can't call it a curb because it obviously hadn't been conceived as one) is too high to allow a door of one of the new cars to open. I had some trouble getting to the right-hand lane but really they haven't altered the park much and I never could find my way to anywhere in that tangle of walks without at least one mistake, anyway. And I thought if I missed it altogether and found myself at the exit I'd walk on back through the park, depending on the time, but I got to it all right. I'd forgotten that it was Friday and the rush had already started though it was well before five. I had thought, naturally enough, to avoid the worst of the blue cloud of car exhaust that filled the avenues, plainly visible at the distance of a block or two, since I would be above it. But the pressures over the city are full of surprises and the exhaust on the flyover was worse from the start. I thought at first that this was simply because the cars on the entrance ramp were moving so slowly, bumper to bumper, with all the tops down or open, and drivers' arms out, hands on the car roofs, the sun-dazzle filtered by the permanent exhaust-cloud. But I realized as we went up that the cloud was actually more dense where it had risen a little, and had merely turned grayer, and less blue. Besides, the construction of the flyover is such that the exhaust is caught in it as in a canal, if the pressures, as they often do, keep it from rising properly. The balustrades are solid, though the die from which the railings themselves have been stamped has made them look as though there were regular slots that you could see through. You know how they are on some of the big bridges, when you want to get a look down at the river, or to see whether it really is a river underneath and I've supposed that they'd made the sides opaque that way deliberately, so that drivers wouldn't be tempted to take their eyes off the road. I thought that must be the reason here too, to keep drivers from gazing down into the park as they crept along, but as soon as we were off the ramp and onto the flyover itself I saw it couldn't be that, and must have something to do with stress, strength in proportion to weight, one more classical feature, a blankness. Because in back of the railings once you get up onto the flyover there is nothing most of the way but high brick walls, the backs of all that new building where they've just been reclaiming the second level and the man was talking about the effects on real estate, the other evening. The exhaust was worse than ever, blowing across my ankles, and I nearly turned back then, but that ramp is longer than any of the bridge approaches, for a start, and it would have taken me far too long, as I thought. And I didn't relish, for some reason, walking back on the left facing traffic, though that's what you're supposed to do, and besides I had a notion that I should have told you about, I imagine, but I wanted to find out a little more. I saw an ad the day before yesterday for what sounded like just what we'd said we ought to find, in the western part of the state, in the woods, and I'd had in the back of my mind the notion that we could have gone, maybe on the weekend, to have a look, and could have taken the flyover and by then I'd know the way, you see, so I thought I'd just walk on to the next exit down on the west side, which must be nearer to the top of the ramp than to the entrance, judging by how far I seemed to have come. I couldn't see back by then because the ramp curves and the exhaust would have hidden it anyway. Motorcycles were racing ahead as I thought about it, and there must have been an accident or a drama of some kind up ahead, and though it was bound to be too far for me to get to before it was all over, or probably to get to at all, I moved on a little faster as they went by, the way one does, and a wave of impatience seemed to flow along the whole stream. The mufflers seemed to have burst or to have been removed on a larger number of cars than before, and the roar, with that wobble in it that we used to imitate as children, accelerated. Squirrel tails on radio antennae actually brushed my shoulder twice. Then you get up a little farther and the really big buildings hover around looking as though they would be silent, just a little higher than the flyover, if it were not for the helicopters blasting back and forth just above them. You know, the flyover is built up through the upper levels so that I don't imagine that that part of it will be visible from the ground when that area is opened again. But you reach a recessed place, some distance along, where a sort of bay is formed to the right of that lane. It afforded a relief at once, as though a pressure had been removed. All along it big trailer trucks were backed in, as they do downtown, to unload. There was a new smell, something cool, wading through the exhaust cloud. I thought it was meat, then I realized it was the smell of slaughterhouses. I couldn't make out what companies or directives have led to the establishment of slaughterhouses up here, whether it is part of a new movement of dispersion, a paradoxical decentralization, or whether these are purveyors to some orthodox belief or to several of them which require special butcheries to maintain their own cleanliness of spirit. There are no advertisements on the brick walls, or none yet at least, and the trucks themselves bore the names of shipping firms, express firms, ranches, and an assortment of meat packers, and a few called for support of the war effort, so I could not reach any conclusions. All the unloading seemed to be taking place without visible human participation: they have managed that by connecting the rear of each truck to its unloading port in the long facade with one of those telescopic caterpillar tunnels they have at some airports. You get no sight of the animals going in. The empty trucks turn out into the lane heading west out of the city, and the metallic tunnel has already been closed off inside before the truck is detached, as I was able to see. The full trucks enter the bay from a special ramp coming up from the level below, which may run under this one, in the opposite direction, for the whole length of the flyover. I was beginning to wonder about the time. I thought I had been walking long enough to have almost crossed the island. I began to doubt whether I would in fact be able to walk all the way back, or would have to take the subway after I got off the flyover. There are no clocks in the bay, that I could see, and there is no way of seeing out to one of the buildings that flashes the time and the temperature in lights every fifteen seconds. I might have asked a truck driver, but I was rather reluctant to call attention to my unauthorized presence, on foot in the place, and I edged past the end truck and out onto the ledge again, walking rather faster than before. It was hotter, out on the flyover itself. It seemed that I must come to an exit, or at least to the first sign telling of one, quite soon. I looked up once or twice to see whether there were gulls, not that I would have been able to tell anything, I suppose, if I had seen any. But the ledge is too narrow; it feels dangerous to look up, as though you were suddenly trying to balance on a rail. It felt reasonably hazardous even to turn enough to look back, with the traffic heavier all the time, and kept moving, as they say. As in the tunnels. As though a certain regulated panic were officially encouraged at some starting point on the structure, and the vehicles fled from there to the end, or to some sign that checked them. But nothing told of an exit. The bay was well out of sight. It came to me with a quick additional rush of heat to the face that I had no real certainty that there was an exit from the flyover on the west side of the island. I had assumed that it would be possible to cross the island that way, and that there would be a way off the structure before it was no longer over the city but already crossing the river. I tried to think back to the entrance, to see whether I could conjure up some image of the signs there. Had I missed one that told of some other lane for traffic that was not outward-bound but merely intended to cross the city and descend again on the other side? Or was there no such lane at all; was all the flyover traffic bound out of the city? I tried to remember what I had heard and read in the papers about the plans for the flyover, about its construction and what it would mean for circulation in the city, to see if I could muster up some clue that would answer the question for me, but it was useless. I ended with images of other bridges, expressways, ramps, and it was dangerous to let the imagination stray from this particular ledge. And the time—how could I find that out? Can you imagine anyone stopping for an overheated pedestrian in that unlikely place, and can you imagine the pedestrian, if he did, asking what time it was? But I realized that I had lost any idea of how late it was getting. You might be back by now, for that matter. Not knowing what to think. Perhaps worried already, puzzled. Going out again. A long way ahead, as far as I could see through the exhaust haze, it looked as though the light were different. Brighter. As though the brick walls were lower and the daylight came in from the sides as well as from overhead. It might have been nothing but some trick of perspective, but it presented a welcome possibility. I did not dare to run, on that ledge, but I hurried ahead, noticing as I did the peculiar walk, slightly sideways, that I had adopted on the ledge, slightly turned out toward the rushing traffic, my usual stride unbalanced and sidling. I tried to guess whether it had delayed me much, but I had been in no hurry to start with, so how could I judge. It was an unpleasant recognition, this one of the effect on my walk which I could do little about changing, in my hurry on the narrow ledge, or not without increased danger and an excessive concentration on the stride itself, which I imagined would be still more distasteful. But the alteration in my walk entered into my sense of myself like some false but powerfully impelled gesture. No passing driver could have paid more than an instant's vague attention to me, or have had time even for curiosity before I had disappeared, but I imagined that the sidelong way in which I was setting one foot in front of the other must look stealthy or ashamed, and I felt both. But up ahead the light really was different. And I saw a sign, looming out of the haze above the traffic; I could not read it, but when I had to look away I saved it up in my mind like a chocolate when I was a child. When I got to where I could make it out, it did not, as you will have guessed, announce an exit, but "Last Turnout before River. Parking for Disabled Vehicles Only." Clearly there was no exit on this side of the river. But I thought perhaps there might be some way off the flyover at the turnout, and the idea of going all the way back without at least going on to see did not seem sensible. The turnout and the river would explain the change in the light up ahead. It even crept into the bricks as I went: the new pinks and yellows looked a shade cleaner. I had a moment of imagining that the change in the light might after all be simply a prelude to the sunset, and the thought filled me with something like fright, but I told myself (quite rightly) that it couldn't possibly be that late. Perhaps the air currents near the river had thinned the exhaust; in any case, the changed visibility seemed to lengthen the distances too, and it turned out to be farther than I had expected to the turnout. Then a lane began to sheer away to the right at an angle so fine that I had walked some distance along it before I realized that there was already a yard or more between the ledge and the rushing fenders that were held away from me by a white line that streaked away due west, while I was heading slightly north on a tangent, and a widening sliver of black asphalt, a reversed perspective, was running ahead, empty and unclaimed and undisturbed. Still, the ledge held me by its narrowness, as much as by its liability to be brushed suddenly by a vehicle making for the turnout, to my slightly edgewise walk. Even the entrance lane, so gradually angled, took up what seemed to be an exaggerated distance before it finally split entirely from the nearest lane of the outbound traffic and slid behind a brick wall about twice the height of a man. But it was not very far beyond that point that the turnout began. Another long bay, two generous lanes wide so that cars could get past each other. There is room, lengthwise, for a dozen of them or so, parked in the usual manner: yes, the bay is longer than a midtown block on one of the avenues. It is hard to judge because there were no cars there when I finally got in behind the wall to the point where the whole turnout became visible, and there are none now as I write. A long irregular oil slick in the middle of the parking lane, beside which the ledge widens into a real plaza, as wide as another two lanes, in the middle at least, for it is shaped in a shallow curve like that of a row of seats in a theater, facing the wall that divides the turnout from the traffic. There are, as you would expect, a number of abandoned tires scattered over the plaza, and ripped treads, half inside out, and crushed oilcans, still with their burnished tops clean inside the greenish ring of oil with the red iridescences, and the two triangular punctures undistorted by what has befallen the rest of the abandoned container. And a few other cans, cartons, cigarette packages, piles where ashtrays have been emptied, torn envelopes and letters, bits of newspaper, a small broken radio, a burst basket of pink plastic, despite the fact that there are large signs at intervals on the walls saying "No Littering $100 Fine," and waste receptacles every two car-lengths or so, with others farther apart over by the balustrade. Still, the place is cleaner than many streets in the city itself. What is pleasant is that the balustrade has great apertures in it, like those of a greatly magnified battlement, and through them one can look down into the city. I cannot understand how I could have walked so far, as it seemed, to be only at the river, even though, it is true, we have been rising and, obviously, passing uptown at an angle all the way. I had no idea how high we were already. I can make out the street, working my way in from the monument. The view of the river is marvellous from up here and I can understand their not wanting it to tempt the eyes of motorists. The barges have that afternoon light effect on their rust that makes them look as though they themselves were fading, beginning to disappear, even as they approach throwing up spray with their prows shaped like old coal cars, and the old bridge is hardly visible, pale and finespun, receding when you try to fix it with your eye. It looks as though the air has cleared down there, since earlier. The details along the drive, the reflections on car bodies and glass, are sharp and distinct. I see an ambulance on a cross-street, but individual sounds do not carry up here, only blurred susurration, like a steady flowing of some simple element—air, water, fire, dust. I thought at least I would be able to telephone from here and see what time it was, and try to reach you, because I thought there was bound to be a telephone at the turnout: it occurred to me almost as soon as I saw the sign, once I had got past the first disappointment at the thought that there would be no exit before leaving the city, and I was pleased with myself for thinking of it. And indeed there are telephones here. Six, to be exact, in groups of two each, at either end of the turnout, and in the middle. But over each pair there is a sign saying that they are police telephones, for emergency use only, for calling the police (number given), ambulance (number given), breakdown service attached to the flyover (number given), or fireman. There is the same penalty for improper use or tampering with the telephones as there is on fire and police telephones in the city. There is a locked iron door in the wall at one end of the balustrade. It may be some kind of exit. And there is a Public Convenience, with a large warning against loitering, and a mailbox, strangely enough, which is what made me think of writing something, in the same notebook I had been using earlier, and I had some envelopes and stamps left from this morning. It says there will not be another mail pickup before tomorrow morning and so of course I will be there long before this even starts on its way, but it gives me an excuse to sit, for a minute, on two of the abandoned tires laid on top of each other, and take a rest in the light, before I go back to the ledge. I have thought carefully about whether to go back to the entrance, or across the river, and on the whole I think that I would do better to go on. I can't imagine that the actual distance would be much greater. There must be an exit on the other side, to the dock area, and its ramp may start splintering off from the main flyover well before the other side of the river. Any possible additional distance would be compensated for by the light, which looked more pleasant, airier, up ahead, where the flyover is out above the river, and where the balustrade, consequently, is much lower than the blank backs of the buildings, over the city. And besides, I would be moving in the same direction as the traffic, which I prefer, whether or not it is in fact natural and excusable; for the moment, at least, I have got used to moving that way, and am convinced I can make better time than I could by working my way back, facing the cars. From the other side I should easily be able to get a bus or a subway back. Even a taxi, to a subway station. Whatever the time is then. Still the rush hour here, judging from the sound of the traffic on the other side of the barrier, and the packed cars on the drive, down there, where no doubt you have got back now, even some time ago. Even if I make it back before dark and you are there, you have sometimes said that I am not always good at saying things, and sooner or later this should help to explain.

THE HAWK AND THE MULES

(1971)

I have looked toward the island, toward the region of my memory where it is, and have seen out of the corner of my eye the word *Hawk* written above it, or the words *Sea Hawk,* and I have caught the smell of rats. I am not sure what these mean. A judgment of some kind, no doubt, but by and upon whom I cannot yet say. These signals were not present before, or at least I did not notice them. It is true that I have not perhaps turned my mind much to the island these last years, especially by day. It goes without saying that I was not conscious of such signs when I lived there.

I was alone. I had a house in a little terraced valley running up the mountain to the east of the village. The moon rose late there, only appearing over the craggy peak long after the village below had been turned pale by its light. Only one house near me was lived in, by a fisherman's family. I lived on fish, which they brought up from the boats early in the morning, and on eggs, which I bought from them too, in the beginning. "Their eggs taste of fish," I was told. And it was true, and I did not serve them to guests. "They mix the hens' eggs and the ducks' eggs together," I was told also. That was true too. I went on buying them just the same, as though it were a game involving a certain risk. "Why not get your eggs at the shop?" I was asked. (I had not been complaining.) Many of those in the village who did not keep chickens got their eggs at one of the two small dark shops, each two steps down from the dirt street, each lined with tubs of sardines and hung with salt cod and dried sausages and little ivory cheeses, all converging on the sacks ranged in front of the wooden counter as in front of an altar; rice, the sack farthest to the right containing the most gravel, that to the left of it costing more and containing a little less, that to the left of it containing still less, until the one all the way to the left,

"The Hawk and the Mules" appeared originally in *The New Yorker.*

which had scarcely been touched, contained almost none. At the right of the counter was a small grilled cage housing fish pies and spinach pies, many days old, which some of the village women made and brought in, warm, a few at a time, in their hands. At the other end of the counter was another cage containing eggs lying on dried grass. Old women brought them in, carrying them in their aprons. The wines from both shops tasted of churches, heavy and musky. It was a taste I grew to like in the wine, but I went on buying my eggs from the neighbors.

Their hands and clothes were often smeared with scales and blood. There were always feathers drifting around their door and mine, and down the path to the village, where the eyeless heads of fish still tried to swallow dust, but the hens would not allow it, nor the dogs, nor the cats. The path slipped into the village between the huddled backs of houses, passing board lean-tos in which, at the sound of footsteps, the voices of pigs stirred like large hollow stones in their huge sides waiting to be fed and cut open.

I bought my eggs finally from a tall mute who lived alone with his mother, in a house by itself, on a spur below the village, over the sea. I had stumbled upon the place one day when I was walking in the hills, and they had invited me in and plied me with bread and fresh goat cheese, and wine that was like a rock to the teeth. He would force up whispers which his mother interpreted to me, and we talked as well as we could, and when I got up to go he disappeared for a few minutes and came back with some eggs and held them out to me. When I showed reluctance to accept them as a gift he made his noise to his mother, who said to me, "He will drop them." With difficulty I managed to learn that they sold eggs, sometimes, to people, and also cheese, and I offered to come and get some of each every week, but the mute was anxious to bring them himself. "They'd sell their eggs to anybody they could," I was told, and also, "Their eggs aren't fresh." And from time to time there was a bad one. And I was told that his dog had run sheep and been shot for it, and that he was not right in the head, and that nobody knew where she got her hens, and, of course, that she was a witch. He brought the things every Thursday he had them and remembered, and would not take as much money as the shop, and would not stay, and no one he passed caught his eye or looked at him when he went by, though they might turn and look after him. Clearly I had taken up with people whom none of them wished to be associated with, and for a long time I tried to discover why, lying in wait for the subject and dragging it suddenly off the path into the bushes. I suppose I thought I would surprise some poorly disguised tale from which all their unforgivings flowed, but I came at last really to believe that there was none—that their behavior toward those two was a matter of pure custom, arrived at gradually, imperceptibly, inevitably, because it was possible and fulfilled a general urge.

On one of the paths below the house where I lived was the olive mill, in a building that was still a palace, though the green shutters of the upper stories were seldom opened. In the courtyard paved with unpolished slabs of local marble a large fountain carved with heads and vines stood empty, and beyond it, in the autumn, the smoke of olive wood slid through a wide doorway and stained the stones above it, and under the smoke came the smell of crushed olives and mule dung and sweat, and the sound of long sticks whacking the spines of two gaunt mules buckled into a framework made for four, turning all day in a track around a stone basin in which sacks of olives, like small black eggs, were poured into the path of two revolving stone wheels. In another room a trickle of oil, warm from its meeting with boiling water, picked up the color of the darkness and made it lustrous, flowing into a stone basin like a sarcophagus, to be dipped out on pieces of bread and praised as though it were the balm of every earthly pain.

At the same time of year the flocks of migrant birds passed, stopping at the island. In the one place in the village that served meals they offered little birds to eat. Men went up on the mountain with fish nets and sticks and came back with sacks. Decoys in cages, some of them blinded, hung outside houses in the afternoon sun, and children limed sticks and set them as though they were showing each other a secret. There were one or two large cages in windows, filled with all kinds of birds flinging themselves against the wires, some of them obviously dying. I stayed away from the village and from the sound of voices as much as I could, but one day when I had been to the sea I came back past the olive mill. It was the end of the autumn afternoon but the dry whacks of the sticks and the creaking of the harness and of the beam presses could still be heard up on the path. And there ahead of me a boy was sitting with his back to the wall, in the dirt, throwing stones at something, which turned out, as I came closer, to be a bird, a goldfinch, tied by its leg, with nine or ten inches of string, to a rock, so that it could try to fly from the stones as they were thrown. I ran up to the boy. I did not touch him. Whatever I said frightened him. I picked up the rock and the bird and broke the string, and when I told the boy to go away he ran.

It was hard to get the string off the bird's foot because the skin of the leg was tangled in it. He must have started to blind the bird and got only halfway. Anyway, it was dying. I took it along in my hands and it died on the way.

While I went along saying, "That was heroic, wasn't it? Rushing at him because he's only a boy, and poor, and ignorant. Why not do something about the mules, if you're so zealous and so pure." And I answered, "It'll teach him a lesson." And I said, "You know it won't." And I went on, "Why don't you stop them liming and caging them down in the village? Why do you just do it to one boy, by himself up on the hill?" "Well it just might teach him a lesson." "It just might make him worse." "Well what could I have done? Walked by and done nothing?" "Do you really think that was the best thing to do, just because it's the only thing you can think of? The heart fails and the mind makes excuses. You just did it so you wouldn't be ashamed of yourself." "That's not true, either." "Prove it." "That wouldn't be a good reason for doing anything, either." And later I was told that I had been imprudent, and might now expect coolness or even hostility from many of my neighbors.

But it was none of these things that took me away from the island at last, many months later. No, and I went on home that evening and threw the dead bird out for the foxes and cats of the mountain, and found that the mute, whom I had given up for that week, had come and left eggs and cheese inside the door and not waited for his money, and I ate my cheese watching the sun go down among the olive trees, knowing that below me the black stream was still flowing in the mill turned by those mules that must have been dead now for years.

AIR

(1978)

The open windows, huge as sails, rise, tall, white, slender, on both sides of the vast room. Room? Barn, warehouse, hangar, hall, nave—what should it be called? It has been all of them in turn, and passed through them. Outside the windows, the white sail of the sky, with shadows moving slowly along it, crossing the glare of summer. The shrill voices of children playing in the afternoon fly up, fly up. I stop hearing them. They go out. Then I hear them again, those voices. The unseen children must be the age I was when I first thought of making the boat. No, they are older. And the children have changed, and changed, but the voices are the same.

Standing with my head back, looking up to the top of the mast just under the main beams of the cavernous raftered ceiling, thinking to see the masthead move in the wooden sky, as one expects to see a body breathe, I hear them. They echo. When I was a child, the building was a church, and the windows were colored. Pale greens and yellows, enfolding bright flowers and heraldic devices. Panes like maps opened horizontally in summer, pulled by long thin ropes that swung in sunbeams through the vacant singing of hymns, first, second, and last verses inclusive. Stones broke them later, here and there, and they were removed and sold, and replaced with plain glass. Wire netting was rigged below them; and roofs like stairs lying down, with ventilator cowls rising through them, came to occupy the spaces from which the stones had once been thrown. For a while the whole structure was left empty, and considered abandoned—but I would not have thought then of making the boat here. In fact, there were times when I seemed to have forgotten about the boat altogether, but then the thought would be there again, and I would realize that it had never been away. Yet I did feel, at certain

"Air" appeared originally in *The New Yorker*.

periods, that it was impracticable, unreal, unrealizable—as perhaps it is. And the reason for wanting it, the object of the whole enterprise, shifted, dissolved, reformed, and occasionally, if examined suddenly, was seen to be completely blank.

The building went through an era as a cheap movie house: Grade B films, old Westerns where everything happened in a hailstorm, early serials, strung together. The tickets were sold in a wooden booth brought whole from some other history, painted white, and fitted into what had been the barn door, facing the street. And upstairs, in the back office, in that era, there was a barbershop, with a view of the harbor from the barber's chairs; the customers went up the iron fire escape stairs, outside. The barber's friends came to pass the time of day with him, up there, sitting on varnished chairs, around the walls, under the yellowed, stained, faded posters showing tall women in tight ball gowns, soldiers with flags, and autumnal vistas of Canadian forests with moose standing in lakes in the twilight. The conversation sank and resumed while the barber stropped and clipped and lathered, and a shrewd eye belonging to neither a friend nor a customer could have told at a glance the friends from the waiting customers by the set of a hat, the angle of a newspaper, the way a spittoon was moved closer with a foot to receive a cigar butt, the way a passage of talk was ignored and then interrupted. Friends, if they chose to, left by the inside stairs that led down into the front of the movie house, through a door marked "Private," and took in a few minutes of the movie on the way out, for the barber, the manager of the movie house, and the ushers were friends as well. The barber retired eventually, for reasons of health, and sat with his friends in other establishments, nearby. The barber's chairs, and some of the varnished chairs and posters, are still up there, with lumber and crates piled around them. One of the barber's friends knew a friend of mine, to whom I spoke, much later, of the old, and still rather vague, plan to construct the boat. And that was how I learned, later still, that the building was available, on terms that I could meet. Behind me, I hear the steady voices of friends of my own, who drop by often in the afternoons and brew coffee among the gluepots on the stove. A few are recent acquaintances. Many of the friends, recent and not so recent, I have met through the work on the boat: a foreman of a lumberyard, an old chandler, a carpenter. Several were friends of the barber's, and have returned to the building through successive stages of its life, to continue the conversation.

They take the whole thing for granted: the building, the boat, the welcome, the time of day, the children. And I? Each of those friends when we met bore some relation to what I imagined I wanted the boat for, just then. Now I have forgotten those iridescent purposes as though I had wakened from them days ago. Images of moments at sea in sunlight, or at night: waves phosphorescent, dark shearwaters skimming them in moonlight; the seethe of the wake. In some of the images, indeed, remembering this age, this place, the boat unfinished, the sounds at home. At one time I was visited by a recurring sense of being pursued, and nursed fantasies of the boat as a means of flight—but from what, and in what direction, and toward what destination? Constructing the boat by myself, doing everything without prior experience, I have assembled some things, I am sure, in a peculiar order. Today for the first time I have put up the mainsail, slowly turning the winch, stretching the cloth, the ratchet clicks echoing off the ceiling. I had said nothing to the friends, in their chairs tipped against the wall, of this occasion. They are used to my going on with my work on the boat, preoccupied with what I am doing, entering and leaving the conversation without formality. The sail has been ready for weeks. They have seen it, lying on the floor and along the boom. Up on the deck of the boat, above their heads, in a different light from the light they were sitting in, I felt just now that I was turning the winch cautiously. More than that. Surreptitiously. I was sure that the clicking of the pawls, at one click or the next, or the next, was bound to bring their talk to a halt, and then there would be a silence, and then a question, a comment on the sail. Why not? What difference would it make? But as I continued, the opposite seemed as likely: that they did not hear it at all, any more than the children did, outside. Or that, if they heard it, they were paying no special attention to it, not noticing that anything was happening, that anything was different. I watched the sail climb toward the masthead— but not clear to the top. Not the first time. I left it for the luff to stretch, and stood—stand—here in midair, looking up the rest of the way. As long as I look, the masthead appears to move among the rafters. The new sail hangs stiff and breathless, one more white shadow, but above it the masthead itself feels a steady breeze, and the rigging trembles in my hand. I hear the breeze distinctly, and for a moment I catch my breath, afraid that the conversation behind me has really stopped, and that the voices of the children outside the window were long ago. But no, they are both still there.

II

The Mediated Past:
Autobiography and Memoirs

A RECOLLECTION OF STONES

(c. 1957)

i

I had heard of that part of the valley of the lower Loire; the river wide and quiet in the early morning, and the mists rising from it. The houses not awake, but not asleep either, with that look they have in the first hour of light, as though they were staring off at some vacancy that they knew about, and their builders were blind to, or afraid of, or both. The wise blank look that houses have in certain lights, along a river.

Breakfast on a terrace that looked out over the Loire—how silent the flat riverbed seemed, and the glassy water under the sliding mist. I had heard of a cathedral. Parthenay. I thought of the name, there on the Loire. On the terrace, looking out over the river at breakfast, seeing, away downstream, the tall spire of yellow stone, with a little of the pink light of daybreak still sliding down it like a drowning man's fingers on a mast.

I was on the way back from southern France, and had turned off the road that led north, and started west over the rolling grain country that stretches away from the wide valley of the Loire. The signposts could not agree about the distance to Parthenay. One series of markers, optimistic, and with pointers at the crossroads to make sure of the direction, would assure me that Parthenay was twenty-seven kilometers, *that* way. But two hundred yards further on, a sullen concrete obelisk would insist, without further comment, that Parthenay was thirty-two; and this series didn't care which way you got there, if you got there at all. They merely warned you of the distance, and the rest was up to you. The two families bickered and insisted in the rainy afternoon, while the wide swelling landscape of grain fields changed, in the watery light, from amber to gray, to green, and back to amber. It was an empty road, in wide empty country, where, apart from the wind in the clouds and the grain, nothing seemed to be moving except the car. The arguing signposts gradually conceded some of their difference, but they never could come to an agreement; even at the edge of Parthenay itself they disagreed, by almost a kilometer, as to how far it was to the edge of town.

Coming at it from the east, the first glimpse of Parthenay is the spire, a lighter yellow than the grain fields and rising out of them, off on the horizon. Only when you get much closer can you see the town puckered and piled at its foot, a huddle of darker yellows and grays, and the weathered colors of the tile roofs. Even when you get into the town you hardly need the signs to guide you to the cathedral: you can see the spire from almost anywhere in the place. From the wide empty *place* with its white statues in the middle, and high slatted-board sidewalks around it, and some very new-looking cafes along one side, where truck drivers and a few fat Belgian tourists in white cloth caps were sitting at tables watching the few cars as though they had never seen any. Even in the narrow overhung cobbled streets one never loses sight of the spire for long. In fact, whether because of watching too closely for the old signposts, trying to see whether they would at last agree, or as a result of watching the town so eagerly, I took a wrong turn on the way into Parthenay, and then had to find the way to the cathedral, through the little back streets, with no guide but the spire itself. It wasn't difficult.

The cathedral stands in one of the narrow old streets where the houses are of a darker stone with wide store windows cut into some of them along the street. The street itself is dark, and it was almost empty; it was the one day of the week when the stores are closed in Parthenay. Everyone was either somewhere else, or indoors asleep, with the doors closed and even most of the dogs and cats and children battened in behind the shutters. The cobbles looked very clean, for a narrow street in France, as though they and the gutters and the sidewalks had just been scrubbed. I caught myself wondering whether people really lived there. Not far down the street you could see that there was a gap in the houses, and that the whole street was flooded with bright daylight. That was where the cathedral was. The light came partly from the gap in the houses, and partly, it seemed, from the reflection of the sunlight on the yellow stone of the church itself. But there is no broad *place* in front of the cathedral. The flight of a dozen or so steps, the width of the facade, which lead up to the main door, are all that set the church off from the street. The bottom step, in fact, is virtually a part of the sidewalk. And I was almost in front of the cathedral before I could look up and see the facade itself, and the spire, rising out of it, falling at a great speed across the sky.

I was disappointed. I knew it, but would not admit it, for the moment. I love that variety of styles which make up the French Romanesque. I had just seen a lot of it, in the south, and by contrast the ruled lines of Parthenay, which is in many ways more Gothic than Romanesque, looked cold and uninspired, while the building itself appeared bare without seeming simple. I looked for a long time at the Romanesque arches and carvings over the doors of the porch and around the tower at the base of the spire. Some of the capitals that apparently had once been covered with carvings had been damaged or destroyed, and replaced with plain, new stone. I went up to the front door and found a bar across it, and I was just admitting that I didn't mind not going in, anyway, when I noticed that a smaller side door was open. The inside smelled of paint, and had recently been plastered over with battleship-gray cement marked out in a brick pattern. It was not as large as the outside had seemed to promise, and the proportions of the original church were hardly visible under the retouching. There was a list of the war dead of the parish on a board. Even the altars of the side chapels seemed apologetic among all the grim newness, and the echo of feet on the stones didn't sound like the echo of feet in a church. I caught myself wondering again about the existence of the people of Parthenay. Obviously, if they did exist, they must worship here; they must have worshipped here for a long time. But the application of a little cement and paint had completely exorcised the ghost of centuries of their worship. I could no more find it there, in their church, than I could see evidence of their physical existence in the clean cobbled street outside. I went out and walked around to the back, and saw that the apse, which at one time may have been Romanesque, had been rebuilt and enlarged into what seemed to be a Gothic sacristy, a rather awkward one. I liked Parthenay better from a distance.

I drove out of town by another road that wound down a hill. And when the road turned and I could see the spire rising from the hunched clutter of roofs, at the top of the hill, it still looked as beautiful as it had when I was approaching it.

The road wound on down through an *estaminet* and crossed a little bridge. Somewhere, on the map, there was Vieux Parthenay, but I couldn't make out whether this was Vieux Parthenay or another village whose name I can't remember. It was now half submerged in the newer developments of the outskirts of a town: warehouses and big garages were muddled up with worn stone houses, small farmyards, and the occasional gabled seventeenth-century bourgeois dwelling, closed up, with the trees untrimmed in front of it.

I was driving slowly, looking back, through the spaces between the houses, at the buildings of Parthenay spilling down over their hill. I passed a farmyard larger than most, with a high white wall around it, and through the arch I glimpsed something that looked like a Romanesque building. The rainy sky of earlier in the afternoon had cleared, and the sun was blazing on the white wall, brighter in the washed air. I might have been in the south again. At the end of the wall the road turned and I looked back and was sure that what I saw was the remains of a large Romanesque church. Not a ruin. If there had been a tower or spire, which there probably hadn't, it had gone, but the high, flat-angled weathered roof looked to be still intact. One end was rounded into an apse, and another building had been built up against it. There was a round window high in the wall, at the other end, but if there had been windows along the nave, they must have been filled in long since. It didn't look as though it was used as a church any more. Could a Romanesque church of that size have been abandoned like that, with nothing to so much as indicate what it was? Surely it was used for something, though, back there in the farmyard, with a skirt of smaller, newer whitewashed buildings around its base.

I went back, and walked in through the arch. There was no doubt of it: no warehouse ever stood that way in the sunlight. Seeing it unannounced, and without any of the context of a place of worship, I was struck by whatever it is that makes a building a church. It was oblivious to the sunny farmyard and the buildings gripping its walls, and to any change. It was still what men had made to stand, not just between them and the weather, but between them and heaven, and to be silent. A shape of stones, whose silence was meant to contain God and man, and interpret the mysteries of the one to the mysteries of the other.

A bundle of cats were fighting around a garbage can at the doorway of one of the smaller buildings. I went around to the rounded eastern end of the church. The apse still had its windows, long and slender, all the way around. They started halfway up the wall, and went on almost to the roof, where the tile eaves still hung out over some carvings of heads and monsters. Down at the side of the apse I saw a door which looked as though it had once been the entrance to the sacristy. It had been bigger, but had been partly filled in with stone, and a smaller Gothic doorway now stood there. There was Gothic carving on the lintel and doorposts. I was starting toward it when a small man in a dirty apron appeared around a corner.

I looked in through the door as he walked toward me. The smell of decaying flesh was as heavy as fog. A flight of wooden stairs led to a floor above, and up there I could see hundreds of small pelts hanging from wires, drying, like tobacco leaves in a smoke house. I turned back to the sunlight. "Is it a fur tannery?" I asked the man.

"It's a rabbit slaughterhouse," he said. He was friendly, and interested that I was interested in the church, and he went on explaining to me that it was a rabbit slaughterhouse. The little man said did I realize that the building was a church; he wanted to make sure that I noticed that. They used it, but it was a church, and people from the Beaux Arts had even come once just to see the church itself. Maybe he thought I had come just to see the slaughterhouse. Of course the smell, as we stood there, was not the smell of a farmyard at all, though in the middle of the yard it wasn't so bad. The little man was beginning to go into detail about the business, so I interrupted him to ask him if it would be possible to see the church. I had to ask him more than once, he was so interested in making sure that I understood the workings of the slaughterhouse from the time that the live rabbits arrived until the different parts of them were sent their separate ways. But, trying not to be rude about it, I made it plain that it was the church that interested me. I asked him again whether there was any chance of being able to see the inside.

He understood. He showed me how one of the buildings of the rabbit-works had been built out of the old cloister, which had stood on the other side of the back farmyard wall. You could still see part of it. But as for the church, he said there wasn't much to see in there that would interest me. They just used it to dry the skins of rabbits in, he said, and that was all that was in there. It was just very old, and you could still see it was a church but it was all falling down. I said I'd like to see it anyway, and the little man led the way through the door and up the steps. The smell got worse with every step, until it beat at your nose and eyes like a barrage of noise against your eardrums. It was surprising to find you could actually breathe it without choking. Upstairs the floor was partly stone slabs, partly heavy oak boards. There were no columns, and the wires ran clear across the nave, about six feet above the floor, and almost all the way to the western end of the church, with aisles between them so they could be reached without trouble; they were all hung solid with drying skins. Once you got past the first rows, which were the newest and dryest, it was a little better. Over the tops of the wires you could see the round window high in the western wall, which was filling that end of the church with a broad beam of hot yellow afternoon light.

"You see," he said, "It's all old." He pointed up at the walls, which had once been whitewashed.

"You can still see some of it from when it was a church, but it's all falling down." Up on the walls there were brownish red patches and lines of brighter red and greenish blue, and what must have been gold. Only spots here and there, and broken fragments of outlines, scattered over the wall. As my eyes got used to the light I moved around to where I would see them better. I could make out most of a lion, or was it one of the beasts of the Apocalypse? In what, as far as I could tell, was the graceful twelfth-century northern Romanesque style of the paintings in the porch at St. Savin-sur-Gartempe. The other wall of the nave was the same. Bits of monsters, or Magi, or madonnas, in a tawny red. And shadowy masses in the white ground of the wall, which may have been the remains of a whole composition, or simply a chemical change in the wall.

"You could still see a whole horse there two years ago," the man said. "You could see a lot of other things. There was a lion there, but maybe you can't see it now. The man from the Beaux Arts said this place is too much ruined to save it. He even copied some things."

We went back out through the rabbit skins to the other end. The floor had been built up into the apse in a semicircular bowl, like the banking around the curve of a racetrack. It led up to the sloping sills of the windows.

"Up there," the man said, pointing to a place on the wall, about level with where the altar must have stood, "there was an animal, I never could understand what it was. But it's gone now. You can only see a little. Next year you won't see any. Do you want to see down there?" He pointed down under the stairs.

I said I'd like to see all there was to see of the church. And we descended out of the worst of the smell, into the crypt. Low arches blackened with smoke. My guide didn't know how they had come to be black, but maybe it was from gypsies and people camping in there before the place was a slaughterhouse. Gothic-letter inscriptions, in the differing styles of different centuries, were cut into stone plaques in the wall.

"There are those," he said. "If you can read them. The man that came said he could read them, but I don't know what they say. He never said. They're in Latin," he explained. The tombs of priests, and of prosperous citizens of the parish. After the church above, there was almost no smell down in the crypt. In the far wall of the chamber there was another arch that had been filled in with stone.

"They don't know what's in there," he said. "Some day they say they'll come back and see. But it can wait," he laughed, "It can wait." He patted the wall. "It's stood there a long time. It's a good building."

We went back out into the sunlight, and I walked away from the door.

"Is this Vieux Parthenay?" I asked the little man.

"Oh no," he said, as though he had been mildly affronted but would forgive me because I was a foreigner. And with pride he told me that I was in a separate village, and had been in it ever since we crossed the bridge at the bottom of the hill. A village, he insisted, with a life of its own.

In the archway of the farmyard I turned to look back. A truck had backed in against one of the buildings, and was being loaded with fresh skinned rabbits, for the butchers. The cats were fighting over rabbit guts. The garbage cans were full of it. The little man was standing near the cats, watching the loading, with a gentle smile on his face. Down the road there was a diesel truck, with a double tanker-trailer behind it, belching out black smoke as it labored up the slope. The road was too narrow for anything to pass it, and there was a long line of smaller trucks and cars inching up the hill behind it. If I ran for the car and started, I might be able to get away before it overtook me.

ii

"How would you like to buy a castle?" the Marquis said, and I laughed, and he threw back his fat head, with the pince-nez and the high-bridged nose, and lifted his double chin and laughed too. Only, I could see that it wasn't one of his jokes, because he laughed less than I did, whereas he laughed quite as long at his own jokes as anybody else did. Giggled or wheezed or doubled over or gave out with a reedy guffaw. But the castle was serious.

"I think I could get one for you," he said. "The oaf who's living there now bought it two years ago for three hundred thousand francs, and I

hear he'd be glad to get rid of it. He's a bourgeois gone to the dogs. He
lives up there by himself and keeps sheep. But then what would you
expect from a bourgeois gone to the dogs? We could go up there this
afternoon, if you'd like to. Wouldn't you like to? I'd like to show it to you
anyway. It's a place you should see."

I had met the Marquis only two days before. I had come to his village,
in the valley of the Dordogne, late in the morning, because it lies
halfway up a deep valley, and is not out of the shadow of the cliffs until
the sun is high in the sky. I had brought a picnic and was just
beginning to look around for a place to eat it when I saw a sign pointing
down to one of the largest and prettiest houses in the place, announcing
that it was a *manoir,* that you could go through it for eighty francs, and
that the proprietor also had antiques for sale. I left the picnic in the
ancient car, and went down into the courtyard and rang the bell.

A boy about twelve, with a butch haircut, a fat face, and long white
legs sticking out of shorts too small for him, answered the door. It was
plain from the sounds of bustling, nearby, that lunch was in the chaotic
process of being prepared. A tall thin woman with graying hair, wearing a man's white shirt and a peasant skirt, extracted herself from the
preparations and appeared behind the boy, and asked me in. Her husband,
she said, would be there in a moment. I suggested that maybe it was too
near lunch to be convenient, and perhaps I should come back later, but
she said lunch wouldn't be ready for a while anyway, and there would
be time.

The Marquis appeared. He was not very tall, he did not have much
hair, he was wearing an old tan sport shirt, a pair of cotton pants, and
espadrilles, and he walked with his large stomach sallying ahead of
him, as though he were leaning backwards to hold up the weight of his
middle. He led me into the dining room and from there through the rest
of the house. He had begun to talk the moment he saw me. His voice
had that papery tenor timbre that heavy smokers often develop, though
I learned before long that he didn't smoke. He took a long time showing
me the house, with digressions about pieces of furniture, some of which
were for sale and some not, and about some of the portraits. I had
suspected, halfway through, that I was being treated to something more
than the eighty-franc tour, and that he was warming to his monologue,
before a new audience. He led me out onto the balcony at the back of the
house, and showed me the long pools, with ducks swimming around in
them, which had been built around the small stream that flowed down

through the valley. When I admired all that too, he led me down and showed me the mill beside the stream, which was part of his property, and the park out past the stream, which extended as far as the orchards and vineyards on the hillside. And the Chateau des Anglais, clinging to the top of the cliffs above, where it had been crumbling since the Crusaders abandoned it. And when he had showed me all these, he asked whether I wouldn't like to eat my picnic in his park, and he brought out a bottle of wine to go with it, and later, when he had eaten his own lunch, he brought out coffee and liqueurs to drink with me.

That was how I had come to know the Marquis. He chattered about his family, about the locality, and at the end of two coffees and several liqueurs he began to expatiate on those local points of interest which tourists, for one reason or another, seldom saw. And ended by asking whether I wouldn't like him to go for a drive with me and show me some of them.

He knew everybody in the countryside. He knew every back road for miles in all directions. He knew which farmhouse had the best cheese and the fastest daughters and we were welcome to stop and sit in the kitchen and sample the cheese and take a good look at the family. He knew the exact spot to stop to get the best view from whichever road you were taking, knew it so well that he would warn you to slow down two hundred yards before you were there (and neither I nor the car wanted to drive very fast). He knew all the little churches in back villages, that weren't in any of the *guides,* and all the castles and beautiful houses that were not open to the public. He knew the families who lived in these castles too—if they were still owned by their families—and would have us drive royally in at the gates, tramps in my old automobile, and stop at the main entrance. Signs which said ABSOLUTELY NO ADMITTANCE were put there for other people. He knew the stories of all the families in these castles, and would recount them as we mounted the steps and swept through room after room. One of the most beautiful of the castles, where he had visited almost weekly as a child, had been sold by its family, and was being used as a summer camp for poor children from the city. As we approached the vast front entrance he launched into a complicated and vigorous account of the love lives of the castle's heredi-tary owners, a story which involved one countess, one local electrician, one attempted suicide by hanging, in an upper bedroom, one shotgun on a spiral staircase ... He told it with sonorous gusto, and the park echoed with his laugh. So did the stone entrance as we started through.

Heads of hundreds of children were being pulled away from windows, and a bad-tempered crone flew out of a tiny side doorway, waving her hands and insisting that visitors were not allowed. The Marquis ignored her, continuing his story, but her gesticulations and warnings grew more violent, and without changing his tone he half turned his head and said, "Yes of course, old dear, we know quite well that it's not allowed," as he sailed past her.

And when the afternoon was over he had asked me to come back, the day after next, and take him into the local shopping town (his bicycle, he said, was a crucifixion to him, and besides he had given it to his son, and besides it was broken) and stay to lunch. Where, after coffee, he was now offering castles.

I said I would love to see the castle he was talking about, even though I wasn't in the market for feudal estates.

The road led up the steep rocky valley onto the *causse*—the high rolling plateau, twenty to thirty miles wide, that lies between the river gorges and rich valleys in that region. In some places the *causse* will be as barren as the uplands of Castille, for miles at a stretch; no trees, no bushes, nothing but small boulders lying on swellings of bare dry yellowish ground—the *causse perdu*. But where we went it was green and tumbling, with farms huddled in folds of pasture, and trees, and disheartened old stone walls wandering absentmindedly over the land, which was not as rich certainly as the valley below, but which would pasture sheep and cattle, and could be coaxed into yielding a few crops. A little farther and the *causse* started to rise and turned into forest: chestnuts and oaks, with pigs running wild under them. The dark oak woods of the river country, with truffles growing among the roots.

We turned off onto a dirt road and drove two or three miles.

"It's up there," the Marquis said, and up to our left I caught a glimpse of a round stone tower just showing above the tops of the trees. Then the thick woods on the hill hid it again, as we drove on, nearer; and there was nothing in sight but forest rising all around us. The Marquis said to stop the car there. A narrower dirt lane, obviously a private entrance, masked with bushes and small oaks, ran down steeply, just in front of us, to the road. A small, antique, dilapidated farm truck that had once been blue came jolting slowly down onto the road. There were two unkempt men in the cab, in dirty khaki. They didn't look like peasants. The Marquis waved them to a stop, and went over and talked to them, half shouting in through the door of the windowless truck. They hardly looked at him; they made monosyllabic answers, and after a minute they drove on without a glance in our direction.

"That was the proud owner," the Marquis said. "It's all right to go up. There's nobody there, which is just as well. We can enjoy the place at our leisure." And he swept his hand, like Napoleon describing his conquests, to indicate the hill, with the castle up there behind the trees.

We left the car and started up the lane that led to the castle. It seemed incredible that even the tiny truck that we had just seen could have managed to get down the lane, to say nothing of getting up it. It was steep, and was washed out at regular and frequent intervals. A man could stand in the middle of it and touch, not foliage, but branches, on either side. The lane led straight along up the side of the hill, then made a hairpin turn and led straight in the opposite direction for the same distance. The scrub and saplings along the road gave way to superb woods: tall oaks and chestnuts, with no underbrush among them, but only the sloping forest floor, dark with their shade, and green with moss. The lane rose through their shadows. Down on the road it was hot and dusty, with the noise of crickets coming from the ditches. But up in the trees it was cool; the air was moist; very far away we could hear a bird singing, and then it stopped, and the woods were totally silent. The lane made several more of its formal, regular, rising turns, and then, at the top of the next straight bit, one could see the chapel. A small stone building, not much bigger than a room, with a cross at the peak of the roof, and a big wooden door. As we came nearer I saw there was a crest above the door; and I was just going to have a closer look at the chapel when up to the right I saw the castle itself.

"Le voilà," the Marquis said. "It's a real Victor Hugo," he said. He had said that before.

Above the turn by the chapel, the lane rose in one unbroken green sweep to what had been the main gate of the castle, but was now nothing more than a gap leading between the crumbled ends of walls. Halfway there, the trees fell away and the hill was covered with lush grass, which rose steeply to the outer wall. This was a low circular gray stone parapet, higher than a man could reach, but it looked low, even from underneath, compared with the rest of the castle. It ran from some no longer well defined spot near the lane, around the base of the castle, and disappeared behind the far shoulder of the hill. Inside, the grassy hill rose steeply again for thirty or forty feet, to another higher ring of stone, within which there was a circular stone platform which skirted the keep itself: a thick round tower of dark gray stone, rising seventy or eighty feet above the platform to a snaggletoothed ring of crenellations, half of them fallen, through which the few clouds slid.

We walked between the ruined ends of the outer wall into a flat grassy expanse with walls and towers and the ruins of buildings on all sides, that must once have been the main courtyard. We stepped through a carved doorway on the right.

"This was the great dining hall," the Marquis said. It had been a long spacious room, with spiral stone staircases leading up onto balconies at either end. The fluted stone vaulting of the ceiling had gathered at the corners and swept down, coming to rest on the stone mantels of the vast fireplaces in each of the four corners of the room. From the fireplaces, broken rays of fluting still rose a little way toward the ceiling, which was no longer there. The sky looked very far away above the jagged walls, and what had been the floor was piled high with a mound of delicately carved rubble, with grass and thistles growing through it. As we stepped through the door a flock of sheep that had been grazing in there vanished with hardly a sound through some opening in the other end.

Across the courtyard was a long square building, with a stone ramp leading up to a wide square door: perhaps the stables, or part of the living quarters. It was being used as a barn. Hay was spilling out of the upper windows. At the corner where it almost met the end of the great hall, there was another tower, smaller than the keep but the same shape; another one stood just beyond, a third stood on the other side of the courtyard, and still another was just visible out among the trees. The Marquis said there had been thirteen towers, altogether, and as far as he knew they were all still standing. But there were thickets between, and perhaps adders in the stairs, and the stonework would be unsafe. Exploring that part of the grounds, I could see, did not appeal to him.

He fulminated and muttered about the owner's disgraceful neglect which had allowed stone after stone to fall and shatter. "It's not as though he were poor, either," he said. "He could take care of it if he wanted to. Only a little care, the least bit of care, that's all. Even yet. The roof of the keep is still perfect. Maybe that's because it's a solid stone platform, up there."

He showed me where the owner had pried loose a few dozen carved stones from the keep's top battlement, and pushed them over the edge, so that he would have stones for an ugly little bourgeois terrace. But whether the owner's heedless abandon affected him that way, or the silence of the place, or something else, his talk, which had been continuous up until then, gradually grew discouraged and then ebbed away, like water into sand, and he sat down on a stone and left me to explore the place alone.

The stone platform that I had seen from below completely circled the base of the keep. On the side away from the courtyard it ended in a low wall that joined the fortifications. Out in front of me the wide saddle of woods that had been the domain dropped away, dark green and unbroken, for several miles. And far out beyond them, and far below us, was the rolling *causse* gleaming gold in the afternoon sunlight. I seemed to be able to see clear to the edge of it, to a place where it dropped away to nothing. There was no movement down in the woods, and the *causse* was too far for me to see anything moving there.

There were a few windows near the base of the keep; the panes were cracked and dirty, but I could see that there were two rooms on the side toward me. The walls had been plastered at some time, and painted a dark cream, which had cracked and peeled in patches, and were yellow with smoke and age. There was a brown table of the sort that French customshouses sometimes use in small stations along the frontier. A rickety chair or two, an unmade iron bed, a stove with some pots on it and the flue going into a hole in the wall, and some plates, rags, shoes, pieces of basket, dirty bottles, lying around the naked floor. A bare light bulb hung down from the ceiling in one of the rooms—the Marquis, with ironic ecstasy, had pointed out to me a pair of wires running out of the woods to two white porcelain insulators which were set into the masonry above the cheap brown-painted door. "We have *electricity*," he had said, speaking for the present owner, and preciously exaggerating all the syllables. "We have *something* to show for our presence here".

But my own presence there was not comfortable. There was a coldness to the place, as of faces turned away from us. The heavy splendor of the towers was forbidding; the silence seemed to listen; the rooms through the dirty panes were like a sudden laugh. At the far side of the keep, back near the gateway again, I found myself looking at an old door, set half below the level of the ground. It was not large; it was black and crossed with heavy beams, with diamond-headed studs in them, and a vast iron lock on one side. The shady, dark side of the keep. The ground was mossy and the stones were pitted with moss, and dark; damp, as though they sweated a little. There was ivy on that side of the tower; the leaves hung there without moving, watching me watching the door.

The Marquis was still sitting on the same stone, and stood up as I approached.

"I thought we might take this back with us," he said, showing me another stone, a fragment carved with a knot and roses. "I don't see why I shouldn't have a souvenir, for my collection. Do you think it would be too heavy to carry down?"

I thought it would, and he left it, with a shrugged "*tant pis,*" and we walked slowly toward the lane. He pointed out the little door as we passed, but said nothing more.

"Do you like the place?" he said, halfway to the chapel, turning to look back up at it.

"It's very beautiful. Very beautiful."

"It is, isn't it?"

"What's its name?"

"Saigne. Saigne. That's quite a name, isn't it? It has a ring to it. A ring—like something." We were almost to the chapel, with the woods rising around us.

"You see?" he said. "There's the name for you. For your stationery." He was pointing to the blazon over the chapel door. It was a carved fist holding a dagger, from which three drops of blood were falling; and the motto beneath: "Je fais saigner." He repeated it, "Je fais saigner." I draw blood. A stone cross at the roof peak.

The motto, or perhaps it was the distance between us and the neglected towers above us, had shaken the Marquis from his brown study, and he treated me to an *explication de texte.* The comtes, or maybe they were the barons de Saigne—if they were called that then—had been there since early in the Middle Ages. He did not know when they came there, and if he told their origins I have forgotten. As far as I remember, the castle was built, in its actual form, sometime in the twelfth century. It figured in at least one of the Crusades, and in most of the small but bloody local wars. The family had been powerful and belligerent, and the castle had probably witnessed the usual feudal changes of those raw times. But no incident of peculiar grace had distinguished it before the Wars of Religion swept through that region. At that time there were several battles, and the castle changed hands more than once. After one particular battle, a group of fifty or sixty prisoners, of both sexes and all ages, were led into the courtyard. Whether the victors were Catholics and the prisoners Protestants, or whether it was the other way around, the Marquis was not sure, and as he pointed out, it didn't make any difference to the story. The prisoners had been herded through the little black half-underground door which I had seen, at the base of the keep. Presumably there had been water there (there had been several wells inside the fortifications, in case of siege). But no light, and not much room. When the prisoners were all inside, the heavy little door was closed, locked, and the victors rode away, taking the key with them. Forty days later someone rode back, unlocked the door, and looked in. Those who were not already dead had gone mad, and fallen to eating the corpses, and each other, and in some cases themselves.

Maybe other interesting *morceaux* of history had occurred there during the next three or four hundred years, but the Marquis simply said that the incident of the prisoners was "typical," and glossed over several centuries, to our own. The last scion of the line to inhabit the castle had been rather eccentric. At some point in middle life he had climbed to the room at the top of the keep, and locked the door behind him. For twenty-odd years he had lived there, never coming out, never so much as showing his face. He had his meals sent up in a basket on a rope, which he let down through a trapdoor in the floor of his room. It is not related why the servants stayed, but apparently they did. For there was someone there to notice that the trapdoor did not open one morning at breakfast time. Nor at lunch time, nor at dinner time. Nor the next morning. But it was not until the third morning that anyone had the courage to break the routine of the castle still further, and climb the rotten ladder and knock at the tower door. There was no answer. The person waited until there were several others with him on the platform, and then they broke down the door, and found the old man lying dead, and half eaten by rats, on a mattress half filled with gold pieces.

Word of his death was sent to other members of the family, who lived in other parts of France. The body was buried; they did not come for the funeral. Several weeks later a convoy of trucks forced its way up the lane; the castle was stripped to the walls; the contents—furniture, tapestries, rugs, silver, paintings—was loaded into the trucks, and then they drove away. And Saigne had stood empty for several years and then been sold, for a ridiculous sum, to the oaf who lived there now, and had a brown customshouse table, and rags on the floor, and porcelain insulators for his naked light bulb, in the masonry over the door, and sheep in the ruined hall.

Two days later I saw the Marquis again. He was radiant. "You can have the castle," he said. When I did not respond immediately he added,

"You remember? The real Victor Hugo. I have called the owner. You can buy it for two hundred and fifty thousand francs. He will be delighted."

He seemed surprised that I did not appear thrilled at the news.

"Two hundred and fifty thousand francs," he said. "Two hundred and fifty pounds. Seven hundred dollars." (Just so there could be no mistake.) "You could probably even argue him down another fifty. You would not even have to pay it all at once. I am sure of that. A deposit, that's all. Maybe a hundred thousand. And keep him waiting for the rest."

ASPECTS OF A MOUNTAIN

(1975)

I went from Venice to the Virgin's Holy Mountain of Athos, with only two nights between.

One would expect such a passage to provide contrast so entire and abrupt as to shock—a leap between opposites. And the contrast was there, everywhere. My ears were still echoing the slosh of dark canals and the anonymous bubbling of crowds in the Piazza San Marco when I began to hear the wind in the chestnut forests that unroll from under the ravens' stone ridges. The reflected water-light of autumn shimmering along facades of palaces built on mud, the evanescent vanities, deceptive lightness, and elusive confidences of the Queen of the Adriatic, marvels of composed acquisition, possessiveness that claimed even the sea year by year, as the sea now claims it, and took marriage as its figure (not by chance was *Othello* set in Venice), an ancient republic whose power and greatness were represented by elected prisoners, a city all leaves and no trees, in late September, had not been veiled but enhanced by the sleep of travel, when I came on foot, alone, around a high bend, and saw, in the early light, far to the southeast, through the woods, the bare shadow rising thousands of feet in one line out of the sea, to the marble point which some have taken to be the exceeding high mountain where the devil showed Jesus all the kingdoms of the world and the glory of them, and which many believe to be, with its northern approaches (including the spot where I was standing), the site that the Mother of God had received for an earthly garden of her own. At a glance it would seem that the two places must have little in common except the planet and its turning, but the very transit between them—the word, and the journey—reveals other links. Both Venice and Athos make reverberating statements about existence, its dimensions and its treasures, and

"Aspects of a Mountain" first appeared in *Shenandoah*.

both look beyond us. Neither of them belongs to our century, yet both provide the transient with that sense that clearly is shared by all periods but that seems characteristic of our time and its furnishings: a vertiginous touch, the feeling of stepping-stones sinking under the feet they help to cross.

Venice, of course, is sinking literally, borne down by its triumphs, succumbing to its own monuments. As the wooden pilings driven deep into the silt and clay have rotted under the marble, more marble has been added to the pavements, raising levels but increasing the weight. On the canals, white marble steps that once led up to landing stages now lead down under the polluted water and disappear. Delivery barges, the curtained launches of the rich, high-powered diesel water-taxis, the nifty speed-crafts of the perennial adolescents with much to prove and motors to prove it with, one after the other send waves ricocheting back and forth across the narrow channels. Annually the waves splash farther up rotting doors and slide deeper into rooms, bringing bits of driftwood, cans, disposed plastic conveniences, black bags of garbage that have slithered off collection scows, oil slicks, detergents, all the latest effluvia. The stone along the waterline is being eaten away. Cracks climb from it into the masonry. Tall belfries lean this way and that on their softening foundations. During the high tides around the autumn equinox the Piazza San Marco, and the streets near it, flood. The lagoon backs up through the drains in the well-laid pavements. It rises into the gorgeous Basilica of Saint Mark itself, where the saint is represented again and again crossing water, and the most prominent dove in the porch ceiling is Noah's. On some days the flood fingers sections of the mosaic floor. Boardwalks laid on trestles allow files of tourists to proceed slowly back and forth across the squares and into the church and out of it. Gondolas made fast to jetties appear to be riding at moorings out in the lagoon. Opinions differ regarding how fast the city is subsiding, but it seems certain that the rate is accelerating as the pilings rot. At the same time, surface—not just the water surface, but all that is superficial: the visible, the outside, the garment, the public, the act of display—has always been integral to the nature, the architecture, and the life of Venice, and if Venice can be preserved even piecemeal, no doubt it will be effected by elaborate, expensive, public attentions, and in order that Venice may continue to be seen. Athos is another matter. There too wealth has mattered, and accumulation has been practised: kings and queens have built monasteries, endowed them, repaired them, protected them, and added to their treasures. And there too the visible artifacts—frescoes, illuminated manuscripts, architecture, and sculpture—are prized and admired, and some of the ikons are revered. But whereas Venice clearly profits, and may in the end be salvaged by tourists and their money, for Athos they and what they represent merely contribute to the gathering destruction. For the essence of Athos, and the element that threatens it, are both invisible.

Geographically, the way to it is through Greece. Three peninsulas, set like fingers of a hand, run southeast from the district of Chalkidikis into the Aegean Sea. The mountain stands at the end of the one farthest to the east, that points toward the island of Lemnos. The peninsula is some thirty miles long, most of it high and rocky, though there is a narrow bit at the northern end where it drops almost to sea level. It is claimed that sections of a faint furrow, between the two shores there, mark the course of a canal that Xerxes, sailing to attack Greece early in the fifth century B.C., ordered to be dug, rather than risk the terrible seas at the foot of the mountain: an entire fleet had been lost rounding the headland a few years before. South of this dubious memorial the land rises in low hills for a few miles and then heaves up into sharp folds running toward the summit. At the start of this century the boundary of the Holy Community of Athos lay considerably farther north than it does now. The Greek government has expropriated a number of square miles of the gently sloping base of the peninsula— much of its best farmland—and turned it over to farmers and to other forms of exploitation. Compensation, in the form of a small regular subsidy, was promised to the monasteries whose land was taken, and they depend on it. Its continued payment is now in doubt. The monastic community, by the terms of its charter, governs itself. But in fact there is a connection with the Greek state which does not seem altogether to content either party. The visitor's first contact with it is likely to be in Thessalonika, at police headquarters. According to the Treaty of Lausanne, of 1923, and the Charter of Athos, of 1924, drawn up jointly by Greece and the monastic community, the monks are Greek subjects, the Greek penal system extends to Athos, ecclesiastical administration is left to the representatives of the twenty monasteries, and there are ecclesiastical police empowered to refuse admission to visitors. Perhaps even fifty years ago pilgrims could arrive on the Athonian peninsula under no colors but their own, and remain there without credentials until their deaths, as some are said to have done. In the ancient tradition, the guest

had been sent from heaven and should be received as though he were
Christ. Now papers are required, in triplicate. They must be supplied by
the Greek police, and necessitate a visit to another office, across town,
and further confirmation from the authorities on Athos. Until recently
there was virtually no time limit imposed on visitors. Now, due in great
part to the annually developing number of tourists, a week is the
maximum, unless the monastery representatives choose to extend the
permit, and normally a visitor is not allowed to spend more than
twenty-four hours in any one monastery.

The road has helped to make, or at least implement, the difference.
For centuries the journey to Athos was long and exacting. It took more
than curiosity, a few hours, and the price of a bus ticket to get anyone,
on foot or muleback, across the hundred-odd miles of inhospitable
mountains between Thessalonika and the base of the peninsula. In the
past few years the road has been gouged and tarred all the way to the
present boundary, which once lay well within the monastic domains.
For most of the journey it winds steeply through chestnut woods and
over barren slopes, connecting a few shrines and small towns, passing
under ruined castle walls at Aristotle's Stagira, where a sign in both
Greek and Roman letters points off the road to a white statue: the shape
of a beard and a gown, a stone with a back. A regular profile, facing the
sea, against a blank sky, as the bus turns; he looks quite new. The
Philosopher, you know. In these towns, a monk told me later, they have
football stadia but no libraries. Another tradition. Hill villages set
among orchards sagging with ripe apples, the cracking boughs weighed
down onto old walls and spilling over them, awash with October
sunlight. Dahlias, geraniums, calendulas. People sitting out at tables in
the shade of grapevines, the remaining leaves turning translucent after
the grape harvest. Dogs gliding through the shadows of the tables.
Towels hanging beside open doors. Families facing the bus as though
they were grouped for daguerreotypes. Firewood. Television aerials. Hens
under lines of laundry. Piles of new red hollow bricks, white mortar,
raw roof tiles. Erissos, down on the Aegean shore, is entirely modern—
the ubiquitous housing (southern European version) that looks as though
every room might be the bathroom. The old town was totally destroyed
in 1932, by an earthquake that killed many of the inhabitants. A little
way down the coast, set back from the shore among trees, beyond little
fields, and pastures with tethered cows and donkeys, are the domes of a
tiny church, an outpost of Athos, and farther along, overlooking the sea,

a bare cement construction, a hotel. There are few cars on the road, but the developers have plans. From the first rather tentative-looking hotel the road rises, and crosses the peninsula to the next long bay. Between one year and the next a huge masonry receptacle has been completed there, on the rocks above the water: sweeping drive, suburban lighting, liveried evergreens, the architecture of a clinic on a postcard, or a chic sector of the Atlantic Wall. And the name, Eagle's Palace Hotel (true), in English so that there may be no mistake. One is assured that it is the first of many. On the shore below, from the small quay at Tripiti, fishing boats cross to the island of Ammouliani. A few minutes later the road descends to the coastal village of Ouranopolis, the end of the line— so far.

The approach to the village is lined with half-finished multilayered constructions: the hotels of next year's resort. But the building that still dominates the place is the thirteenth-century tower of Prosphori, on the rocks by the shore. It was once a dependency of the monastery of Vatopedi, and it may mark the site of pagan Dion. At the beginning of the present century it must have stood almost alone, by the water. There is a small old house beside it, that has been run for some years as an inn, and facing the sea are the vestiges of a few other cottages converted to shops and eating places. I had seen the town last in September, the year before, and in that month the season, though waning, was still in swing: many of the tables under the pergolas and in the few restaurants were occupied by Germans—I was told that that nation's penchant for Greece had been turned to account by the proprietor of the new attentively landscaped beach hotel at the edge of town, who had connections with travel agents in Germany. More and more busloads of mixed Germans were confidently expected every year. A foreigner is addressed in German as a matter of course. But on the first of October, still, the high life goes home. Most of the tables are put away, most of the restaurants close, the antique dealer returns to Thessalonika, and doors are left open toward the sea so that women with cats at their feet can get the afternoon sun to their needlework. Most of the village was built after World War I, to house two groups of settlers of Greek ancestry brought from Turkish Asia Minor under the provisions of a League of Nations arrangement for resettlement of populations. In the year since I had seen it, a startling number of the remaining structures from that original period, and the lanes between them, had been removed to make way for hotel launching pads. But in October the locals still sit under the vines of the one open cafe, the half-inch of retsina in their glasses glowing with the long light off the sea. Beyond the tables, the wharf, and the sand of the shore. When I had left my things in the inn I walked down the empty beach past a hauled-up fishing boat, a truck out to pasture, a shuttered hotel, a jumble of fallen rocks running into the sea. Birds in the thornbushes, conversing about evening—pipit, wagtail, or lark voices, the glassy trill of some finch, none of them quite familiar, but the ancient words clear. Shadows swirling on the darker side of rocks, and then on the side from which the light was draining. The sun descended into gold-bordered clouds. The last breeze died. The blinking of a buoy on one of the small rock islands was echoed finally, more steadily, by a few lights thin as stars, over Ammouliani, where I have been told there is no electricity. The peninsula beyond it, to the west, faded into the dark sea. This one was sacred, once, to the sea-god, and its peak was named for his son. Suddenly clouds of tiny insects appeared, hovering above the waterline, in the dusk, and the moon, almost new, gathered light over the sea. As I turned back, a little dog ran toward me along the beach, as though it knew me.

The Greek geographer Strabo, at the beginning of the Christian era, wrote that those who lived on the summit of Mt. Athos saw the sun rise three hours early. Doubtless he did not come to check on his statement: the summit is an uninhabitable steeple of rock. But it may be that his assertion should not be read as the offering of fact that we have come to expect every statement to be, but meant instead "a high place, half legend, on its own terms with morning." Those who live now on the western shore, at the base of the long promontory, are up before the sun, like inhabitants of fishing villages elsewhere. There seems to be no hurry: they shamble through the mist, collars up, shawls over mouths, carrying sacks or empty-handed, as though waiting for something to come or go. Eventually a few figures gather on the cement wharf beside boxes of fish, baskets, oil drums; three or four have knapsacks, there are several black-robed monks with goat-hair bags; last come the fishermen, boatmen, the inevitable policeman. It is not many years since most of the fishing and the coastal traffic were conducted on sailing caiques, and small steamers anchored off the villages fairly regularly, if not often. Since the last war the fishing boats have adopted a less distinctive shape, and motors. The pioneers of the changeover still have tillers and wooden railings with dowelled banisters. Their replacements are big steel diesels with broad sterns for trawling or loading, and stertorous engines. Both kinds of vessel make the run to Daphne, the port of Athos. The boat leaves at seven. In October the first sunlight has just whitened the east face of Prosphori Tower and the sea at its foot. The boat noses down the coast, keeping close in. The monastic state begins a short distance below the village. The present boundary is a collapsing stone wall, beyond which the ancient ascetic rule of Athos, instituted, according to the story, by the Virgin herself, obtains.

They say on the mountain that the Virgin and St. John had sailed from Joppa to visit the resurrected Lazarus, who was then living on Cyprus. A storm had blown their vessel to the mountain, where the Virgin went ashore near the site of the present monastery of Iviron. In that day there was a temple to Poseidon on the spot, but at the appearance of the Mother of God the idols crumbled to pieces. She blessed the mountain, said that it would be her garden, and forbade any other woman to set foot there. For the most part, the injunction has been strictly kept. In the twelfth century Wallachian shepherds moved into the northern part of the promontory, three hundred families of them, and the women proved fatally attractive to large numbers of the monks. When the shepherds were finally expelled, the erring fathers were excommunicated in numbers that considerably reduced the population of the mountain. At different times the Empress Placidia, and the Serbian prince George Brankovic's daughter Maria, married to a sultan, are said to have come to visit Athos. Both of them were benefactors of the monastic state. But at Vatopedi the ikon now known as the Antiphonitria of Placidia is said to have spoken to the empress, warning her to go no farther, "for another queen than you reigns here." Queen Maria, in the fifteenth century, is reported to have stepped ashore at the monastery of Agiou Pavlou—St. Paul's—bringing with her gold, frankincense, and myrrh that the Magi had offered to the Christ Child, but a voice not of the earth had been heard forbidding her to take another step, and for the same reason. Village girls from north of the wall occasionally cross it to pick up olives or fetch goats home, and in 1948 guerrillas, including twenty-five women, occupied Karyes, the capital, briefly. But in general the commandment has been not only observed but extended to include female domestic animals and all "beardless persons," though the ruling on animals varies from monastery to monastery—there are cats about in most of the houses, and hens around some of them—and the ruling on beards, where visitors are concerned, is taken, in practice, to mean simply "old enough to grow one."

As the sun climbs, the misty rays tilt into ravines full of scrub, and rocky clefts leading up from the sea. The morning of a place apart. No visible habitation. It looks as though the sound of the boat could not be heard on the shore. Green water over rocks, and around a point, a boathouse on the shingle, a walled meadow nearby, with a few vines and olive trees. No one in sight. Farther along, another boathouse and a rambling two-story stuccoed building, with a porch along the upper story; a monk out airing bedding on the banister; no one on the jetty. The cliffs rise higher from the sea. Up on tiny ledges, over the water or over narrow gorges, ruins begin to appear. Some of them as large as big farmhouses, with the stone domes of their chapels still intact. They had been *sketes*—the word translates as 'cloister': an assembly of monks attached to a monastery but living apart from it under the rule of a prior. Or, if they are smaller, *kelli,* which are settlements housing three or more monks, who work on the land. Or hermitages. The roofs of many of them have fallen in. The sky shows through the walls. Vestiges of garden enclosures and terraces the size of kitchen tables hide in the wild growth, still catching the morning sun. Another point is drawn back, revealing the first of the monasteries on the coast: Docheiariou. Stone boathouse half barn, half fortification; arches and porches, square pilasters and stone chimneys. The monastery rising behind it: high walls, long balconies flung out over nothing, tier above tier of rough masonry, pink and blue painted plaster, wooden struts, rows of windows, russet tiles, cupolas and domes and chimneys all rising to the massive square crenellated keep, at the top, with its back to olive terraces and the foot of a steep wooded slope. Monks waiting; the boat puts in, a monk gets off, and with him an arrangement of sacks and boxes. The process is repeated a few miles along the coast at the next monastery, Xenophontos, which rises straight from the shingle's edge, another fountain of crenellations, towers, balconies, domes. And at the third, St. Pantaleimon, a Russian monastery, and until the Russian revolution the largest on Athos: enormous, dark, relatively modern (most of it built late in the nineteenth century), one whole wing burnt out, never repaired, looking like a ruined factory. At the turn of the century this monastery housed nearly fifteen hundred monks. There is a harbor where seagoing steamers could dock. In one of the towers hangs the second-largest bell in the world, transported from Moscow. Now there are no more than twenty monks, and there is scant prospect of others coming from Russia, or of the Greek government allowing them to stay if they did come. Around a point after St. Pantaleimon, Daphne appears: a jetty, a building at the end of it, a short string of white-stuccoed houses facing the sea.

The traditional uniform for the police of the monastic state includes a red, gold-trimmed jacket over a white shirt, shoes with pom-poms, and a hat that manages to combine the shapes of a garrison cap and a beret. Parts of the costume, no doubt, are very old. For everyday use, almost the only article of this finery that is worn is the least impressive: the hat. The wearer of one of these, looking cross, was waiting at the entrance to the customs-shed, at the end of the jetty, to flag down each visitor, with a handout in four languages: a brief blurb about the Holy Community of the Holy Mountain of Athos, leading up to the point of it all in the final paragraph—"You are consequently requested that, since you intend to visit the Holy Mountain, your appearance in general, both in regard to clothing as well as hair, should be appropriately restrained. We shall regret being obliged to refuse entrance to those who do not comply." Whatever else it may mean, it means No Hippies, whatever that may mean. More specifically, and most usually, it equates appropriate restraint with the canons of the present-day straight, secular, Greek middle class, and it means No Long Hair—though the monks wear theirs up in a bun, in back. The German boy with blond locks brushing his shoulder blades did not realize it yet, but if he wanted his permit at Karyes, which he would need in order to stay on Athos, he would certainly be led around in back of a building to a barbershop of raw boards, a recent edifice, something between a do-it-yourself privy and a fortune-teller's booth, and there would have his curls appropriately restrained—to above his collar, all around. Two vehicles were waiting in the dust between the customs-shed and the row of shops, in the one street. An ancient bus, with a ladder up the back for luggage, including boxes of fish, and gardenia plants. And a natty gray Landrover, property of the Greek police. I wandered off into a shop to pick up a new map of Athos (there are several available editions, but none is much of a practical guide to the maze of footpaths that wind from ravine to ravine over the ridges) and to look at the hermits' wood carving, and the objects there for sale to the monks and workmen: heavy cloth, thick dishes, lanterns, soap, flashlights, axheads, rope, rice. Everywhere the same and everywhere different. Beyond the third or fourth shop was a pergola, with cafe tables under it. I put down my sack, in the shade. At one of the tables was a tall monk with a long gray beard, talking with three men clearly from the outer world, in holiday attire. The conversation was in English, and as I repacked my sack so that the new map would be handy, and put away the no longer needed sweater, I heard the monk, speaking with an American accent, explaining to the visitors, who proved to be Roman Catholic priests, the rules in the different monasteries regarding the wearing of religious vestments other than those of the Orthodox church. They depended largely on the views of the respective abbots. One of the visitors said that he had missed his cassock in the evening, and had felt chilly. The monk spoke apologetically about the severity of some of the houses. The bus beeped, but I let it go rumbling and lurching away over the dirt road. I knew that bus trip: an hour of rattling in the old tin cookie box, up the jeep road and straight over the spine of the peninsula. The backs of monks' heads bobbing sharply in unison. Pin-up ikons. No This and No That signs. The road of the flogged engine, and its smell. I was glad I already knew it. This time I would walk.

The road follows the sea for a short distance and then turns sharply to the right and starts up the steep slope. A row of poles for a telephone line between Daphne and the mainland runs parallel to the shore, and drops behind as the road swings up away from the water. Gates into overgrown terraces, in the bright sunlight; mules and horses browsing under olive trees. Sounds of horsebells, finches. The road switches back and forth, climbing; heads up a wide ravine, doubles back to a point above the sea, turns inland. Holly oak, arbutus, bay trees. Bees. Large languid butterflies in the morning stillness. At the top of the first long rise, suddenly a level shady plateau, and off to the right, among big trees, the high walls of a monastery, a small worn bas-relief of a horseman with a spear—St. George?—set into the corner nearest the road, and a fountain with a tin dipper facing it. A peasant stacking firewood under the trees. Xeropotamou: a huge hollow square of stone. Founded in the tenth century on the site of an older village whose name is now disputed. A monastery that survived earthquake and fires and has been rebuilt by several rulers, one of them a sultan, Selim I. He had seen in a vision the Forty Martyrs of Sebaste—Armenians who, in the fourth century, had been set in a lake to freeze to death—and they had instructed him to restore the monastery, which had recently been burned down by pirates. The Martyrs, for their part, would help him fight the Arabs. Long after the sultan's death in 1519, his successors continued to provide oil for the lamps before the ikon of the Forty Martyrs, in the Xeropotamou church.

The ascent continues as steeply as before; the monastery, seen from above, dwindles until it looks like a farm on a ledge above the sea. The sun climbs, but the heights grow cooler. The limestone scrub gives way to chestnut woods, mules wandering loose in the sloping shade. The last mists have burned off; the road winds higher and higher. Then, without warning, a sudden presence, off to the right, across a great empty space: the first view of the mountain. Once it has been seen, the sense of it remains wherever one goes on the promontory, whether or not the peak itself is visible. The road clambers on over the ridge, and the eastern sea, the Holy Sea, comes into sight through the chestnut leaves, and down through the woods the roofs of Karyes appear: tile and rusting iron, vineyards, gardens, *sketes,* and *kellis* straggling out from the center, a tilted village turning as the track winds down to become its one street.

Karyes, named for its hazel trees, is the capital of the monastic state of Athos. Except for Koutloumousiou, which is considered to be too close to need one, each of the monasteries has a house in town, known as a *konaki,* for its deputation to the Holy Epistasia, the governing body, which meets in the Mansion of the Holy Community, a large, relatively modern building dominating the upper end of the town. The road fans out into a dusty plaza: in the northwest corner, monks and muleteers load and unload the scraggy goat-footed gelded mules and horses that manage to pick their way all their lives over the steep twisting mountain paths, often no more than a series of narrow, rubbly depressions in the rock. The street itself begins with a flight of stairs—with a cobbled path around them: it runs for the distance of a couple of short city blocks, past the few shops, most of which seem to be in the hands of laymen. Windows display the wood-carvings and other handwork of the hermits, hardware, dry goods—in one I saw a cartridge belt and a gun case. Cobblers' shops, saddlers. Halfway along, the street crosses the eastern end of the square on which the main church of Karyes, the ancient Protaton, stands, and then turns downhill, toward the woods. There is a rule against riding down the main street, and the monks dismount and lead their horses and mules over the big, worn cobbles. The rule does not seem to apply to the Greek police jeeps—no doubt a jeep is harder to lead. That vehicle had roared past me as I climbed from the sea, driven by a young man ostentatiously in tune with his uniform, his face, and the station in life to which he had risen: the James Bond of Daphne. The jeep was parked on the otherwise empty square of the

Protaton, jacked up and wheelless, with a layman on his back under it, and the driver bent over slightly to extend helpful unconcern from his relative height. The police station was still open, and I picked up my passport, but the Mansion, which amounts to the town hall of Karyes, was closed until three, and I would not be able to get my permit until then. Downstairs to the beanery, where the two head men from the police station—the only other customers—were already installed. Some days are fish days, some are squid days. This was neither. Pistachio walls with posters advertising the 21st of April, and a fly-specked photograph of the incumbent caudillo (October 3, 1973) tilting out from on high like a family portrait. In case the decor tempted one to linger, the cook made it clear that he was in a hurry to close: he was late for his siesta. The street was empty. I looked into a tailor's shop, with a tin window-pane to hold a stovepipe, and dusty sewing machines older than anyone on the mountain. A year before I had spent an hour in there, with a thin white-bearded monk, a muleteer, and a French priest in mufti, whom I had met on the Mansion steps, and with whom I had agreed to visit the north of the peninsula; he had wanted to engage a guide and a mule to carry the knapsacks. An hour of delirious bargaining, in a wash of languages, while I tried to see into the crannies in the back of the shop—attics of lives I had thought I had forgotten. I had watched the monk's shoes: black leather boxes, half *sabot* and half slipper, made more for shuffling than for walking, and for standing in through the all-night vigils. The shop was closed; we might never have been there. In the summer, in the middle of the day, Mediterranean Karyes bakes on its hill. But in the autumn, in the shade of the street, a coldness comes out of the stones that is the cold of the mountain towns far higher than those hazel groves, a cold shared with ancient settlements well to the north of Greece, nestled on heights, between limestone and granite. A chill that flows through the empty streets at noon, with the sound of many small streams running down from the chestnut forests and through the sleeping town. I went back to the square, to the west of the Protaton, and sat in the sun, on steps leading up through the late-flowering rosemary and hollyhocks, to wait for something to open. With the knapsack for a pillow, I dozed off to the sound of bees, and a tinkle of horsebells almost overhead woke me: it was the muleteer from the first day of the year before, going up the path, and we wrung each other's hands and exchanged congratulations and pantomine. The church was open. Inside, a young monk was moving a ladder around, replacing beeswax candles in the great brass *corona,* the ring-candelabra suspended in the nave. Strangers are not invariably welcome in every church on the mountain—the French priest had told me of his cold reception at the Protaton, on an earlier occasion—and I slipped through the open doorway quietly, to look at the murals wall by wall.

The paintings of Athos, indeed those of any of its major churches, demand, and in some cases have received, studies to themselves. The ikons, in building after building, even after centuries of natural disasters, recurrent fires, raids, occupations by alien empires, are still of a bewildering richness. The ordinary lay visitor seldom has a chance to do more than look briefly at a few of them, in each place, perhaps during or just after one of the divine offices. The churches are not museums—yet. Even if he is shown in by a welcoming monk, it is unlikely that he will be allowed to linger as he pleases, and unless he is Orthodox he will seldom be allowed to see anything behind the ikonostasis, where some of the most beautiful of the ikons are hung. Most of the monasteries house one or more ikons that are themselves the subjects of legends: pictures said to have been miraculously painted, or preserved, or transported to their present places, paintings said to have wept or bled or spoken, instruments of divine intervention. Athos, besides, has always maintained schools of ikon-painting, and many of the finest ikons are native to the mountain. The murals are another of the great treasures of Athos. They do not represent the historic range of the ikons; most of them were painted between the fourteenth century and the eighteenth. But they are even more obviously integral to the place, its walls, its roofs, its weather, its fate. They were painted where they are; they have suffered damp, smoke, mutilation, and restoration where they are; even if they could be moved, or if the use of their buildings were to change, they would not be the same. Some of the murals are famous, and art historians come to study particular groups, details, progressions. Of the painters whose names have survived, the most celebrated is Emanual Panselinos of Thessalonika, an artist of the sixteenth century about whom legends have gathered on the mountain: monks are to be found who will state positively at what period of his life, and in what order, certain murals were painted. But there is no single mural anywhere on Athos that can be indisputably attributed to him. The murals on Athos vary greatly, even on a single wall, and the scholarly purist does not always do justice to the peculiar importance, to the great works, of their settings, including, often, the humbler, cruder patchworks of the tradition around them, and the aging buildings of which they are a part. Anyone who has once seen, high on the two walls under the dome, separated by the arch of the apse, the two balanced protagonists of the Annunciation, the Angel Gabriel on the left, the Virgin with the book signifying the Word, on the right, silently conversing across the dark abyss lit only by a gold crucifix, and has then seen that composition repeated, with greatly differing artistry, in church after church on the mountain, is unlikely to think of the separate figures afterwards in isolation from the significance of their placing, and their relation to the whole drama. The thematic arrangements of the murals in each church follows, besides, liturgical and initiatory patterns: it is not by chance, nor for aesthetic reasons, that the entrance to the apse, into the holiest part of the church, should be traversed, above, by the Annunciation, and lead into the place of death, resurrection, and elevation. The ikonography itself, where the art is as rich and as functional as it is on Athos, is sometimes rendered with great vividness by a painting which, taken by itself, would seem neither especially gifted nor forceful. I think, for instance, of some of the images of fish, symbols of Christ, in the frescoes, linking the paintings of the Baptism with those of the Harrowing of Hell. They are crossed in the river Jordan, where Jesus stands on them. The doors of Hell are crossed in the same way, and the dead and resurrected Christ is shown standing on them. The crossed doors need only be shown, then, above the west entrance to the church itself, to convey a whole symbology of the body and the spirit, baptism and resurrection. The paintings themselves, as is the case with most genuine symbologies, embody both a conscious and an unconscious tradition, and much of this aspect of them is lost in isolation.

The Protaton at Karyes is the oldest church on the mountain— a basically tenth-century building on the site of a still earlier one, but restored in the sixteenth century. It contains some of the most famous murals on Athos, including some of the ones attributed to Panselinos: contemplative saints, haloed knights and rulers in armor, historic and legendary protectors, along the nave. The paintings above the door have been damaged, and they rise into fresh cement. Even at midday, with the doors open, the church smelled of incense and the beeswax of the long candles that the young monk was setting in place for the night's vigil.

Outside, the Mansion was open, and the Athonian policeman, whose manner when dealing with a batch of new visitors at the routine hour had been irritable and forbidding, received me with affable curiosity and served up my permit in the official kitchen, where he and the cook and bottle-washer were passing the afternoon over coffee. It was late to set out for any of the more remote monasteries that day. The shadows of the autumn afternoon were already lengthening. The massive, iron-plated monastery doors that stand open all day are shut and bolted at sunset: a custom that is said to have come from the days of raiding pirates.

Just above Karyes, off the Daphne road, is the *skete* of St. Andrew, a rambling mass of architecture, like a child's cardboard palace that has been left in the rain. It looks Russian, and it was, in fact, one of the buildings that resulted from the great nineteenth-century influx of Russians to Athos. The rank of monastery, with the right to a representative in the Holy Assembly, is accorded to only twenty monasteries on the mountain, a number that has been maintained despite Russian attempts to change it for nationalistic purposes. Before the Russian revolution the *skete* of St. Andrew housed some eight hundred monks, far outnumbering many of the Greek monasteries, yet in the administration of the mountain it remained a dependency of the monastery of Vatopedi. A lane leads off the road below the *skete* and follows the walls to the main gate. From the windows I could hear boys' voices repeating lessons and singing in unison: since 1930 part of the *skete* has housed the Athonian School, a seminary run by the Holy Community with the support of the Greek Ministry of Education. The cobbled courtyard, sloping up to another portico and a pair of heavy doors, looked older than some of the structures facing it. The doors of the inner portico were shut, chained, and padlocked. There was a gap between them, and it looked as though a vast abyss full of ruins overgrown with shimmering trees was inside there. Somewhere within the walls of the *skete* —but perhaps not in there—was the huge church of St. Andrew, recent, like most of the Russian buildings on Athos: it was finished in 1900. And parts of the *skete* are indeed ruins: a fire, in 1958, raged there for four days, destroying whole sections of it, and many of its manuscripts and other treasures. One of the three or four old monks who are all that remain of the *skete* itself, hatless, long hair hanging loose, venerable shoes that had collapsed into slippers, was sitting out on a stone bench in the sun, chattering with a workman, as I came in. He leaned back against the stone, as I approached the chained and padlocked doors, and asked me about myself, and said that now it was no longer possible for me to go in there. The government, he said, forbade it, and he grew stern as he told me. I tried to find out which government he meant—that of Athos or that of Greece. Yes, yes, he said, the government. The restriction did not seem to make him unhappy, but rather to fill him with a vague satisfaction: things were being properly looked after, mysterious though the process might seem. And the sun was warm, and he was enjoying his conversation and returned to it. The voices of the boys echoed in the courtyard. From a ramp at a lower level, several laymen beckoned to me, and I went and found a small knot of cronies sitting on benches in the sunny end of a long corridor. A single visitor was an object of curiosity, and we found out where we had each come from. Most of them had been peasants from that part of Greece; one of them had traveled, working in a ship's galley. He disappeared and came back with a glass of water and another of *raki* (grape alcohol slightly flavored with anise). He, too, led me to understand that neither the *skete* nor the school, at the moment, were open to visitors. But he insisted that I must be hungry, and popped back into the kitchen to fetch me a big tin bowl of cool lentils and onions, a tomato, and a fistful of good heavy sour bread, and I obediently consumed the lot while they watched and pressed me to more: there was plenty, they insisted, because they had all those students to feed and to prove the point one of them got up and took a large basket full of broken ends of bread out into the courtyard, tipped it into a wooden trough, and led a fat donkey around to the trough to munch at leisure. Another old unkempt monk, tall but bent with rheumatism, came in and sat on the end of the bench—clearly a favorite: a wit and a man of style. It was a lighthearted session, and when I got up to go, the cook popped into the kitchen and came out with more great wads of bread, which he pressed into my hands, to eat on the way.

I went back through Karyes and downhill toward Koutloumousiou: a cobbled path, steep as stairs where it left the town, between walls, and dropped into woods. Hazels overhanging the turns. Little streams running alongside and trickling across. Mud at the foot of banks dotted with cyclamen. More chestnuts. The sea far below, to the left: scattered cypresses, and the tin and stone roofs of small *sketes* and *kellis.* The great east wall of Koutloumousiou was in shadow when I reached it and stopped for a drink at the fountain facing the gate, under the trees. The armored doors stood open; a tunnel the length of a room led into the courtyard, already full of luminous twilight, where a fine grass grew between the stones. As I stood looking in, a white horse ambled past me and in through the blue light of the tunnel, and began to browse in the courtyard. When I followed I saw no one, at first. The hollow square of stone was silent. The center of the courtyard is taken up, in the familiar way, by the church—at Koutloumousiou, the Church of the Transfiguration. Tiers of arcades and balconies face onto it, from the surrounding walls. Cats were running up and down the stairs between the rows of arches, like pieces of shadows. A marble *phiale*—a cupola over a basin for blessing holy water—facing me, was tipped toward the door of the church: the streams running down the mountain and through the courtyard had softened the ground at its base, and over the centuries it had subsided into the grass. Behind it a massive square keep rose high above the rest of the monastery. Empty wine barrels on the grass. Water dripping from pipes by the arches. Tethering rings in the brick columns. Painted plates and jugs set into the brickwork of the arches, and of the church, as ornaments. I heard the sound of wet cloth being shaken, and looked above my head: a monk was hanging out a bit of laundry on a balcony railing. He asked where I was from, and told me that someone would be along to welcome me. An old monk appeared in one of the arcades and started to do some ironing, watching me. After a few minutes a younger monk appeared around the base of the tower, greeted me, and led me up echoing wooden stairs to a broad, recently converted dormitory on the top floor, that looked as though it might be the back room of a country store filled with cots for some annual occasion. A modern tile screen divided the front part from the back, and I chose a cot at the back, by a window that overlooked the chestnut woods. But I had to move a little later, when two Greek visitors—middle-aged men with plastic shopping-bags—were shown in: many of the monasteries make a point of lodging the Greeks and the foreign visitors separately. It is customary, on the mountain, for guests to be presented, on arrival, with a little tray containing a cup of Turkish coffee, a piece of Turkish delight, a glass of water and a shot glass of *raki* or *ouzo*—to be consumed in whatever order the guest decides upon, but the underlying assumption is that he will knock back the homemade *raki* first, follow it with the candy, and then the water, and finish up sipping the coffee. At Koutloumousiou the ceremony was dispensed with altogether. The monk who had led me up to the dormitory had told me that he would wait for me downstairs, and when I arrived again in front of the church he unlocked it and led me in to see the paintings, including miraculous ikons—many of the features, both of ikons and frescoes, hard to make out in the shadowy building already being overtaken by dusk. The monk indicated a spot at the base of one of the great brass candlesticks where he said money would be gratefully received—the only time such a suggestion was ever made to me on the mountain. The frescoes inside the church, some of them dating from the sixteenth century, are impressive works, but the upper parts are hard to see; those in the church porch get more light. They are cruder, but the themes that are traditional in that part of the building—the Creation and the Apocalypse— lend themselves to naive treatment, which in turn benefits by the conventions of ikonographic composition. Outside, the monk said I should sign the guest book, and I in turn asked whether I might see the library. It was locked, he said, and hurried off to fetch the book, or the key—I was not sure which. He never came back with either. In the dormitory, a boy from the States was engaged in stuffing bushels of camping gadgets and clothes into a huge knapsack. He was on his way to the Near East, and had heard of Athos and stopped off to see why anybody would live in such a weird way. He had wandered around the empty corridors, looking for something to eat, and an old monk had given him some apples, and a few figs that were being dried on a balcony. In the dusk, a monk came to lead us both to the dark kitchen, seat us at a table with a kerosene lamp beside us, and serve us each a bowl of eggplants and peppers stewed together, a salad of tomatoes and onions and olive oil, all from the garden, and a pitcher of water from the mountain, while he shuffled around in the shadows beyond the mighty stove. The monasteries' traditional hospitality, instituted in an age of foot travel and pilgrims, has been taxed to breaking in recent years by the swelling current of tourists brought by motors, each summer. As the spate of visitors has increased, the number of monks, and the resources of the monasteries, have been dwindling. The situation—one hears again and again on the mountain—is encouraged by the Greek government, whose tourist office, it is said, is impatient to break the monasteries, round up the remaining monks and get them out of the way, and turn the buildings into museums and hotels. The light drained out of the courtyard. I walked down the corridor and found my way to a balcony hanging over the chestnut woods. The moon was drifting above the ridge, already silvering the eastern slope. The monastery was still. A pair of tawny owls echoed each other in the forest to the south. Beyond them the peak of Athos gleamed in the moonlight and the last pallid emanation of day.

The evening turned cold. A couple of smoky kerosene lamps had been brought into the dormitory. The American boy was still wadding his infinite impedimenta into his finite bag: the loose bits were piled on the surrounding cots and it looked as though the process might go on all night. The Greeks, in the other section, were talking over a table. In a while they began to snore: deep, determined reverberations. I picked up my sack and some bedding and went out into the arcade to sleep there. The courtyard had filled with moonlight. The domes of the *katholikon*, a few paces away through the air, looked frosted over. Cats slipped along the arcades and fought above the plank ceilings. I was wakened by a grunt: an old monk with a lantern was looking down at me, startled. When I stirred he hurried on, and clattered down the stairs, and the sound was taken up on other stairs, and the beat of the semantron suddenly overtook them all.

The semantron is a cousin of the oar. The two arrived by different routes at a kindred form. The semantron looks like an oar blade rising out of its reflection and joined to it by a handle: a double-ended oar, two blades with one handle, made for calling, wakening, warning, announcing. A monk in a black veil carries it on his shoulder and strides around the courtyard, circling the church, turning to the four quarters, striking the forward blade rapidly with a mallet, a toccata rising and falling as the mallet moves up and down the board, faster, slower, pauses, starts again. The echoes leap from the board: dark fireworks. They rebound from the walls of the courtyard and the unlit corridors behind the arches. They rattle the doors. The first of them shatters sleep. The monk pauses at different points in his circuit, and the rapping stops. Then it begins again, urgent, sharp, the insistent wooden syllables forming the name of Adam over and over, the whole summons repeated three times, the calling of Noah to the creation to come into the Ark: first to the things that go upon their bellies, then to the things that go on four feet, and last, to man, who stands up, and knows. Besides the portable semantron there is a larger one in most monasteries, swung from chains in an arcade, or outside the refectory or a church door: a massive beam cut in roundels at the ends. And in some monasteries there is also a huge omega-shape of iron, suspended in a commanding position; on certain occasions these, too, and the bells in the towers, are all sounded together. But the plain semantron, half beaten and half resounding, from a shoulder, each blade in a different part of the same note, announces the hour of most of the services, and of

some of the times prescribed for private prayer. The hours themselves
are reckoned according to different systems, in different monasteries. In
most of them—eighteen of the twenty—time is told according to the
ancient Byzantine system, in which sunset is twelve o'clock. Iviron
observes the traditional Georgian custom of calling sunrise twelve
o'clock. And one monastery, Vatopedi, counts its hours according to the
custom prevailing in the secular world, with twelve o'clock at noon.
The services also vary somewhat from monastery to monastery, upon a
basic pattern: nones, vespers, and complines in the latter part of the day,
and on some of the nights vigils lasting through the hours of darkness
until daybreak and the opening of the outer doors. In some of the
churches the office is read and attended now by only a handful of old
monks, nodding, chanting, bowing, in the light of candles, among the
glinting of ikons and brass candelabra, and small flames in red glass
ikon lamps, and the smoke of incense rising toward the dim faces in the
ceiling, to the sound of the worn words.

I was outside the blue doors in time to see the sun appear at the end of
a pink, gold, mother-of-pearl path of mist that blurred the sea. The peak
was clear, catching the first light, one wisp of cloud trailing from it
eastward toward the sunrise. Looking up and back to the walls of the
monastery, I saw two old monks out on a high balcony, sitting watching
the light before their first meal of the day. They waved me on my way,
down the path through the woods, to the southeast. Jays flashed uphill
among the trees. The low rays of the sun rebounded from the mist on
the sea, and slanted under the chestnut branches. Figs hung out of the
woods, over the narrow walled path, with its accompaniment of trickling water: breakfast. Arbutus, the red berries splashed on the ground
below the bushes, some of them overripe and broken open in the fall,
showing the yellow, mealy, gritty interior: *arbutus unedo*, or *monedo*,
as I have seen written: "arbutus eat one," the name in Latin referring to
the effects of the fruit, its property of loosening the bowels, or the notion
that it contains an insidious narcotic, or both. But I like the flat dry
taste, and as usual did not limit myself to one—and as usual they did no
harm. A twist of the path under their foliage. A dry fountain like an
empty shrine, set in the mouth of a wooded ravine. Flocks of warblers
flying through sunbeams, with silence all around them. Whole banks
covered with cyclamen. The smell of pines mingling with that of the
mold of chestnut woods and the scent of honey, as the undersides of the
leaves warmed with the morning. Mysteries farther on: the unmistak-

able sounds—and the sight—of hens in the woods, from some stone-roofed *skete* or *kelli* on the slope, and at the same time, fox droppings on the cobbled path. The cobbles do not run all the way. They play out, they have washed out, they are abandoned for shortcuts gnawed by the tear-shaped iron shoes of mules, they resume suddenly on a curve skirting a gorge, or at the approach to a stone bridge: on the way down from Koutloumousiou to the south there is a high arch over a rocky torrent, quiet in the autumn. Stone-covered runnels cross the path, the hidden water whispering and splashing like mice. Rags of cloud appeared up on the ridge, and vanished over it. Bright sun on the slope to the south. Where the path followed the side of a small valley, in sheltered woods, I came on a monk down on all fours, gardening, clearing the weeds from the wall below a long bed of flowers that had been tended with love. His hat was off and it was clear that he had been absorbed in the work since first light, and that his heart was in it. Wild dianthus were blooming along the path a few feet from the nodding yellow heads of campanulas. The soil was black and crumbly, and his hands and knees and cassock were covered with it. Just beyond him was a small chapel newly painted reddish-brown and white, with painted tin cans full of basil plants around the door, and rosemary in bloom at the eastern end. Then the path came out into the open, dropped toward bare ground. Cypresses marking far slopes, giving scale. Autumn squills, Saint-John's-wort with enormous flowers, that late in the year. The green brush gave away to olive trees, each on its separate half-moon of carefully built dry stone terrace, and over the shoulder of the hill came the sound of breakers. I rounded the corner, eastward, and saw below me the huge monastery of Iviron, on its eminence dominating the shore. Gardens, orchards, vineyards around it. One facade with a white-columned neoclassic portal: the main gate, from which a broad cobbled way led down, past roofed fountains and garden walls, to a wharf, and a fortified tower by the sea.

It is there, the legend says, that the Virgin came ashore out of the stormy waves. When she had prayed to her son to be given the mountain, a voice from heaven had granted it to her, to be her garden and paradise, and a place of salvation.

The great ocher walls of the portico lead under a large ikon to a cobbled entrance hall with the gatekeeper's office on one side, and the bright interior at the far end. Fountains, the spouts emerging from slabs of carved marble: bas-reliefs of thistles and birds, angels, suns, crowns.

There is a magnificent *phiale* facing the entrance: even the curtain drawn back between the marble columns is carved in stone. And a cluster of churches in the broad level courtyard, besides the *katholikon* itself, which dates from the eleventh century, and contains frescoes of different ages, from the sixteenth century on, some of great vigor and beauty. The chapel of St. John the Baptist, near the church, is said to stand on the site of the original temple of Poseidon, destroyed by the presence of the Virgin, and replaced in the third century by a small monastery named for its founder, St. Clement, Bishop of Jerusalem. The present monastery was built by three Georgian-Iberian (whence the name Iviron) noblemen, late in the tenth century.

Another chapel stands near the site of the old gates, and is dedicated to, and houses, the "Portaitissa," the Virgin-of-the-Gate, the guardian of the monastery: one of the most revered ikons on the mountain, and one of the oldest and richest in legends. Traditionally, it is one of the seventy paintings by the hand of St. Luke, and it is one of several ikons which are said to have been consigned to the sea, to save them from ikonoclasts, and to have been brought by miraculous means to the mountain. The Portaitissa traditionally came from Constantinople, where an imperial messenger had pointed a sword at her, and had been frightened off when the picture had begun to bleed. (Another story, about a scar on the painting, says that it marks the place where the sword of an Arab pirate struck the Virgin below the chin, and the wound bled; the sight of the blood converted him, made him a monk, and at last a saint—Saint Barbaros.) The widow who had owned the ikon is said to have taken it down to the sea and watched it sail away, upright, westward. Seventy years later it appeared at the base of a pillar of light, off Iviron, and a voice from heaven named the one monk who would be allowed to carry it ashore.

It was as well that I had been to Iviron before and had a glimpse, at least, of its treasures: apart from a young monk mending a black garment at the outer gate, who looked at my permit and waved me in, there was no one to be seen, and the church and chapels were locked— except for the porch, with its remarkable frescoes. I crossed the court-yard and climbed the long staircase leading to the rooms for receiving guests, and was met by a layman who insisted on speaking German to me, and urged me to go somewhere else to eat. Iviron is one of the monasteries that has suffered most from the recent influx of tourists: too famous, and too easy to reach, by road directly from Karyes, or by boat, during the summer. It must have been a great relief, there, when the season was over. I carried my pack down to the church porch again, for another long scrutiny of the murals, and then back out through the main gate. Mules were tethered by a column, and mules and horses by the fountain at the bottom of the cobbled incline, facing the sea. Near the wharf, between the shingle and the wall at the foot of the gardens, firewood had been piled shoulder high. More pack animals were tethered beside it, and an assembly of monks, muleteers, and boatmen were sitting on logs following a heated discussion between an old monk—obviously in charge of the transaction—and a boatman. They were both red in the face and beyond concern for decorum, though not for drama: they danced their indignation back and forth around one symbolic log, on which they visited tokens of their passions, kicking it, pushing it toward each other, snatching it back again, putting a foot on it, turning their backs on it, walking away, and whirling around to deliver a terrible rejoinder. The wind was off the sea. The argument seemed to have been going on since sunrise. The audience swayed like the waves, and the mules swished and stamped. I watched one complete but inconclusive round and then threaded my way among them, between the walls of firewood, stepping over the log; I was scarcely noticed. I went on, along the road that runs parallel to the water, to the end of the wall, and then turns inland, uphill. Much of it is recent, and raw. Jeep-tracks in the mud. Mutilated swaths hacked across the slopes for telephone poles, and bright new wires humming above them. The new divine right. The road overruns bits of old footpath here and there, climbing. Made for wheels, and the body can feel it. At the end of a long ascent through woods, it levels out in sand and granite rubble glinting with mica. The woods on the north slopes were still green as spring. A few rain clouds suddenly gathering. The sun hot, the air cool in the shade. Around a bend, sitting on a lap of vines and gardens at the head of several small steep valleys, Philotheou rose out of the thinning leaves.

It is not one of the largest monasteries, and its walls, surmounted by no towers, are plainer than many, though hung with old, windowed balconies, some of them used now only by pigeons. The road turned into a cobbled lane that ran along between the garden wall, on the left, and overgrown vineyards tumbling toward abandoned *kellis* in the woods, on the right, and it led to a cobbled space surrounded by grapevines, big trees, benches set along the wall facing the sea, a fountain under the shade of the vine-arbor, and the doors of the monastery, opening under balconies to the grassy courtyard bright with the autumn sun. I had sailed, a year and a month before, along this bit of coast, and looked up at the monasteries and *sketes* half hidden on the slopes, silent as paintings, and they had passed from sight, and here I stood. There had been great activity at Philotheou since that first glimpse from the sea. The sound of hammering echoed around the courtyard; a saw joined the music; a young monk hurried past me carrying a board and another saw; a monk balanced on the top of a ladder, painting the stucco window-surrounds of the church dark red. The monk with the board and the one on the ladder both saw me but went on with what they were doing; their lips were moving; they were praying as they worked. An old monk, by a walled flower bed, to the right of the entrance, shuffling under balconies, with a fat cat at his heels, smiled and waved me in toward the dahlias and marigolds, the smell of woodsmoke, the wine barrels lying on the grass with water running into them to swell them; he told me to make myself at home.

A young monk with a hearing aid and a saw and crowbar came from behind me, greeted me with a nod, and wasted no time on his way to join the work on the far side of the church. I put down my sack and stood looking across the courtyard into a wide doorway on the other side, painted cans of basil flanking the door, and inside, a staircase newly painted bright blue, with a red carpet in the middle of the steps, climbing into the darkness. As I looked, two monks (they were all young except the old man with the cat) came from outside the monastery, struggling with a huge reluctant sheet of hardboard which kept collapsing in the middle. I grabbed the sagging section despite their polite mumble of protest, and we proceeded across the courtyard to the door I had been considering, and up the blue stairs, and then on up another flight, before we stopped at the entrance to a large empty room. There, while they caught their breath, they asked me about myself, and one of them led me down into the courtyard, while another disappeared to look for somebody, and in a moment several monks called me from an upper balcony, and I was directed up newly painted stairs, along newly painted corridors, to a pale green room full of light, jutting out into a balcony over a courtyard. A long table down the middle, with a white crocheted tablecloth, and seats on either side, took up the whole room. A shelf of books along the east wall, high up, half of them in English. One monk who looked scarcely old enough to have grown his beard, showed me in, vanished, and returned almost at once with the guest tray, its napkins neatly ironed; he nodded shyly, and left. As he went, another monk entered, greeted me in English, and told me that he was busy at the moment, that he would be back shortly to talk with me— meanwhile I was welcome. His gesture included the shelf of books.

I had opened one of them, but was looking out into the courtyard, listening to the urgent sounds of carpentry, and the few words, sharp and abrupt—not a conversation—that broke over them at intervals, when he came back: thin, grave face, fine features; always, in talk, leaning a little forward, as though in the act of bowing, looking up at the last minute, but the eyes never straying from my face. It was obvious that the time for this meeting had been set aside, taken away from something else. He spoke with a constant watchfulness: level, gentle, low-voiced, a slight smile, benevolent, but neither personal nor effusive. His attention was mine, but almost all of his life was elsewhere.

He had learned English as a child, at the American school in Athens. He spoke it softly, carefully, with little hesitation. I remarked on the youth of many of the monks—a sharp contrast to most of the monasteries —and the surge of manual work. He told me that it had been going on only since January. At that time the monastery of Philotheou had dwindled to eight aging monks. He himself was one of a larger group of young monks who had been living farther up the mountain at a *skete* called Provata, and the *kellis* around it; his own had been the *kelli* of Agius Artemius. Their enthusiasm, fired by a remarkable elder, had led growing numbers of new monks to the *skete*, and in a few years it had become crowded. Most of them had been moved, in January, to Philotheou, where the running of the monastery was divided between them and the eight old monks who were there. A similar takeover, he said, was planned for Koutloumousiou, where only five old monks were left, and perhaps for Simopetra, across the peninsula. The transition, at Philotheou, had not been without difficulties, for anyone. There was the inevitable friction between the older monks, set in their ways and used to having the whole echoing place to themselves, and the sudden overwhelming invasion of youth and ardor. The newcomers, for their part, did not take readily to the life of a monastery. They were solitaries; at their beloved *skete* they had been trying, under the guidance of their elder, to restore what they believed was the all but lost Orthodox mystical tradition of constant prayer, the prayer of the heart, which Athos in particular had nurtured for centuries. In their *kellis* they had been able to devote almost all of their waking hours to private contemplative prayer. In the monastery there were more activities to be undertaken, many of them in common; administrative duties were far more demanding, and more time was devoted to liturgical worship. True solitude was harder to achieve. And the young monks' fervent devotion both to doctrine and to practice, also contributed to a current of dissension between them and the older men. He told me that as the monastic calling had waned in numbers, in recent generations, the monks had come increasingly from among the less educated parts of the population. Some of them were scarcely literate; very few of them could read the ancient Greek of the early texts. Gradually their understanding of many passages became patchy and distorted. Many things were forgotten altogether, and the process was accompanied by a growing laxity of habits and attitude, and a perfunctory performance of the divine services. My questions about the particular tradition of contemplative prayer to which he referred were met with an inquiry as to whether or not I was Orthodox, why I was interested, and a suggestion that I look carefully into the book that I had open on the table: Kadloubovsky and Palmer's translation of St. Nicodemus of the Holy Mountain's *Unseen Warfare*. "Now," he said, "I will show you to your room." And he led me along the corridor to a green room facing northwest, with a view of chestnut forests climbing the ridge. "I will go and see that you have something to eat," he said. "You will be called." I asked if I could help with the carpentry or, if possible, with the gardens, where I had seen a layman hoeing rows of cabbages and eggplants. "No," he said, "most of the summer's work is over. We can do it all easily now." I had come a long way, he told me, and what I should do was to rest, and eat, and read the book, which he had urged me to bring with me. I said I would like to have more chance to talk with him, and he told me he would try to find time later in the day. And with a slight bow, which may not have been a bow at all, but simply his way of turning, he left me.

Bare wooden floor. Iron beds painted white. Even the sheet on the bed seemed not to have been used more than once or twice, and here it was, the end of summer. The door opened without a knock. It was a Dutch student, another who was traveling to the East; his knapsack was at the foot of a bed by a window across the room. The sheet on my bed, he told me, had in fact been clean the night before, when he had used it himself; if we swapped sheets we would both be sleeping in luxury. His subject was agriculture, but the methods of its practice at present had disheartened him, and he had decided to see a little of the world while there was time; he hoped to help with some farming in India, where he had friends. India, agriculture—Sir Albert Howard? I asked. But Howard's work on the soil of India, even in the early years of the century, had been at odds with an age in which farming was already becoming an adjunct of the chemical industry, and I was not surprised that his name was not mentioned in the curricula of agricultural schools in the Netherlands. The boy had come to Athos simply because he had heard about it after he had got to Greece, and had been curious. He liked the quiet of the mountain, but could not see what *good* the monasteries did. Footsteps, at that point, on the flagstones of the corridor, and a light knock on the door. It was Father Mark, the monk with whom I had been speaking, come to tell us that something had been prepared for us to eat.

From the long walls of the refectory, and from the end rounded like an apse, remnants of superb frescoes dominated the room, as though it were the fragment and they were the whole. Faces, haloes, bodies of saints standing, bowing, raised hands, wings, walls painted on walls, boats on the last flakes of seas, among deserts of white plaster. They had survived—as far as is known—for more than four centuries, through periods of poverty, neglect, damp winters, invaders, and a disastrous fire a hundred years ago. Long tables flanked by benches traversed the entire room, leaving the middle empty: the tables were half set, and at two places near the door, bowls of lentils, tomato and onion salad, oil, olives, bread, apples, water, had been placed. Again the bow, and Father Mark disappeared through the green-painted wooden partition that separated the refectory from the kitchen, and we were left to eat in a silence that imposed itself. Sounds of dishwashing came from beyond the partition, and two young monks came and went, continuing to set the tables; others came in, spoke with them briefly, went out again. When they caught our eyes they nodded, and their lips went on with their prayers. The correct greeting of a monk on Athos is "Evlogite" —"Bless me"—and the reply is "O Kyrios"—"The Lord." At Philotheou the exchange is often dispensed with. But one small bright-faced monk, the cook, came to ask whether the food was good, and to tell us to eat more, bustling, permanently amused—he laughed at the very idea of our bringing our plates out to the kitchen, where he was washing the last dishes, a few minutes later, and at our offering to help there. We had scarcely left the refectory when I saw him, clutching a saw, pattering downstairs to join the carpentry, as though it would not wait.

Outside the monastery, one of the old monks was sitting on a bench in the sun, gossiping with a lay workman, their backs to the sea. The gardener was still hoeing the monstrous eggplants and okras, and made it clear that he would have welcomed a bit of willing help, but plainly it would have offended some rule of hospitality or some monastic restriction, if the Dutch student and I had ignored Father Mark's evident unwillingness for us to participate in the work of the monastery. The Dutch boy went off one way, exploring, and I another, around to what appeared to be a muleteer's house behind the monastery: a farmhouse with an upper porch, an old whittled banister, pack saddles, horse blankets hanging on wires, tack, old sewing gear, axes, pieces of olive presses, rope—hanging, leaning, waiting in someone's sleep: it was the siesta hour. Around to the newly painted cemetery door, past a storehouse with part of a new floor laid, to some abandoned *kellis* sitting in their arbors of unpruned vines. Up into the woods above a pile of new-sawn lumber stacked to dry. The monastery derives part of its income from the sale of timber. Clearings, up in the woods, healing, full of cyclamen. By the time I got back, the bench was empty and I sat to read, where I could look up and watch the pigeons under the balconies, the shadows moving along the whitewashed garden wall, the sea far below—until I saw a monk in a black veil stride into the monastery with a semantron on his shoulder, and heard it, moments later, sharp and brisk. I got up and went in, but a monk met me in the church door and asked politely whether I were Orthodox. No one who was not was admitted to their services, he told me. I had encountered hostility on Athos before—the feeling of being regarded as a heretic intruding upon holy ground. I had been forbidden to pass behind the ikonostasis, when Orthodox visitors were being shown in to see miraculous ikons kept in the holiest parts of churches; reliquaries had been closed lest I should catch sight of the relics. But such acts had been great exceptions. Never before had I been forbidden to attend a service—and it was done without overt hostility, as though it was perfectly natural and I should have been expecting it. A while later, reading at the window above the chestnut forests, while the shadows darkened on the ridge under the gathering clouds, I heard the service end, and the clatter of feet on wooden stairs, and then the monks chanting in the refectory below. They clattered out. The light knock came on the door. Father Mark, to lead me, in my turn, to the refectory. On the way he said that he would have some time, after I had eaten, to continue our conversation. The

Dutch boy was not yet back, but they brought him along when he showed up. A cold light came through the refectory windows. There was no sunset. The merry cook came in to say that his soup (cold on the table) was a triumph (which it was) and should be eaten in quantity, along with everything else—chestnuts and okra and olives and bread, in whatever order seemed appropriate. Father Mark was waiting, after the meal, and led me past the guest room, along the corridor, to an old parlor: yellowed lithographs and photographs of czars and archbishops tilted out from the walls into the early dusk. We sat down at a large round table; the white crocheted tablecloth hung to the floor. In the twilight the table seemed to be growing. There was light enough for some time for me to miss nothing of Father Mark's face: hollow, tilted forward just as it was when he was standing. Watching me out of the tops of his eyes, with their steady burn.

He asked me what progress I had made with the books on the shelf, and what my plans were for the next day. I had originally thought of going on southeast, perhaps to Great Lavra, down in the craggy country near the end of the promontory, the first in rank, one of the oldest, largest, and most beautiful monasteries on the mountain. When I had been there, the autumn before, I had seen only a few of its celebrated frescoes and its other treasures. And on the next memorable day I had left at first light to round the steep end of the peninsula, making for the *skete* of St. Anne, on the western coast. It is generally considered to be an arduous trip, along the rubbly edges of precipices, across stretches of scree, up and down over the spines and buttresses that line the south face of the peak. I wanted to have the whole day for it. The footpath ravels into scrub more than once, and is lost. Looking for it, I had pushed through thickets into a high shady meadow ringed with chestnut trees and holly oaks and shining with yellow autumn daffodils; horses without bells, half wild, bolted into the woods at the far end. A little way beyond the meadow an icy spring trickled out and crossed the resurrected path—the place may have been the "Krya Nera," the Cold Waters; snow is said to lie near the place throughout most of the year. And in the woods below, a hermitage not long abandoned, the hearthstone hollow like a shallow sink, the back of the fireplace rounded in the same stone, and the projecting ends of the small stone mantlepiece carved round. The shutters and the cupboard doors were still intact in the one hushed room with horse droppings on its rotting floor. At a farther spring I had mistaken my way and followed the sound of horsebells up the steep slope, thinking that the path led over a shoulder of the mountain. I had climbed through a grove with another spring, far up into clouds and cold winds, the stones wet, the path growing even steeper and less probable, but the horsebells still rang from above me, in the cloud. Until I came in sight of a long low building like a metal tent, on the bleak, foggy, buffeted slope. The horses were loose on the scree above it, and as I came nearer I heard the sound of scraping and the slosh of water. A few monks were establishing themselves there, a bare thousand feet from the summit, where the slopes on both sides drop more than five thousand feet, straight to the sea. They were rebuilding the small chapel of the Panayia, mixing cement in the clammy wind. In one corner of the earth-floored room where they lived and ate, a fire was smoking under a pot. Their ambition included new frescoes. I had left them and clambered down again through the clouds, and the evening woods full of low west light, and at last the miles of steep marble stairs leading to St. Anne's, just above the sea, where they were bringing in the grapes of that year, and the monks and their kittens welcomed me. And from there, in the next days, I had followed the path through the New Skete, to the monasteries crowning the looming rocks of the southwest coast: St. Paul's, Dionysiou, Gregoriou, and harder to believe when actually seen, than it is in pictures—Simopetra, held up, apparently, by pure faith, standing on its cliff as though on a wave. And back to Daphne. I had thought this autumn, perhaps, to see Lavra again, and if the weather permitted, to make my way on to visit the wood-carving and ikon-painting monks at the *skete* of Kafsokalyvia, on the south coast. If the rains broke, I thought I would take the boat back from Lavra. But there was no boat from Lavra now, Father Mark told me. The one going around the end of the peninsula stops running anyway, in October, because the sea, which is dangerous even in summer, becomes savage after the equinox. And the fishing boat north to Iviron stops its runs after the first of October for the same reasons that the cafes close in Ouranopolis. The path over the cliffs to Kafsokalyvia, and the whole of the end of the peninsula were not to be recommended if the heavy autumn rains broke, and though the weather on Athos is hard to predict, the clouds on the ridge that evening looked ominous. "Stay if it rains tomorrow," Father Mark said, and he explained that the rule forbidding visitors to stay for more than twenty-four hours was more or less at the discretion of the different monasteries, particularly after the tourist season was over.

It would have been hard to guess his age. A detached authority, on the one hand, that was clearly mature, and on the other, a simplicity and candor that seemed distinctly youthful. The features, emerging from the fine beard, left the matter in doubt, though they themselves were sharply drawn and clear, the bones prominent but delicate, the large eyes set deep. Early thirties perhaps. He was twenty-two. He had become a monk five years before. His mother was devout, but his father was opposed to any religious manifestations, and had at first refused to allow his son even to visit Athos. And the boy had gone, during the Easter holidays, to the monasteries of Meteora, looking for a spiritual guide, and there had met an abbot who had urged him to go on to Athos and seek out one monk, the abbot at Provata. His own father's consent had finally been obtained, after some difficulty, and the young man had come and met the brothers, but not the abbot until several visits later. By that time he had decided that he wanted to be a monk at the *skete;* he had asked, and been granted, the abbot's permission to come, and he had gone and said good-bye to his family, and come back to take the vow of obedience to the abbot, and be given a monk's name in place of the one he had grown up with.

The abbot, he told me, was a man now in his forties; he too was the son of a devout mother. After she had been left a widow his mother had made part of the house into a chapel, where she and friends met to pray. She had tried to live like a nun, and she had asked her son, who was a priest as well as a monk, to come and consecrate her chapel. While he was there she had asked him to make her a nun; several of her friends had taken the vows at the same time, and they had formed a small convent, with him as their confessor.

The abbot had received his own training, and had been instructed in the sacred teachings, by an elder, named Joseph, a holy man secluded somewhere on Athos, who had spent his life trying to rediscover the true hesychast (Hesychasts, "the Silent," from Greek *hesychia* 'silence') tradition, of immeasurable age but certainly going back as far as the Desert Fathers, in the fourth century. The practice of hesychasm had involved, from the beginning, a constant inward awareness and invocation of God, a fervent meditative discipline of thoughts, and a corresponding struggle with distraction. It was, and it is, both a way of living and a state of being; it centers on a form of continual inner prayer, the prayer of the heart. Silence, asceticism, self-emptying, all directed toward a more intense focusing: at the dawn of the monastic age the Abbot Bessarion, in the desert, as he was dying, had said, "The monk should become, like the cherubim and seraphim, nothing but an eye." For centuries the monks who had practiced the prayer of the heart had borne witness to it as the way to the kingdom of God that is within. In the thirteenth century Nicephorus the Solitary, or the Hesychast, on Athos, had added to the already considerable corpus of writings on the "rule" or "keeping" of the heart, a discussion of the control of breath in prayer, a technique that may well have been an unwritten legacy from much earlier. It was developed in greater detail, by later writers; the technique fostered a wave of monastic enthusiasm, and another of reaction. There was heated controversy over its importance, and over the theological value of the inner light that it produced, which some of the method's adherents claimed was indistinguishable from the essence of God, the uncreated light that had shone on Mount Tabor. The movement had survived the controversy and had suffered from the general decline of monasticism in the centuries that followed. The whole tradition had been revived in the eighteenth century, and many of its scattered texts gathered together and published as the *Philokalia* ("Love of Beauty"), a collection that exercised a powerful effect in the following generations, not only in the Greek world, but in Russia. But the ardor had again drained from monasticism, and the tradition had faded in the monasteries for lack of succession and zeal. It had withdrawn to the remote *kellis* and hermitages on the mountain, and it was there and in the ancient texts that the elder Joseph, Father Mark assured me, had found it and breathed it back to life. The twilight had gone from the room, and the young monk's eyes were still two points in the shadow. He had not himself told me the story of the tradition, but only of his confidence that it had been found again and resurrected, and that it was the one true way set forth by Christ and the apostles, the unbroken promise. He spoke, he said in his low voice, from experience. When I asked him more about the prayer itself, he said that I was welcome to read about it—more and more of the old texts were being published— but that the reading was only preparation; the learning itself required the guidance of an elder—and of course it assumed the Orthodox faith, the only one that could claim to go back to Christ and the apostles without a lapse. The Roman church, for him, was simply not Christian— a limb amputated, a schism. He spoke of it as hopelessly lost, rather in the way some conservative Roman Catholics speak of Protestantism. The entire contemplative tradition of the West he considered, *a priori*,

to have no value whatever. He was also severely critical of a seculariz-
ing movement within the Orthodox church itself, which had drawn
many of his own generation away from monasticism, into a more active
life professing a modern social consciousness; he believed that it had
encouraged doctrinal indifference, a hostility to the contemplative
tradition, and a disregard for prayer itself.

But it was prayer, the quest for it, that had drawn the young monks to
the *skete* of Provata, and its abbot. The night, Father Mark told me,
was—at least for beginners—more favorable than the day, for silent
prayer, and most of the hours of darkness had been given to it. They
woke there at sunset (midnight on the Byzantine clock) and spent the
next hours, until six on their clock (some time around midnight on
ours, depending on the time of year) in silent prayer. Then they had
gathered, by candlelight, in their church, for two and a half hours of
liturgical worship. After that, they had breakfasted on porridge and at
the same time received instruction in the holy texts, and discussed
them. Over their meal they had pronounced prayers for the dead. When
the meal was over, the lessons and the inquiries into the texts had
continued into the daylight, and then they had gone to sleep for three
hours before starting the day's work, which occupied them until early
afternoon. Then reading, and vespers, followed by the meal of the day,
and sleep until sunset. The monastery routine still chafed them, and it
was hard not to feel that time was being daily stolen from prayer; the
acceptance of the change was an exercise in obedience. At Philotheou
they went to bed at sunset, and slept for four and a half hours. The long
session of private prayer that followed was two hours shorter than at the
skete, and the hours of liturgical worship were proportionately longer.
An hour or so more was spent in manual labor, instead of reading and
solitary meditations. The difference was great enough for a monk such
as Father Mark to feel it as a constant yoke. Weaker brothers, he said to
me with a slightly ironic smile, are allowed to sleep longer, and urged to
eat more. The long services in the church, particularly the vigils, were
physically exhausting: the stalls are so built that one leans back onto a
shallow shelf, and props up the elbows but remains standing. Some
monks develop hernias from remaining from four to six hours at a time
in that position.

The rain was falling heavily in the dark chestnut forest. Father Mark
had lit a kerosene lamp and we were talking across the flame. The
hollows in his face were more pronounced in the unsteady glow. I asked

him about his sleep and he dismissed the question at first, saying that there was always time, as long as I was interested. But at last he admitted that he was one of the "weaker brothers" he had spoken of: his health was bad, and the doctors said that he must eat and sleep, because his lungs were not sound. The damp from the woods was bad for him. He shrugged. The Dutch boy came in just then. He had heard our voices and seen the light under the door. He wanted to ask about the life there. What made them come, to be monks on Athos? What made them stay? And his real question, which he asked with diffidence and hesitation: what *good* were they doing? The young monk asked him what he meant by "good," but it was not an attempt to dodge the question—only to get the boy to consider it for a moment. And the answer, predictably enough, was "good to others": active altruism. "Yes," the monk said, "it is important. But it is not the only good, and we are not even certain that it is always good. How can you know?" The Dutch boy thought for a moment of how one might judge of goodness, and the goodness of works, and he said something about what they did, their effects. "What your works do will never be known to you," Father Mark said. He tried to make it clearer. He spoke of goodness as a cause. He said, "until you have the good inside you, how can you do good; what will it mean?" He said it in several ways, straining his command of English, while the Dutch boy listened skeptically. "It is there," Father Mark said, touching the air as though to wake it, trying to remember something. "How do you say it?" he asked, as though we did; he was whispering Greek words, groping to bring them into English. "The good man . . . out of his heart . . . out of its good riches . . . " *The good man, out of the good treasure of his heart, bringeth forth good things.* I listened to him making his own translation.

By sunrise the rain was over; the forest was dripping. Father Mark was out in the cold corridor and breakfast was waiting at the foot of a painted saint facing east: heavy bread and apple butter, tea, and a boiled potato. I left my sack and went out through the gate into the morning mist. An old monk tying up a mule—where had he been at that hour?—discoursed to me in Greek, and a few words of English, about the path down the slope to Karakallou. Evidently something about me amused him, and so did the thought of all the wrong turnings I might make and where *they* would lead me. The path splits off, without warning, from the new sand road and the swath for the telephone wires, and in a dozen steps leads over a bank out of sight of them, to where the woods seem not to have changed for a thousand years. Trickling sounds, in the granite rubble. Flurries of cyclamens, jays diving through the trees with light folded in their wings. A robin, keeping just ahead of me, then following just behind me. The sea appearing in patches, far below, through the branches and mist. Slate roofs and cypresses on the lower slopes. Mushrooms, smell of chestnut mold in the early morning. Mingled sounds of sea and wind in autumn leaves not yet dry. Where the path straightens and starts to drop, a narrow wooden flume, on rickety stilts, keeps it company, dripping all the way. Near one of the biggest leaks, a tin can suspended for drinking from. Rail fences, new rails set into them; sign of young monks in the *sketes*. A gate post, entrance to a *skete*, with a pot of basil in a can wired to it, just watered, still overflowing. Seen from above, the skirts of vines run up from all sides to the roofs of the *sketes* and *kellis*, so that windows, doors, and walls are invisible. The first sight of Karakallou from above: an immense stone tower, wading in the monastery walls. Horsebells in the woods. Sound of wood-chopping, smell of chestnut smoke. The cobbles in the path become more regular, winding down among the trees; the path turns into a lane between outbuildings. In a porch, an old cross-eyed layman, splitting wood. To the left of the stone area before the main gate, overlooking the sea, the long vegetable garden, with terrace walls around it. A small cross tied to the top of one of the bean poles. One dry cornstalk standing in the tall eggplants, rustling among their black fruit. Loud sounds of water running: incessant stony bird voice. Gray head, gray coat, bent harvesting red peppers, on the far side of the water sound. Beyond the garden, on the terrace above it, a row of wooden crosses, some painted blue, some green, and a small stone house emanating neither menace nor sadness.

Pink-washed entrance tower, and no one near the open doors. Karakallou is one of the least visited monasteries on Athos. The flagstones inside continue the outer slope, though less steeply. Bones from a whale over a door, and a racket of carpentry filling the small cold courtyard with echoes. On the tower, facing inward, a blue-washed balcony with a bell, on a level with the tops of the lime trees. Limes glowing in the shade. A huge stone basin near the red church; ancient carved slabs set into walls. Heaps of firewood. An old monk and a layman were putting a new corrugated iron roof onto a flight of steps leading up to a balcony: the racket came from the hammer on the sheet of iron held up on its raw struts, the layman crawling out onto the bending sheet to where the whole tipsy structure was supported by patient divine intervention, and there banging big nails while the old monk approved. Other old monks sorting nuts in the sun, and doing their sewing. The carpenters waved me toward a building that turned out to be the refectory: dark, empty of decoration, spilling out of its farmy kitchen where monks were wandering back and forth. Catching sight of me, they herded me to a table as though I might be wounded, and then dispersed, and in a moment the place in front of me was garnished with bread, lentils, tomatoes, peppers, olives, and a large carved double wooden salt bowl. Monks came and ate in silence. A rounded monk drifted in, selected peppers from wooden trays, slipped them into the folds of his robes, gazed into the kitchen for a while as though into an infinite landscape, and drifted out again. A thin old monk, bent with rheumatism, a delicate open face, came to talk with me. He had been to America, he told me. Working on a ship, fifty years ago. "Now you fly," he said, "don't you?"—with a hint of admiration for the idea, looking at me closely to see what strange effects it might have had. I told him that I preferred boats. He shook his head. "You fly now," he said, and showed me how, with his hands. In between talking to me, he talked to himself, his smile changing from the one to the other. He asked me whether I would like to sleep there. I tried to explain that my sack was at Philotheou. "But you're here," he said, and got up to show me the guest room. I followed his thin bent back across the courtyard, watching the neat patches on the holes of his faded woolen socks. His rheumatic walk was clearer than most words: his health, the love of his monastery, the pleasure of being hospitable. With his back to me I thought of his long large slender hands resting on the dark table, flying up and setting again, under the gray eyes, as he talked. Up stone stairs between tumbling bushes of basil and marigolds. He flung open a door off a balcony. It was all mine, he said. The whole place to myself. I had to tell him again about Philotheou.

Karakallou is not as old as Lavra or Philotheou, but there was an abbot there within a generation of William the Conqueror. The origin of the name has been lost. Monks with the kind of historic perspective one sees in medieval paintings have been happy to credit the Roman emperor Caracalla with the foundation of the monastery, and I was curious to see his portrait, which is somewhere among the eighteenth-century frescoes, but it escaped me. Up on the tower, in the sunlight, a fig tree was growing out from among the stones, above new paint and corrugated iron. The old monk led me back out through the gate, since I was going after all, and stood in the sun describing to me the whole path to Philotheou. I was not to turn off to the *sketes,* uphill or downhill, nor to the *kellis,* which he named (there is one nearby where a king and a general, in the sixteenth century, retired as hermits, after building much of the present monastery). His hand wound in the air, taking all the right turns, and then he stood and watched me climb, waving me on, each time I looked back, until I took the right turn, out of sight.

In the afternoon, at Philotheou, I walked up into the valley behind the monastery. The path winds over rocks, along a ledge, following the south side of a gorge, back into the chestnut forests, the far side bright green and gold, the sound of splashing coming up from rocks below. Not far inland, the ravine widens out, the trees are enormous and dark, the water lies in black mirrors at the foot of boulders big as the insides of caverns. A long tenuous bridge of crooked sticks, tacked to looming black trunks, crosses the pools, water striders and chestnut leaves flying over its reflection. On the other side the path climbs again, looks down to where the ravine narrows above the dark glade: rocks set in vast ferns, under chestnut boughs that bend toward the water. In the deep fallen leaves, a small elegant bronze frog watched me climb past, into the sound of a waterfall and a glimpse of the high sunny ridge through openings in the branches. It was still possible, not long ago, to cross over the mountain, on that same path, to Simopetra on the western coast, but Father Mark told me that the forest has blocked the way now. If the young monks move in at Simopetra, as they have done at Philotheou, then maybe, he told me, they would be able to open the footpath over the ridge again. They were supposed to be moving in within a few days, he said, but nobody was sure. The government was rumored to be obstructing the change; Simopetra is one of the most famous of the monasteries, and the thought of a full complement of young, enthusiastic monks there might not delight the Tourist Office.

Father Mark and I talked together again, at dusk, in the room with the round table. Wagtails were running on the rocks at the edge of the woods, below the monastery walls. I asked him about the wandering monks on Athos, several of whom I had encountered on the mountain. Little is known of them, he said, and nobody knows how many there are. Most of them are not true wanderers but have hermitages or caves somewhere, where they make carvings to sell, like other hermits. Many had left their monasteries in 1924, at the time of the dissent over the

adoption of the Gregorian calendar, going as an act of defiance against
the patriarch responsible for the change, whom they regarded as a
heretic. Some had gone and pretended to be fools, in the ancient way.
Some had really become mad. Only when they die, he said, do we find
out about them. Then anybody who knew anything about their lives
tells it. Some are no good, and some may be saints. There was a Yugoslav
who had once worked the garden at Chilandari but had moved away
and lived in a hut—a man who spoke five languages and preferred to be
thought an unlettered peasant. Nobody knew who he had been, before
he came to Athos. He died sitting in his chair, with a bowl of vegetables
in his lap. He was thought to have been a man of great spiritual
advancement. But there would be no more of the wanderers, so-called,
when those now living had died. A man must be admitted to a monastery before he can legally wear a monk's cassock, which means that he
must have an abbot's permission to live outside the monastery walls. To
obtain permission to live as a hermit is not easy, and to live as a
wanderer, attached nowhere—how could permission be granted for
that? We talked of the elders and holy men living in remote parts of the
mountain, all but unknown, and the tradition of which they are a part.
And from them, Father Mark turned the subject to the ancient texts
which were now being published at last, a number of them for the first
time, and many of them in English. Several of the monks at Philotheou
were learning English just so that they could read the translations of
these words, since the Greek originals were unavailable. But it was hard
getting books from anywhere; hard to know what had been published,
to have things sent from abroad and pay for them in foreign currency—
it was hard to find enough money of any kind. It seemed particularly
ironic that it should be so difficult, when many of the originals had
been written on Athos. But I was keeping him from his sleep. The
chestnut leaves were beginning to give off moonlight. With my few
words of Greek I said that they were beautiful. He echoed the word.
"There are so many words for that, in Greek," he said.

In the morning, after a breakfast of chestnuts and tea, I took the back
path down to Iviron. Very different from the new jeep road. A narrow,
winding footpath, like others on the mountain, cobbled here and there,
along old walls. The sound of the sea carries up into sheltered ravines
where the sea is out of sight. I came to the monastery from the side
facing the ridge, passing its gardens, and horses tethered near a drinking trough, one of them with its bell stuffed with green grass. I went

into the courtyard once more, to look at the frescoes in the porch, and the carvings. The German-speaking layman from the kitchen hailed me as I came out—no one else had noticed me. I assured him that I had not come to eat, but that I had had a drink from one of the fountains in the monastery. "Which one?" he asked. I told him. "That's all right," he said. He pointed around a corner to another one. "That's the colic one," he said. And when I asked about that, he explained—what I had already grasped—that its water was apt to produce acute abdominal discomfort and other unpleasant symptoms. And he warmed to his subject and assured me that the two fountains in front of the main gate were the same way: one good, and one colic. "Why do they have a fountain of colic-water?" I asked. He said that the horses could drink it without ill effect, and it flowed into the trough. "And the one inside the monastery?" I asked. He raised his empty hands to indicate that he knew nothing about it, and shrugged, and I walked down to the sea with a new riddle to ponder. The thought that I was not staying to eat had led him to proffer persistent instructions about my route—but I already knew the way.

It led to the sea's edge and then north along the shore. For a half mile or so it followed the road to Karyes, and then a barely visible path dove from the level sand into the shadow between bushes and began to thread its way through dense arbutus thickets, along the cliffs above the sea. It came out onto treeless rocky slopes brilliant with heather, the smell of the sprays of heather in the sun overpowering the sea smell, and the deep hum of bees, in spite of a strong east wind, muffling the sound of the heavy surf. The path dropped to the shore, ran along shingle of white marble. Stones, of different sizes, at intervals of surprising regularity, broken in half, and the broken surfaces, worn slightly round, the shapes of soles of human feet. Climbing past a shuttered house, fisherman's house; a boathouse near it, and beyond, a massive tower commanding the water's edge, empty and doorless. Across the marshy mouths of streams, and up again into heather, over headlands. On one of them the monastery of Stavronikita, built on the end of a long jutting sea-cliff. The path dropped and approached it through rocky pastures; beyond them a garden with a scarecrow in it, dressed as a monk. Horses by a newly painted gate. Young horses, with groomed coats. But from the gate, the sound of a gasoline tractor.

Stavronikita is another monastery that has been turned over recently, at least in some respects, to a group of young monks, but the change has

not taken the same form as at Philotheou. The aim, apparently, was
different to start with. At Philotheou the manual labor is obviously
undertaken with zeal and occupies most of the hours of daylight—all
the time I was there, the monk at the top of the ladder was painting the
outside of the church with a narrow brush, carefully picking out the
window surrounds and the moldings, and as I left in the morning mist
another monk was rearranging the slates on the dome; but even while
working, both of them were consciously praying, their lips were moving,
there was a silence around them. At Stavronikita the fervor of prayer
may be as intense, but it is less apparent. The monks there have
undertaken to reorganize the agricultural life of Stavronikita—which
had long been known for its orchards and gardens—and they have
resorted to a modest program of mechanization. At the top of the path,
before it turned into an arbor leading to the main gate, a monk was
sitting on a small tractor attached to a trailer. His gown was tucked up
in his belt, and his beard almost reached the steering wheel. He was
talking to a couple of laymen, agricultural workers, one of them sitting
near an attachment for a power tool. Above them ran a line of stone
arches, an ancient aqueduct, that descended from a spring on the upper
slopes. The way to the gate led past the row of stone pillars supporting
the end of the aqueduct, square stone cisterns at their feet, surrounded
by flower beds. Late grapes still hanging from the dense arbor. From the
wall, a view down over the gardens, to the sea.

Someone had been filling the lamp that hung above the main gate: it
had been lowered to chest level in the doorway, with no one near it. As I
started to walk around it, a middle-aged monk appeared and hustled me
aside to a reception room, of recent furbishment. I had sat there the
autumn before, in the company of the French priest, once a Benedictine
monk, who had admired the fresh beige paint of the walls, with the
hand-done frieze at the top depicting agricultural activities, and the
solid newly made furniture: signs of industry, somebody caring. The
monk said that I and my pack must rest, and he left me, for some time.
Young monks bustled past the door, in and out, with the abstracted
haste that arrives with machinery. A Greek bourgeois entered, sat
down; a monk came and greeted him and sat with him. The one who
had led me in came back and prepared the traditional guest tray for
him. I rose to go, but the monk insisted that I should rest a bit longer,
and disappeared again. Quiet talk while the guest tray was consumed,
and then a layman, an agricultural laborer, appeared in the door and

questioned the monk about the tractor. The guest joined in the answer; the voices changed. They grew urgent, opinionated, jostling each other, until all three of the men left together. When the monk who had led me in returned at last, he asked me whether I had hoped to sleep at Stavronikita. I said I thought not. "That's good," he said. "We're very busy here. Have you been to Pantokratoros?" "Yes," I said, "but last year. I think I'll go back." He approved of the idea at once, and said, "Come." He led me briskly into the courtyard and upstairs to the refectory, half filled with sea light, where a place had been set for me at the near end of the one long table: a bowl of boiled eggplant, cucumber and onion salad, even cheese. Up near the farther end of the table, several other places had been set, more elaborately, it seemed, and I noticed wine. I thought of the Greek bourgeois in the reception room, and remembered, on my first visit to the monastery, sitting up at that end of the table, facing the remnants of fine eighteenth-century frescoes on the walls, while a monk and two of the guests discoursed learnedly about the monastery's paintings and the history of the building. When I had finished the meal, this time, and carried my plates to the kitchen, the monk met me again and led me down to the church, to give me a chance to look again at the magnificent sixteenth-century frescoes there. When we came out, the monk pointed up to the massive tower rising above the gate, and told me it dated from the year one thousand (there was supposedly a tower on the headland in the eleventh century) and had withstood pirates and fire. He was busy, as he told me again, and I had seen the library—in the aimless manner of the utter layman who looks obediently at what he is shown, usually without understanding what he has just been told about it—the year before. All at once, as he stood telling me about the history of the buildings, all the libraries I had seen on Athos kaleidoscoped in my head—Lavra, Iviron, Chilandari: the padded doors, the black-curtained windows, heavy smell of mothballs, cloth covers on glass cases. Which illuminated page (the only one that would be seen, lying open under glass) of which water-colored gospel had been where? How far away I had stood from each sample offered to view, and how cursory had been each glimpse of things made to be looked at again and again through whole lives. I thanked the monk and picked up my pack. He must have felt that the welcome at Stavronikita had been somehow wanting, and he told me to wait once more, while he went into the kitchen behind the guest room, where I had been relegated upon arrival, and there he wrapped up several pieces of Turkish Delight in a paper napkin, and handed them to me, with some apples. He walked with me under the arbor, and along the flower beds. Had I no staff? he asked—and thinking I should have one, he selected a bamboo for me from several in a corner. I paused by a flowering bush of rosemary to pick a few leaves to crush and smell on the way, and he turned and tore off a whole branch of it for me. When I had said good-bye he stood waving me on to the right path.

Through the thickets and woods along the sea-cliffs again, and up onto small plateaus, past *sketes,* some of them empty but apparently still used at times: glass in the windows, crockery near the fireplaces, patches of overgrown garden. Like Stavronikita, Pantokratoros rises on a stone headland above the sea; its own small harbor is nestled into the rocks at the foot of the promontory, and the approach, from the south, is again, as at Stavronikita, a descent to the level of the shingle to cross a broad steambed that circles around and among the well-kept gardens and orchards below the monastery walls. A cobbled ramp, like a lane in a fishing village, leads up along the south of the main enclosure, behind outbuildings, under the shade of large trees. Hens were exploring among the cobbles as I climbed, and a small pink pig was scratching his side against a stone. At the top of the ramp a wooden gate, open; more pigs and hens and a mule wandering loose on the area in front of the monastery, whose domed and columned portico faces the sea. Firewood neatly stacked under an olive tree. On the seaward rim of the open space, a wooden summer house with benches all around it hangs over the harbor and the view of the coast, the cracks between its flagstones neatly bordered with whitewash. A round-faced toothless old monk with a long white braid down his back wandered out through the brilliant blue iron doors and vaguely shooed a nearby pig. I had set down my knapsack under the dome of the portico and the old monk beamed at me and said to come in when I liked; he stood for a while gazing toward the matchless view, and then went back in, himself. I had become interested in the paintings on the vaulted ceiling of the portico, and in the afternoon light on the coast and on the Holy Mountain, and in the intent lives of the pigs. There were swallows nesting in the porch. The paintings clearly were not very old; the monk had not known their age, or else (more probably) he had not understood my Greek; but their symbolism was more than usually abstruse. A central Godhead in a triangular halo. Below the halo, three vertical rows of circles, each of them of three colors, each of them winged, and each bearing inside it a smaller circle, like the pupil of a downcast eye, and in the smaller circle a head, full face, eyes left. Each row of circles flanked by two angels, from a ring of ten; each angel holding a sphere marked with two Greek letters: *omega* over *chi.*

I remembered, from the year before, the huge basil plants in the courtyard, standing in the crisscrossed line of whitewash, under the lemon trees, and the red katholikon at the top of the flagstoned slope. A new varnished banister rail flanked the steps leading to the balconies on the east side of the courtyard. A monk emerged from a doorway and signaled for me to go on up, and up again: the wide corridors of the balconies, too, were flagstoned, and whitewashed, and cool. I sat on a massive bench in the mixed smell of fish, frying, and outhouses. An immense monk with a plastic bag of fish passed me and smiled and told me to take it easy, and come to church when they called me, and a few moments later I was hailed by a young monk inviting me down to vespers. He came to me after the service and introduced himself, in English—Father Theodoros—and led me to a kitchen off the corridor where I had been sitting. The room with its huge stove under a hood, and its table covered with oilcloth, opened onto a balcony high above the cliff and the sea. Pantokratoros, like several others on the eastern coast of Athos, is an idiorrhythmic monastery. There are two kinds of rules on the mountain, and each monastery professes one or the other. In the cenobitic rule, all property is held in common; meals are eaten together, and absolute spiritual obedience to the abbot is mandatory. Eleven of the twenty monasteries on Athos are cenobitic, and they pride themselves on being better disciplined and more austere than those that follow the idiorrhythmic rule—a later (fifteenth-century) development which allows for a more democratic administrative system, and greater individual scope either for asceticism and prayer, as some of its defenders insist, or for laxity and worldly indulgence, as the cenobites scornfully declare. The idiorrhythmic monasteries permit the holding of a limited amount of personal property, and the monks have apartments of two or three rooms, instead of a single cell. Theodoros, speaking to me with a play of grave irony, told me—after a few moments of conversation—to make myself comfortable. He shared the kitchen with another monk, Cyriac, the giant with the plastic bag full of fish, who came in while we were talking, laughed about the fish, laughed about my presence, welcomed me to their hearth, and was gone again. Theodoros led me out onto the wooden balcony and invited me to sit down at the weathered table, where I could look at the sea, while he made some coffee. None for him, he explained: he had a delicate stomach, and it had been troubling him for several days. Fasting, he supposed, was probably indicated, and he had resorted to it, more or less.

The rays of the sun had left the water. The sky was still full of day, but the moon was beginning to gleam, east of Athos. From the balcony the whole coast was visible—headlands and towers, the surf catching the first moonlight, and the abrupt crags clustering at the base of the peak. The sea began to glitter before the stars appeared. An old monk with a bloodshot eye entered the kitchen and came out and sat down, and another, younger monk, behind him, and the coffee-making grew more ambitious. Cyriac came back and we all sat on the balcony, watching the evening. We discussed—chiefly with gestures—the old monk's blood-shot eye (the result of bumping into something in the dark)—a theme whose comic possibilities were trotted out for my benefit. Then we discussed Theodoros's stomach and the mysteries of digestion, with Theodoros providing conscientious translation. Cyriac, looking earnest, rolled up his sleeve to present, in the manner of a contribution, a patch of dry skin, which clearly fascinated him, on his huge forearm. Theodoros and I pronounced it an allergy and agreed that his chances of survival were probably fair. It seemed that the young monk should be able to provide a malfunction of some kind, but he passed; and as for me, I could offer nothing more interesting than a bit of stiffness, contracted by sitting in the shade. We laughed at the orgy of hypochondria; the balcony rattled; the water in the basin where the fish were soaking, on the other table, shimmered with scales of moonlight. The young monk and the old one left; Cyriac went in and began to clatter at the stove, and Theodoros came out and sat down to look at the evening. Supper was half-ready, he said, and Cyriac would do the rest. He opened a newspaper—partly to show that he had it. The moonlight was bright enough to read it by, but he gazed at the sea with a deep familiar satisfaction.

I learned that he was in his early thirties. He had been a monk for seven years. He had even lived for a while at Philotheou, but he was not one of those, he said. The place was not for him. He twirled his beard. Too regimented, he explained. His calling, as he had quickly seen, was not the same as theirs. He had become a monk, in the first place, not from an overwhelming desire for the monastic life, but—he began to tell me about life in Greece as he had seen it. He came from near

Athens; his father had a restaurant in Piraeus (but not fresh fish like this, he told me). He described the workmen in Piraeus, sitting bored in their cafes, bored in their houses, drinking and centering their lives on their television sets, watching other people kick leather balls around fields: he gave an imitation of his secular contemporaries coming home, ignoring their wives, slumping into armchairs to face the box, as he was facing the Holy Sea. That was not a life he had managed to look forward to, he said. Television, to him, was the symbol and one of the forms of absolute debasement, an abdication of life. "They think cars would be even better," he said. He had not wanted any of that. And then there was politics: both the right and the left, he had concluded, led naturally and avidly to police states. He did not want to live in a police state—and he believed in God. He had felt that that was a good thing to base a life on, and he was not troubled by the thought of living extremely simply, without material ambition. But the fervor of Philotheou had seemed too narrow, and he had not much liked living as a hermit, either: there was a *kelli* up on the sea-cliff where he had stayed from time to time, and which he still could use, when he chose to. We could see it from the balcony, up in the moonlit olive trees, above the heather, with its low garden wall around it, and its cypresses—I had passed it that afternoon, and admired it. Too lonely, he said, sleeping up there. He liked to go up and spend the day and look at the wild flowers, but for living he preferred to have his friends around. His frankness was encouraging, and as tactfully as I could I brought the subject around to women— didn't he miss them? That was another matter, he told me. It hadn't been easy, especially at first. He liked women. He had almost got married. It wasn't the girl who had changed his mind. It was marriage, as he had seen it in Greece, at any rate. Everything that came with it. For the rest of your life. With some difficulty he had decided against it, but if he had stayed in the world it might have claimed him just the same. And in his view, if he was not going to marry, relations with the opposite sex, as things were at present in Greece, would not have been very satisfactory. "But Cyriac!" he laughed, and nodded toward the big monk padding back and forth, cleaning fish and preparing supper. "He never had a moment's peace." In Crete, he told me, where Cyriac had been born, he had been widely and eagerly sought after, and had become terribly—entangled. "What about it?" Theodoros called, and he asked Cyriac to explain how things had been. Cyriac paused in his cooking and, fixing me with his eye, ran the fingers of his right hand lightly up his left arm to the shoulder, raised his eyebrows, ducked, heaved a great sigh, and laughed. Then he picked up the basin of fish guts and heads, and looked over the railing. In the mingled dusk and moonlight, among the shadows at the base of the walls, one could make out hens, pigs, and one kitten, waiting under the balcony for Cyriac's nightly offering. He aimed in front of the kitten, which subsequently disappeared under the scrimmage of pigs and the flapping hens, but reemerged a few moments later. Then he aimed to the side and tried to distract the pigs and catch the kitten away from them. The kitten appeared to be in more danger from trampling than from starvation, but it seemed to be taking care of itself.

"This is one of the best times," Theodoros said. "Beautiful. Autumn. The season's over at last. I never thought, when I came to be a monk, that I'd spend half my summer washing dishes." And the tourists were worse every year. They came in boatloads. Now that there was a road down from Karyes, they came in busloads, too. Two thousand—three thousand—something like that, at Stavronikita and Iviron that summer, and Pantokratoros had not fared much better. "Most of them don't know anything and don't care," he said, "about anything. Do you know why so many come? It's very bad of me to say it, but half, more than half, much more than half, come just because it's cheap." I sympathized. I pointed out that I was prolonging the annual burden. "Oh, that's different," Theodoros said. "You're a guest. In the summer we almost never have guests—there are too many. Even the ones we'd be glad to talk with are usually part of a crowd. You're alone. Make yourself—at home."

How did I feel about eggs, Cyriac inquired. That is, did I *like* them. I said I thought highly of eggs. "Eggs?" Theodoros asked. "I thought we were having fish." An apologetic nod to me, and a hurried consultation between my two hosts. Cyriac had decided that the fish would take too long, and should be kept for the following day. He had prepared a large salad of mixed raw and cooked vegetables, and now was about to complete the meal with some cold scrambled eggs out of a cupboard. There were even some cold noodles. "No, no," Theodoros said, "*I* will do the eggs." And he leaped up and with a practised hand heated the pan and fried me two eggs, fresh from the hens under the balcony, in oil from the trees on the hill. Cyriac set out the cold scrambled eggs for himself—not all of them: he saved some for a future meal. Theodoros, observing his own medicinal fast, made himself a pot of tea—English tea. He vanished into the corridor and returned in a few moments with lemons from the lemon trees in the courtyard, picked by moonlight, for our greens and his tea. Their cat followed him in and was served a bowl of fish remains, and Theodoros settled in earnest to his steaming cup, which was going to do him good. He moaned a little after each hot swallow, and laughed, and after a moment he reached for the transistor, by a pile of gray and black laundry at the end of the table. "The news," he told me. "I try to keep informed. I listen to the BBC when I can." But all that came out of the gadget was a pair of voices selling something, interspersed with snatches of bouzouki music. Theodoros snapped it off. "The usual garbage," he said. "We'll get the news at eight o'clock. It must be too early." But at eight we were talking about other things, and forgot. Theodoros was telling me about the history of the monastery, founded in the fourteenth century by two Byzantine noblemen who are now buried in the church. The frescoes were originally sixteenth-century—it is claimed that some of them are, or were, by the great Panselinos; but they were restored in the nineteenth century and, for the most part, ruined. Only here and there patches of the older work remained. I had had a chance to look at them, at vespers and afterwards. The light in the katholikon was better than in many of the churches on the mountain at that hour. I said I was glad to have seen them, restored or not, and to be eating with my hosts, in their kitchen. "Where did you eat at Philotheou?" Theodoros asked, and I told him. "Didn't you eat with them there?" I said that they chanted, during their meals, and probably had not wanted an outsider and a heretic to be present. It seemed consistent with their not wanting a non-Orthodox visitor at their services in the katholikon. But Theodoros was shocked by the whole idea. "Phariseeism," he called it. He strode up and down the kitchen, indignant. "You are *welcome* here," he said. And to prove his point he led me into a dormitory above the surf, the windows overlooking the rocky moonlit coast, and when I had chosen my bed he insisted on making it himself—with clean ironed sheets. The pillow, which he dropped into the ironed pillowcase, was covered in red velvet.

The night's liturgy in the cold church undid whatever good work the tea and fasting might have begun, and the next morning Theodoros had a fever. "Colic," he said mournfully, and prescribed a light breakfast, which he ate, green-faced. I went walking, that day, on the slopes. From the north Pantokratoros appears to be huddled into a crook of cliff, beneath ruins of tall buildings and of an old aqueduct. I passed a fat wagging puppy, and a thin one, both tethered with yellow ribbons.

Olive trees growing in the lee of crumbling walls, to the exact height of the masonry: pollarded by the sea wind. The path runs along the cliffs through brush, overgrown olive groves, passing under great pines and holly oaks. It splays out into tracks made by mules and horses turned loose to browse on the sparse wiry growth. The soil there, a decayed granite with flakes of mica.

I had come down that way, the autumn before, from the monasteries at the northern end of the peninsula: Kastamonitou, first, reached in the twilight after hours of threading wooded ravines and ridges, and winding down through chestnut forests to the shadow of an immense walnut tree in front of the entrance gate, not long before it was closed for the night. Tall forest-circled walls and towers resting on foundations laid in the eleventh century. There an old monk, finding me alone between the evening services, as the glass of the windows was misting over, had fetched a second kerosene lamp to the table by my cot, and hurried off to bring me, volume by volume, his infinite stamp collection, the accretion of a whole lifetime, and had pointed to the empty spaces, as yet unfilled, between stamps arrayed in series, had tapped them with his finger and smiled: those spaces still beckoned to him. The pleasure of having an audience for his collection warmed him. Increasingly he seemed to be sharing a secret, and he grew more and more hurried for fear I might not see—if not all, at least the most interesting, some of the most interesting. At last he had bundled all the volumes under his arm, picked up a lamp with the other hand, signaled with his head for me to follow, and crept out the door, down the creaking stairs and along a corridor to his cell, where more volumes were piled precariously on a table no bigger and no sturdier than a hat, and covered with green baize; he had scarcely entered and turned round to welcome me, when a younger monk, whose eyes matched his black beard, arrived in a rage and ordered him to lead me back at once to the guest room. Kastamonitou is a cenobitic monastery: the cells are strictly forbidden to visitors.

And the following morning, the path down through woods and gorges to the shore. There, boathouses, heavy towers, porches, balconies, high stone buildings apparently uninhabited, in the early mist; then climbing again over cobbles and along grooved rocks, above twisting ravines, to Zographou, one of the mountain's Slavic monasteries, enormous and silent, at the edge of a steep slope. The big courtyard with its striped churches of red stone and red ocher, empty. Roofs, covered with broad irregular pieces of glittering greenish slate held in place by gravity

alone: repairs under way on them, and patches of roof laid bare to the
gray boards strange to sunlight, gazing upward again at a particular
morning of autumn, slates stacked around them, no one bent over
them, for a while. The clocks in the courtyard had stopped at different
hours. At last a young monk with a cavernous face came and unlocked
the church: the frescoes not ancient but in the great line, and one of two
ikons of St. George hung with coins, medals, watches stopped at different times, all clinging to a legend. In the story, the three noblemen of
Ochrida who are said to have founded the monastery in the tenth
century, built the church but then disagreed over its dedication, and to
resolve the matter locked a panel of wood inside, while they stayed
outside, praying. When they opened the door the panel was covered
with a painting of St. George. The name Zographou means "The Painter's."
A doubting bishop once touched the ikon, it is recounted, and the little
crater beside the nose is all that remains of his finger-tip, which had to
be cut off. In the thirteenth century, when the Eastern church and Rome
were rejoined for a while, and the union was widely resisted on Athos,
soldiers of the Latinizing emperor burned twenty-six stubborn monks
alive in a tower in the courtyard; now there is a stone that claims to
mark the place—after seven hundred years.

From there, on over the spine of the promontory to the vast Serbian
monastery of Chilantari. A peddler with a donkey and a display of
mirrors, combs, flashlights, paper ikons looking like candy wrappers—
a one-man bazaar, in the shelter of the main portico, tolerated by its
frescoes. Who was he expecting, by way of customers? He had gone off to
sit on a wall. A monk who had lived in France, a man of learning,
opened the church, led the way over its twelfth-century inlaid floors,
past frescoes of the fourteenth century—restored, and badly—the great
ikon of the Virgin of Three Hands, she and the child gazing out through
the incrustation of worked gold, with the third hand, in silver, beneath
her right hand which supports the child. Standing in front of the ikon,
the monk told the story of John of Damascus, Greek, a saint of the
eighth century, who had written against the emperor Leo the Iconoclast,
and had been betrayed, in letters forged by the emperor himself, to the
caliph, John's protector, so that the protection was withdrawn and
John's right hand cut off in punishment, and hung up to rot. It was this
ikon, then known as the Virgin of Guidance, to which John had prayed
for his hand (though historians declare that the ikon was not painted
until six hundred years later). She had rejoined it to his arm and the

caliph had been moved to pardon him. Other legends of John and his age arose from that one: stories as conventionally and intricately wrought, and as dark as ikons, most of them on the twined themes of humility and charity.

From Chilantari, in the afternoon, a descent along the paths of the east slope of Esphigmenou, seeing it from far above, down on the shore: the massive square of walls set among gardens and vineyards. Arriving at the siesta hour, no one in sight near the entrance with its looming keep. The white limestone giving off a cool light of its own, in the shade of old trees, water trickling through a pond at the foot of the walls, freshness and sweetness in the hushed air, a courtyard full of lemon trees. A young monk, hurrying to the garden, speaking English. And then an older one, portly, stern, and spectacled, inquired as to whether or not I was Orthodox, lectured me severely on the perilous folly of my heretical state, and thrust a publication instructing me on how I should proceed, step by step, to rescue myself from this condition, before he admitted me briefly, and with a reluctance born of distaste, to a quick glimpse of the church. The courtyard was more beautiful: the smooth pallor of the stones in the open air.

And from the pool at the gate I had gone on, along the sea-cliffs, taking the rest of the day to reach Vatopedi, a monastery like a medieval city, rising and opening out of itself. Sloping courtyards inside the immense gates, stepped like waves on long beaches, dry grass growing in the cracks, in late afternoon light (so that the French priest, who was also there, pursed his lips at the neglect and backwardness of the place: what a difference just a little weed-killer would make to the look of things!) and cats and their long shadows straying through it. Churches open, frescoed; the refectory door ajar for workmen, and the long room elaborately frescoed above the rows of carved marble tables, each set in the embrace of a stone bench the shape of a horseshoe. From my high window overlooking the trees near the gate, and the sea below, I watched a stately monk, his beard still black, trying to catch a stray pullet in the bushes at the foot of the walls, without loss of dignity. The branches took his hat—which involved a separate rescue, and he set the black crown carefully on a ledge, for the duration. Then a twig untucked his hair and a bush caught at his cassock, and both had to be readjusted. When he finally got right into the bush, the pullet, exercising its full genius, dashed out the other side, but was cornered at last, and picked up and smoothed with the same hand that smoothed the cassock, retucked the hair, replaced the hat. Unruffled once more, the monk straightened his shoulders, glanced around at the evening as at an audience, and strode in through the gate, bearing the bird to safety from foxes and the night on the mountain. I had gone down, in the first twilight, to sit in the church porch looking at the frescoes, and an ancient monk with a white beard worthy of the patriarchs in the paintings had come by and beckoned me to follow him—into another courtyard, up flights of stairs, to his room, a cell of white plaster, with only one small window. Dirty; a few clothes, papers, books, strewn here and there. A jug of pink wine in the middle of the floor—Vatopedi is one of the idiorrhythmic monasteries scorned by the stern cenobites— from which we both partook, scarcely conversing (my lack of Greek and his lack of teeth) yet touching on his rheumatism and arthritis, the paintings in the church porch, age—he laughed about them all.

It was from Vatopedi that I had walked, next day, along the coast to Pantokratoros, and had come down to the bit of path near the sea-cliffs that I recognized a year later among the brush and olive trees. The veins worn in the ground by browsing animals disappeared among the bushes. I followed them seaward, over a rise, onto a promontory; the sharp mint smell of pennyroyal crushed by my feet; one wild apple tree; white heather blooming among the purple. I came to a small chapel, the old plaster walls shadowed with age, the apse toward the sea, and a porch almost as large as the chapel, at the door to the west. Stone steps up to the porch, then down inside it again to the stone floor, as though into a pool; a railing around it to the west and south, to keep the horses out, perhaps. And a wall to the north, and benches of stone, rimmed with wood, like mangers, on the four sides. The afternoon light came in under the eaves to the western facade, and filled the cracks in the gray unpainted boards of the door. Empty niches to either side of the doorway, and above it a third niche filled with a dim fresco of St. Nicholas and a head of Christ above him. The door fastened with a hook; inside, another silence with another age. In the center of the dusty blue-painted ikon-screen an eye was carved: a left eye. From the south side of the porch the sea could be heard, but not from the other side. There only the sounds of bees and of the soft wind in the olive leaves came through the sunbeams. The bench faced south over the coast, to the blue peak of Athos: a little cloud to the west of it, full of light.

On the way back to the monastery I stuck my head through the doors of the agricultural outbuildings, to look at the garden tools, the storehouses, the olive mill. Outside one of the doors a pile of baskets stained purple from the grape harvest was leaning against the stone wall under the eaves, and through the open doorway I could make out the towering form of Father Cyriac, legs braced wide apart, grasping a thick pole which he was plunging up and down into the grape-filled vat below him. He laughed about the wine he was making—a job that he obviously loved, though he himself drank nothing but water, even with meals. The purple stain was splashed everywhere visible in the dark building, and a gathering of fruit flies hung in the beams of light, swirling in time with Father Cyriac's massive dance. His face was red and shining and he informed me, as though it were a great joke, that *all* of last year's wine had been drunk up a few days before.

Theodoros was ironing his clothes in the kitchen, with the silent transistor among the spilled piles of garments. His stomach was much better, he said, and he was going to Athens to visit his family. We sat on the balcony again, in the evening, above the tongues of mercury slowly licking the coast, and discussed his life. One of the things he loved was wild flowers. In the spring he sometimes went with a few other monks, up onto the peak, where we could see the glaciers of moonlight, and camped there for a few days. He had a pup tent, and he took his books—he brought them out to the balcony: botanical guides to the Mediterranean, most of them in English. By candlelight we pored over the photographs of autumn squills and of the three kinds of cyclamen that grow on the mountain and the several yellow flowers that color the sea-cliffs at that season. An owl flicked past in the moonlight. "Athena's bird," Father Theodoros said, and made the sounds of each kind of owl to be found on Athos. "The bird of wisdom," he informed me portentously, "that sees in the dark."

We had our fish at last; Father Cyriac urged me to eat, eat, and Father Theodoros caught the news—the invasion of Israel: war. When the bouzouki music came on again Father Theodoros switched it off and we sat back to discuss the event. Few facts, so far, and when we had run through the first expressions of dismay it began to be clear that Father Theodoros's sympathies were with the Arabs, less because of any inherent sympathy with them than because of a frank anti-Semitism, a prejudice not vehement but ingrained, obstinate, deaf, and imbued with a familiar obscurantism. There was the old ghost story about an international conspiracy of Jews—financiers, Rothschilds, the veteran figments which sympathized, I found, in a traditional way, with free-

masons of the old stamp and rotarians of a newer one, for equally hazy
reasons. Even the documentations of the concentration camps, and the
history of the Final Solution, were doubted and minimized. Father
Cyriac echoed the chief prejudices, at Father Theodoros's invitation,
and a moment later, when the subject had returned to the evils of war,
he told with horror of what he had seen and remembered of the German
invasion and occupation of Crete.

I left in the morning as the sun was striking the portico above the sea.
Father Cyriac was out in the early light, working under an arbor, with
the pigs and hens busy near him, among dry stalks and shadows. The
path inland dropped below the monastery walls to the bed of a small
stream quietly trickling seaward over rocks and a bed of black and
bronze leaves. Both sides of the stream were bright with the new
leaf-fall, and the light coming fresh through the trees overhead after the
night and the months of summer. Up a lane across the stream, an
abandoned *kelli,* a large one, perhaps a mill, and farther along, on a
bare rise, another, the door hanging open at the top of a few stone steps;
inside, all the rooms open, ruins of beds and a kitchen, ivy creeping in
at the windows, a porch facing the sea; one room a chapel full of
cobwebs, bran, bits of straw, as in a house that has passed through an
old age as a barn. And farther again, a ruin among trees in the gold
light, with horses browsing beside it, coming to inspect me as I passed
along the wall. The path wound back and forth across the stream and
found the old cobbles where it began to climb into the wiry brush of
that part of the peninsula. It is not far from Pantokratoros to the big
skete of the Prophet Elias, as large as some of the monasteries, which is
one of its dependencies: the cobbled mule path looped and twisted and
led finally between walls of terraces: pastures and vineyards of the *skete,*
arbors shading walls, walnut and olive trees in grass with colts running
among them, roans and one black one. The path turning among the
walls as in a maze; at one turn a ruined windmill at the end of a grape
arbor, and a large wooden building faced with sheets of tin once painted
white, the rust bleeding through, the edge chattering in the wind.
Crows wheeling and racketing around the sinking crown of the windmill,
black flashes reflected in the broken window panes.

The arched entrance is on the side away from the sea, shaded in the
morning. The inner courtyard capacious, paved. A church, clearly
recent, facing the doors. A well with green-painted tin roof, very trim:
bucket, rope, spindle. A cement table to the south of the church, with a

chair beside it, and newspapers on the table, weighted with rocks, blowing in the wind. No one about but an orange cat on a bench—it sounded as though the bench were purring. The whole *skete* is of recent construction: the first monks who were drawn to the spot were followers of the great Russian monk and elder Paisius Velichkovsky in the mid-eighteenth century, and the *skete* is a Russian dependency of a Greek monastery, just as St. Andrews, near Karyes, is. It was instituted in 1839 but the building and expansion continued through the rest of the century, and the original church was greatly enlarged between 1880 and 1900. Unlike older establishments of its size on the mountain, it is not entirely enclosed by high castle walls: the seaward end of the courtyard looks out across a terrace balustrade, over the lower pastures and orchards and the wild slope of Pantokratoros and the coast. The open end makes the courtyard seem like a spacious flagstoned square, with a church in the middle of it.

Voices to the left. I peered into a windowed gallery like the wall of a greenhouse. Inside it a second row of windows, a darker interior; at one of the inner windows a hand beckoning me in. I found my way through a series of storerooms—wood, fruit, baskets, potatoes, dark jugs—to the kitchen, containing a further glass enclave hung with shellacked prints of saints, and barely large enough for an oilcloth-covered dining room table. In the kitchen an old Russian monk, pale and thin-skinned, in a pointed hat. And the owner of the beckoning hand: a monk of my own age, born in Pennsylvania, not far from where my father had grown up. Blue eyes set in a flat Slavic face: Father Gabriel's family was of Czecho-slovakian origin. His mother had been so strict in her Orthodox obser-vances that she would not cut bread on Sunday—it had had to be sliced on Saturday night, for the following day. He had served in the army during the Korean War, had not minded it, and had gone to an Ortho-dox seminary afterwards, in eastern Pennsylvania, near a place that I had known as a child. I learned these elements of his life sitting on a bench at the dark kitchen table, under a small window high up in the thick whitewashed wall, where I had been set to consume a bowl of vegetable borscht, a plate of eggplant, potatoes, and peppers, and a salad, all from their garden, and wine and ouzo from their grapes, while Father Gabriel sat facing me and chided me for having failed to become Orthodox—a bad habit, dangerous and inexcusable. He him-self had obtained permission to stay on permanently at the *skete,* but it had not been easy, with his American citizenship, to acquire the consent of the Greek government, and it would not be easy for anyone else. Talk of Philotheou led him to tell me of the practice of hesychasm at the *skete*—evidently less tightly scheduled than Philotheou. He gave me to understand that they at the *skete* of the Prophet Elias were certainly no less fervent than the monks of Philotheou, though they might not *seem* so obsessed with their prayers. (It was obvious at once that the *skete* did not indulge in the free and easy ways of Pantokratoros, where even the monks' title of *patir* had quickly become optional, in addressing them.) Father Gabriel informed me, as a rank outsider, that in time one must hope for the silent pronunciation of the Jesus prayer to become a part of one's nature. He might be repeating it to himself at that very moment, while he was talking to me, and I would not know it, child that I was. He implied that his brother monks repeated the prayer without ceasing, as a weapon against the devil—indeed against the devils in the plural, who were presences and creatures of great immediacy for Father Gabriel, and for many of the monks.

The Jesus prayer itself—the simple invocation "Lord Jesus Christ, Son of God, have pity on me, a sinner!"—had evolved out of the long tradition of hesychasm and the prayer of the heart: "pure" wordless prayer. At certain stages of the tradition the repetition of the formula, or simply of the name of Jesus, has been used as introductions and aids to wordless prayer, the "recollection of God." At others it had virtually absorbed the entire practice of silent communion.

The Russian *skete* was a good place to ponder its history. One of the great modern resurgences of the tradition was the wave of enthusiasm that had sent pilgrims, beggars, and fools of God praying over the roads of Russia in the nineteenth century—a movement that had caught the imaginations of both Dostoevsky and Tolstoy. As the surviving writings of those pilgrims make clear, the Jesus prayer was important to the whole movement. The pilgrims came to the tradition through the Slavonic translation of the *Philokalia* by that same Paisius Velichkovsky through whom the *skete* of the Prophet Elias had come to exist. A battered copy of Paisius's translation, and a Bible, had been the only possessions of the most famous of those now anonymous pilgrims. And the first biography of Paisius, written by disciples of his and published in 1847, was another of the works that had inspired the movement.

Paisius was born in 1722, in Poltava, in the eastern Ukraine, the eleventh of twelve children. His father, a priest, died when he was four. His eldest brother John also became a priest, and from early childhood

Paisius read the available patristic writings and dreamed of becoming a monk. When he was thirteen his elder brother, John, also died, and his mother had taken Paisius to the Archbishop of Kiev to bespeak for him his father's former place in the Poltava church, and Paisius had remained in Kiev to study for the priesthood. But after a falling-out with the school prefect he had been severely punished and "his soul had become fired with the love of wandering." He had run away. First to the Holy Monastery of Lyubetz, at Lyubich, on the Dnieper, and then—when a new abbot there frightened him—to the monastery of St. Nicholas, on an island in the river Tyasmin. It was a time of Uniate persecutions of the Orthodox, in that part of Russia, and Paisius had fled, in turn, to a monastery at Kiev, where he had been put to work in a printing shop. There his brother John's widow had found him and told him that his mother, in her anxiety about Paisius, had had a vision, as a result of which she had decided to become a nun. Longing, himself, for a monastic life, Paisius had set out, with two monks, for the *skete* of St. Nicholas the Wonderworker, in Wallachia. From there, in a quest for the lost patristic sources of the Orthodox contemplative tradition, he had gone to Athos, where he had spent three years in solitude, and afterwards had been joined by a single young monk, at first, and then by many others as his reputation as an elder spread. The *skete* of the Prophet Elias was founded and grew to number some five hundred monks before Paisius decided that it was time for him to return to the Slavic world: Wallachia, again, where the governor gave him, and the sixty-four followers who went with him, the Monastery of the Descent, called Dragomira, near the city of Sochava. There he had been formally invested, by another monk, in the Great Habit of the Schema-Monk, a garment which had been shown to an early ascetic in a vision, and denotes particular spiritual advancement and authority. And there he had made the Slavonic translation of the *Philokalia*, which was published in 1793, a year before his death.

It was not, in fact, the first modern edition of the work. Eleven years earlier, the Greek text had been published, in Venice, under the patronage of a mysterious Rumanian prince, John Mavrocordato—nothing else is known about him, for certain. The entire edition had been shipped back from Venice to the East: until the independence of Greece it was common for Greek works to be printed in the West and reexported. The Greek compilation may have been known to Paisius long before it was published. It was the work of two men younger than he: Bishop

Makarius of Corinth (1731–1805) and Saint Nicodemus of the Holy Mountain, Nicodemus the Solitary, the Hagiorite (1749–1809), who knew of Paisius early in his own life, and at one time had sailed from Athos to Rumania to see him, but had been driven by a storm to the island of Thasos, had taken it as a sign, and returned to the Holy Mountain, to a cell in the *skete* above Pantokratoros.

Discovery and resurrection were the clear themes of the lives of these men: the unknown in the known, the forgotten in the present, the relic and the breath, dust and freedom, sea light, cave shadow, mountains and islands. Nicodemus was born on Naxos and sent to school at Smyrna. As a young man he met Makarius on the island of Hydra, and at twenty-seven he went to Athos, to the monastery of Dionysiou. It was from there that he had tried to sail to find Paisius, by then a legend on the mountain. After his return to the region of the *skete* of the Prophet Elias, a monk named Arsenius of Peleponnesos came to share his solitude, and taught him mental prayer. Together they sailed to the island of Skyrapoula, 150 miles from Athos, where they lived as hermits for several years; then Nicodemus returned alone to Athos and there moved from place to place, settling at last among the cave-dwelling hermits, called *kollybades* (from *kolleva,* rice eaten in memory of the dead, the ritual mentioned by Father Mark at Philotheou), at the rocky end of the promontory. Makarius came and visited him on the mountain, and persuaded him to help in the compiling of the *Philokalia* and the *Sayings of the Desert Fathers.* They collaborated on a number of other works, and Nicodemus, by himself, became a prolific and important writer, one of the chief heralds of the nineteenth-century revival of Orthodox mysticism. His works did not altogether escape the ironies of history: one of his manuscripts, a study of St. Gregory Palamos, Bishop of Thessalonika and defender of hesychasm, was seized in Vienna, where it had been sent to be printed. The Austrian authorities had taken it to be a subversive work, a (three volume) proclamation of Greek independence.

Nicodemus's attitude to Western Christianity was not simple. He had translated and adapted the *Spiritual Exercises* of St. Ignatius, and Scupoli's *Spiritual Warfare* into Greek, to make them available to the Orthodox world, but he attacked Thomism as "love of darkness," declared the Roman church to be totally deprived of grace, and inveighed against joining in prayer with the non-Orthodox.

I was shown over the buildings by Father Paul, who had been invoked during the answers to most of my questions of the morning: "Father Paul will be able to tell you more about that." When I met him, at the main meal of the day, he ignored me, pronounced the long grace to the paper ikon, and carried on the conversation in Russian until the meal was over. Even so, it was clear that he spoke, as he seemed to do everything, with a remarkable mixture of magnetic ardor, authority, severity, and charm. He was only a visitor, he explained to me almost at once when he turned to me after the meal, but he had stayed fourteen months. And as he led me into the courtyard, the *skete* seemed, for the time being, to be his domain. Heretics, outsiders, pagans, were at liberty to join in prayer with the Orthodox—he informed me when I asked, as we entered the church—whether outside or inside Orthodox buildings and ceremonies, but the Orthodox should not join in the ceremonies or prayers of heretics, on pain of becoming, themselves, anathema. The Orthodox should not even pray for pagans, inside the church building, he said, though they were free to do so when they were out in the world. The strictures were set forth with a blunt promptness, courtesy, and a flicker of humor, and added to the impression that Father Paul was, however temporarily, the heir of the place, a feeling that was further enhanced by my seeing it and learning something of its history, and something of his, at the same time.

He had been born in Smolensk, thirty-three years—and six days— before. After the war his family had left Russia, and he had been brought up in Austria and in different parts of Europe. In 1951 his family had sailed from Bremen to New York, where they had friends. He had gone as "summer boy" to an Orthodox monastery near Utica, and his mother had encouraged his interest in the place: he had stayed and gone to school there, and when one of the monks had suggested that he join the monastery, he had said, "Why not?" This many years later the answer seemed out of character—vague and unformed. But he had been hardly more than a child, and clearly once he had made the decision he had had no regrets. His eyes burned as intensely as Father Mark's but their flame appeared to be fed by a heavier element. Utica, he said, was better than most places he had seen in the States, because of the Catholics there. They were believers, at least, even if they were heretics.

The church building at the *skete* was of little interest, he said (and it was true). The ikons and the architecture both had suffered the unfortunate Italianate influence that had run through Russian Orthodoxy in the eighteenth century. There was one miraculous ikon at the *skete:* the

Virgin who wept—and one of the monks saw it—on the eve of the Russo-Turkish War. But almost none of the ikons at the *skete,* in Father Paul's forthright opinion, deserved the name: they were merely pictures, and their real purpose, as one could see, was aesthetic rather than spiritual. He showed me one of the older chapels, set into the building flanking the courtyard, the only one in the *skete* which he said kept the feeling of the old basilicas. It too was recent—compared to the great monasteries of the mountain. A small room, the paint looking almost new, the ikons lacking distinction, but its intention and its simplicity moved him, as the larger church did not.

On an upper story we walked through the long, creaking ceremonial reception rooms painted in the pastels that had pleased the figures in the processions of huge framed photographs and portraits from the last decades of the czars: abbots, bishops, archbishops, and the czars themselves. Black bentwood furniture, black horsehair furniture, tight to the walls. Round tables covered with white embroidered cloths, the fringes touching the floor. On one of them an obese unrecognizable fruit grown in a bottle. To show guests. The silence of the portraits possessing the rooms. Father Paul showed me a picture of the *skete* as it had been in 1880: smaller, simpler, plain, with cypresses in the courtyard. Outside a window of the present reception room a kestrel hovered for a moment around a stone cornice, and then dropped away into the ravine.

One series of rooms—parts of two floors of the west wing—had been used as a hospital in the days when Chekhov was a doctor. Father Paul and I lingered with equal fascination in the dilapidated dispensary and the long paneled pharmacy with its ranks of inscribed jars still full of powders, crumbled leaves, crystals, stacked envelopes with faded labels containing crumbs and dust, drawers where the mice had nested; and in the small consulting room with its horsehair sofa like a burst black doll, its cot for emergency cases and for the dying. The desk of that room was still full of papers, and the cabinets were crammed with tarnished scales and tumbled surgical instruments. A large zinc washstand with a mable back stood in one corner. Piles of rags. And from there Father Paul led me out to a small building on the slope just west of the entrance to the *skete,* and opposite the window of my room. There was no lock or latch: the door was held shut with a string. Inside, the walls were lined with shelves as in a library, or the pharmacy behind us, and the shelves were filled with rows of skulls, some of them with names written above the sockets, some of them without. Behind the shelves facing the door was a recess full of bones, all piled together. There were the bones of monks who had died in the *skete* and had been buried in its cemetery, and then, in accordance with the tradition of the mountain, had been dug up after three years, to make room for others. Sometimes, he told me, the bones had a sweet smell when they were uncovered after that length of time, and that meant that the life through which they had passed had been holy. Some of the skulls were white, some were tan. Both colors were good. Often the saints were tan, as one could see from the bones in reliquaries. But sometimes the diggers found black bodies that had failed to decompose: the earth had rejected them, and special prayers had to be said over them, and they had to be buried again. Once it had happened three times, and at last the abbot had asked God in prayer what the wretched monk had done, and he had been told the sinner had worshipped with heretics, and was anathema. After the Crusades, Father Paul told me, there had been many black bodies—monks who had been forced or persuaded to pray with the Catholics. And again we turned to that subject. It was forbidden to pray, inside the church building, for the souls that had inhabited the black relics. In fact, one might pray inside the church according to Father Paul, only for the true Orthodox, who represented a very small fraction of those currently professing that faith. The search for the true faith was what had brought him to Athos, he told me, "and even here ———." He dropped the theme and led me into the disused wagon sheds and carpenters' shops, and around the wine presses. "The Protestants," he informed me, "think that drinking alcohol is of great importance. Like the Mohammedans." The long black robe swept past the empty vats.

Great energy and passion. The circuit of the monastery buildings kept shifting the foreground of the conversation. Basil is grown by the doorway in the monasteries, he told me, when I asked, because the crucifix is decked with basil at the great feasts of the cross, in particular the seven-day feast of the Elevation of the Cross, in late September.

Father Paul loved clouds, the light in them, and he stood and gazed up at those on the ridge and told me of their conduct on the mountain. Sometimes they would move in, low from the west, emerging over the tree-tops high above the *skete,* and at the same time others, higher still, or a little to the north or south, would be coming from the east, with different light in them. Sometimes they would move landward, to the south, and seaward, to the north, in a great circling current of wind rebounding from the heights; and the whole thing could change in half an hour. (Father Mark had described the same things, as though talking about a distant age.) Father Paul was making a collection of seeds of wild flowers to take back with him when he went: flowers that he liked to find and to smell. He knew none of their names. And he was not yet certain when he would go, but he believed that he had accomplished almost all that he had come for. He felt that there was little more for him to find on Athos, and he had no wish to remain much longer. He had been helped, on the mountain, but not in the way that he had expected. And he felt that what he must look for next was elsewhere— perhaps back at his own monastery. He believed that Athos as a whole was degenerate; that most of the monks, and whole communities (Pantokratoros, for instance) had fallen far from the true faith, and that nothing could be learned from them. I spoke of Philotheou and Provata, but he was skeptical and not interested: even if the true faith indeed existed there, he himself must move on now. He conceded that there might still be a few holy men, scattered in remote corners of the mountain, but he felt certain of the purity and faith of none except the Zealots, many of whom were living as hermits on the sea-cliffs of Karoulia.

He had come to the mountain looking for an elder, a *staritz*, who might guide him in the pure uncompromised faith, in the light of the original apostolic vision. The Russian *skete* founded by Paisius had been the logical place for him to stay, even though it was almost empty (at the moment there were only three other monks living there). He had not, in fact, found an elder, but in answer to his fervent prayers the Virgin herself had helped him, clearing his mind, answering his questions, leading him to the very books he needed. Purity of faith, he explained, implied purity of doctrine, and Father Paul, with the Virgin's guidance, had grown more than ever convinced, on Athos, that the true Orthodox were a dissenting minority within the church (part of his guidance had come to him, almost certainly, in the form of a periodical, *The Orthodox Word,* published by the St. Herman of Alaska Brotherhood, in Platina, California: the brotherhood holds the *skete* in particular regard, and the *skete* library contains a relatively complete file of back issues). One of the recent conditions of doctrinal purity was an insistence on retaining the old Julian calendar, instead of the Western, Gregorian, one, which had been adopted by the Greek patriarch in 1924. The official acceptance of the Western calendar had been accompanied by the insertion of the patriarch's name in the liturgy: the dissenters refused to include his name in their prayers, regarding him as a heretic. The calendar affected the entire liturgical year, for the Julian calendar had become an organic part of the liturgical cycle of the early church. Father Paul assured me that the Julian calendar provided symmetries and simplicities that were lost in the Gregorian arrangement. The Paschal cycle, for instance, was said to repeat itself exactly every four thousand years in the Julian calendar, and illiterate peasants could calculate the cycle on their fingers. And in the old calendar, Easter always came after the Jewish Passover—in accordance with the Gospel—whereas in the Gregorian calendar it was not always so. But these were minor objections. The real argument against the calendar change was one of principle: an opposition to any alteration of the essentials of Orthodoxy—any change in the church itself. I failed to elicit from Father Paul a clear rule for distinguishing what was essential to Orthodoxy from what are mere accretions however distinctive. But the essentials, whatever they were, make up the Church itself; and the Church—so the argument ran—is Christ's body, and therefore perfect. There can be only one, and it cannot be changed to accommodate it to other religions, or to anti-religious pressures, without implying an imperfection in Christ, hence in God Himself. It was in part their rejection of the calendar reform of 1924, therefore, that had led Father Paul to believe that the true Orthodoxy, on Athos, was virtually restricted to the dissenters there who went by the name of Zealots.

They had taken their names from the Holy Apostle Simon Zelotes, the bridegroom at Cana of Galilee (John 2:1–11) who was converted by the miracle of the changing of the water into wine, and left the feast and his bride to become a disciple of Jesus. (In *The Golden Legend,* de Voragine notes that he was called Simon Zelotes or Simon the Cananean, both names having the same sense, for Cana meant "zeal.") Their leader had been Schema-Hieromonk Theodosius of Karoulia, who had died in 1937. He had studied at the Kazan Theological Academy, and had been rector of the Vologda Seminary. In 1901 he had come to Athos in search of spiritual guidance, and after years of searching had found an elder, a Bulgarian named Ignatius—and also a Greek adviser, Callinicus. He had edited works of Paisius Velichkovsky, and had translated writings of Nicodemus the Hagiorite into Russian.

Only one monastery on Athos, Esphigmenou ("the Tight-Girdled One") had embraced the Zealot position, breaking off communion with the commemorators of the Patriarch of Constantinople who had adopted the Western calendar. But there were Zealots at the *skete* of St. Anne, the New Skete, Kafsokalyvia, and the monasteries of Xenophontos and St. Pantaleimon. And there were other contemporary movements of pronounced opposition to the authority of the official Church: the Catacomb Church in Russia, the Russian Church in Exile, and the True Orthodox Christians of Greece. It was hard to obtain news of their activities and persecutions: the St. Herman of Alaska Brotherhood, and its publications, were one source. In any case, an undue regard for the mere numbers of the faithful, Father Paul insisted, was the sort of thing that had always typified the West, rather than the true Church, which had always cared instead about the fervor of its converts, the quality of their faith. The remnant of the faithful, in the Latter Days, was bound to be small.

We stood in the courtyard as the warmth went out of the daylight. Father Paul pointed out the places where the cypresses had once stood, before the church had been built. One thing he would like to see sometime, he told me, was a line of trees he had read about, leading to a church—he had forgotten where it was. In the story, one of St. Luke's portraits of the Virgin had been taken to that church at one time, and all the trees, as it had passed them, had bowed down to the picture and then straightened again, with a bend in their trunks.

It was the hour for him to go and get his veil and semantron, and ring the bells. A Russian belfry; he was a virtuoso. Books and periodicals on subjects that I had asked about had been put on my table, and I read until dusk. Owls back and forth in the trees outside my window. The tinkle of the bells from the service in the church, echoing in the courtyard on the other side. I lit the lamp to follow the stories of the persecutions of the Orthodox in Russia. Among them an essay by Boris Talantov attacking the Metropolitan Sergius of Moscow for collaborating with the Stalinist repression. The legitimacy of Sergius's authority had always been disputed by many Russians who called themselves Orthodox. In 1918, in the blaze of the Revolution, the Russian church had elected its first patriarch since Peter the Great had abolished the office two centuries before. The new patriarch, Tykhon, had been imprisoned in 1922 and had died in prison three years later. A series of *locum tenens* who succeeded him had been arrested, and the Soviet government forbade the election of another patriarch. Sergius, the *locum tenens* in 1927, in that year came to terms with the Soviet state. He obtained a legal recognition of the church, on the one hand. On the other, he publically denied that believers were being persecuted by the government, and he declared that there was no essential conflict between Orthodox Christianity and the *praxis* of Russian socialism—self-sacrifice was the basis of both. "We want the achievements and happiness of the Soviet Union to be our achievements and happinesses," he had written—in what Akhmatova described as a "relatively vegetarian" period, before the great purges of the thirties. He had introduced a prayer for the Soviet government into the liturgy, and forbidden prayers for political prisoners. There had been a wave of opposition to the settlement, within the church. Sergius had excommunicated Archbishop Dimitry Gdov, of Petrograd, one of the chief opponents, and in the years that followed, others were executed—among them Metropolitan Joseph of Leningrad, one of the leaders of the opposition. The accounts of the Catacombs martyrs read like echoes of the Final Solution. Talantov's essay accused Sergius and his "adaptation" of reducing the religious activity of the Church to external rites, and he listed a series of recent (1960s) governmental restrictions even of those rites—restrictions which he declared had been imposed with the knowledge and support of the official Church. The dean of the sole remaining Orthodox church in Kiev, he said, had told him that the local authorities forbade the administering of supreme unction in the homes of believers; as a result, Talantov's own wife died without the last rites, which she had asked for. Talantov himself had been arrested on June 12, 1969, and had died in prison on January 4, 1971.

Outside, the long empty corridor was crossed by rungs of dim reflected moonlight; the roof of the church, the courtyard, and the Holy Sea beyond, ran through shades of silver. I went down to the vigil liturgy which had begun in the large chapel on the north side of the courtyard. Sound of chanting, more melodious than at Philotheou. Russian. Music was another of Father Paul's interests, and the *skete* contained some manuscripts of ancient music. He and the student from Los Angeles were singing some of the liturgical passages together. The voices filtered out into the moonlit courtyard. A few candle flames, and ikon lamps reflected from gold frames and paintings, shone through the windows; huge shadows wheeled past them. Inside, out of the moonlight, the chapel seemed almost dark. Candles at the lecterns scarcely lit the few monks cowled in their black veils, and the gaunt tiny features of one old Russian in brown tweeds, who read the passages of Scripture, occasionally stumbling over words, without dropping his high monotone. Father

Gabriel, with a censer, bowed, swooped, and whirled: the movement of censing became a slow dance before the ikons and into each part of the chapel. The language, the pace, the voices, the undertone of feeling, all different from those of any of the Greek monasteries. I listened without understanding any of the words. When I went out, the shadows had moved around the courtyard, and the night was colder. I went back to the kerosene lamp, and the books. Some of them I would not have a chance to see again: I meant to start early in the morning. But my eyes rebelled at last, and I turned down the wick and blew out the light and watched the moon's shadows on the hill. The owls were silent. A few bright clouds. I heard the vigil end, and the monks come from the chapel, scuffling across the courtyard and up the stairs, and I went to bed.

I hoped to walk across to the other side of the peninsula the next day. It was a long way, and most of the route I planned to take would be unfamiliar. I got up with the first light and went down to the courtyard to see the red sun rise, magnified and elliptical, in the mists over the sea toward Lemnos. A fishing boat appeared, puttering along the coast. In the kitchen, Father Gabriel was up, discussing the day's meals with a workman who was cleaning fish and squid at a dark sink. The squat peasant figure of the gardener, half asleep, in a jacket faded colorless, was wedged into a corner behind the table, by a lighted lamp. No one else was awake. Father Gabriel promised to say good-bye to the others, but he insisted that I stay for breakfast: Turkish coffee and rusks with dark honey from the hillside. A cat and kittens growled over pieces of fish too hot to eat yet, flipping them on the stone floor. News of the war in Israel. The Moroccans said to be sending troops. Father Gabriel stuffed apples and even a piece of cheese into my sack, before I picked it up and went out the gate and up the path along the garden wall.

Cobbles leading up into the scrub. Mushrooms in grass: *marasmius oreades* dried by the sun of the past few days. Some kind of *tricholoma.* The path led out onto a small barren plateau of weathered stone, with a view of Karyes, and the peak far beyond; then it dropped to join the road, the dust leveled for wheels, with canned-beef cans, chocolate, and cigarette papers, toilet paper, cigarette butts, occurring along the edge, contributions of the summer's visitors. Small *sketes* with gardens, along the road, some empty, some inhabited. A plank stile into a pasture full of olive trees, with horses under them. One plank of the stile painted with a stencil: "Return to Monsanto Fawley." A new cement bridge. Sound of a motor: a miniature tractor driven by a young monk, with an old one, white beard flying, and a workman, rattling in the cart behind. Small-flowered knapweed with grayish leaves. Chicory in flower, and the sight of the mountain above its blue.

After an hour or so, Karyes again. The morning cold, and a cold wind swinging between the east and the south. My map showed a path from the *skete* of St. Andrew over the ridge to Xenophontos, and I walked into the courtyard at the *skete* to ask where it began. Nobody seemed to know. A fat layman in a sport shirt, eating tomatoes, with the juice and seeds running down his face, told me that there was no such path: I would have to go to Daphne and take the road along the sea. He appeared to be a surly representation of simple Atrophy: once the wheels have come the paths cease to be real—retroactively. I showed a young monk the map, but he said the path was too complicated. He had never taken it, himself, and I was sure to get lost. I thanked him and walked up the road that leads to Daphne, to a branch at the top of the ridge, which was marked unclearly on my map, but should, I thought, take me eventually to the coast. The mountain, to the south, was pale, and wrinkled with shadow. Dark clouds were racing across the sky. I turned up the side road, following the truck ruts through the chestnut forest that straddles the spine of the peninsula there. Almost at once it began to edge down the western slope, and the other sea appeared, far below. The mud became sandy, and the chestnut forest alternated with regions of scrub. The wind turned colder, and the clouds darker. Hours, the road, the woods, empty. Some time in early afternoon, rumble of a motor: an ancient truck overtook me, with two laymen in it, and turned off down a fork that led south again toward a small bay.

The road wound back behind hills, avoiding the tops of ravines, and an upland valley opened before me: the rusted domes of a church, and high monastic buildings of wood and tin. Panes of glass reflecting gray sky. Beyond the building, terraced green meadows with trees, and horses grazing. An old cobbled path dropped away from the road, toward the sea, through heather and marjoram: the link between a small *skete* near the shore, and the rusted church of Sts. Catherine and Barbara, below me. The dome was an octagonal wooden structure, and there was another wooden tower at a corner of the locked main enclosure. The ground among the buildings was marshy, and the grass bright. There is a lake in a hollow of the hills above there, and water trickles into the still valley. The flapping of tin, in the wind. Ravens. The horses were grazing behind a small house tucked into the far slope, under trees; it was almost hidden by its piled firewood. A dog asleep under the eaves, so unused to travelers on the lumber road that it went on sleeping. The wind covered the sound of my feet.

An arm of a steep valley; suddenly, on the left, it opened out toward the sea. Groups of *kellis,* tile roofs, a church, all far away on the other side, facing south. The sound of a chain saw in the woods. Abandoned truck tires and oil drums by the road; missionaries. A peasant with sacks and a smile full of gold teeth, riding a white horse, told me where I was, and turned aside into the gate of a *skete,* under big trees. The valley much warmer than the ridge behind me, and the woods. In mid-afternoon the long descent brought me to the coast just above the gardens north of the Russian monastery of St. Pantaleimon, and I turned north on the path that followed the shore, through olive groves. Over one of the terraces above the sea, two kestrels looped around and around each other until the aerial dance carried them over a hill. A large, half-ruined *kelli* in a meadow, the main room used as a stable, full of trodden horse-dung. A broad bat fluttered away from me into a cupboard, and when I went to look, it had disappeared. The chapel, off the main room, was still intact: on the shelf of the ikonostasis, stumps of candles, and a faded paper ikon of St. George.

I approached Xenophontos from behind: it faces the sea. Ruined stables extending back into the trees. Masonry built of boulders: gray, russet, black. Lichens. Thickets of henbane, the flowers closed in the dark day. Another outer building, a *skete* or habitation apart from the monastery, with a porch along the upper level, and white plaster rooms at either end. Windows broken, doors jammed open, but black garments hanging on the walls. A niche for an ikon above the arched doors under the porch, martins still flying in and out there. A long-tailed wren warning from the bushes on the shore. A stick footbridge across the boulder-lined bed of a wide torrent, dry at that season, to the high woodpiles and sacks of charcoal under the monastery walls. An old monk—long, intelligent face—was sitting among the firewood mending a cassock; he motioned me on, through the open gate under the tower.

The ironshod doors painted bright blue. A circling cobbled ramp led up into the cold. In the first courtyard inside, a bell suspended in a brick arch, above a basin. No one in sight. The northern end of the courtyard flanked by the small church of St. George, locked, but the porch, even in poor light, revealing the remains of great frescoes, including one of several series on the same theme, in the monasteries of that part of the peninsula, depicting St. Jerome and his lion: the human-headed beast wincing as it holds up its paw for the saint to extract the thorn, rubbing its head on his knee, carrying his waterpots, leading his white mule by a long cord held in its lion teeth. In the porch and passage to the inner courtyard, imposing seventeenth-century frescoes of the Apocalypse, half-ruined. It is said that the frescoes inside the old, locked church (not the main *katholikon* of the monastery, which was built in the nineteenth century) were originally painted in the mid-sixteenth century by the great Theophanes of Crete and another painter of exceptional gifts, named Antonios, but the paintings have been damaged and badly restored.

The main courtyard is crossed by a runnel of water; a stone pond is sunk, beside whitewashed arches, in the middle of the open space. The semantron had sounded and the monks were sailing toward the main church, its massive doors older than the building. The black robes reflected in the water, and the white arches. The *katholikon* houses a rich assembly of ikons—two of them said to be miraculous—and two ancient mosaics: St. George and St. Dimitrios.

The stone corridors of the living quarters were empty. Off to one side of a long hall, a chapel no bigger than a cupboard, inside glass doors, with an ikon light burning, and benches outside it. My footsteps were heard, and a young monk, limping, appeared behind me, led me to the guest room, returned a moment later with the tray of coffee and *raki*, and left me alone with the two walls of windows, west and south, over the sea, and the photographs of kings and the current dictator of Greece. After the hours of wind, the room sounded like a wooden shell, a steady echo of the shore under the high windows. The building itself was silent. I might have stayed: The monks who had spoken to me in the courtyard had been friendly, and the one who had brought me the tray had made me welcome. I was tempted. I would have liked to see the old chapel of St. Dimitrios, which had been there no one knew how long before the monastery was built around it in the tenth century. And the remains of the frescoes locked away in the church of St. George and the chapel of Lazarus. Perhaps even to try to find and converse with the few Zealots living there. But even if I had been shown the paintings, the light of that dark afternoon was already going. I had only one more night on Athos, and I had started that morning hoping to see Docheiariou. Rain was surely on the way. I looked for the monk who had brought me the tray, but he was not to be found. I left him a note, and picked up my pack. Down in the courtyard a layman working with a length of irrigation pipe led me out through a small door in the wall above the sea, and along the terraced vegetable garden—rows of cabbages and tomatoes in sandy dark soil—to the path through the olive groves. It was no great distance to Docheiariou, he told me.

Olive terraces most of the way, the path looping and descending a few times into small wooded gorges made by torrents, full of tree shadows and looming rocks, the foliage greener than the slopes above. Over a shoulder of cliff, Docheiariou appeared suddenly, as beautiful as it is from the sea. Cobbles came to meet the path and climbed among walled gardens, past fountains, under arbors, beside a pavilion that looked out over the water, to the massive iron doors barely ajar, under the tower. The adobe-colored *katholikon* takes up most of the main courtyard, but around it stone stairs, small paved terraces like minute *piazzas* surrounded by raised stone flower boxes, balconies, stone roofs, clamber higher than the main dome: a city in an Easter egg, until one has climbed to the top balconies that look out over it all to the sea, and far beyond, faint on the horizon, the mountains of Chalkidikis. The rain had begun. I sat in a wooden porch near the topmost level, waiting for the guestmaster. Grape vines climbed around the balconies. Geraniums, late marigolds, zinnias. Basil. Yellow lichen on the rounded rough slates of the roofs. Huge pomegranate trees. One of the towers connected to a wing of the monastery by a covered wooden bridge. The wooden doorway off the porch was cut in the shape of a shallow Moorish arch. All at once, soft bouzouki music and the smell of Turkish tobacco drifted out through it together. I coughed, and a round old monk in a gray robe emerged, red-faced, surprised, turned back to put away his cigarette, thought better of it and brought it out with him, to welcome me. His eyes were watering and he was in the pulsing clutches of a terrible cold; affable, and bored. The room where he had been sitting alone was an enormous kitchen, dark only because of the weather, about which he grumbled as he shuffled back and forth making me Turkish coffee, between sneezes. There was a bottle of misty *raki* on the table, and he poured me a bit, into a misty glass, with a fat trembling hand and a few words of warning pronounced from the cloudy heights of age and experience.

We tested his French, which was original, but better than my Greek. When he sat at his bench behind the long table, and leaned against the wall, under a crooked calendar (Gregorian) depicting Leonardo's Last Supper with bright improvements, his heavy left hand lay on the curled white back of his cat, and occasionally stroked it. Before I had finished my coffee he had other company, who entered casually and made themselves at home: evidently my host's kitchen was a meeting place for a wide circle of cronies. The first was a tall slender graying man in a neatly ironed orange sport shirt, with one bloodshot eye, and a trim mustache: a man about some nearby town, with many relatives and his hand on a few slender ropes. He pulled a handful of special coffee beans, wrapped in newspaper, out of his pocket, and unwrapped it slowly on the table, explaining their provenance and virtues. Then from a shelf he brought the monk's old cylindrical brass coffee grinder, poured the beans into it, and began to grind, with majestic satisfaction, while his friend explained about his cold, laughed and shook his head each time he sneezed, and fiddled with the dials of the transistor. The grinding ceased and the mustached visitor took the coffee to the small burner in the corner, by the window, and started to make another brew, with a style born of practice, and long familiarity with that kitchen. A fat workingman in faded farm blues came in and sat down wearily, and laughed, and fixed us all with a melancholy smile, and he in his turn learned about the cold, the coffee, and the other's family, and then told of his own troubles, which sounded remote but insoluble. The monk opened a tin box on the table: his cigarettes, and a razor blade for cutting them in half. He divided one with his second guest, and then, seized with a thought, got up and left the room, returning a moment later meditatively examining the box containing a jar of Vicks Vap-o-rub. He sat down again between the table and the wall and held it up in his hand like a crystal he could see into, and he extolled its wonders as though he were thinking of selling it. The coffee came to the table and was poured, in the middle of his pitch, without interrupting his enthusiasm, and ignoring it, he opened the jar and gouged out a generous finger-load of the stuff and worked it well up each nostril, tears streaming down his face, laughing, and passed the jar on to his guests, each of whom obediently imitated him, and with watering eyes pronounced themselves deeply impressed. Until it was my turn, and I explained with heavy use of gestures that the traumas of my childhood, in which salves and unguents very like this one had figured regularly, had deprived me of impartiality—which was not to say that I did not retain the deepest respect for anything of the kind. By that time nobody cared. The product was already relieving the monk, in a way, and it seemed to have suggested to his guests that they should leave. They were all on their feet. The monk showed me out, and pointed the way up the

stairs to the balcony that I would have to myself, and the room at the
end of it, white and open and freezing, with a plaster fireplace, and a
window looking west over the whole monastery. There was a bench on
the balcony, and I sat out watching the rain sheet down, and the clouds
sag over the sea. When I was about to go in and light the lamp, the
monk called me down and asked me whether I had eaten. I answered
vaguely, and he told me that I must eat; it was important; and he
invited me to sit at the table opposite the cat, while he got over a bout of
sneezing. I urged him to take some hot *raki* and go to bed, but he had
decided to try aspirin, which he showed me, and he said that his day's
duties were not yet done. He heated up some old noodles for me until
they were tepid here and there, and watched me conscientiously eat
them, accompanying me with aspirin and water.

All night the rain beat on the roofs and ran from the eaves over the
grapevines and the balcony railing, and in the morning it had not
abated. I splashed down the puddled white-washed stairs, avoiding
water-spouts, to the dark churches.

The monastery was founded in the tenth century, nearer to Daphne,
and was moved later to its present site, bought from Xenophontos ten
years before the Norman Conquest. But the present *katholikon*, dedicated
to the Holy Archangels, was built in the mid-sixteenth century. The
frescoes, in the Cretan style, attributed to a painted named Zorzi, a
master of Panselinos, must be among the most beautiful on the mountain,
and ordinarily it is easier to see them than it is to see many of the others:
the placing of the dome and windows allows more light to reach the
ceiling and walls. But on that dark morning it was hard to make out
anything very clearly, and it is a church where the figures form large
compositions—a Tree of Jesse, a detailed sequence of the Creation and
Fall. The covered passages outside the *katholikon* are also frescoed; dark
maroons and golds glowed against the rain light in the courtyard. In a
chapel down a dark frescoed hall, a litany was being sung. The visitor
with the neat mustache was standing in a stall, listening, telling a
string of beads, and I stood for a while in another stall, and heard the
rain stop, and went off to see whatever paintings might be visible. There
is a series around the roof of the Well of the Archangels, in the courtyard.
Scenes from a legend: a shepherd finding a treasure; monks in league
with the devil, trying to drown him. The Archangels had saved him
and set him down in the monastery—that was the story.

The rain started again. The guestmaster barked and hailed me feebly
as I went past his door to pack. He was not feeling much better, and the

rain and cold did not help. The boat would pass before long on its way to Daphne. I might wait and catch it an hour or so later, on its way back, but he said that if I did so I might miss it: if the sea got much rougher the boat might not put in at all, at the cement wharf. And it was better for foreigners to go through the exit customs at Daphne. I thanked him and said good-bye and went down to the boat shed by the wharf—a tower and squat walls—until the fishing boat appeared, and I hailed it.

The deck empty. As we backed off and turned down the coast again I thought I was the only passenger, until I saw a face at the hatch opening. There were a few others, below there: monks, one bishop, two or three Greek boys on a first visit. Once again I watched the coast to Daphne. The customs-shed steaming, the bags of Greek pilgrims, and my own, searched to make sure that no one was smuggling ikons, relics, manuscripts, the mountain's portable treasures. Even my books and notebooks were opened, leafed through, shaken. The service is said to be in the interest of the monks, but the uniforms, of course, are Greek. And again the boat, back the way I had walked the day before. A scholarly Dutch Orthodox priest and I, sitting out on deck, fell into conversation. He had been cataloguing the libraries of Athos for years—St. Pantaleimon this time. The library there contained wonderful things, he told me; manuscripts of great importance and beauty, in a terrible state of disorder and neglect. It was typical, he said to me, cheerfully. He showed me one of his monographs, in Dutch and Greek. As for the *information,* he said to me, the situation was rapidly improving: every year more of the works in the libraries were being microfilmed. From the point of view of scholarship it was becoming simpler to work from films, in Thessalonika. As for the rest —— . He got off at the arsenal of Zographou to look at a few manuscripts, and I traveled the rest of the way up the coast in silence.

The mountain itself had been hidden in cloud all morning. The rain stopped. For a moment the clouds separated and a part of the peak could be seen—then the blank clouds closed over it again. I could not tell which part it had been. Then in time Prosphori Tower came into sight, in the opposite direction. From 1928 until he died in 1954 it had been the home of an Englishman, Sidney Lock, who had spent his later years writing about the mountain with learning, wit, love, and a sharp eye. How changed the place would look to him, after twenty years! I boarded the new bus. The clouds were clearing as we crossed the mountains of Chalkidikis. To Thessalonika. The night train, and Athens in the morning.

FLIGHT HOME

(1958)

(In August 1956, Merwin flew home after seven years in Europe. The notes that follow are taken from a journal he kept at the time.)

Aug. 27, 1956, a barber shop in St. John's Wood

They say that after seven years every cell in your body has changed. You are a different person.

I wish I could remember what day it was, in July, 1949, that I landed in Genoa. Or the day (one or two days before?) when we first came in sight of the Spanish coast.

Strange, now I am going back, to think that I have been in Europe without a break, ever since I was a minor. Ever since I was twenty-one.

On the chart one does not see the long line of wanting to go back. Beginning in my case before I set out, and rising through delight and hostility and wonder and everything that has been the experience of Europe. The line rising clear off the chart at last and stabbing into the air above it, without footing, but without coming down, for how many years now?

Part of the confusion, once the desire to go back got off the chart, arose from the suspicion that this was simply, at least in part, the first shock of maturity: a realization that home, where you grew up and belonged— belonged with and without your own volition—no longer exists. The desire to return to it, the moment you know it no longer exists. I had been away long enough, and surrounded by Europeans thoroughly enough, to get these mixed up. European friends wondering, as they say, what I will make of it. Probably nothing at all. Wishing, they say, that they could be here, like a fly on the wall, to watch, when I get back. How can I explain that I do not want to go back in order to form opinions.

"Flight Home" first appeared in *Paris Review.*

That, unless I am very wrong, opinions will have nearly nothing to do with the main thing of being back. Home is a place that does not exist, about which your opinions are irrelevant.

Aug. 27, 1956, 11:30 P.M., PAA Clipper Carib

It is nearly impossible, afterwards, to remember at what point I began to believe that I was really going. Believing comes elusively, not when you expect, most often, but both earlier and later, only gradually filling in the place where it will be. Unpredictable, like a season changing.

It would come over me all at once that I was, say, sitting in that barber's chair for the last time before I went. It would take the imagination by shock. The next minute I didn't believe it at all. I was sure I'd go on and have the next haircut in that same chair (with the barber who'd learned what I enjoyed was not having him talk to me, but having him carry on animated conversation with other customers, to which I could listen), and the one after that, and the one after that. When I got around to having haircuts at all. Somewhere else in the mind the imagination suddenly looks down the long vistas of time where one will not walk. The possible lives that one will not lead.

And twenty-four hours before I was due to go, when everything was reminding me that it was happening for the last time—a rhythm that had gathered speed until it was unbroken—I would find myself going through the motions of the place's most familiar habits, and not be able to believe.

I was sure I was going in a thin way like a hum in your ears, yesterday, as the desk gradually grew bare and everything in the study was either packed or put away. Not feeling anything about it but a certain emptiness independent of the emptying room; but sure. Feelings? I suppose they were there, after all, but like beasts patient as immigrants, waiting to move in on the emptiness when their time came.

And sure yesterday as my key case kept getting lighter, and the keys one by one were used for the last time and then packed in intelligent places where I will never be able to find them again.

Then with all but a few things done, except things that could wait till the last minute, or things that would take too long anyway and must be abandoned, suddenly finding that everything was ready. And time all at once was heavy. Between the intense activity of getting ready, and the farewells and rush of getting off, time was heavy. More so not because I was anxious to go. I'd forgotten that, days before. A week ago. But because of all reasons I did *not* want to go. Wanted not to be going, but since I was going wanted to be gone. How different from most times when I've been going somewhere, thinking almost entirely of where I was going, savoring the whole trip, from the moment I was ready to go. Different entirely from when I left America, for I didn't know how long, seven years ago. Even though a great part of me wanted to stay in America then, and even had an array of reasons. (Why go to Europe when I knew so little of America?) I know just how much and in what ways I'm fond of Europe, but I didn't know what I felt about America. I regretted leaving, before I had even gone, but I didn't know what I'd really miss until I'd been away for some time. Foreign places, however familiar, defining your feeling about home. But stay away too long and you're bound to confuse that with homesickness. (Which I never in my life felt, except in the mildest ways, until these last few years. Unprepared for it.)

The lassitude that descended, in that pause of an hour or so between the end of getting ready, and the time to go. Not calling the taxi, after all, until almost too late. That dazed lassitude that does not believe in time; or, at the moments when it has to countenance the minutes' passing, panics, and protests, protests, flailing in molasses, shouting under water: "Not today, no, not today." But dazed, languorous, just the same. The lassitude hand in hand with the emotions themselves of good-bye. And they, together, swelling the occasion with their heavy, bewildered, helpless dumbness. The daze still there (like the feeling when you have been in a pub for several hours at lunchtime, and suddenly find yourself out in the sunshine, alone) in the taxi, all the way to the air terminal. Feeling bulky and clumsy, as though your ears had just stopped ringing. The traffic so heavy that the taxi barely made it in time; the excitement of almost missing the bus to the airport, rising through the numbness of departure, and I was grateful for it.

Odd that passing sense of panic that wants to put it off till tomorrow, that hangs around and wants to go all right, but not today; trying to jump back into yesterday. A feeling that can, in the end, find nothing to focus on, and no grounds for itself. Maybe just an intensification of the familiar conviction (when going out to the theater, or leaving a hotel room) that you are leaving something vital behind. As, of course, you always are.

In the rush at the air terminal, again almost missing the bus. Never having felt any departure so contradictorily, I was never before so aware of the way the efficient bustle, the professional voices on loudspeakers, the assembly line rounding up and processing of passengers, resembles the ward-walking manner of nurses. Admirably impersonal. Cheery. For the benefit of everybody especially, designed to brisk, shame, and cozy you along. I've always found this amusing, a tiny bit irritating (making me want to ask them stupid questions and delay everything, and see just how long everything could be made to wait, just how elastic it could all be), and rather pleasant. And this time I wished it wouldn't all rush through so fast, so that I could have a chance to watch the effects of the helpful manner on the other passengers, especially those who were parting at the air terminal itself. (My incurable vulgar curiosity.) Partly to get away from too clinging a concern with my own departure and what I was leaving.

But in England, up to the very last, there's always the weather to concern you. The morning had been overcast and rainy, but as the taxi drove away the sun came out. And the airport bus was stuffy and hot, turtling through the Kensington and Hammersmith traffic in the sunny muggy London late afternoon. The sort of weather that would have women swanning up and down Knightsbridge, and the London shopkeepers and charwomen groaning. A nice summer day, or a bit of one. One of the Bright Periods whose Second Coming the London papers will mendaciously prophesy for months to come. The few English people in the bus quietly sweltering in their dark inconspicuous tweeds (one splendid man with a white mustache and a dirty gabardine raincoat on over his) and the many Americans peeling off their conspicuous pressed, newly bought-in-England woolens. Two collegiate characters, each just twelve pounds overweight, in white shirts, talking seriously about expansion of some kind, somewhere in Connecticut. A glum, brown-dressed, green-faced thin, young New Yorker next to me, filling his embarcation card with that particular expression of unimpressionable, slightly sour-natured boredom which is peculiarly New York. Two ugly girls from Baltimore talking to a handsome woman from further south, up ahead of me. Several South Americans, Brazilians. A collection of Turks, and one family with Turkish diplomatic passports. A group of American Greeks going back to Greece, with the accent of the mother country, the intonation of my country, driving through England.

England, where nearly all intonations of the language except the few variants of what they call "standard English," tend to be considered comic, or ugly and undesirable if you have to take them seriously. A system which, I can see, is good for acting, but strikes me as deadly in most other ways. About as healthy for writing, I should think, as the French deliberate limitation of their literary vocabulary was for French poetry. Socially handy, it seems. This preoccupation with class distinction which no longer means much. A preoccupation which, after five years off and on in England, I still find as foreign as sampans. Continuous effort and argument with myself, not to find this amount of preoccupation with class distinctions more than a little vulgar. In a way which, to me, looks sterile. Probably this is a case, among so many, where the illusion that we speak the same language registers against my ability to understand.

When we got to the airport the day had gone dark with clouds; there was a raw wind, and the rain had started again. There must have been several inches of water in some places on the tarmac. Rain sweeping over the wings of the waiting planes. The big planes taxiing around on the wet runway, and the rain and real wind skating across it in gooseflesh streaks like flaws rushing across mica. The slipstreams of the planes tore up long plumes of spray, the water streaking out flat and whipping away like grass does out on the airfield. The engines, idling or warming up, actually bared and dried the tarmac, for a second, just in back of the wings. And when a plane would take off, as one did right in front of us, the water on the tarmac would lie gashed and open for a moment, bared over a bone, and then flow back hesitantly to fill the place and smooth it over, after the plane was airborne, just as it would have over a ship that had sunk. The genies of controlled violence reminding you that the control is artificial, that they're all one family and never forget each other and that two-thirds of the world is violence.

With everything so organized and sterilized and herded and heated and air-conditioned, it seemed strange that one should be walking in real rain, even for a minute. The taxiing around the airport, that always robs me of the last shred of my sense of direction, wherever I am, as though you had to be robbed of that before you could be hurled straight toward your destination as the crow flies. The houses and allotments around the airport turning and turning. You have to be dizzied, after being robbed of volition; be the Blind Man. The voices in the plane coming from far away, as through the sleep of a child, over the noise of the engines; the pressure of everything seeming to build up in the plane. Wanting to sing, as always, when the engines, one by one, were gunned and roared, at the end of the runway before the takeoff, and the plane shook itself free of the ground. As excited as a child, as always, by the takeoff. And at the same time, this time, suddenly caught in an immense depression, as though all the dead weight of the lassitude of an hour, two hours, before, had fallen on me at once, and was carrying me down. As the plane rushed down the runway and the wedge between us and the ground widened, and the line of houses streaked by, I had a distinct impression of a cloth being violently torn. I would have rushed out of the plane that minute, had it been still; or have been tempted to. And back onto it, the moment my feet touched the ground.

England looked soaked, sodden, from the air. Whole fields lying under water. The standing water in sheets of glassy gray, no color, white, no color; showing the contours of all the hollows and low patches. As though a sheet of some sort of metal had been slid through the land. The ponds looking higher than their banks, and the Thames looking as though it lay on top of the countryside. Landscape and sky all lights and shades of gray, in every direction. Even the sunlight gray and laden with rain: pregnant. The sky dark with tons and tons of water as we flew toward Wales; and the towns beneath looking as if they had never been dry.

A nun looking like an albino buffalo with dyspepsia had got on at London, with another of her cloth, and I with my superstitions had to keep my fingers crossed all the way to Catholic Shannon because where could I find two dogs on an airplane to cancel the nuns? Though we were flying over towns full of Englishmen all loving dogs as Americans are supposed to love their mothers.

We were in and out of long feathers of black cloud, over Wales; after dusk with the lights on in the towns, but the dark not final yet, and the coast of Wales clear and sharp as we flew over.

Next to me a young thin Jewish doctor, my age, from Philadelphia, who has been all over Europe as surgeon to a traveling Black basket-ball team.

He has been to see his grandfather's four ancient sisters in Liverpool but I have been able to extract few details from him other than their ages (69, 72, 78, 82), the fact that two of them are almost blind, and that they are too old to cry. This last seems to be quite a drawback, since although they had never seen him before they apparently all wanted to cry as soon as they knew he was there, their brother's son whom they thought they'd never live to see; and it seems they were all of them pretty choked up as long as he was there. But enjoyed it, if he is any indication. Probably quite genuinely glad to see each other . . .

Cloud over Ireland until we got to the west. And then the low-running hills looking green as in the storybooks, in the almost dark dusk. Long pennons of water winding in from the coast, with lights along them, and everything low. We came in over water.

And Shannon was better than I could have hoped. The low, dark green buildings, temporary and whorish. The feeling that they'd sell you their genuine Machree grandmother if you expressed an interest in such baggages and had the green money. People lined up ten deep at the liquor counter, buying the limit. Watches, perfumes, Irish linens and tweeds, pipes, souvenirs of olde Erin impossibly clean and already looking like the belongings of tourists. A long waiting room with asbestos walls, where fifty travelers sprawled and smoked and drank and sat guard over packages and looked as dejected as though they had just learned they were going to live there. None of them seemed to be speaking to each other. Loudspeakers in the walls asking for Father O'Brien every two minutes, or if not Father O'Brien, Father Malloy. We were led into a dull supper of thumb soup with pretensions to mushrooms and flannel beef.

Taking off from Shannon, we had a searchlight beam on us, and the light in the propellers made big, slow-widening spirals of light, with spirals of shadow inside them that spread outward from the propeller shafts. Like those tops I had as a child, where the colors melted outward as the top spun.

12:35 A.M. London time

I wonder whether it is raining in London. Probably. I wonder whether the rags that I left in the attic joists won't get too heavy in the ceiling and bring it down with a sodden crash all over the floor.

The Dipper is as bright as I remember it in Spain, just outside the window. A regatta of little triangular clouds, far below, as we fly west. And one great mountainous cloud which we have just flown through had a long promontory which ran out into nothing, and made me feel vertigo for the cloud. I remember seeing a promontory in Majorca, on a day so still that its reflection in the sea was as sharp and clear as its own shape; they made a single shape running out into the colorless sea that looked like a sky, and it seemed they must certainly fall. And that first summer in France, the day when I swam out into the Mediterranean trying out a pair of underwater goggles, which I'd never worn before. Warm with pleasure at the first long view of the jagged seafloor shifting with light and blue shadows. Fish, fronds, sea anemones, swimmers, and sliders and weeds washing. The pocked snags and sloping ridges maybe thirty or forty feet below me as I rocked and swayed and swam out. They deepened a little and then rose toward the surface again, a hundred feet out. And then suddenly ended. The sharp edge dropped off into dark blue nothing, in which occasionally a tiny fin would flash light for a second. I was out over nothing at all, and it felt cold, and nowhere but in my dreams had I ever known such vertigo.

Every time you leave it is the last time.

Even if passionately addicted to talking about myself, how difficult it would have been to explain to friends in England (and to some Americans) this thing of *not expecting anything* from going back. I know things have changed. I know too that, as I've felt it all receding from me, I've made it up, invented it. I knew at the time that I was doing it.

I don't expect to be disappointed at finding that my invention was false, that the place isn't like that at all, that even the things I never liked, and remember disliking, have changed. I expect to be immensely relieved to be able to abandon the fiction entirely, and let the real thing take over. Because the real fiction was a fence to keep people away from what of America I felt I had managed to hang on to. And I was aware that it would end by keeping me away from it too. I look forward to being able to admit to an honest dislike of something right there and my own. A thing that I've hardly allowed myself to do for months, not because I was concerned with anyone's opinions, but because of a fear that such admission might push the smallest detail of home, even an unpleasant one (especially an unpleasant one) further away from me. But remembering, in private as deliberately as anything else, sordor, squalor, waste, ugliness, injustice. One thing I do not expect is to respond to the place simply, with delight, or admiration, or repulsion, as I do in Europe. Not one feeling at a time. But several of them or all of them, all me, at once.

I have loathed that fiction, and myself for fostering it. Like finding oneself insisting that the person one loved was pretty. Finding myself betraying everything, out of my desire not to betray it. Only let me waste no time now even for penance. It redresses nothing, least of all balance. Let me find instead a hard eye.

I don't think that Europeans get the same sort of passion for home. Generations and generations having worked out a way of regarding the place, taught them where to fix the feeling, what to see and how to communicate with it. And just the confidence which must come from the awareness that it all has been there so long already. And allow themselves even nostalgia without so much danger of sentimentality running riot. They can do it all more gently, more gracefully. Two qualities that we, quite often, must manage without.

I suppose it would be simpler to say that they have loved their place for generations, centuries; and know it, without having to make a fuss about it. Whereas, by comparison, we begin as a loveless people. Generation after generation having cared little for the place. Our fathers began by caring little enough about Europe so that they could leave it. We've used the place, wasted it. It has made us prodigal, restless. And we are attached to it in still-raw ways that we aren't aware of, most often. We ought to know that we couldn't hate it as fiercely as we do sometimes without there being something honest in our attachment to it. But there is always the sense of surprise, of inarticulate awkwardness, at discovering that the name for what you feel is love.

The black sea down there doesn't even need sleep, all the way to Labrador; and the night is splendid, and above it all.

AFFABLE IRREGULAR
Recollections of R. P. Blackmur

(1982)

How old we all were! It is harder to believe than to remember, even when I cast around, one more time, for reasons, explanations, and manage to persuade myself that I have spotted a few. They don't add up, and they explain nothing. John Berryman's cadaverous features and vaulted intonation—he was in his early thirties, still the young man of the Cornelia Walcott drawing in the 1946 edition of Oscar Williams's *Little Treasury of Modern Poetry,* but he enacted an imperious need to be one of his elders. He talked as though he were a contemporary of Allen Tate's, at least. And Blackmur, only ten years his senior, seemed already older than he would ever, on the calendar, live to be. He had the gravity, the voice, the deliberation, the walk, even the smile, of a man far into his sixties. Fortunately I could not know, when I met him, that earlier in the same year he had concluded that his life was really over. Russell Fraser's exemplary study, *A Mingled Yarn,* reveals that on January 14, 1946, Blackmur, then a week short of turning forty-two, had written in his notebook, "the days or years that remain after this date I consider posthumous." What he anticipated was merely a "pre-mortem interlude." The actual semblance of age, whatever it told of his own will, must have been his for a long time. He had always been precocious. Fourteen years before I first saw him, his friend Sherry Mangan described him as "that artificially aged dodo, our old friend Dick Blackmur." When he wrote that, Blackmur was not yet thirty.

There was some corresponding assumption, a little ahead of time, of the unspeakable burden of years, among those of us—there were really very few, in that era—who considered ourselves to be, whether formally

"Affable Irregular" was published first in *Grand Street.*

188

or not, students of Berryman or of Blackmur, or of them both. Some of the false-ripe manner may have been nothing but a perennial phase of the student role, a donning of impressive earnestness and the long face of the acolyte. And some of it was noted and considered special even at the time, and was praised as a new seriousness, attributed to the ending of the war and the return of veterans who were said to have grown to appreciate the real importance of getting an education, and who wanted to make up for lost time. Some of them really were several years older than was usual for undergraduates, and some were married, which in an exclusively "men's" school gave them enviable privileges and a distinction usually associated with later years. For the aspiring literati among the students, as for Berryman and Blackmur themselves, one of the looming figures of the period was Eliot—at forty, and perhaps long before that, the aged eagle. But it was not a matter of a solitary imposing model. It was only twenty years since the legendary 1920s and F. Scott Fitzgerald's Princeton, and the cult of novelty and youth that supposedly had characterized that time. It all seemed as remote as the Civil War, and Blackmur and those he spoke of as colleagues clearly hailed from an authority that was at once more immediate and more ancient. More honorable, in our eyes, and more interesting. More profoundly unconventional, and more mysterious.

Money—the lack of it—no doubt contributed to the loyalties and preferences that evolved among those of us who liked to see ourselves as already writers. Students were still not allowed to have cars on campus, nor, I believe, in town, but many alumni and undergraduates, and some among the faculty, continued to cherish the reputation of Princeton as the country club among universities, a view which, after all, antedated Gatsby and roadsters. On the other hand, many of those who then wanted, or imagined they wanted, to write, represented a kind of unorganized and unacknowledged dissenting minority not peculiar to Princeton and the times, yet the more conspicuous for appearing in what was traditionally a rich man's college. Some even then surely cherished a lively regard for money, and some went on to acquire substantial quantities of it. But a number of them, as students, had and were used to having very little of it. Some were there on scholarships, or eked out GI Bill checks from month to month, or both. The image of the bohemian artist helped somewhat—or I imagined it did. It provided a model drawn from other ages and situations, of dedication and behavior that mocked, and affected to mock, not only the conventions and pieties in which most of us had grown up, but also the presumptions of the young sports with Princeton banners or Confederate flags above the rows of steins on their mantelpieces. Neither Blackmur nor Berryman, as we knew, had been students at Princeton, and we were sure that, in respects we could not even guess, they were out of all that. Blackmur had been moneyless all his life, and even when I knew him his salary, as rumor soon told us, was pinched and its continuation uncertain. He and most of the following that gathered around him and Berryman tended, or were forced, to be outsiders. A kind of necessary privation which both of them built into the basis not only of a virtue but of an ethic of fierce devotion to an art in a philistine society. To art itself, and a view of life in which its importance was beyond question, preeminent and predominant.

I had finished two school years at Princeton before I met either of them, and for most of that time I had not even heard their names, though I imagined that I was determined to be a writer, indeed a poet, of a vague, variable, but feverish variety. I owe the meeting, as it came about, to Anne and Keene Fleck, who ran the Parnassus Bookshop in a small, pretty, old, yellow-painted (at one time) house on Nassau Street. I was led there first by a friend, Don Cook, and I took to haunting the shop, alone or with a crony or two, though I had no money at all to buy books. The pair of downstairs rooms off the hall were lined with old and new volumes, and there was often someone in a corner chair, or sitting on a low stool—a round green-velvet stool with three legs made of steer horns held together by a chain—reading, and someone else browsing, in library-reading-room quiet that began at the front door. Anne, or more rarely Keene, might be deep in hushed conversation, repeating what seemed to be esoteric gossip with an intimate, and once I came to know them, Anne would tell me, after they had gone, who *that* was. I was in my third semester there, and was busy being Shelley, mostly, and a bit of Beethoven, in ill-fitting pieces of discarded army uniform passed on to me by my father, who was a chaplain and whose sizes were different from mine. If I was alone, I walked everywhere reading—Shelley or Milton, Keats or Spenser. I was, in important respects, a rather retarded seventeen.

It was Anne, with her gaunt gypsy face and smoker's laugh, who suggested that I meet Blackmur—Blackmur in particular. Berryman certainly occupied a conspicuous place in her pantheon, but she may have been somewhat afraid of him. Of the two, he was more obviously aloof, unpredictable, savage, whereas Blackmur's manner, at least, was usually benign, formal, courtly. She spoke of them both with evident awe, showed me their books, and also a small anthology called *Bred in the Bone* by poets who had been students at Princeton in the years just before I had arrived, at which I glanced from too great a height to make it out distinctly. She told me of Blackmur's perspicacity with a poem of her own which she had shown him. He had pointed out, almost at first sight, the very passage from which she had just cut two lines, in the previous version. She extolled Blackmur's kindness, his humor, his wisdom, the range of his learning, and his love for Maine, where he then was. She and Keene suggested that I send him, in his summer retreat, some poems of mine. It must be said at once that this was apparently a normal procedure in applying for admission to the still quite recently formed writing program at Princeton. And from my point of view, the suggestion came at the right moment. I wanted to know for sure how you could tell whether a poem you read, or (a little shifty) one you wrote yourself, was really good or not. Some of the professors pronounced upon specific poems and poets in categorical fashion, but when asked how the judgment had been reached their answers had not contented me. I suspected that they did not really know. And I thought it possible that this Professor Blackmur, who had no degree and was not a professor, might. Heaven knows what I sent him.

After all the buildup, my memory of the first actual meeting is hazy. One rainy autumn afternoon in a small office in McCosh Hall, I stood in a dripping crowd of students, the whole assembly steaming, and smelling of wet rubber. On foot in one corner a severe, bony, superior figure all in browns managed to whirl, flash papers, snap answers, ignore most of the callow hopefuls. I learned that that was Berryman. By now I see him there in his brown porkpie hat, which is likely enough. But the long maroon-and-yellow-striped knitted scarf, insignia of high days at Oxford, and the gabardine, may have formed on him later, though it is true that for a while he seemed always to be wearing them. And was it not Blackmur, sitting behind a desk, smiling up in answer to questions, all but inaudible, and eclipsed, much of the time, by the students who had come to register for courses? I think I saw him without meeting him, and was out of the room before I knew it was he—if it was. Such an encounter would have been typical of the man and the relation to him: the low-voiced benevolence on the one hand, and the remoteness on the other.

I never formally took a course with him, nor did I visit him with any designated regularity. Our acquaintance, then our friendship, accumulated imperceptibly through chance encounters, often with mutual friends, on the campus, on the street, or in that echoing cafeteria with its shower-room decor, across Nassau Street from the campus gates: the Balt. Occasionally, after a while, at his house on a Sunday afternoon— visits to which my shyness and his own reticence lent a stammering awkwardness on my part, at first. Gradually we circled a bit nearer to each other. The will was there. What I recall of Blackmur's speech during those years survives from such conversations, from the weekly talks on Joyce, Dostoevsky, Flaubert, and Mann that he gave regularly in the evenings in Clio Hall—one of the neoclassic temples in the middle of the campus, which were attended by a small fervent band of aficionados, and from a graduate course or series of seminars on the history of criticism which I sat in on toward the end of my time at Princeton, after the dean of the graduate school and I had agreed— mutually, if somewhat precipitately—that I was no longer a graduate student.

My abrupt break with the graduate school was something that Richard regretted, at least in the form of it, which he felt had been quite unnecessary—a misunderstanding on both sides. Dean Taylor, he assured me, if properly acquainted with the circumstances, would have been sympathetic to my situation. He reproached himself, he told me later, for not having made things clear to the dean in time. I am not sure just what in my situation Richard supposed would have elicited the dean's forbearance. I can hardly imagine that anything more enthusiastic could have been expected, even by Richard. I learned in roundabout ways, over a long time, of some of Richard's efforts, before that fateful conversation, to make it possible for me to continue as a graduate student. As he understood matters, according to the letter of the law if someone attended classes for one year as a registered graduate student, and read the books on the relevant department's reading list, that student was entitled to sit for the examination which, if successfully completed, entailed the conferring of the master's degree. At the time of the rift I had finished a year of graduate courses in the Department of Modern Languages, and was working my way through the reading list in French. I was spending my days in the library and living in Morrisville, across the river from Trenton. Yet I had never been entirely certain whether I wanted to take the examination for the degree even if I was allowed to do so. Richard's own lack of degrees was more to my taste, and continued to claim my admiration. I had considered ignoring the bachelor's degree that I had earned, or at least skipping the graduation ceremony, and had bowed finally to various persuasions, notably those of my parents. Richard seemed no more eager for me to acquire graduate degrees than I was, myself. Once, in a rapidly passing mood, I mentioned the possibility of working toward a doctorate, and he asked me what on earth I wanted a doctorate for, if I wanted to be a writer. It was my own question as well as his, but at that point, whatever I may have said, I was perhaps less ambivalent about the answer than he was. On the other hand, it seemed to him a good idea for me to stay on in Princeton for a while after graduating, unless some remarkable alternative offered. I would be able to use the library, and as for the graduate school itself, a good education, as he put it, would do me no harm.

But I had done my undergraduate work in English, and if I stayed on I wanted to read, and try to translate, the poetry of other languages. I had barely met the entrance requirements for the graduate school in the Department of Modern Languages, and my admission put me in a position roughly analogous to his own, on the faculty, where the allies, known or unknown, regarded the very irregularity of his presence, with no degree and no academic background, as something of an adventure, a welcome exception, while the more conventional among them ground their teeth and waited for the chance to set things straight again. I was an erratic graduate student from the start, impatient with what I considered the duller stretches of the canon of French literature, and eager to indulge instead discoveries and enthusiasms of my own. I was being Ezra Pound, by then, in the same seedy bits of old uniform, but with a ratty pointed beard which Bill Arrowsmith referred to, not altogether accurately (with respect to the shape), as an armpit. Pound's criticism, which I was avidly ingesting along with the required French literature, did not help my tact or my status as a student there on sufferance. Blackmur's arguments in my defense (which were needed sooner than I knew) did not have to do with scholarship, of course, but with that far more debatable presence, talent, and the university's role in recognizing, encouraging, and making exceptions in order to harbor it. His urging on my behalf may not always have been much more tactful than my own conduct as a student. I was told recently that once, when the subject of my continuing in the graduate school came under review, Blackmur asked one of the deans, "What do you know about so-and-so?" "Never heard of him," was the answer. "Well," Blackmur is supposed to have said, "that's not surprising. He's only remembered because he was the don who expelled Shelley from Oxford."

Whatever the relation of the story to what really was said, it is interesting as an example of a continuous campaign of Blackmur's, not, of course, merely on my own behalf. During his teaching life, Richard repeatedly displayed a patience, generosity, and kindness that have become legendary, toward certain of his students whose talent he seemed to take on faith, for there was little enough evidence of it, and whose academic conduct stood in need of apologies. His personal writings make it plain that he was far gentler to us than he was to himself. In defending us, obviously, he was speaking out for the Richard whom he wished, or thought he wished, with a great part of himself, that he had been, or that he might have become. The faithful, unswerving outsider, rather than the salaried teacher however untenured, underpaid, and uncertain. The unpredictable, the insecure, the risky, the unrespectable. The writer in him, or his image of the writer in him, which he went on feeling that he had betrayed by committing himself to the university life. Whatever its general truth, the conflict represented a dichotomy of his own and was relevant to him first of all. Others have managed to combine writing and teaching more or less happily. And others have suffered from something like his guilt, self-hate, and disappointment without transmuting those poisons into generosity toward the young.

And it is also worth remembering his own history of unbroken poverty, the years of living on pittances earned from reviewing, the unpublished and unfulfilling novels. And that the time when he started his defense of such inconvenient students of his was the 1940s. For another fifteen years, respectability and a steady careerism would be the dominant mode in most quarters, even among the young, quite as though there was no alternative. Richard was speaking for alternatives. To be discovered, invented, made. He was insisting that the artist—and by extension, the individual life—can have no formula for survival.

At least occasionally his influence in favor of finding one's own way corresponded with a half-formed, ill-articulated, floundering (he would have said "inchoate") urge that was integral to a particular student. I think it was so in my case. My friends there almost without exception were older than I was, and most of those with literary leanings took it for granted that they would teach. I took it for granted that I did not know what I would do for a living, and even more strangely I took it for granted that I would not know, for a while. My friends spoke of their own assumptions as proofs of maturity, in contrast to my own unrealistic childishness. I learned, to my surprise, that Richard abetted my improvidence, and although he was generally chary about what he saw as direct meddling in other people's vital decisions, he discouraged me from considering a university career. More than a decade after I had left Princeton, on a visit to Boston, where I was living, he prefaced an invitation to give a series of lectures at Princeton by saying that he hoped I would not teach, but that if I was thinking of it he would like me to consider, first, a proposal that he had come to make. His reluctance echoed my own.

By the time I sat in on his graduate seminars on the history of criticism I was no longer a graduate student, and the irregularity of my presence in the course clearly pleased Richard. A university was there for the students who could use it, in his view. As for the institution itself, an order, as he would put it in his ponderous but muffled diction, was strong and rich precisely in proportion to its ability to contain within itself the seeds of its own destruction. I could not quite see myself as anything so ominous, looking out the window, watching spring unfold in the trees above Nassau Street, listening to the revolving talk about *Antony and Cleopatra*, Longinus, Aristotle, Croce. Blackmur had set up the course taking *Antony and Cleopatra* as the single central text, to be read afresh each week, along with the work of a different critic whose theories were then to be exercised in relation to the familiar play, to see where they led us. They led us, as I recall, nowhere very definite, and certainly not to any fixed, dogmatic notion of the real function of criticism or of one absolutely right methodology, in the way of Babbitt or Winters or Leavis. Blackmur thought of a good critic as a house waiting to be haunted. Which was fine with me: I loved the play, loved reconsidering it regularly, was fascinated by the form of the course and above all by listening to Blackmur on the subject before us, or on any other. Yet something in the course, no doubt, wound down, lost not only impetus but form as the weeks passed and the days grew longer and the windows opened onto days nearer and nearer to summer and the end of the school year. Blackmur held the talk, spun it, handed it back, wandered off from it into his own meandering improvisations which veered from startling insight to mumbled incomprehensibility, and I suspect that some of the graduate students who had taken the course for

orthodox reasons may have been disappointed. I remained more interested in the teacher than in the course—and I was leaving. Some of the
Blackmurisms promised to be inexhaustible. One heard them and
missed the next five minutes, or one went on listening and lost them.
Some may have been scribbled down in notebooks, and Richard himself
may have used some of them again, elsewhere. But most of them, by the
nature of the talk itself, were probably lost.

For some of us the course was simply an extension, employing a
certain amount of dialogue, of those evening sessions at Clio Hall that
Blackmur had been giving during the time I had known him. They
were the most heady, suggestive, illuminating, and bewildering lectures that I had ever heard, and in the years since then, nothing has
replaced them in my mind. They were monologues, lasting several
hours each evening, and in considerable part they were improvisations
from notes and from annotated texts and marginal jottings. They were
not transcribed. The click of the cassette box was not yet with us. Some
of the faithful—most of the faithful—came equipped with hardback
notebooks and tried, session by session, to take down the substance and
the phrasing, but I think no one managed to keep up the practice
consistently, or in reliable detail. Some of the material, in Blackmur's
own decoction, saw the light in later essays of his, particularly in those
on the European novel. But much of the real body of it, its character and
force of suggestion and evocation, its humor and its intimation of
discovery, survived only in the recollection of those who were present.
And the fact that most of us have so few nuggets of language and
perception to show for the hours spent listening to that unpredictable
voice must be as maddening, or as gratifying, to Blackmur's detractors—
who for years I could scarcely believe were serious—as the opacities and
infelicities occurring in his written work.

The novels on which I most distinctly remember him expatiating
were *Ulysses, The Magic Mountain,* and *The Brothers Karamazov, The
Idiot,* and *The Possessed.* Each of them, read and reread with his
massive, rumbling commentary, took on the nature of an initiatory
process—a situation, certainly, with built-in dangers. But those lectures
fostered and deepened, in a number of us who had the luck to hear
them, a veneration for the human imagination as it makes and finds
and moves in language. It is ironic, and altogether consistent with
Blackmur's nature, that the two fragments I remember most clearly
from those hours of monologue are what they are. One has to do with

character, and arose in reference to *The Brothers Karamazov*. In Blackmur's judgment, at that time, at least, Dostoevsky had characterized more profoundly than any other novelist. His characters were founded so deeply, in fact, that they acquired what Blackmur termed "potential reversibility." However he used the idea later, at the time of those sessions this meant that Dostoevsky's personages were able to act in ways inconsistent with what one had thought of, until then, as their true characters, without the reader's ceasing to believe in them. It was a statement of Blackmur's own vision of the bewildering intricacy, and beneath that the unseizable depth of human individuality. The other shard was not even commentary—or not in its intent. I am not sure, either, what led him to bring it up, though I believe it arose in the course of his chapter-by-chapter perusal of *Ulysses*. It was simply Blackmur's quotation, in his doughy Italian, of Virgil's line to Dante (Inf. III, 18) explaining that the tenants of Hell are those *"c'hanno perduto il ben del'intelleto"* —"who have lost the *good* of the intellect." He rolled the word "good" with his remarkably small mouth. The quotation emerged from his own most intimate, familiar, and continuing perception, and for me, at least, it leapt from the context of the talk. Neither his own personality and upbringing nor, it must be said, the time and company, would have tolerated any suspicion of private plaintiveness in the delivery; but, whether or not I was immediately aware of it, I came to realize that the line spoke to him of what he thought, much of the time, of himself.

Part of the quality of those talks, their richness, and their freedom, arose from the fact that they did not represent a course, were not part of any curriculum, and that no one attended them for university credit. They too were irregularities; and I recall, as clearly as the Dante, Blackmur's smiling relish in repeating Yeats's line "an affable irregular" —another, and happier, image of himself. In the tradition, as he saw it, of Flaubert and Yeats and Pound, he believed, or said he did, in the work that was formed out of the life *as against* the life itself, whatever that was or is. For decades, he insisted on the distinction between them, and on something like the autonomy, or at least the sufficiency, of the latter. But despite my admiration for his written work, it was the man who impressed me, first and last, whom I am happy to have known and to remember, and toward whom I have felt, since those years, a continuing debt and affection. When I met him, as I see now, I was in search of some kind of absolute touchstone, and I saw both him and Berryman through the lens of my own expectation. Neither then nor since have I doubted the authenticity of either of them.

And with Blackmur, as with Berryman, most of what I remember, and remember with deepest gratitude, survives from private conversations. Axioms. Blackmur telling a student who complained of not having enough time to write that "you always have as much time as you need." Or remarking about a possession, "in order to keep it you have to use it, and in order to use it you have to add to it." Helen Blackmur's story of his sitting up in bed suddenly, one night, and mumbling, "a good sinner makes mighty good eating," and then lying back and going on sleeping. (He said that he dreamed of Coleridge often at that time.) His confiding, while talking of something I had written, that he had wanted for years to get the word "inchoate" into a poem—a glimpse, when he said it, of his own humility. His walking down Nassau Street in a Harris tweed overcoat that he mentioned buying years before in Filene's basement, talking of his own coming birthday, of the late starters such as Conrad, or of Titian saying that at forty-seven he was just beginning to learn to paint, and going on from there, somehow, to discourse on the theme of Molly Bloom's fart, which he described as "the spiritual extension of the animal soul."

At times I felt that, even in his talk, and often in that of students around him, nodes of experience, literary or nonliterary, got involved in intolerable cocoons of abstraction, where they seemed to perish, and sometimes he revealed a similar impatience. He helped some of us not to take ourselves as seriously as we imagined was necessary. "Stop talking to me about Aristotle," he said one day to one of the Balt habitués, "I don't sit on his pot." When I mentioned, some months before I left, that I was thinking of applying for a grant offered for the study of diplomacy he smiled and said, "You're incapable of diplomacy." The first translation that I published happened to be of a poem by Richard Coeur de Lion. When I showed it to him, or told him about it, he quoted with pleasure, *"O Richard, ô mon roi, l'univers t'abandonne."* I was slightly disappointed because it came from a nineteenth-century opera. He thought, finally, as I did, that it was important for me to get away from the university, to live in some other milieu, and without constant reference to literary criticism. Shortly before leaving Princeton I told him that I was reading through his essays again. "Oh, you shouldn't do that," he said. And he went on to urge me to avoid criticism entirely, for a few years at least.

I wrote to him a few times, but we did not correspond. Over the years there were happy reunions. In Princeton, and at his favorite Greek restaurant in Boston. One afternoon, we went together to the Boston Museum of Fine Arts, and in the Asian collection he talked of the concept of the Bodhisattva. That afternoon he seemed inexplicably yet unmistakably like a father. A father to me. Particularly when he was turned away, was looking elsewhere. But the meetings were rare. Years after leaving Princeton, when I finally had a book of poems that I wanted to show him, I dedicated it to him. I wrote to him beforehand, but by then it was no longer his approval that I wanted so much as a way to thank him. For what, it is still impossible to say. For confirmations that have survived him, among them a tenacious esteem not for the human alone but for the inchoate in humanity, as it struggles inexplicably to complete itself through language. In the purity of impure human language, in language as a vehicle for the unsayable. A faith in empty words. I still send him my poems.

III
A Public Conscience: Essays and Statements

ON ECOLOGY

From "Ecology, or the Art of Survival"

(1958)

When I say that as I perused these two books the question of survival kept
up a dull continuo in my head, intruding itself on my pleasure at intervals
like the sound of a faucet left running somewhere, I do not mean to comment adversely on the books. Nor am I perversely stretching their scope in
the interest of a needless topicality. I am talking about survival of human
beings as well as of birds, and I am using the word survival in its
familiar contemporary sense—as distinguished from the perennial objec-
tive which impels flocks of Magnolia Warblers to migrate over vast
distances at night at the risk of crashing headlong into obstacles and
perishing by thousands, and which has taught the marvelously camou-
flaged Stone Curlew, in southern Spain, to keep as still as the ground it
nests on and the eggs it broods. In its natural sense, of course, the
question of survival has been with us since we were amoebas, or
whatever we were. We may have developed ears, at first, to listen to it,
and minds primarily to be haunted by it. For Homo sapiens it has a
peculiar meaning: one of the essential things that separate us from the
other animals is our awareness of our mortality; not a day passes, in the
life of an ordinary man, when he is not reminded of his eventual death.

In our time, however, the question has developed a special sense.
Nearly as close and insistent as the old "how long will I survive," we

keep hearing "how long will anything survive?" We have this all to
ourselves too; the other animals are not aware that tomorrow they may
be blasted to nothing, or deprived of the necessities of their existence.
But there are important differences between the two questions: the old
one, for example, is posed by the nature of existence, and there is,
finally, nothing that can be done about it; the more recent one is a
reverberation set up by human action, and the inference is that human
responsibility might be effective in controlling it. I am not talking just
about the Bomb. I go on the assumption, which I cannot avoid, that
there is some link between a society's threat to destroy itself with its own
inventions, and that same society's possibly ungovernable commitment
to industrial expansion and population increase, which in our own
country remove a million acres from the wild every year, and which
threaten more and more of the wild life of the globe.

I am told that this is a rash assumption; alas, the subject at times has led
me to entertain notions which were even crankier. A bird of prey—or a
warbler, for that matter—requires such-and-such an area to range over
in order to survive; I have wondered whether a society in which there
were not a given minimal area of wild land for every human being,
whether or not he cared about it, knew about it, or ever laid eyes on
it—any more than he ever sees the fields his potatoes come from—might
not also be on the way out. The bird ceases to exist through starvation,
or because his breeding conditions disappear, or through encroachment
and slaughter. As for a society, when it possesses the means of its own
destruction, and grows daily more crowded, restless, tense, unhappy,
and disoriented, in situations without precedent, what is likely to
happen to it? If it survives might it not do so only under circumstances
so artificial, restricted and neurotic as to resemble captivity? I am
reminded that man is, after all, a civilized animal, and not a bird nor in
most senses comparable with one. And I hurry to state that I am not
proposing a return to some Never-Never Land in the past— indeed I am
not nearly as long on proposals as I would wish. However, I am addicted
to both birds and men, and that faucet keeps running somewhere.
    Neither ecology (which in Mountfort's *Wild Paradise* is described
simply as "studying the relations of animals and plants to their environment and to each other") nor man's usually disastrous influence upon
it, is the main subject of these books. But for one thing we are confronted,
as in so much contemporary writing about noncivilized animals, with
a more or less overt feeling that a sentence has been passed and is

gradually being executed; undoubtedly this will continue to be usual at least as long as the words "wild" and "waste" are practically interchangeable when referring to land. For another thing, the detailed evidence of how well most species have adapted to their different environments, with their various perils and intruders, is inevitably contrasted with the bafflement, diminution, and defeat of a growing number of species in the presence of man. So the Chestnut-Sided Warbler, in whose nest the parasitic cowbird often deposits an egg, "sometimes responds by covering the intruding egg with an additional nest flooring," and vultures are able to gather out of an apparently clear sky because with their extremely long-range eyesight they "watch each other and the smaller scavengers as they patrol the skies; a downward movement is the signal awaited and this is instantly passed on for miles around, as one after the other follows suit." On the other hand kites, which in Shakespeare's London were "well protected and became so confident that they would take crusts from the hands of children on London Bridge," have dwindled until in all of Great Britain "only about twenty-five pairs of our kites survive, in a closely guarded hill area in Wales." The "Demoiselle Crane and Black Stork used to nest on the Coto; given continued protection they may yet do so again," though when a pair nested north of the Coto in 1952 the nest was robbed by egg-collectors. Still, not all species are vanishing; some of them, particularly some of the smaller insectivorous ones, including certain warblers, are actually on the increase. And not all ornithologists are specially anxious: indeed Ludlow Griscom, in an introductory essay to *The Warblers of America*, waxes grumpy over the fact that "sentimentality" and protection threaten to make bird-nesting and egg-collecting lost arts.

From "On the Bestial Floor"

(1965)

These are four books about man, the same who once heard his deity exhort him to "Be fruitful and multiply, and replenish the earth, and subdue it; and have dominion over the fish of the sea, and over the fowl

Review of C. P. Idyll, *The Abyss;* Colin Betram, *In Search of Mermaids;* George B. Schaller, *The Year of the Gorilla;* and Ruth Harrison, *Animal Machines,* in *Nation,* 200 (Mar. 22, 1965). Copyright © 1965 by *The Nation Magazine;* Nation Associates, Inc. Reprinted by permission.

of the air, and over every living thing that moveth upon the earth." Together these recent publications illustrate a curious development in the later days of the species, which has come to devote to the aforementioned command a zealous, and what sometimes appears to be a slavish, observance long after the author of it has fallen silent and been given up for dead. In the new silence, man's superiority to the rest of creation and his right to hold over it the powers of life and death, evolution and extinction, are questioned scarcely more often or more seriously than they were when he boasted a soul as his excuse. Now in the rare instances where his convenience alone is not taken as ample justification for his manipulations and erasures of other species, it is his intelligence, or some aspect of it, that is held up most regularly as the great exoneration. This, according to the myth, was the property which gave him the edge on the other creatures; and in the process it became endowed, in his eyes, with a spontaneous moral splendor which now constitutes between him and the rest of nature not a relative but an absolute difference, like the one which separates him from the silence. Indeed, by now, this difference and its exigencies are normally deferred to like the great necessities themselves, as though they were not only ordained but everlasting. It is true that this justification of man to man is voluntarily accepted only by man. To the beasts there must often appear to be little essential distinction between the force of human intelligence and other kinds of force. It is not a relevant view, of course. And the animals will not have appreciated, either, that it is this same faculty of intelligence that has recently given man the power of life and death over his own species, thus relegating him to a position which until now he and his gods had reserved for beasts devoid of reason. At the same time as he was preparing this coup his restless intellect was already perfecting a system of promoting living creatures which he had never made to the status of mechanical objects expressly contrived for his advantage. And yet as man's power over other living things has become, if not more perfect, at least more pervasive, his dominion over himself, however conceived, seems here and there to be escaping him despite analyses and institutions, and taking, it may be, the route of the departed divinity.

LETTER FROM ALDERMASTON

(1960)

On Falcon Field, on Good Friday, in the countryside of Berkshire, England, I met a young English playwright whom I knew. We compared impressions. Spreading around us, the gathering had something about it which was faintly reminiscent of a football crowd. And more than a hint, here and there, of a Sunday school outing in unpromising weather. All of the English political parties of any importance, from Conservative to Communist, were represented, but the atmosphere of the assembly was not (and never became) appreciably political. In the end we agreed that these ten thousand people, spread out over a large meadow, eating sandwiches, strumming musical instruments, rubbing their feet with alcohol, sitting in little bunches and talking, wandering back and forth under their banners and placards, many of which were obviously home-made, were not quite like anything we had ever seen. The 1960 Aldermaston to London Nuclear Disarmament March had established its own character before it ever set out on the fifty-four miles to Trafalgar Square.

There was clowning. Girls in Bardot hair and leotards, boys in carefully bashed top hats and outlandish costumes; bearded ragtime musicians, warming up on "My Old Man's a Dustman." There were many Quakers, nothing conspicuous about their dress except the heavy shoes and the knapsacks. A large group of Catholics. Another of Methodists, Unitarians, Baptists, Presbyterians, Franciscan monks. Country gentry in impeccable tweeds, doctors, medical students, businessmen, nurses, a representation of Black and Asian people in many of the groups. There were contingents from the different boroughs of London, from scores of English towns, from Eton and other schools, from what seemed to be dozens of universities, both in England and elsewhere. An international ex-servicemen's group. And the international contingent itself, with sections from France, the United Arab Republic, Israel, Ceylon, India, Pakistan, Iraq, West Germany, Sweden, Switzerland, Canada, Australia, Italy, Denmark, The Netherlands, Guyana, Nigeria, Ghana, South Africa, Japan, Ireland, New Zealand, Cyprus, Tanzania, Kenya. And the United States. The Japanese section consisted of a half-dozen students who had come from Japan expressly to join the march. Their way had been paid for by the donations of other Japanese; their cameras and other equipment had been supplied by Japanese firms. They carried no banners except the small one which told where they came from. Japan's special place in the demonstration needed no emphasis.

Falcon Field faces the heavy wire fence which surrounds the Atomic Weapons Research Establishment, Aldermaston. Inside are what appear to be miles of low, pastel-colored buildings laid out like an army base. Between the fence and the buildings is a concrete road. A closed truck passed on this road from time to time, like a satellite in a planetarium. A guard truck? Just inside the enclosure two or three men stood with a big police dog on a chain. Behind them, in and among the buildings, there was not a sign of life. But elsewhere it was obvious that we were not popular around Aldermaston. The pub keepers near the field were noncommittal, but local children shouted "Cheers for the Bomb" and "Marchers Go Home," obviously expressing their parents' attitude. The Aldermaston Establishment has, of course, brought employment and business to the locality.

Canon Collins, the precentor of St. Paul's, London, and leader of the march, conducted the assembly through a hymn, pronounced a simple, apposite prayer while Catholics, Communists, and Quakers stood silently beside each other; then he headed the march out of the field, down the road toward London. Beside him were other members of the clergy, writers, journalists, and Joseph Rotblat, nuclear scientist from the University of London, who had been on the British team at Los Alamos. He was one of a number of nuclear physicists who marched. The day was cold, blustery, with spatters of rain. As we left Falcon Field we had a first glimpse of one visible characteristic which would stay with the march. On the field where 10,000 people had been having lunch, there was scarcely a sign of trash, paper, or garbage. The march would have its nuisance value, all right, but that was not the way it would go about it.

The procession went on walking for four days, from Good Friday to Easter Monday. On the first day, as we passed through the countryside, there were few spectators. The rain settled in, wet feet began to blister. But it was on that afternoon that most of us had the first exciting view of the march. As the country lane wound through open fields we could see the column moving four abreast under its banners, stretching ahead of us for more than two miles until it disappeared over the horizon. Behind us, at a distance nearly as great, the end of the line was still not in sight. The line, in fact, was four and a half miles long as we wound into Reading, to make our way to the schools assigned to us, where local women were waiting to sell sandwiches, hard-boiled eggs, and soup at cost, and where we would collect our blankets and sleep that night on the schoolroom floors, laid out like bullets in a belt.

On the second and third days the march was at its most distinctive. The distances were longer, the weather, at least part of the time, got better; it was still cold but the sun came out, and all through the second day there were larks overhead. Feet got worse; spectators multiplied; so did the marchers. On the second day, to cover the nineteen miles, there were 15,000, and on the third, Easter Sunday, the column that moved into Chiswick, in outer London, was 20,000 strong and stretched for seven and a half miles. The police had traffic problems. They also had apparently endless patience. Theirs was part of a huge wave of patience and goodwill which seemed to envelop the whole enterprise, and with so few exceptions that many of us found it hard to believe. It was partly because of this, I imagine, that many who had come to march only for a day stayed on to the end.

And as the march wore into its second and third days, details of it began to pile up and make a picture which surprised everyone, including the organizers. Pathetic and funny details, some: the turbaned Sikh who stood rigidly saluting the column as it ambled past; the man with the briefcase who walked the whole way, alone, on the other side of the road. The antics of the clowning teenagers; the skiffle bands. On the first two marches, in 1958 and 1959, these eccentricities and capers had been played up in the press, and the demonstration had been largely written off as a stunt carried out by weirdies and cranks. This year, what with the numbers present, and the quiet demeanor of the demonstration as a whole, it was impossible to overlook the seriousness of the procession; in any case the press no longer seemed disposed to do so.

The seriousness was neither earnest nor scouty, and it did not preclude a good deal of gaiety quite apart from the self-appointed clowns. "They *can't* ignore us now," Canon Collins kept saying as the march grew. "They *can't* say we're just a bunch of cranks now." The details which helped to underline his conviction were as homemade as any of the instruments in the skiffle-groups, but they made less noise. Blind men being led the whole way, after having traveled from remote corners of England to march. Disabled people going as far as they could. A gray-haired Quaker who pushed his paralyzed wife all the way in a wheelchair. Old people. A man from Brooklyn, a Princeton graduate in his seventies who has sent two sons through Princeton, a victim of throat cancer, whose larynx has been removed; he was on the march every day, and has participated in every march since the first. Middle-aged people joined the procession in mid-morning, with bulging knapsacks; when the line broke for lunch, they opened these packs which turned out to be full of food to be given away. Several people appeared in the line with plastic buckets full of peeled oranges for the marchers. Couples pushed their babies and lunches in baby carriages.

On the second and third days, too, people began to walk in the "wrong" contingents, not by accident but as a way of fraternizing. In most cases the effect was not obvious. They carried one another's banners and the result looked about the same. But in the international contingent, where this practice was most prevalent, there were some odd results. At one time the Nigerian banner was being carried by two whites who had never been near Africa—a Canadian, as I heard it, and a Dane—and there was only one Black marching in the unit. Arabs and Jews marched together in several instances, and black and white South Africans. Quakers from far parts of England, Blacks from the West Indies, Japanese, writers from London and Paris, marched with the Americans. A Swiss boy and an English girl once carried the American banner for miles while the Americans marched with the Japanese, the French, the Swedes, the Italians, and the Irish (who had an accordion). So that part of the time when the spectators cheered the "Yanks," as they did, they were cheering half of Europe without knowing it.

On the second day the column passed an American car with two American officers in it. As the internationals appeared, one of them was heard to say to the other, "Well at least there won't be any Americans here." "They're right back there around the bend," several of the marchers told him, "you just sit tight." If the officers waited long enough they saw not only a huge U.S.A., but a separate banner from the University of California, marching among the European universities.

There were hecklers, but astonishingly few. I could count on one hand the number of jeers I heard on the whole march, and I am not sure that all of those were seriously meant. The main opposition came from Fascist fringe organizations which sent cars up and down the road through the middle days of the march, going too fast, usually, for us to hear what they shouted. One of their slogans, apparently, was "Let Britain Lead," and it is said that the marchers simply picked it up from them to use themselves. Certainly many of the improvised placards bore that same legend, sometimes with "There's Still Time, Brother" or simply "No Nuclear Weapons" written underneath.

The last day the distance was shortest. All the way into London numbers (including the entire large cast of a very successful West End play) stepped off the curbs and joined the march. In Hyde Park, at lunchtime, it was possible for the first time to compare notes with the spectators. Then one heard story after story of chic couples who had come to watch and say amusing things to each other and who had looked quite different after an hour. And of men who, asked what they thought, said, "Up until today I was neutral." The silence of the column, we found, had more effect than its songs. It was too late to impress this on the marchers, but as the procession entered its last half-mile, from Parliament Square to Trafalgar Square, it marched, by agreement, in silence. By that time, according to police figures, the total procession numbered 74,000, marching six and eight abreast (there were about one hundred in the American contingent at that time). At the head of the whole march a single drummer in kilts slowly beat out the Morse for Nuclear Disarmament. Behind him the column, banner behind banner, advanced up Whitehall into Trafalgar Square and the end of the march. There had not been so large a peaceful procession through England, we were told, since the days of the Chartists, if ever. There had not been so many English banners since Agincourt. Quietly the procession came to a stop at the foot of Nelson's column. Some began to disperse. Some stayed for the speeches. One of the last was given by a nuclear physicist who announced that the police estimated 126,000 as the total of those who had been in and around Trafalgar Square to take part in the demonstration, and pointed out that the first small and relatively primitive A-bomb which was dropped on Hiroshima had killed a comparable number of people in one second. At the end of the ceremonies there was a minute of silence for the dead of Hiroshima and Nagasaki.

Some of the banners, some of the marchers, moved on toward Waterloo Station to cross the channel and form a procession to the Summit Conference at Geneva. The rest of us straggled off on wobbly joints. (Waiting for me, in the mail, was an insurance statement in red warning that the insured objects under the old policy were not and would not be covered against nuclear radiation. Waiting for all of us was the news that one more victim of the Hiroshima bomb had died of radiation poisoning while we were actually marching.) As we left, we were impressed, in retrospect, by the *quiet* determination of the whole demonstration in which we had participated. We kept asking each other whether it *could* be ignored now. Whether "they" *could* say that it was just a political demonstration, or a cranks' carnival. Two reporters came up to us in the American contingent and asked—among other things— whether we minded giving our names, because they'd quite understand if we did, and "the Embassy, of course, might take views. . . . " We gave our names. Considering how many able-bodied Americans there were in London, we wondered why there had been no more of us from the land of the free and the home of the brave. Or we tried to wonder. Those tourists missed something. We remembered how people all the way along had behaved to us when McCarthy was mentioned, or the McCarran Act, or Little Rock, or the American South, or America's policy on disarmament and the arming of Germany. How those people had always been sure that there must be good reasons for all·those things. How we had always agreed, naturally, trying like mad to remember what the reasons were.

ACT OF CONSCIENCE

(1962)

It was as well for its reputation that the wind was hesitant, slipping across San Francisco Bay toward the Pacific on the early morning of May 26, 1962—and that it was not a citizen of the place whence it was blowing. In moving the thirty-foot sailing vessel *Everyman* from a mooring in Sausalito toward the boat's published destination in mid-ocean, it was helping to violate an order of the United States District Court for the Northern District of California, and other accessories in the departure would shortly be unable to prove that the sailing was not an act of criminal contempt.

The three men on board the *Everyman* were used to considering their proposed voyage in other terms. It was their illusion that they were acting in contempt of no one—they supposed that there was some possible distinction between disobedience and scorn. They had stated repeatedly and publicly what they took to be their purpose: to sail their craft into the "danger area" which the United States Atomic Energy Commission had defined around Christmas Island, in the Pacific. Somewhere in the area, the commission was currently engaged in carrying out the *Dominic* series of nuclear tests, which President Kennedy, with a statement of his exceeding regret, had announced in late April. The crew of the *Everyman,* and the people who had sponsored and abetted the departure, conceived of the trip as a protest against the resumption of nuclear testing by any government, even their own. Once in the "danger area," the sailors said, they intended to stay there until they were themselves destroyed, or removed, or until the tests had stopped. If they survived, they had further plans for sailing toward the Soviet

Union to protest the nuclear explosions which the Russians said would follow the American ones.

Participants in the *Everyman* project, most of whom were affiliated in some way with the Committee for Nonviolent Action (CNVA) which had organized it, had claimed from the start that their activities were dictated by their consciences, for which they professed remarkable respect in spite of the fact that these consciences were at variance, here and there, with the incentives of duly elected government.

They had built, then, this plywood sailboat: a three-hulled affair officially classed as a trimaran. Symbolism, it is said, had nothing to do with the decision. They had merely considered that this sort of craft would be fast and, they were persuaded, seaworthy, and that it would be possible to build it more quickly and cheaply than any more conventional rig which could possibly carry three men three thousand miles into the Pacific. It was their opinion that, with the use of local materials and the donation of local skills, it would be less expensive to build such a boat than it would be to buy one. So they had done it themselves, putting the vessel together in the course of a few weeks, earlier in the spring.

Logic of the Symbols

But symbolism was never far from their efforts, as perhaps is inevitable with acts of conscience, and the builders were early reduced to consoling themselves with considerations of what their project might signify, rather than what it might accomplish. Some of their symbols were simply given to them. It did not take much discussion, for instance, to decide that the mainsail would serve as backing for a large cut-out of the Aldermaston insignia, dark blue on the white cloth. This mark was already traditional to world peace movements, and the CNVA may have entertained hopes that it would mean something to such members of the general public as might have it brought to their attention, but events were to show that any expectations of this sort were overoptimistic. The sign:

This character is most frequently explained as a representation of the semaphore code letters N for "nuclear" and D for "disarmament." At one point when the symbol was being evolved in 1958, a cross had been suggested, but it was pointed out that the cross had been used to sanction violence by the Crusaders, had been a military decoration in several countries, and had been invoked to bless the dropping of A- and H-bombs over Japan. But with the arms of the cross shown drooping as a symbol of human grief, the figure was the same as the combined semaphores for N and D. Apparently the sign had been anticipated in older symbology, as well. Lanier C. Greer, in a letter to *The Nation* (June 23, 1962) refers to Robert Krock's *Book of Signs,* where the following interpretations, dating from the Middle Ages or earlier, are given:

Man	Man Dies	Fire
		Eternity
		Unborn Child

The suggestion is that the sign stands not for an abbreviation which is necessarily exclusive to the English language, but can be read (and for that matter might have been so read, in cultures that were in ruins before ours began) with a more ample interpretation, to mean "Man Dies in Fire" or "Man Dies Unborn." It was to these ambiguities, at any rate, that the CNVA invited the wind.

The Christening

Then there was the naming of the boat itself. The keepers of the free world have had the luck to find places called Holy Loch and Christmas Island ready to hand for their uses in opposing a godless ideology. Obviously the same facilities were not available to the CNVA and its abettors, and their christenings were open to plain eclecticism. The naming of boats, like the naming of most things, is apt to be a sympathetic rather than a strictly rational process, and the naming of the craft that was meant to sail into a bomb-test area as a protest would require special sympathies. And this was not the first time the problem had arisen.

In the spring of 1957, when the British were conducting a series of nuclear tests at Christmas Island, a British Quaker named Harold Steele had tried to assemble a crew and acquire a vessel to sail into the restricted area. He himself had got no farther than Japan, and his project had never had a boat to name, but his plan had received admiring attention from some Americans who frowned on nuclear tests, too, and who were planning dissident gestures of their own. When in September, 1957, the United States government announced that it planned to set off a series of nuclear experiments near Eniwetok in the Marshall Islands, in April, 1958, certain members of a committee which was then called Non-Violent Action against Nuclear Weapons began to work out details for a protest voyage. The captain would be Albert Bigelow, who had commanded warships in both the Atlantic and the Pacific theaters of action during World War II, and had become a Quaker some years after the bombing of Hiroshima. With him would sail William Huntington, as mate, and George Willoughby and Orion Sherwood as crew, in a thirty-foot ketch named, after many suggestions had been considered, *Golden Rule.*

At Honolulu, on Thursday, April 24, 1958, the *Golden Rule* was restrained by a federal court from so much as leaving the dock. Its sailing, the restraining order declared, would violate an Atomic Energy Commission regulation. The captain and crew appeared on May 1 before Judge Jon Wiig, who welcomed the chance to justify the ways of the AEC for the record, and to turn the temporary restraining order into a preliminary injunction. The *Golden Rule* sailed anyway, and was overtaken by the Coast Guard, whereupon those responsible for the sailing were given sixty days to consider it in the Honolulu jail. (Mr. Bigelow wrote a book about the whole thing.) One effect of their venture had been the impairment, for further possible use, of the phrase they had sailed under; for Judge Wiig, in preparing to sentence them, had announced to history that they had "tainted the golden rule." Their successors, making for Christmas Island in 1962, would do well to find another name.

Other possible names had been more or less ruled out, too. Before the 1958 tests had finished, Dr. Earle Reynolds, an American anthropologist, had deliberately sailed his ketch *Phoenix* (full name *Phoenix of Hiroshima*) into the AEC prohibited zone. Dr. Reynolds, who at one time had done major research on the radiation effects of the Hiroshima bomb on the surviving children, had with him his wife, their two children and a Japanese yachtsman, when he was boarded by the Coast Guard and forced to sail (or be towed) out of the area and through admittedly unrestricted international waters to a trust territory. He had spent over two years and a good deal of money and effort before the Court of Appeals in San Francisco had ruled unanimously that the regulation he was convicted of violating was itself invalid.

Emulators, considering the treatment Dr. Reynolds was accorded by different departments of the government, may well have questioned the luck of repeating the name *Phoenix,* even if they were deliberately trying to establish a tradition. Besides, even in legend the bird that rose from its own ashes was said to be rare, and the relation of Hiroshima to the first *Phoenix* was one which no American city was yet qualified to imitate.

It was, finally, an old suggestion which persisted and settled itself as the name of the new boat even before construction was under way. When the planning of the 1962 protest voyage was in its first stages, Albert Bigelow, who had been the *Golden Rule*'s captain, had flown to the West Coast to help with the organizing of it, taking the experience of the earlier sailing to the fitting out of the projected one. The vessel they would build would bear a name which had been proposed originally for *Golden Rule.* It would be called *Everyman.*

The Launching

The name speaks to its own source, obviously, which no doubt is why it was used in the first place in a mystery play, or interlude, at the close of the Middle Ages. The protestors must have hoped that it would convey something of what they thought of as their cause even to observers to whom history means nothing; in any case, the allusion was considered to be relevant, and it went on conversing with their purpose. "The somonynge of Everyman called it is . . ." (I quote from an edition printed in the first part of the sixteenth century by Richard Pynson); "The story sayth: man, in the begynnynge / Loke well and take good heed to the endynge."

They had hoped to have the boat in the water in early May. The launching itself was planned as a gesture: it was to take place on May 8, the same day that a nuclear-powered Polaris submarine was to go down the ways, with the graceful blessings of Mrs. J. F. Kennedy, on the country's opposite coast. But the schedules of the two boats had not been joined in heaven, and it took considerable effort to get them to approach each other. It looked as though *Everyman* would be late, with the press waiting and everything. (Or at least with reporters waiting: it is in the tradition of the American press to recount "peace activities" as local news, when they are so far dignified as to be considered news at all, while many war activities, reasonably enough, are by contrast national and international features.) Some of the participants in the *Everyman* project were oddly uninterested in the public-relations angle and went on with preparations for the voyage rather than for its image in the papers. Finally, the elements of a ceremony were assembled just the same, but where officialdom is likely to be well practiced in this sort of thing, individuals are as apt to betray that they are amateurs, and this is roughly what happened.

The first swing of the bottle missed *Everyman* and felled an onlooker—the boat's official owner, Carl May. On the second, glass flew and first aid had to be applied to the nose of the pretty girl who had performed the rite. The trimaran was barely afloat and the photographers were not yet finished, when hands started to haul it ashore again: the first coat of paint, hastily administered the night before so that the boat could be launched at all, was scarcely dry and would not be improved by a real soaking. Altogether it is doubtful whether the dipping of the three plywood hulls stirred any more of the citizenry to apprehensions of man's fate than did the smooth christening in Groton, Connecticut, of the blunt instrument named as an honor to Lafayette and designed to use two-thirds of the globe as its ambush.

(It was a week which had had a full complement of futile gestures: on May 6—that was the Sunday—an elderly Japanese, Seiichi Matsushima, who had been irradiated at the bombing of Hiroshima in 1945 and had been a patient at Hiroshima University Hospital, had stood in front of the tomb erected to the memory of the victims of the Hiroshima bombing, in the Peace Memorial Park there, and had committed suicide. He had left behind him a note addressed to the American and Russian embassies asking why men could not live peaceably, and declaring that all his survivors are brothers. Local news.)

Publicizing the Crime

From the moment that the CNVA had begun to organize the 1962 protest voyage, it had made its plans public. The members of the committee shared a belief that nonviolent actions should always be performed "in a spirit of openness"; the authorities concerned should be informed in advance, in as much detail as possible, of exactly what they might have to deal with. This approach is considered to be more than simply an extension of the protestors' own exercise of nonviolence; it is supposed that, in some cases at least, it may help the authorities to a measure of nonviolence of their own. For instance, at a demonstration at the AEC building in New York City, in March, 1962 (while bruises were still fresh from the famous club-swinging charge of the mounted riot squad into a gathering of demonstrators, men, women, and children, some of them sitting down in Times Square), Bradford Lyttle, former national secretary of the CNVA, had put the principle in his own way. "We must make sure," he had told some fellow demonstrators, "that the police are aware of the full limits of our intentions, and we must do nothing to surprise them, because if you watch their faces you'll see that they're frightened. If they're startled, they're liable to behave like frightened men. We must try to help them not to." At that time, with the riot squad's action still uncondoned by the city officials, the police were reluctant to comment on anything at all, and it is not known what they thought of Mr. Lyttle's sympathy for their faces.

The practice of notifying the authorities of plans as soon as they were formed had become a matter of tradition as well as one of principle. In January, 1958, George Willoughby and Lawrence Scott, for the CNVA, and Albert Bigelow and William Huntington, for the crew of the *Golden Rule,* had sent identical letters to President Eisenhower, John Foster Dulles, Lewis Strauss of the AEC, and leading officials of the United Nations, including Dag Hammarskjold and the chairman of the United States delegation to the United Nations, Henry Cabot Lodge, setting forth in detail their decision to sail a boat into the test area and the reasons therefor. The letter and an accompanying statement giving further information were released to the press twenty-four hours later. The material evoked no official response from the American incumbents, at the time, but was used later by the government's prosecutor to prove that the government had known all along of the plans for the *Golden Rule's* voyage. In view of the tardy and, in the end, uninspired use which the authorities had made of that knowledge, it might seem rather surprising that they were willing to call attention to how long they had had it, but they may have been confident of some final invulnerability in their case.

In the Reynolds sailing, the decision to enter the test area had been made when the *Phoenix* was actually on the high seas, proceeding from Honolulu to Japan on the most convenient course, which if kept to would pass straight through the 400,000-square-mile forbidden zone. It was not until they were nineteen days out of Honolulu and less than two days' sailing from the restricted area that the Reynolds family and Nick Mikami, the Japanese yachtsman who was sailing with them, had all made up their minds to continue on their course and sail into the zone. On the same night they had communicated their intention to a Coast Guard vessel which had nearly run them down, and on the following day they had broadcast a statement of their plans on the ship's radio. Dr. Reynolds was actually well inside the test zone when the *Phoenix* was halted by a Coast Guard vessel and boarded, and he was put under arrest and forced to change course and sail to Kwajalein.

Dr. Reynolds' unarmed invasion of the forbidden area is not known to have affected the course of the 1958 test series, to have jeopardized the national defense, nor to have disclosed to the American people knowledge which might have endangered their welfare—eventualities which had seriously perturbed several branches of the government. On the other hand, the fact that Dr. Reynolds actually had managed to get inside the zone itself, and that he had done so by stating his plans when he was already on the high seas, were points which figured in many later discussions of protest voyages.

Argument for Secrecy

It was not necessary, for instance, for protestors or their sympathizers to be able to answer critics of the principle of openness who, in due course, would declare that the organizers of protest voyages had no real intention of ever having to face the unpleasantness and dangers of a long sea journey followed by exposure to radiation and possible blast effects— that, in fact, they did not mean to risk having to carry out the voyages they projected, and that they announced their intentions in order to make sure that they would be stopped. But it must have been convenient to be able to point to the fact that one group of protestors had actually carried out their stated plans. (There were other answers, too, of course. Harold Stallings, of *Everyman,* in 1962, would say that other people might, if they chose, decide that he never expected to go through with the voyage, but that for his own part he could remember how scared he'd been.) Still, the evident likelihood that Dr. Reynolds had made it only because he had announced his purpose when he was already at sea and close to the test area lent persuasiveness to those who believed that the only way to get into the zone in 1962 would be to keep any such purpose secret until the last possible moment. Many who shared this opinion went so far as to suppose that the government had set itself absolutely against any such challenge as might be implied by a sailing into a test area, and would prevent such a voyage by any means it might consider necessary, legal or not. But other organizers of the *Everyman* voyage, accustomed to addressing themselves to the best in everybody, clung to a notion that the authorities were not yet so arbitrary in their use of force.

It was not a comfortable position to defend, in view of the histories of the earlier test series and voyages. Some of the Marshall Islanders, for instance, might not have agreed that the United States had been visibly scrupulous about observing any law, national or international, once it had decided to use their islands (a trust territory, consigned by the United Nations to the United States for safekeeping) for the 1958 tests. Again, the AEC, in arrogating to its peculiar uses hundreds of thousands of square miles of the Pacific Ocean, had never been made to hesitate by the existence of Article 13 of the Laws of Maritime Jurisprudence in Times of Peace, which reads: "No state or group of states may claim any right of sovereignty, privilege or prerogative, over any portion of the high seas, or place any obstacle to the free and full use of the seas." (Admittedly, international law is hard to enforce.)

Again, at the time of the Reynolds arrest and during much of his subsequent treatment, the representatives of the U.S. government had behaved with a disregard for the processes of law, which, in an ordinary citizen, might have been considered dangerous. Among other things, upon arresting him in a place where their jurisdiction was eminently debatable, they had issued no warrant, refused to inform him of the charge against him, neglected to remand him from military to civil custody until it suited them to do so, interfered at the same time (and on the high seas) with a citizen of another country (Japan), failed to allow the defendant to introduce evidence in his own behalf at his hearing, and made it impossible for him to have the counsel of his choice. These violations, and others like them, were apparently not in contempt of anything which the law necessarily protects, and no one had been troubled by them except their victims.

Even so, some of the CNVA would have contended that the government wanted to obey the law if it could, and they might have reminded skeptics that when the authorities had decided to stop the *Golden Rule* in the spring of 1958, and had had no law to invoke in order to do so, they had gone so far as to enact a special AEC regulation—three months after the project had been announced and three weeks after the boat had actually sailed for its avowed destination—aimed at preventing it from continuing. The regulation, officially designated as "U.S. AEC Title 10, Part 112, Section 112.4, *Prohibition,*" had read: "No United States citizen or other person who is within the scope of this part shall enter, attempt to enter, or conspire to enter the danger area during the continuation of the Hardtack test series (the name of the tests has been brought up to date since 1958 and the statute has been amended) except with the express approval of the appropriate officials of the Atomic Energy Commission or the Department of Defense." (As time had been short and the sailboat constituted an emergency, the AEC and the Department of Justice had even waived the public hearing and the statutory waiting period which would otherwise have been necessary before such a regulation could have been enforced.)

The organizers of the voyage had fitted out *Everyman* with water and supplies for weeks at sea—food for forty days, water for sixty: they thought it would be best not to risk putting in at Hawaii on the way to the zone. There were seventeen days between the launching of the trimaran and the date of the proposed sailing. The time was spent in checking off the supply lists which had been compiled by Albert Bigelow and others, in working on the craft's radio equipment and in shakedown cruises in the bay and open ocean. The preparations were slowed up a little by the fact that the *Everyman* project was news by now— locally—and that visitors kept appearing at the boatyard with questions.

The Crew

The crew could well have used months. Quite apart from the readying of the boat itself, there was the problem of sailing experience. Crew members for a voyage such as this—or at least such had been the view of the CNVA—ought to have clear convictions on the relations between individual conscience and nuclear tests, the arms race, and what Lewis Mumford (*The Atlantic,* Oct., 1959) has called "the morals of extermination," and they should have some basic sympathy with the essential aims and principles of nonviolent resistance. Then, of course, they should be experienced sailors. But the moral and philosophical qualifications, or so the committee believed, were indispensable, whereas it should be possible for one member of the three-man crew, at least, to pick up a rudimentary but perhaps sufficient nautical experience in the weeks before *Everyman* was due to sail.

And the final makeup of the crew bore witness to this opinion. One of the original choices for the project was Edward Lazar, whose experience of opposition to institutionalized violence was extensive and the result of careful deliberation. Mr. Lazar is a quiet, steady, twenty-seven-year-old New Yorker who had graduated from Columbia and served in the Army. In the early '50s, a sojourn on Formosa in a military capacity had convinced him of the criminal futility of force, and in 1959 he had joined a civil-disobedience protest at a missile base in Nebraska and had been imprisoned for five months. He had also spent six months in India studying the achievements of Gandhi and his followers, and had been a member of the San Francisco-to-Moscow walk and participated in a demonstration against Soviet testing held in Red Square at the end of the walk. But the first sail in his life was on board *Everyman,* some days after its launching.

Harold Stallings, the thirty-year-old captain, represented a more even balance of sailing experience and nonviolent principles. He is a Quaker and had served on the staff of the Pasadena office of the American Friends Service Committee. And he had once owned and sailed a boat of his own, somewhat larger than *Everyman;* it had been offshore and not open-ocean sailing, but it had been sailing. Mr. Stallings was the least conventional looking member of the crew: all his actions display the directness of a gentle bear, and he confronts the world through a rust-colored Ulysses Grant beard. He was also the one family man on *Everyman;* he was leaving behind him a wife and four children—sailing, as he explained, not in spite of them, but as a step toward providing his children, and those of other men who were unable to do such a thing, with a world in which they might reasonably expect to be allowed to grow up. He was also leaving behind him a good job as director of Pacific High School in Palo Alto, California.

The member of the crew with the most considerable experience at sea had come most recently to a personal moral position on the subject of nuclear weapons and individual protest. He was Evan Dedrick Yoes, Jr.—serious, unobtrusive, a graduate of the University of Texas, who had studied electrical engineering at Stanford University and served in the Navy (he would later write, "Prison is rather like the Navy. 'Now all the following named men, lay down to the [Guard] Captain's office . . . ' "), where he had learned navigation. After his discharge, he had worked as a radio engineer and as an announcer. He had felt for years that the arms race, nuclear weapons, and testing were regrettable, but had thought that individual opposition to them was pointless. He had read, for instance, of the Nevada protest on Hiroshima Day (August 6), 1957; on that date eleven men, including Albert Bigelow, after standing in meditative silence for some time outside the gate of an AEC test site near Las Vegas, and after informing the authorities of their intentions, had walked onto the site as a protest and had been arrested.

At the time, Mr. Yoes had thought their action was rather silly. A little over four years later, in the winter of 1961, he found himself working as a radio announcer in a small town in the mountains of northern California: little to do, nowhere to go, plenty of time to read. He read. The more he read and reflected on history and on the development of the cold war and the race in nuclear weapons, the more he was drawn to an opinion which had been expressed in *Life* magazine (though he had not read it there) in the issue of August 20, 1945: "Our sole safeguard against the very real danger of a reversion to barbarism is the kind of morality which impels the individual conscience, be the group right or wrong. The individual conscience against the atomic bomb? Yes, there is no other way." He realized that he no longer thought the Nevada protestors had been silly.

In the spring, when he had quit his job and gone down to Berkeley, some of his friends there had mentioned the *Everyman* project and he'd thought it an admirable idea. A while later he had heard that the organizers of the project needed crew members and he'd hoped they would find them. Later it had crossed his mind to send his name to put on their list, but he had dismissed the thought: he had felt awed by his notion of the kind of men who would undertake such a venture. He was sure that they must be saintly and rather heroic types who would not be interested in his offer.

A Matter of Conscience

Then one evening at a party he had heard that what the *Everyman* organizers were really looking for was a navigator, and he had felt at once that this brought the matter to his doorstep. He found himself asking himself where he got off pretending to approve of what these people were doing if, when he was perhaps in a position to give them the help they needed, he didn't at least offer to do so. (The lines had been waiting in *Everyman*, numbered 237–38, saying it for Felowshype— who defected later—and for him and others who did not: "For he that wyll saye and nothynge do / Is not worthy with good company to go.")

Once again he told himself that acts of this kind were futile, and the thought stopped him, and then he recalled the 1957 Nevada project and reflected that he was himself a proof that the action had not been entirely futile, for if he was standing there at that moment pondering a step that might lead him to participate in a similar venture of unknown scope and consequences, the example which had stayed in the back of his mind for four years and had gradually impelled him, as much as anything else, to his present position, was that same protest action at the base outside Las Vegas, which at the time he had thought was silly. He had picked up the telephone and told the voice at the CNVA office (they do not keep regular hours—some of their detractors are quite right) that his acquaintance with the history and principles of nonviolent resistance was limited, but that he was sympathetic and would like to discuss the matter, and then he had outlined his qualifications as sailor, radioman, and navigator, and had offered them to *Everyman.* They might, he said, if they wished, put him on their list. They told him the list of possible navigators was very short and that if he was in fact essentially in agreement with their aims and means and would present himself the next morning, his chances of qualifying were excellent.

He took his qualifications along, and it was clear before long that he was being allowed to include himself in the project, and not long after that it was plain that he would be the third member of the crew. Not that many questions were put to him directly. The CNVA is not a Quaker organization, but some of its members are Quakers, and a great many of its ways of approaching situations and decisions have been molded by Quaker traditions. It is not consistent with the Quaker view of the dignity which is available to human conduct for a person or a group to grill someone about his beliefs. Besides, in this case the circumstances themselves were revealing: no one but a heedless adventurer or exhibitionist would have been likely to volunteer for the *Everyman* project, with its stated purpose of "putting men under the bomb," unless he had some basic sympathy with what they were trying to do. And having volunteered, it would be unlikely that an intelligent person could pass the whole of the shakedown period in complete unconcern about why he had made his decision and was doing what he was doing. It was a fair guess that, during the two weeks that Mr. Lazar would be concentrating on picking up as much seamanship as possible, Mr. Yoes would probably be applying himself to a scrutiny of his own motives and their implications.

Meanwhile the plans were worked out in final detail. On Saturday morning, May 26, the boat would sail across the bay to pass near Marina Green, at the foot of Fillmore Street, San Francisco, where any who wished to wave good-bye would have been asked to assemble. From there the craft would turn and pass out to sea under the Golden Gate Bridge. Ahead of them to the southwest would lie twenty-five hundred miles of open ocean before they reached the nearest edge of the Christmas Island test area; 750 miles out, the vessel should run into the northeast trade winds, which should take it toward the restricted zone at an average speed (estimated on the basis of other Atlantic and Pacific passages made by this class of sailing vessel) of around 175 miles a day.

First Legal Blow

If they managed to get outside the three-mile limit, onto the high seas, without official interference, the crew planned to continue toward their destination unless physically compelled to stop. In the weeks before the announced departure date, the Coast Guard had been approached on the subject, and a spokesman had stated that they had no grounds for preventing the sailing.

But the government had evolved its own traditions for dealing with this sort of gesture. As in the *Golden Rule* sailing, where the regulation which was to be used to obstruct the voyage had been enacted after the voyage was in fact already well under way, so here the authorities had waited until the last possible minute—and then a little bit longer—before producing their impediment. This was a further reminder of *Golden Rule:* a restraining order, based on a new AEC regulation resembling that which the San Francisco Court of Appeals had ruled invalid in the Reynolds case. It forbade Messrs. Stallings, Lazar, Yoes, Carl May (owner of *Everyman*), and Roger Moss and Robert Swann of the CNVA, as well as the committee itself, to move *Everyman* from its berth at Sausalito harbor. The order had been requested of Judge William T. Sweigert of the U.S. District Court for the Northern District of California by the office of the U.S. Attorney, Cecil Poole, who had submitted that the proposed voyage of the boat into the test area would be "an interference with the conduct of operations engaged in by the United States of America in its sovereign capacity to provide for the common defense and security and to protect the health and safety of the public." Furthermore, "the United States of America, the plaintiff herein, will suffer immediate and irreparable injury for which it has no adequate remedy at law." As far as is known, this restraining order had been asked for with a straight face and granted in like spirit—after office hours on Friday, May 25, 1962, the evening before *Everyman* was to sail. The lateness of issue meant that the order could not be contested before the following Monday, at the earliest.

At the same time the U.S. Attorney had filed a complaint asking for an injunction against the same defendants, for the same reasons. This too was granted, and it too, as the judge later pointed out, might have taken its turn and been contested in the courts. The papers containing these official restraints were accompanied by a solemn document from the AEC recounting its regulation and professing its legitimacy, and by another from Vice Admiral Herbert D. Riley, U.S.N., director of the Joint Staff, Joint Chiefs of Staff, stating his belief that the sailboat in question would ruin the nuclear explosions he was supposed to take care of.

Bundles of these informations were made up for the defendants, one for each individual named and one for the CNVA, "their agents, servants and employees, and all other persons in active concert or participation with them . . . "; and the bundles were, as the phrase goes, served on the defendants. This meant that the United States marshal, Edward A. Heslep, and his assistants saw to it that the people named got the orders which referred to them. The U.S. Attorney's delay in asking for the papers, and the fact that they were finally issued less than thirteen hours before the announced departure time, gave the marshal a lot to do that Friday evening.

A thankless job, too. At the harbor Mr. Lazar, for one, declared that he was not interested in the literature which the marshal had brought him, and there was nothing for that officer to do but to lay the writs on *Everyman*, where they promptly blew off. (It was not Marshal Heslep but another who had been bespoken to take the word to *Everyman* in the first place, viz., line 63: "Where arte thou, Deth, thou mighty messengere?") It was after midnight, according to the office of the U.S. Attorney, before most of the papers had been delivered, and on that point the CNVA would contend that it had been "improperly served" since there was no indication of who, in particular, the papers had been addressed to.

Decision to Defy

The committee was convinced of its moral right to sail; but this move on the part of the government surprised no one. Knowing what they were dealing with, they had not only foreseen the possibility of such an action (though its timing seemed exaggerated even to their experience), but those concerned had just about decided what they would do if such an eventuality occurred. It seemed clear to them that the authorities were planning to use the courts to delay their sailing until it would be too late for them to reach the test zone. They themselves had no way of knowing how long the tests would continue, and the U.S. Attorney could not know either, exactly, though he might have the benefit of some official estimates. But they had had some experience of judicial delay. They remembered Dr. Reynolds's case—the judges shrugging him on from court to court. If they stayed to contest the order, they might be kept in the bay area until the end of the test series was in sight, and then the case might be shelved. Their protest, conceived in moral and human terms, would have been diverted into legalities and nullified. And if they were to go into court, discover that some such process was entangling them, and then decide to cut loose in the middle of it and sail, they would be in a far weaker position than they were in now. These were some of the reasons why Mr. Lazar was not as friendly as he might have been when Marshal Heslep, in cowboy hat (his summer one) and modified cowboy boots, arrived with the message.

The committee's interpretation of the government's intention was fortified by the manner in which the authorities had acted quite as much as by what they had actually done. Of course, it may have been impossible to get a restraining order at any time except after office hours and the late newspaper editions of the Friday afternoon before the Saturday morning on which the boat was to sail, but it did seem unlikely, considering that the authorities had known of the committee's intentions—and had made a point of the fact that they were familiar with them and took them seriously—for nearly two months. Whether or not a restraining order might have been obtained earlier (in which case it might have been contested earlier, with less danger of the legal process delaying the sailing until it was too late), it was customary and would have been courteous for U.S. Attorney Cecil Poole to warn the committee that he intended to apply for such a paper. It was plain that he would have had time to do this much, at least, for the affidavit from

Vice Admiral Riley which accompanied the restraining order was dated May 5—nearly three weeks earlier.

Mr. Poole, when asked on May 26 why he had waited until so late to apply for the order, declared that he had not known until that late when the boat was really going to sail. It was true that the departure date had been postponed from the 13th of May; on the other hand, the sailing had been announced for the 25th some two weeks before, and Mr. Poole had had notice of it. He did not explain why he was willing to take the committee's word about its intention of sailing into the test area, but was reluctant to believe it on the subject of the departure time. Mr. Poole might have acted no differently if he had been under some obligation to present the committee with a surprise order, synchronized to catch it within a few hours of the announced departure. After a brief consultation, the crew and the committee announced their determination to sail in spite of the order.

The Sailing

It was not an elegant part of the harbor, where the *Everyman* was moored. In the cold, early morning light, on the 26th, a Coast Guard boat passed close, at intervals, on a patrol which might have been routine. Shortly after daybreak there were already spectators. One woman was standing by herself, in silence, conducting what was described as a vigil in sympathy for the enterprise that was about to begin. Mr. Lazar was already on board *Everyman;* Mr. Stallings arrived. The departure was scheduled for 7 A.M. Near the hour, Mr. Yoes arrived. The Coast Guard vessel moved in very close, but then moved out again. A few minutes after seven the mainsail went up, the lines were cast off and *Everyman* stood out into the bay.

It sailed past Alcatraz to Marina Green, where a demonstration with placards and banners was waiting to wave good-bye. A press boat, the *New Merrimac,* followed. At nine o'clock *Everyman,* on a port tack, passing close to an atomic submarine, slipped under the Golden Gate Bridge into the ocean named for peace. A Coast Guard cutter, the *Taney,* and the *New Merrimac* moved out to sea behind it, keeping it in sight.

The sea was rough, there was an overcast and a stiff wind. Bright-colored oilskins and life preservers appeared on the white sailboat. When it was nearly 10:30 and it seemed that *Everyman* had made it and was happily beyond the three-mile limit, in international waters, the press boat turned back. There were lawyers on board; they might have known that the three-mile limit does not apply to U.S. citizens (on vessels registered in the United States, at least) if the United States government chooses to extend its care to them beyond that point.

And so, when the U.S. Attorney had been informed that *Everyman* had sailed, he had at once requested of the court an order for the three crew members to return and show cause why their sailing was not in contempt of the temporary restraining order. The "show cause" order, as it was called, also named the other defendants: the officials of the CNVA, their agents, servants, and all those other instruments. It was granted, according to the U.S. Attorney's office, at around noon on the 26th, and with it there was an order attaching *Everyman* (which the judge would say he had thought necessary in order to insure that the defendants would show up in court). The U.S. Attorney and his assistant had then hastened across town in the company of the marshal and a deputy; some time around 2:20 they had boarded a ninety-five-foot Coast Guard cutter at the Fort Point Life Boat Station, and the chase was on.

The Boarding

It was nearly 4:30 in the afternoon when all the vessels drew together: *Everyman,* doing seven or eight knots in the rough sea, the large Coast Guard vessel *Taney,* and the *CG95310* carrying the marshal with the orders and a U.S. Attorney suffering from qualms such as the administration of the death penalty had not been known to rouse in him when he had served as Governor Brown's clemency secretary. Overhead a small seaplane had been circling for a half-hour or more in the low overcast. Land was out of sight. The wind, which had dropped shortly before noon, was up again, and bitterly cold. The *Taney* lowered a motor whaleboat with a five-man crew, which made its way over to the cutter, picked up the officers of the law, and made for the trimaran. All the vessels moved closer to *Everyman,* the several Coast Guard craft signaling to one another with semaphore flags. With some difficulty the whaleboat narrowed the gap between itself and the trimaran, and hailed it. Mr. Yoes, on board *Everyman,* asked the officials their purpose, and said, "Ours is to sail into the nuclear-test area of Christmas Island." He was told that theirs was to serve him with papers, which they described into the wind.

The three crew members had foreseen such a possibility and had discussed what each of them hoped he would do in the circumstances. They had planned not to stop unless physically compelled to do so; they were on the high seas and clung to a quaintly literal belief in "freedom of the seas" and in the San Francisco Appellate Court's ruling that the earlier AEC regulation was invalid; they were convinced that they had a legal right to refuse to stop, and that the government had no right to detain them. On the other hand, the marshal had made plain his intention of boarding them, and with a rough sea running it seemed apparent that someone might be injured in the process unless the *Everyman* crew cooperated. In the end they hove to and allowed the authorities to board their sailboat.

The marshal had come equipped with enough handcuffs to go around and enough chains to have taken a light truck over the Rockies in winter, but in the end they went unused. He had left his Stetson behind, but he was still the man who does not mind informing the telephone that he is "not afraid of the devil in his own backyard," and he raised one cowboy boot to be the first aboard *Everyman*. At that point the trimaran shied, and it was nothing but the natural promptness of a Coast Guardsman in grabbing him by the belt that saved him from going in. As it was, he sat down hard in the bilges of the whaleboat. But Marshal Heslep loves his job and the thing to do is to get right back on it, and he did, followed by his deputy, who is proud of his job, too, and shows it by wearing a tie clasp replete with a motif of handcuffs.

This time, when the marshal got aboard the boat with papers, he did not entrust them to *Everyman*. The crew members behaved as they had planned to behave. They heard him out, and Messrs. Stalling and Yoes, realizing that the marshal was not responsible for the legality or lack of it in his action, agreed to accompany him. Mr. Yoes showed a Coast Guardsman a few details to help him sail *Everyman* back into the bay. Mr. Lazar, however, as a protest against what he regarded as an illegal restraint made upon him in international waters, went limp, and while not resisting the men consigned to remove him, refused to cooperate and had to be carried from the vessel. It was Mr. Yoes's and Mr. Stallings's impression that when the marshal had requested them to go along to the Coast Guard cutter, they had asked him whether or not they were under arrest and had been told that they were. This was an impression which the marshal could not later account for. There was no doubt about Mr. Lazar's arrest, but he was indifferent to whatever name the authorities might choose to give to their action.

The First Hearing

All the boats returned to the bay and Mr. Lazar, that same night, was removed to the county jail. On the following day, a Sunday, he was arraigned before a U.S. commissioner and charged with "willfully obstructing a duly authorized officer in serving proper court process." Bail was set at $1,000, but Mr. Lazar, for reasons which he would give later, was not interested.

On the same day, all three defendants appeared in court in answer to the show cause order. Mr. Stallings and Mr. Lazar spoke for themselves without attorneys. Mr. Yoes was represented by Allen Anderson, who was appointed by the court, and Marshall Krause of the ACLU. A spokesman for the CNVA informed the court that Mr. Lazar had been brutally treated in jail, when he remained limp; judo holds and knees in the back had been used to encourage him to move. The U.S. Attorney declared that this was not called for and directed the marshal to make inquiries; but the report, some days later, had not yet been made, nor had the complaint been dropped.

The first main hearing, however, was put off until the following Thursday, the 31st, in the morning session. The corridor outside the courtroom was crowded that morning and barricades had been put up to contain the waiting crowd. In San Francisco, the Federal Building houses the post office as well as the federal law courts; downstairs on the sidewalk a picket line was already filing back and forth past the recruiting posters, with placards reading "Free *Everyman*" and "Free Ed Lazar." Mr. Lazar, convinced that his individual consent had been treated with contempt, still refused to give it to the authorities, and since he would not walk he had been brought into court this time, as on the previous Monday, in a wheelchair. The suit came up after one involving peculation in Laos and another whose protagonist was a soldier from Connecticut who pleaded guilty to charges of mail theft and forgery, and expressed through his counsel a belief that the discipline of the Army was helping to straighten him out. When Mr. Lazar's case was announced, Judge Sweigert called for a recess.

During the respite, a young man entered the courtroom who stood up, when court resumed session and the rest were seated, and unfolded a paper banner reading, "Freedom Cannot Survive Nuclear War." He was taken in hand by the marshal's deputies, whereupon he went limp and was dragged and carried from the room and from the building and deposited outside.

Legal Fencing

A great part of the morning's session was taken up with sorting out the question of legal representation for the three crew members in the several criminal and civil suits which had been instituted against them. The chief addition in this matter was the presence of A. L. Wirin, one of the most distinguished civil-liberties lawyers in the country, who was there to assist Mr. Stallings and to help with the presentation of the argument against the restraining order and the AEC regulation. The restraining order and the order attaching *Everyman* expired that morning, and Mr. Wirin mentioned the fact that legally a restraining order could not be extended without a showing of good cause. He himself requested a week's continuance of the case. The judge extended the restraining order and the attachment. The U.S. Attorney also desired a continuance of the criminal action; it was granted, and the trial was fixed for the following Thursday, June 7.

Before the session ended, the judge raised the question of Mr. Lazar's bail. It had been fixed at $1,000, he said, but Mr. Lazar had declined to make any promises. The judge remarked that he was now considering releasing Mr. Lazar, since the court could, after all, issue a bench warrant for the defendant's arrest if it seemed likely that he was trying to escape. Would Mr. Lazar, the judge asked, return? Mr. Lazar answered that since he had been seized outside the jurisdiction of the United States, he felt no obligation to return. The judge, it was plain, would have been happy, nevertheless, to see Mr. Lazar out of jail at that point, but the possibility disturbed U.S. Attorney Poole. Judge Sweigert so far yielded to Mr. Poole's scruples as to confine himself to suggesting to Mr. Lazar the reduction of his bail to $250. Mr. Lazar replied that, in his own view, he was a free man who had been brought to court unjustly and would refuse to buy something which was freely and rightfully his. In a level voice he told the judge that if the amount of his bail were reduced to one dollar he would not pay it. When the other two crew members left the courtroom, he was wheeled back to the ministrations of his jailers.

Having achieved the first part, at least, of what he wanted, and got everybody together, Mr. Poole dropped the proceedings against the CNVA and its vaguely enumerated abettors. The government, he said (having instituted the case), was not sure that it had sufficient information to represent that these defendants participated in aiding the sailing. This sounded like willful ignorance in view of the fact that accessories from all over the country had been recording their names and addresses to help him out, indicating as they did so that they should be included in the suit against *Everyman,* for they had given the voyage whatever support they had been able to manage. Whether or not Mr. Poole read them, the declarations were no longer of service to him.

Outside the Courtroom

Outside the post office, the picket line had grown. The placards reading "Free Ed Lazar" and "Free *Everyman*" were still there and had been joined by others, among them "Bomb Tests Are in Contempt of People," "Resist Tyranny with Your Own Life, Not with That of Mankind," and "Humanity Is Everyman's Concern." The picketers had small signs, bearing their name, pinned to their clothes. Some of these included *Everyman* as a Christian name, so to speak. There was a certain amount of discussion among the demonstrators about the likelihood of being arrested, or of an incident of some kind occurring. On the raised stones flanking the post office doors, and along the sidewalk, stood lines of spectators—male for the most part, and for the most part hostile.

Around the curb sat the city police in cars, several of them nursing shotguns. Here and there among the picketers was a beard—one of the natural growths which so enrages the familiar type of American male who is anxious to demonstrate his masculinity by displaying the fact that he is exceptionally like everyone else. "Bums," one of these gentlemen remarked, looking for any eye to dodge; "they're bums, the lot of them, nothing else to do."

They had planned something else and the authorities had been notified. At 2:30 a small number of demonstrators intended to go into the building to the U.S. marshal's office; once there they meant to sit down on the floor as an act of civil disobedience in support of *Everyman.* If they were not allowed into the office itself, they planned to sit wherever they were stopped. Of course they expected to be arrested.

When the civil-disobedience protest was planned, it had seemed likely that not more than five or six demonstrators would take part, including the unofficial leader of the action, Ira Sandperl, a high school teacher from Palo Alto. But well before the time when they were to enter the building, it was plain that there would be more participants than had been expected; in the end there were more than twenty of them who filed in and, when civilly requested not to make a difficult situation for the staff by blocking up the small office, sat down in the corridor outside it. "Now," said a mail shifter as they walked slowly past him, "you're messing with the government. Mess with the city all you like, but now you're messing with the government." He pronounced this discovery many times and it yielded him an inexpensive pleasure; he seemed to expect that if he waited long enough, he might witness a public execution.

In the narrow hall the seated demonstrators, expecting to be removed to the jail at any moment, scribbled notes to friends instructing them whom to call up, where the keys were, what errands had not been finished; they handed the missives to sympathizers standing crammed among the photographers, to be passed on. They had been sitting there for some time when it was announced that they would be allowed to stay there, unarrested, until five o'clock. It was rumored that a telephone call from Robert Kennedy's office in Washington had discouraged more arrests than might be necessary. The *Catholic Worker,* bearing a large woodcut of the Crucifixion on the front page, began to pass from hand to hand and was caught in the pictures. A woman who, with her husband, had been on the San Francisco-to-Moscow walk, sat with her small baby asleep in her lap. One spectator remarked that it was a mistake to bring the child along, and a demonstrator replied that everyone there would do what he could to see to the child's safety, and asked why anyone should be more concerned about the protection of this one baby than about the millions whose futures were being jeopardized by bomb tests and the arms race.

Night Vigil

At five o'clock the expected mass arrest was again postponed; the marshal, wearing his Stetson to protect him from photographers' flash bulbs, reminded Mr. Sandperl and the sit-ins that they were on federal property and could be arrested at his pleasure, but said that they would be allowed to stay in the building until it closed if they would move out into the main corridor. The demonstrators complied, picking up their possessions and themselves and taking them to a broader stretch of corridor facing the post office boxes. There they spent the evening watched over by General Service Administration guards. It must be made plain, to the credit of these civilized officials, that they are in all respects distinct from the San Francisco police force—the shotgun cherishers

whose barely repressible boyishness had had a moment of public fulfill-
ment a year earlier when they had turned fire hoses onto a crowd of
demonstrators at the City Hall hearings of the House Un-American
Activities Committee. These guards rarely wear firearms and appear to
have been selected with a view to keeping the peace by other means,
including force of example.

Between the beginning of the sit-down and the end of the day, some of
the guards and some of the demonstrators had reached a degree of
mutual sympathy which no one had expected. And at midnight, when
the marshal asked the demonstrators to leave so that the building could
be closed, again reminding them that they were liable to be arrested,
and they explained that they had come to stay until removed and had
expected to be arrested when they came in, the guards removed them—
lugging them out to the sidewalk on stretchers—with unimpaired civility.

The picketers who had been on the sidewalk since the afternoon, and
the crowd of spectators who had assembled at the back door of the post
office, on a side street, to watch the removal of the sit-ins, were used to
the cold of the San Francisco night by this time. The sit-ins piled on
clothes, deciding what to do next. They had considered some of the
possibilities before they had known for certain what would happen to
them at midnight, and now agreed on one for which tentative preparations had already been made: they would stay outside the building all
night and go back in as soon as doors were opened the next morning.

Along Seventh Street, between the sidewalk and the front of the post
office, there is an area six or seven yards wide, paved with black and
white marble tiles, which is federal property; at the back of it a ledge
low enough to sit on and perhaps a yard deep runs along the building
itself. During the course of the day, the tiled area in front of the
building had become a gathering place for demonstrators, their sympathizers, and their hecklers, and the ledge had turned into the place
they went back to. In the afternoon it had begun to look lived on: books,
clothes, hampers, picketers' signs (turned face downward, in accordance
with a regulation about nonfederal signs on federal property) had
settled there, taking their chances under the pigeons on a higher ledge.
As it grew colder, after the sun had gone, blankets and, eventually,
sleeping bags began to appear, and well before midnight the front of the
post office had begun to look like an encampment. After midnight it
became one. More sleeping bags arrived; some of the picketers and most
of the sit-ins (including several students who had final examinations

on the following day) arranged themselves as comfortably as they could on the stone, and some went to sleep, while others sat up and talked, and a few kept a thin picket line going.

The Delilahs

At eight o'clock the next morning, when the post office opened, those who prepared to sit in and others who were simply cold picked up their gear and went back into the corridor that runs past the mail boxes. Some spread out blankets and went on trying to sleep; the rest sat along the wall. They were asked to keep the middle of the corridor clear, and they tried to. Ladies in crisp hats and men with ventilated shoes and little identities in their lapels picked their way past to collect mail. Some of the demonstrators, catching the eyes of these citizens, ventured to wish them good morning, but either their civility did not elicit much pleasure or the citizens were shy about showing it. Some passersby went so far as to ask the guards what the government thought it was doing, allowing this sort of thing; and their criticism of the authorities and of the Constitution itself, in some cases, attained a pitch of freewheeling dissent which left the demonstrators themselves far behind, and started the guards on a week-long course in learning how to explain to Americans about the essential rights of Americans.

Already on that first morning the demonstration, both inside and outside the post office, had more or less the appearance that it would keep as long as it was there. Most of the participants, though by no means all, were under twenty-five: many were students and spent a good bit of the time studying for finals, surrounded by a small high-water mark of belongings; almost all looked tired and untidy (they could hardly have looked otherwise, sleeping on the street). The post office sanitary facilities were denied them, but the Greyhound terminal, across Seventh Street, was more public-spirited. The need for baths was taken care of by the demonstrators themselves: those who had apartments or rooms nearby offered the use of them to the others. They had this one worked into a system and were taking turns departing with keys and coming back washed some days before the ladies in eyeleted gloves began to suggest that only the bathed have rights.

The ladies developed a principle which implied, among other things, that all men with beards except Abraham Lincoln and that Jew before whom Pontius Pilate washed his hands automatically smelled. They defended their own sex against the rising danger of uncut, unrinsed, unpermed, and unnetted hair, and for unnecessary reinforcement in their cause they recruited passing husbands, and were joined by a flying squad of plainclothes persons from the League of Decency, who had come along to keep an eye open for That Sort of Thing, too. The ladies spoke out as though they had arrived only recently at a discovery, but their viewpoint had been foreseen by many of the protestors long before this demonstration and was the recurring subject of one of the never-resolved discussions with which veterans of the peace movement were familiar.

One faction had long argued that they should make their point by doing what they could, as far as appearances went, to "make a good impression." The other side of the argument saw nothing in this notion but compromise; they believed that nothing lasting or valuable would be gained by giving in to the conformist ideals of the public and being "more middle class than thou," and they insisted that some of the best energy in the movement came, and inevitably would come, from the kind of individualism which insisted on its right to such harmless freedoms as the freedom to dress as the dresser pleased, whether conventionally or not.

The U.S. Attorney's point of view on this subject was no more surprising than was that of the aroused ladies. It was not very different, either, in anything except vocabulary. Mr. Poole's job involves knowing how to align himself with power. After the second night and the second carry-out (in which fifty-three demonstrators had been lugged from the building), he told the press that he had conferred by telephone with his superior in Washington, and was not contemplating further arrests at the moment. He did not express joy at the decision, but felt called upon to produce justifications for his clemency. He preferred, he told the press, not to turn personality problems into criminal problems. Someone was interested in knowing what he meant. "Go look at them," he said. "Some of them are sick."

Signs of an Epidemic

The sickness was catching, whether or not it was frightening. One of the guards who had been exposed to it for a day was approached by a woman who asked him what these people were demonstrating about and he answered that they were intelligent and articulate people, and suggested that she try asking them herself. Another guard, after talking with a few of the demonstrators for some time, expressed sympathy with their purpose and asked some of the older and more experienced ones what they thought would happen to him (he was looking forward to a pension in a few years) if he were to join the sit-in or the picket line when he was off duty and out of uniform. Still another guard's wife asked to be allowed to join the pickets. Obviously a free society cannot be guarded if this sort of freedom is tolerated, and one of the guards was eventually removed and transferred to another beat for a time, and when he returned to his duties at the demonstration, he was in disgrace. As a mark of his shame, he had been ordered to wear a gun. It is not all American law-enforcement bodies that regard a weapon as a degradation.

On the fourth night of the sit-in, the patients decided to help their keepers. There were some thirty of the protestors in the corridor waiting for the usual carry-out, and with them were perhaps as many more who were friends or fellow demonstrators who planned to do as they had done before, i.e., to leave under their own power when they were officially asked to do so. (The marshal's nightly request that the demonstrators leave had become part of a ritual; those who remained after that, though they might not be arrested, were technically committing civil disobedience, and regarded their act as such.) Toward the end of the evening four large young men in black leather jackets stepped into the corridor.

Judging from the appearance and manner of these four, the demonstrators supposed that they themselves were about to receive some of the physical punishment which the picketers outside the building had been promised by angry hecklers since the beginning of the demonstration. Instead, the new entrants engaged them in conversation, asked in detail what their pitch was, and before long decided to join them. One of them announced that these were the first people he had met in a long time who weren't phony. On the other hand, the leaders of the sit-in thought that the newcomers, however interesting, were liable to present a problem. It seemed doubtful that their allegiance to nonviolence was either considered or dependable; their sympathy with the demonstration appeared to stem less from a profound dismay at nuclear weapons and the arms race than from a desire to make things hard for the authorities and not get arrested for it. The finer points of the difference between the post office guards and the city police, and of the arrangement that had developed between the guards and the marshal's men, on the one hand, and the sit-ins on the other, did not at once appeal to the new entrants;

they were determined to get themselves carried out with the sit-ins, as a gesture of their own.

In the circumstances, the demonstrators conferred and decided that they themselves should not stay to be carried out that evening, but should walk out when asked to leave, rather than have the seriousness of their protest called into question. A few minutes later when the marshal requested them to go so that the building could be closed, they did so. The new entrants left, too—their faith shaken—and did not spend the night, nor come back again.

The Fixed Core

By Sunday it was possible to work out an overall plan for the demonstration. It would continue, unless prevented, until the trial, or until Mr. Lazar was released from jail. A further decision was made with the seriousness of the protest in mind. Mr. Sandperl and the demonstrators discussed the possibility of fasting as long as the demonstration continued; the fast would be a voluntary and individual act, and no one would take any pledges or do anything of the kind. Its purpose would be to intensify the protestors' own sense of what they were doing, rather than to try to put any further pressure on the authorities.

By the time the fast was begun, it was plain who made up the more or less fixed core of the demonstration. The total of picketers and sit-ins varied, and at one time there were well over a hundred, but there were not more than thirty or thirty-five who stayed at the post office day and night and were determined to go to jail when the government decided that it was no longer politic to be patient with them.

Of this number, more than half were students, but there were also a handful of laboratory technicians, an elevator operator, several painters, a frame-maker, a carpenter, a teacher, and a truck driver. One of the younger demonstrators still belonged to a street gang; he came with a friend and spent his nights in a blanket in front of the building. Members of the gang would come during the day and visit him, teasing him a bit, with an eye on the cops; his brother had been in the service, he said, and had been exposed to radiation from nuclear explosions. His brother's child had died of leukemia. The connection between the two facts, of course, could not be proved, but the possibility of it could not be forgotten (so it is, we are told, that superstitions are born), and when the uncle of the dead child had stumbled on these people building their boat over in Sausalito, he had thought they seemed to make sense. He had thought about it, and when they got in trouble he had felt like helping them. That was what he was doing there.

There were other unexpected representatives of the American tradition. One demonstrator who ended in jail was named James Thurber, a clerk. And another, who also went to jail and was brutally treated there by the police to punish him for "going limp" was named Tom Sawyer, a laboratory technician. Mr. Sawyer had been at college in Walla Walla, Washington, until he had led a demonstration there at a time when the vice president of the United States was visiting the campus, whereupon the college had taught him its final lesson by expelling him. He had begun his own fast on May 26, the day of the seizure of *Everyman,* so that he was a week ahead of the others when they began.

The truck driver was a burly man from a small town in Idaho, and obviously he had not often fasted before. He said that he had worked his way in his mind from a distaste for killing to a distaste for capital punishment, and eventually he had decided that nuclear explosions were not commendable even if they were ours. He had found some people in his home town who felt the same way—about ten of them. And they had made placards and got ready to have themselves a little demonstration. Only, when the police chief (an old friend of the family, too) heard about it, he had come along and said, "You go out there with those placards and I'll give you thirty days," and after a little while it had seemed best to leave town. But this time, the truck driver said, he would go to jail, he would fast, he would go all the way. Fast or no fast, he was heavy on the stretcher every night when the guards carried him out.

As the stretchers came through the door at midnight, the rest of the demonstrators would be waiting, surrounded by a crowd of spectators, some sympathetic, some hostile. Then those who would spend the night there would drift around to the front of the large building to start assembling some bedclothes.

Questions in the Night

By two in the morning, most mornings, the sidewalk would be nearly empty. Often a few of the demonstrators, usually including Mr. Sandperl, would walk up and down for hours after that, in no organizational capacity but simply because they did not feel like sleep. Sometimes they would dutifully carry placards, sometimes not. They would talk; they would address themselves to the question of what they were doing there; what made them believe that their way of acting was the right way?

They were aware that their gifts and knowledge and their characters were quite ordinary, and that they were trying to do something — among other things, to bring themselves to a kind of behavior, a way of confronting circumstances, which was probably beyond their capacities.

U.S. Attorney Poole was not the only critic who had suggested that "these people" thought they had all the answers: they were concerned, themselves, over the twin perils of a closed smugness, on the one hand, and of hopeless resignation on the other. It began to get light, some mornings, as they walked back and forth past the sleeping bags, accompanied finally by nothing but the mist coming in off the Pacific. What would they do, they would ask, if they were confronted by such and such unpleasant but possible circumstances? Most days they were faced with no tests more searching than could be supplied by angry hecklers threatening violence, but there were other moments which called their principles into question, and some of them had nothing to do with the arms race.

There was a man, for example, who sat every day, all day, in front of the post office, with the demonstrators and slept on the stone among them at night. He got into conversation with no one, so for some days no one knew anything about him. Then one of the guards told a demonstrator that he was known to the police, and was using the demonstration so as to be able to spend a few days loitering without being disturbed. It was also said that he had a psychopathic history, would almost certainly steal if he thought he could get away with it, and that it was likely that he was armed. The information was not accepted without question, but it probably did affect subsequent conversations, such as they were, with the figure sitting there on the ledge in dark glasses and baseball cap, with his knees drawn up.

The Face of Nonviolence

Then one night he appeared, stepping among the sleepers, smelling of alcohol, stumbling over guitars and books and a set of crutches, fumbling among belongings, muttering to himself. First one and then another of the men in front of the building spoke to him, but he ignored them. They went closer to him and began to talk to him, asking him what he was looking for, but when he answered it was violently and he went on with what he was doing. After a while he went over to the ledge and sat down, and when the men who had been talking to him went away he got up and started over again. This time he began to pick up the corners of blankets, whether or not there were sleepers under them, and examine them. It became plain that several of the men were awake and watching him. A few more got up. Mr. Sandperl was awakened; they discussed what they should do. Mr. Sandperl, whose education in nonviolent resistance surpassed that of most of the others, was opposed to calling the police. No one wanted to put himself, or the others, under that kind of protection. Most of the men went back to their sleeping bags, but stayed awake, watching; a few stayed up to learn how you protect, if you have to, nonviolently.

The man went on with his activity. Finally, he began to haul a blanket off a sleeper. The men who were standing nearest him pushed themselves between him and the person whom he had awakened; they pointed out that the blanket was not his and offered him his choice of bedclothes elsewhere if that was what he wanted. He turned on them with a knife. They continued to stand there, talking to him quietly, ignoring the weapon. After some time he stepped back and walked away. Later the police themselves kept the man away from the post office, but by that time a few of the demonstrators, at least, felt that they had perhaps learned a little about facing threats without violence. They reminded themselves that things had not been quite fair, since there had been several of them, and the man with the weapon had been alone. They were wary of exaggerating the importance of the incident. But they thought they had learned that it was possible, in some circumstances at least, for a person to confront a weapon simply by putting himself between it and other possible victims, without preparing or intending counterviolence. And they thought they had found out that it was possible to act in this strange way even when thoroughly frightened. It was, as one of them remarked, an awkward and maybe rather a dangerous thing to have learned. But then there was no reason to assume that nonviolent resistance must be less physically dangerous, for its practitioners, than the exercise of violence itself.

They were there, they kept telling themselves, to "awaken consciences" —and first of all their own. "I don't know anything about conscience really," one of the picketers who was there every day said; "I'm here mostly to protest against the violence in myself."

The Lookers-On

To those waking up early in the morning, lying there watching the citizens of San Francisco emerge one at a time on their way to the day, no assumptions seemed safe. A man in a good summer suit, not a person to pay attention to this sort of thing, would come along the sidewalk, slow down, seeing them all asleep there, and sneak up close for a good, long, slow look. Then he would suspect that he was being watched, straighten up looking scornful, and walk on. One of many. It was in the first daylight that the question would walk boldly up and down the street: are *you* your brother's keeper, and who said so, and if you are, how do you go about it, how do you talk to your brother in *his* world, of which you don't know any more than you do about your own? At least I have at firsthand that this question was met there at that hour, and no sudden conversions of skeptics and scorners the night before (there were quite a few) and no recollection of single acts of sympathy or faith or any of those other creatures were proof against the encounter.

Echoes of the question, it has been said, would be heard during the day too, but the destruction that wasteth at noonday was different. It was not composed of the bitterness of the daily increasing number of hecklers: the anti-Semite who declared that all demonstrators were Jews and should be boiled to death as Hitler would have done, the militarists shouting Obey in all its conjugations and variants, the Pole calling out "U.S. citizens" and laughing, and then saying, "I wish I had a machine gun, I'd mow you all down." It was made up of the mixed complacency and despair which seemed to characterize the public whether or not they showed any awareness of the demonstration and what it was about.

The complacency needs no citation. The despair was most economically summed up by a man on a park bench in front of City Hall, one lunchtime. The demonstrators, he had said, were utterly futile, and it seemed that that was his last word on the subject. He picked up his reading matter; and then he put it down again and looked at the ground and said,

> "But I guess they're the conscience of the country. On the other hand a conscience is a liability. You can't run a business with a conscience. I've compromised with mine all my life. We see things that are wrong, but we don't do anything about it. A conscience is a thing to brag about at banquets, but it's too uncomfortable to live with, for most of us. Those people down there, they're trying to wake up our consciences, but it won't work because what most of us want is to deaden them. Maybe that's why the human race isn't justified in looking forward to a long and happy future. They've temporized with everything. It's too late for an act of conscience, any act of conscience, to be effective any longer."

The gentleman's counterpart was a middle-aged Negro woman on a bus who used the same facts to arrive at slightly different conclusions. She said first that those bombs were just the worst thing that could be. Put them, she said, in the ocean and what do you think the ocean's finally going to do? Going to rise up. Going to blow up and destroy the whole beautiful earth God gave them, and God is going to let them do it because they don't care for each other at all any more. Those people at the post office, she said, she felt for them, giving themselves over to hardship to free everyman who was in bondage. (The lady was not aware of the boat, unfortunately.)

The Trial Opens

On June 7, Mr. Lazar and his crew mates came up for trial for threatening their country with irreparable injury. Somebody, one of the hecklers had said, has got to be government. For the next two days, as far as *Everyman* was concerned, somebody consisted of U.S. Attorney Cecil Poole.

Mr. Yoes's lawyer, Marshall Krause, suggested that there had been irregularities in the seizure of the boat and the returning of the crew, that the government had been acting beyond its jurisdiction, and that a notice of arrest had been improperly given. He cited a phrase meant to regulate criminal procedure: "The government may not use the fruits of wrongdoing in its officers." Mr. Krause went into detail about its being illegal to serve processes outside the territorial limits of the United States; he objected to the manner in which the court order had been got up, with the U.S. Attorney alleging an emergency when, in fact, he had had weeks to act. Mr. Krause said that the U.S. Attorney, through this delay, had effectively removed the possibility of a hearing before the announced departure time. Secrecy, and this sort of underhanded procedure, he said, had characterized the government's actions in this case from the start; evidently Mr. Poole had had so little confidence in his legal power to restrain *Everyman* that he resorted to these sleights to avoid a hearing and invoked an emergency of his own contriving.

Mr. Wirin, for the defense, then declared that the restraining order was void. The AEC regulation on which it was based, he pointed out, had been pronounced invalid by the San Francisco Appellate Court. He moved that the show cause order be quashed, and there were other motions for the defense. All were heard in full, and denied. Then there was a recess.

After that, the government read from its affidavits concerning how dangerous the trimaran would have been to the United States if it had been allowed to sail. The marshal, when asked about how he had worded things at the time of the seizure of the boat, said that he had told Messrs. Stallings and Yoes that he was "taking them into his physical possession"—which, of course, was not the same, as they should have realized, as saying that he was placing them under arrest, which he had done in the case of Mr. Lazar. In the course of the questioning that brought this verbal precision to light, there were those in court who thought they had heard Mr. Stallings address the marshal as "Friend Heslep," but the marshal, later, had not received that impression.

At the noon recess, the press caught a rumor and asked a CNVA representative whether or not it was true that another sailing was planned on another vessel. They were told that it was and given details. When court resumed session, Mr. Poole, for the government, called Roger Moss, of the San Francisco office of the CNVA, and cross-examined him about the committee's intentions. He learned, for the record (over a number of objections), of the plans for *Everyman II*, a ketch, formerly the *Patsy Jean*. This vessel, the committee hoped, would sail from Honolulu within a few days. The crew would consist of Dr. Monte Steadman (a distinguished San Francisco physician and head of a department of the Kaiser Foundation Hospital there), George Benello (a teaching assistant at San Francisco State College and former Harvard classmate of Robert Kennedy), and Franklin Zahn (prison secretary for the Pacific Southwest Office of the American Friends Service Committee). Mr. Poole also asked whether the committee planned to sail the trimaran for the test area again if they could, and the committee admitted that they hoped to do just that.

An Unlawful Law?

Having established that the defendants were incorrigible, Mr. Poole turned to his affidavits again, and then with a single easy slur he ran through the list of freedoms which had been mentioned in the course of the affair—freedom of the seas, conscience, etc.—and dismissed them. They were not relevant. The AEC regulation, he said, gives the United States jurisdiction over its citizens and its vessels in areas restricted by the AEC anywhere in the world.

It was again Mr. Wirin's turn to argue the validity of the AEC regulation. The Atomic Energy Act, he says, nowhere empowers the commission to carve out a section of the high seas and forbid people to enter it. The United States Court of Appeals had made this point in the Reynolds case. Furthermore, he said, the act requires the Atomic Energy Commission to comply with administrative procedure which had been violated in this case by the manner in which the restraining order had been arrived at, among other things. Then the law pertaining to freedom of the seas was brought up, and the sense in which the regulation in question—and the action of the government which, in this case, had been based upon it—violated that law. And then it was submitted that the regulation violated several specific guarantees which are set forth in the Constitution of the United States.

Again referring to the second Reynolds case, Mr. Wirin submitted that the court had no jurisdiction to prevent the crew from sailing to the test area, whatever might have been the position about their entering it.

As the regulation had been used here and in the earlier protest sailings, Mr. Wirin argued, the government has simply found a formula for jailing inconvenient protestors without trial by jury. No citizen, he reminded the judge who was the representative of the citizenry, had had a chance to pronounce on the AEC regulation in question before it had been adopted. A powerful process of government had been invoked against citizens without notice having been given to them. Mr. Wirin adverted to the secret processes of the Star Chamber. The court, by issuing the restraining order, he said, in effect had made the AEC regulation apply not only to the testing area, but to the whole Pacific all the way to Sausalito Harbor. And before he had finished, Mr. Wirin had said what could be said, in the circumstances, about the dangers to freedom of speech and of religion which, he declared, were being threatened by the government in this case.

Mr. Poole, in denying the relevance of the Reynolds case, was anxious to point out that amendments to the Atomic Energy Act were there specifically to regulate the relations between private industry and the AEC. The AEC, he contended somewhat later, has the normal rule-making powers of other government agencies, and these are sufficient to let the commission do what it wants to do to further its purposes. It is true, he admitted, that this is the only civil agency with jurisdiction of this kind over such a large area (Mr. Wirin had mentioned that the 1962 test areas approach in size the land area of the United States, exclusive of Hawaii and Alaska). Mr. Poole said that it was presently the position of the attorney general of the United States that under the said act, the commission can do all that he wants it to do, and that the Reynolds decision did not represent the attorney general's point of view. (The relevance of the attorney general's opinion in the matter escaped some of the people of the United States assembled in the court, but perhaps it was clear to their representative on the bench.) Having argued that the Atomic Energy Act was quite adequate, Mr. Poole then went on to argue that it was not as strong as it should be and therefore should be enforced with the utmost possible strictness.

Marshall Krause, for the defense, spoke of the dangerous vagueness of interpretation with which the government had applied the regulation in question. And then the judge found all three defendants guilty of willful disobedience and contempt of the restraining order and allowed them each to make a statement.

The Accused Speak

Harold Stallings made his first. Nothing that he said, he told the court, should be misconstrued as a defense intended to mitigate the penalties to himself that might result from his act. He said that he could lay no claim to absolute certainties, but that he found himself "on a path the walking of which is becoming more important to me than its destination." He set about trying to dispel what he thought were some current misconceptions about his character. He had been referred to as a captain: the image conveyed was one of command and resource, and "did not even hint at the seasick guy unable to even think for his own fear, willing to have his friends endanger themselves on that boat before himself." Words such as "conscience," "morality," "Quaker," had been used in referring to him and his actions, invoking an image of "the gentle religious, the otherworldly searchers after truth and salvation," and not "the greedy child—the guy who postures and grimaces—the one who delights in hiding from tough daily decisions behind a façade of big words and then runs to escape the consequences of his own indecision. . . . " But the weaknesses were there, and how could someone who knew that there were such flaws in him find any justification for being there in court under such circumstances:

Why didn't he run in shame from the hypocrisy of presenting himself there? Simply because I am a man. . . . Cecil Poole's question yesterday always hits me with fresh new import. "Hal Stallings—

are you flagrantly doing what you 'durn well please?' Where did you get the *right* to think you alone might be right?" I don't *know* that I'm right. Here is the paradox I find in myself: recognizing . . . that I am terribly human . . . I have had to try to act. I have tried to indicate my weakness, my propensity for selfishness. There is another side. What do I aspire to? To once in a while put some other person's comfort and safety before my own. I can't tell why . . . but sometimes I yearn to love another person as much as I do myself.

He indicated a desire for a world in which his children had a fair chance of growing up, and his sense of indebtedness to the orphans of a Japanese policeman who had died as a result of radiation received after the Hiroshima bomb blast there, when he had gone into the city to help the hurt.

Once in a while [Stallings said], it comes hard into me that there are fathers all over the world who have heard it said in my name that for various reasons if the situation so develops I will burn up their homes and their families. I yearn to tell them different. Sometimes I yearn to go unarmed to them and promise with my whole heart that no matter what may come into my hands, no matter what the threat to me or mine, they are safe to live in the same world with me. Pretentious as it may seem . . . I feel that I have acted out of my humanness. I hold no contempt for law, this court, or any person involved. . . . Yet I have come to that place where there are no alternatives. What may seem terribly complex to some seems terribly simple to me. I must not kill or hurt or threaten to kill or hurt. I must not, insofar as I have any power, let any be killed or hurt. These bomb tests and the getting ready for war are killing and hurting. I must go in weakness and confusion to put myself in the path of that killing.

Then he told the judge that he would accept the judge's decision and penalties "in the same spirit of goodwill with which you've accepted what I feel I must do."

It was Mr. Lazar's turn. His view of his arrest had not changed and he would not stand to speak. He said he believed that he should not cooperate with injustice. The judge consented to hear him even so. His tone was level, deliberate, and rational. He said that this was simply in the nature of a comment; the voyage had been his real statement. He had felt that he must act, that words were no longer enough. Our defense of freedom, he said, is robbing us of our freedom. We are becoming a centralized military state in which armaments and their institutions are considered to be of more importance than are individual rights. He knew, he confessed, that the United States was freer than some other countries and that freedom could not be absolute. But the tendency in this country is toward a continuing lessening of freedom. In opposing totalitarianism, we are becoming totalitarian ourselves. That, he suggested, was one thing which the voyage had been trying to say. By what right, he asked, did the government's attorney presume to speak (as he had done) for the "free world"? Would Japan, if asked, have approved of bomb testing? Would India, among others? Would the UN (whose secretary general had openly condemned the present test series— most recently on June 5, only three days before)?

The Pacific Ocean, Mr. Lazar said, is not a laboratory. Every test kills and pollutes and leads closer to a nuclear war, and the people have not been consulted. Is testing, he asked, adding to our security? The nuclear club is growing. The dangers of small wars turning into a nuclear war is increasing. Was this, the judge asked, relevant? Mr. Lazar said that he had been accused of behavior likely to cause irreparable injury to the United States and that he was addressing himself to that charge. He continued with suggestions for disarmament, foreign aid, and conversion to a peacetime economy. He said the voyage had been an attempt to appeal to people all over the world to challenge the military preparations of their governments. He had been called irresponsible, he said, but he believed that it was a citizen's responsibility to challenge irresponsible government. He asked to be released so that he could continue the voyage.

Mr. Yoes made a short statement. He said he believed he was standing in court representing other people who were unable to be there. He was asked whether, if he were released, he would observe the conditions of the restraining order, but he answered that as long as men like Mr. Stallings and Mr. Lazar were prepared to undertake acts such as these and could use his help, he could not promise not to help them.

Everyman had already made his statement some time earlier. He had said:

> Indede, deth was with me here. . . .
> Methynke, alas, that I must be gone
> To make my rekenynge and my dettes paye,
> For I se my tyme is nye spent awaye.

The government had one more motion to make. It asked to have the demonstration at the post office forbidden until the end of the test series, on the grounds that the demonstrators were acting in concert with the organizers of the voyage; according to Mr. Poole the word "conspiracy" might be applied to them. But the court decided to risk it just the same—anyway, Mr. Poole had other means at his disposal.

The Sentence

After lunch, Judge Sweigert made his statement. The government, as he emphasized, had composed the Atomic Energy Act and was carrying out the Dominic tests. The law, he said, could not satisfy all consciences. The assassination of Lincoln, after all, could be described as an act of conscience. The struggle for religious liberty appeared to him to be a record of the state's attempt to accommodate itself to the demands of conscience. From this remarkable view of history he turned to the Constitution of the United States and said that that document and its interpreters had tried to respect conscience "as far as possible"—even in war. In this case, however, no such former accommodations need apply, for the defendants had not been encroached on by the law, but had willfully and gratuitously gone out of their way to break the law. The courts, he said, are the zealous guardians of individual liberties, and the defendants have enjoyed the benefits of their protection. Nevertheless, the defendants' rights to freedom of speech, religion, travel, and the like were not involved in this case. But even if they had been, they would have to be exercised within limits imposed by the courts. The courts were the people's protection against dictatorship, he said, and the defendants had committed an act of violence upon the law and therefore against the whole of society. He sentenced them lightly—to thirty days each, but he had sustained the AEC regulation in question, and in the Pacific the United States government, respecting law in its own fashion, and unmenaced for the moment by sailboats or consciences, could continue to defend the free world with nuclear tests whether the free world wanted to be defended that way or not.

Not the Last Word

And around the post office itself, once the trial was over, a shift in feeling occurred. Marshal Heslep told Mr. Sandperl that the authorities would now have to get tougher and Mr. Sandperl replied that the demonstrators would have to get gentler. The marshal said that that was just what he was afraid of. A little later the demonstrators and some of the press heard the marshal announce that they would be charged with a felony if they remained in the building. The announcement later turned out to be incorrect. Thirty of the demonstrators sat in, in the familiar corridor, until they were dragged out. When they returned, under warning, they were arrested. Some walked and some were carried to the paddy wagons. (They would be booked on a charge of committing a nuisance—not a felony.) The picket line continued. The crowd blocked streets around the post office. Some of the crowd and some of the demonstrators were singing; the shouts of hecklers ("I was the toughest Marine in my outfit and I'd like to show the sons-of-bitches") and of the city police cracked above the songs. That afternoon a record peacetime arms budget was approved in Washington and the fifteenth test bomb in the series was exploded.

At the end of the play, after Everyman is dead and the angel has spoken, a learned Doctor comes on stage to propound the moral. As befits his office, he is dreadfully certain:

> None excuse may be there for Everyman,
> Alas! howe shall he do then?
> For after dethe amendes may no man make,
> For then mercy and pyte doth hym forsake.

But we have not reached that point yet. The angel has not even spoken. Or if he has, he has not been heard.

A NEW RIGHT ARM

(1963)

The nature of man is not what he is born as,
but what he is born for.
                                        —Aristotle

Apparently criticism has not yet vanished entirely (Oct. 27, 1962) although
our leaders have informed us that we are all behind them. Even in the
midst of those events which have been teaching us most recently what
we have in common (I mean the American quarantine of Cuba, and its
consequences), voices have been heard repeating that nuclear test ban
conferences are insufficient, since it seems likely that nuclear tests will
continue. And I have heard others who, in the face of circumstances,
have not ceased to take exception to peacetime military conscription. It
occurred to me that it might be possible for the government to disperse
or at least to baffle both criticisms by joining their subjects in a way
which should prove constructive and which might be adopted with no
revolutionary change of present policies. I confess that the plan which I
refer to was suggested to me by the problems themselves as they have
filtered through to the general public, and not by any specially classi-
fied material. Nevertheless, since this notion, so far as I know, has not
been advocated by anyone else to whom it may have occurred, I should
like to put it forward, with the reticence appropriate to a civilian.

Along with their expense in terms of money, their stimulating action
on the arms race, and their role in contaminating our food, our water,
our air, and our earth, one of the frequently raised objections to nuclear
explosions is the effect which they must be expected to have, and must
have had already, on the genetic structure of animal life, including, of

Reprinted from *Kulchur*, 3 (Autumn 1963).

course, man. It is scarcely surprising that there is wide disagreement about the number and gravity of the mutations which are inevitable in future embryos as a result of radiation exposure. Mutations in some cases may not appear at birth, and they may be spread over some thirty generations; these factors and others render estimation more difficult. However, certain essentials are clear. For instance, there is no dosage of radiation so small as to be "safe," generally speaking. Between conception and reproduction, any radiation that reaches the germ cells may produce mutations; the probability of its doing so is in direct proportion to the amount of radiation. The earth's crust, including elements in the human body, naturally produces a certain continuous level of "background radiation" which varies from place to place. The effect of this natural radioactivity on human genetics has been studied and the incidence of mutations normally resulting from it is known, within rough limits. The average proportional incidences of specific kinds of mutations are also known. As the amount of radiation in the environment increases, the total percentage of all genetic mutations will increase.

Not all mutations are harmful, but some 99 percent of them are. Unless a greatly accelerated mutation rate were to overwhelm them and endanger the future of the race itself, the remaining 1 percent can be considered as contributions to the evolutionary process. It is a view which requires a certain perspective and an ability to be philosophical about the cost, but some experts have met both requirements and have derived from the attitude a settled and articulate satisfaction. One can fancy their pleasure in the thought that man, having struggled against nature for so long, has found himself, in this if in little else, on her side at last. In 1959 the chances of genetically defective births were, at a low estimate, about two in a hundred.

In any considerable tally of genetic mutations the greater number will result in death, prenatal, perinatal, or premature. This again, in the opinion of experts, has its advantages. If he dies without reproducing, a mutant human removes an entire mutant strain from the current of human heredity. He may remove more than one, if he has been the recipient of more than one genetic mutation. In any event the dead are dead, past, present, or to come, and they are not the subject here. My concern is with that unknown but increasing number of future genetic defectives who may be expected to survive pregnancy, birth, infancy, childhood, and adolescence, and come eventually to man's estate: mature, if not complete human beings. The compassion which some of the experts have professed for these creatures has seemed to me rather conventional. Our century has taught us a great deal about the part which a sense of helplessness frequently plays in the experience of suffering. If there were a way of making these mutant persons feel that they had a normal, even a special responsibility for maintaining the circumstances of which they were a part, it might be possible to reduce the expressions of pity which decency still seems to require.

I should like to invoke for a moment the other critical theme I mentioned. Those who make a practice of decrying peacetime military conscription are apt to do so on several grounds. I shall give scarcely more consideration than I imagine the government does to their frequent but basically old-fashioned claim that the draft is an extensive erosion of the rights of American citizens. There is no need for the advocates of this plea to direct their discontent at the military services. They have only to look around them to discover suppression of choice, imposition of goals, regimentation of opinion; bureaucratic authoritarianism, uniforms, the logic of force, systematic waste, overwhelming destructiveness, and extensive erosion of individual rights in contemporary civilian life—and all these without economic security and the inculcation of military skills. From what is sometimes called a realistic point of view (and it is to such a point of view that I address my suggestions) some of the plaintiffs' other arguments are more respectable. For example, it is worth considering their contention—often implemented with quotation from prominent legislators—that the draft is inefficient both as regards our military and our civilian forces. As for the latter, it is argued, the draft disrupts education and careers both of which might be valuable to the national makeup. And for the former, there are those who maintain that a conscript system can scarcely meet the needs of a modern army, not because it cannot supply enough manpower, but because what is required is not quantity for a short period, but specialized skill available over long enough terms to justify the expensive training that is necessary to produce it. Besides, it is suggested that since the conscript has not chosen to spend months or years in the army, he may not regard the military calling with the enthusiasm which would make him most receptive to his training and might in the end bring him to identify himself with the service and regard it as an extension of himself and a second nature. What is wanted is a growing core of youth who are unalterably dedicated to the military profession as a way of life, a raison d'être, and who are committed to it as completely, and therefore

as early, as possible. From childhood. Even from birth. And there I have
returned to my earlier preoccupation.

I should like to inquire whether such an elite might not be supplied,
and well supplied, by the increasing population of genetic defectives
that exists and is guaranteed among us. Of course I am thinking only of
those defectives who could safely be counted on to enjoy a serviceable
longevity, and obviously I am ruling out the few among those—and
they would be very few—who would be totally or virtually inert. But
within these limits there is an often unappreciated and untapped reser-
voir of human functions, and some of the possible advantages of drawing upon it for military purposes suggest themselves at once. The
endowment, or even the potential endowment of these functions with
military capabilities might dissipate what is now a discouraging and
presumably hopeless attempt to hit upon the maximum number of
defectives that can reasonably be expected in a given generation, and it
should encourage scientists, both those employed by the government,
and others, to concentrate instead on the possible minimum figures.
Here they might reach an agreement more easily, adding thereby to our
understanding of our environment. The consideration of mutant persons not in terms of their handicaps but in terms of their possible
usefulness as soldiers would permit the government to extend to them
medical benefits and compensatory training such as would scarcely be
possible, or could not be administered with the same liberality, if the
defectives were simply left to their civilian fate and the hazards of
individual resources. Training thus given would not, as might otherwise be the case, appear to be leading nowhere. From the very beginning
the mutant trainee would have a specific end in view, one which
promised security and status both among his fellows and in relation to
the world at large. He would be relieved of the strain of competition, for
his functioning, once it had been turned into a military capacity, would
be in permanent demand. The stability factor is important. For whereas
a conscript may be assumed to have other courses open to him—jobs,
travel, a certain degree of choice in the use of his leisure—in the case of
a defective such alternatives are likely to be more limited and in some
instances virtually nonexistent. So that the mutant, if he is left to
discover his special condition by himself, in civil isolation, could be
expected to embrace with warmth a career which offered him a rank,
tenure, pride in having an official part in enormous power, and a
uniform to prove it. And this should be true at whatever moment the

opportunity is given to him after the age of choice—whether that age is taken to be the one at which candidates are now admitted to our military schools, or the one at which conscripts are now inducted, or the one at which citizens who meet the other qualifications are presently allowed to vote for the first time. (As regards the current age of conscripts, it is sometimes objected that they are inducted when they are too young to know their own minds. Without commenting on the general practicality of this contention, I note in passing that it cannot be considered applicable to defectives, whose choice, as I have indicated, would scarcely be improved by waiting.) Personally, however, I should think it preferable if the defective were not simply abandoned until so late to the more or less solitary and profitless exploration of his handicap. I should like to see him considered in his military potential as soon as such things as estimated longevity and average probable responsiveness to stimuli had been found adequate—if possible in the cradle. Aside from such mutations as manifest themselves only with later years, increasing experience with mutants and their statistics should add steadily to the probable accuracy of early selection. And the advantages of having the defective grow up in uniform should more than repay the additional cost. His military education and his compensatory training could, wherever feasible, take the same forms. In any event they would become inseparable in his mind. No matter what physical and mental processes finally allowed him to make such peculiar use of his imperfect organism as might be possible, they would be military. He could not fail to identify them with the context in which they became a part of himself, and the purpose which gave them to him in the first place. If any alternatives to a military future ever occurred to him he would be unlikely to think them attractive, for whatever his intelligence, he would come to feel that it was only as a military man that he was a man at all. In his case the term of enlistment would pose no problem.

Indeed its farsightedness, the provision it makes for unborn generations extending into a future as remote as anyone can imagine, is one of the most winning features of such a plan. It would not, after all, be a question of substituting mutants for the present personnel of our armed forces. According to some estimates there might not yet be enough defectives, within the lower practicable age limits, who would be usable, as the services are now organized. And even if the different estimates were to be reconciled and it was discovered that the current supply more than met the need, the expanded training facilities required could not be instituted overnight. At best, for the present, it would be a matter of feeding in defectives gradually, through training centers, to those military uses which they could fulfill, and the number of these would surely increase with experience in handling and placing such persons.

Nevertheless it is only to be expected that such a suggestion would be greeted, at the outset, with a certain amount of skepticism. In this it would be no different from many familiar and convenient expedients of our age, when they were new. Such initial hesitation, except in times of crisis, is one of the ornaments of our democracy.

It will be objected, and perhaps with some insistence, that the mutants produced would not be capable of adequately supporting the burden of any military tasks. The objection, though sweeping, is understandable, rooted as it is in established military practice. Until now it could be assumed that the decisive situation toward which military planning must be directed would be an encounter of armed units in the field. Even the advent of air power did not change this essentially; certainly it did not alter the theory guiding the selection of military personnel. Rather, it called forth a new, and perhaps a final flowering of the process whereby the best physical specimens and the most perfect coordination and mental alertness and adaptability available were quite naturally singled out to be sent to the front lines, whether these were on land, at sea, or in the air. Even if it were nothing more than a profound attachment to this older tradition which encouraged some military theorists to cling to the possibility of a limited war and to claim that infantry is not obsolete, their plea should not be simply passed over. Police actions, undeclared guerrilla warfare, lightning invasions of aggressors in order to negotiate from established positions, assistance here and there of beleaguered allies, all of these may continue, in default of a full-scale conflict, and it should be considered whether the individual operations which make them possible could be carried out, in whole or in part, by defectives. Again I think the answer is gradualism. There would be few, even among the opponents of such an idea, who would maintain that a man with a cleft palate is automatically incapable of shooting a gun, of pointing it at a given person or thing when told to do so, or of marching, running, or creeping to the place where his capacity for disciplined killing would be of most use. Cleft palates, of course, are not typical of mutants, they are simply one deformity among many. But they are an example of a kind of congenital affliction which, while hampering in some civil pursuits and pleasures, need not be considered a military liability. The classification, it is true, extends to malformations which may in fact be reparable—web (if not fused) fingers, absent knee caps, bony obtrusions, flaps, curvatures, missing extremities, some sexual inadequacies, etc.—and includes at one extreme deviations so slight as to border on the norm. And deformities which can be cured or ignored might neither require nor profit by the special occupational provisions I am suggesting. Indeed, the triviality of some mutations, I believe, has been recognized already, on some occasions, by some draft boards. I think it is plain, however, that my chief concern is with those mutations which, while not destroying nor completely paralyzing existence, may render civilian life peculiarly featureless, colorless, vacant, and unproductive. I cannot think that their number will be so small as to be negligible, and I shall consider their possible uses in further detail. What I am advocating, for a start, with regard to general policy and the practice of local draft boards, is a simple reversal of emphasis: not the induction from time to time of the minor mutation in a spirit of carelessness or tolerance, but a sustained effort to find places for mutants in the military future wherever possible. Individual cases would still have to be considered on their merits. The important thing is the establishment of a principle.

Even if we continue to envisage hostilities more or less conventionally, it is obvious that a great deal of modern military activity does not require physical alacrity or wholeness. A person without legs or with a comparable degree of immobility might be taught to navigate, to be at home at a desk, to handle accounts or statistics, to manipulate a radio, a direction-finder, a computer or other machine or instrument, or to engage in any of the military operations of this kind which can be performed without rising. Still with the traditional scene in mind, it would be unfair not to consider the uniformed roles which might be opened to that other and numerous category of mutants, the mental defectives. It seems obvious that such mutants could be used for a number of time-honored military functions where little is required of a uniform except that it be complete, be filled, stand upright, and move in concert with other uniforms at the enunciation of certain loud and simple noises. It might be profitable to determine how far below the intelligence level at which some rudimentary literacy is still possible the manual of arms can still be mastered if training is begun early enough. It might be practicable for a large mobile corps of exquisitely disciplined mental defectives to be organized for the sole purpose of parading at public functions in whatever uniform the occasion required, thereby freeing the rest of the armed forces from an activity whose chief surviving use in contemporary circumstances is to arouse an unreasoning empathic response among the civilian spectators.

It is not impossible that, if such a corps were instituted in the immediate future, and without a public relations campaign, there might be scattered objections on grounds of taste, but they need not be taken seriously. There is no reason to assume that mental defects (with certain exceptions) would be physically obvious in parades, and even if they were, the most elementary consideration of justice should forbid us to discriminate on grounds of sensibility against personal attributes which their possessors cannot help and which we may already have been instrumental in producing. With regard to the effectiveness of the public image, or the plan as a whole, such objections would scarcely merit attention. They have been heard before but they have never yet prevented any realistic enterprise in our society. Instead it has become a matter of commonplace observation how easily the other pressures of the economy manage to effect sweeping and profound changes in taste— one has only to consider how quickly the public ceased to be shocked by pictures of the victims of Dachau and Hiroshima, and how readily it accepts the annual changes in the appearance of automobiles.

As for combat functions, while there have been exceptions in practice, modern theory, as I have implied, has been inclined to assume that the front lines were not places for grossly subnormal intelligence. The theory is debatable at best, though it must be admitted that there is a quaint fastidiousness to it reminiscent of the duelling scruples historically attributed to gentlemen. But since in present-day warfare it may no longer be possible to choose which section of the population shall supply the casualties, perhaps the moment has come to consider whether it is really important what sort of brain works the trigger finger if told to do so. A certain accuracy with weapons can be acquired, frequently, even by the possessors of a very limited intellect. This, in combination with an automatic obedience to commands which the defectives had been taught to associate with the elementary fabric of existence, might well fit them (if they were reasonably sound and adaptable in their other limbs) for use as assault troops or for other costly but essentially uninventive military operations. It would be as well to anticipate the possibility of an objection here, arising from a nostalgia for individual responsibility in situations of individual danger. Such objections, however, can be expected to come, if at all, from those few civilians whose bent is philosophical or historical rather than realistic. There should be few hesitations, of this kind at least, from the military. I am not relying, for my confidence, on the career soldier's traditional reticence about matters not within the competence of his rank. I am simply considering that such a view of individual responsibility, proffered as a general criticism in a military context, would be likely to sound incongruous. From the moment a recruit enters armed service at present, his individual responsibility is systematically narrowed to the carrying out of certain prescribed and codified functions, and his total situation is conceived of as, ideally, a command. Vanity apart, it is hard to see how the logic of military efficacy on which this procedure is based would be outraged by the combat use, in specific simple circumstances, of human organisms capable of predictable and adequate obedience, even though otherwise poorly endowed.

Until now I have been concerned with recruits destined (at least at first) for the ranks, with conventional and indeed rather old-fashioned circumstances in view. The matter of officers is, as always, more special, but some of the same principles apply. The presence of a genetic defect does not exclude the normal possibility that a mutant may have the other prerequisites of officer material, whatever these are taken to be at a particular time. And of course many deformities which, if properly allowed for, would not incapacitate a private soldier, need not incommode an officer either. I envisage a certain, and perhaps impressive, number of defectives working their way up from the ranks and receiving commissions in the normal way. On the other hand the officers thus obtained have never yet represented more than a fraction of those required, and a large percentage of officers has been fed into the armed forces as a matter of course through both private and government-run military schools. In considering the supply of mutant officers I should like to follow the example of these institutions and try to look well into the future.

As everyone knows, the amount of specialized training currently needed in the armed forces, and the consequent desirability of long-term enlistments, have been occasioned by the steadily growing importance of complex machinery in virtually all kinds of military operations. As the tendency increases it seems more and more reasonable to suppose that it will continue to do so, and it is possible to suggest that, as a result of this trend, the concept of the officer has already undergone a modification. To be sure, the traditional image of the officer as a military person in charge of the military functioning of other military persons still exists and of course must continue to do so, though here too, machinery, as I hope to indicate, may acquire an increasing importance in the actual transmission of military authority. Alongside this image a new one has begun to grow: that of the military person who is an officer not so much because of his authority over other military personnel as because of his role as an operator of key military equipment. (The distinction is likely to remain practicable as long as the conventional one between personnel and equipment is of use.) Looking for an example, the civilian is apt to think first of such machines as aircraft or spacecraft, recognizing that the operator of a one-man fighter or satellite comes closer to this contemporary image than does the commander of, say, a bomber which carries a more or less numerous crew. But the new concept would be equally applicable to persons in charge of specialized computers, firing systems, tracking systems, communication systems, and other delicate and ingenious instruments for measuring, tabulating, adjusting, regulating, evaluating, and choosing—machines which have come to assume immense and indeed crucial importance in the total structure of military power and the operation of command centers, and which, as the intricate process of military administration has been brought closer and closer to the actual process and delivery of kill, have themselves become weapons.

Let us consider for a moment the possible future of the traditional image of the officer, and the opportunities it may present to the mutant. It is worth observing that as the gap between the top command centers and the process of kill has been narrowed by technological advances in communication, and other faculties, the gap between actual personnel units has tended to grow wider in many branches of military activity, and in a large number of instances has long since assumed the status of an institution, with a system and equipment of its own. The crew of a bomber may serve again as a familiar if somewhat pedestrian example. At no great distance from each other—at a distance, in fact, which at other times and in other places would have permitted them to converse easily without raising their voices, to toss small objects to each other, to recognize insignia and even eye color—the members have adapted themselves to the expedient of communicating through a machine, a convenience which in itself effects the form and therefore the substance of their communication, and while it joins them does so in a manner which resembles a separation and makes it relatively unimportant whether their distance from each other is a matter of inches or a month's walk. The example can be multiplied throughout the armed services, irrespective of the actual distances which are usual between communicating instruments; the use of walkie-talkies by field units of nearly all ground forces is an obvious instance of the same tendency in relatively conventional disciplines. Quite simply, machines have been adopted in a rapidly increasing number of military circumstances in order to "maintain contact," and naturally enough the contact has come to depend on the machines. One result has been a growing simplification. Distance, as I have indicated, has been reduced in importance until it is possible to say that it has been virtually suspended from such contacts except in circumstances where it is relevant to the desired communication. It has, for practical purposes, been rendered irrelevant unless it is part of the subject of the message. And distance, as might have been expected, is not the only condition whose relevance has been reduced by such methods of contact. It need not be important to the contact maintained whether the human initiator is tall or short, whether he walks normally or can walk at all, whether he is color-blind, totally blind, or was born with congenital amputations of hands, feet, arms, or legs, with multiple deformities of the tubular bones, with improperly formed skull bones or a cleft spinal column, with Waardenberg's syndrome, "cat's ear," "bayonet hand," or "lobster hand," provided only that none of these interfere with the actual transmission of his message. Everything about him, in fact, except his function as an input at the other end of the contact, is irrelevant. Of course I am speaking theoretically, and in practice this point has probably seldom been reached yet (though studies which might make it more usual are progressing, and I shall mention them). I am merely describing a tendency to render irrelevant those attributes of military personnel which do not serve a military function. The potential applicability of this tendency to mutant personnel, including mutant officer material, is readily apparent. As an officer's contacts with those above him and beneath him come increasingly to consist of messages mechanically transmitted and received, it should be more possible to use officers, even within what we have called the traditional image, without regard to anything except their specifically military function, viz., their ability to receive and transmit appropriate military messages. Considering this possibility in its simplest and most practical light, it is easy to envisage how a large number of those sensory reflexes

and motor capacities which might be deficient in the officer-input
might be compensated for insofar as might be necessary; thereafter it
might be simply a matter of application of already existing mechanical
aids. If, for example, closed circuit television is an adequate implement
for teaching history to civilian children, it could perhaps be adapted for
such military purposes as teaching the manual of arms to recruits,
normal or others, for giving instruction in missile control, biological
and chemical warfare and similar military subjects, and in transmit-
ting orders involving visual material. Two-way television, as has been
suggested, might be of use in preserving and indeed improving discipline.
Monitoring sets might be provided in all barracks, offices, mess halls,
washrooms, and other installations, and their use would allow officers
to impose whatever aspect, or to retain whatever degree of anonymity,
they desired. Mutant officers within the traditional image, who preferred not to have their faces seen, for whatever reason, would of course
profit by such a development.

As for the new image, in which the officer's concern is essentially
with machines themselves, the potential field for mutants is perhaps
still more promising. Among the many branches of research which are
encouraging in this connection, I should like to mention one recent
growth of applied psychology which is aimed precisely at the reduction
of irrelevant factors from the output of transmission systems whose
input is supplied by human operators, and consequently at improving
the possibility of being able to regard the human operator simply as a
function. The study is known as Operational Analysis. Recent pioneer
work on the subject has been undertaken as a result of suggestions
stemming from the Armament Laboratory, Air Matériel Command, and
experiments have been carried out under contract with Psychology
Branch, Aero Medical Laboratory, Engineering Division, Air Matériel
Command. Operational Analysis is an investigation of human responses
with a view to designing machines capable of filtering out unwanted
fluctuations (or "error") from the input of the human operator. At
present the study seems especially valuable in developing tracking and
pursuit systems. Ideally, and in general, however, it should be possible
to design equipment which, whatever its purpose, could be run by any
simple and dependable motor response, whether or not the operator
who delivered the input could understand the possible uses of the
equipment's output. The immense practical advantages of such a possibility, of course, might well include the ability to use heretofore

inadequate human systems to operate intricate equipment whose end function was beyond their knowledge or indeed their comprehension.

Regarding the mutant soldier or officer himself, as these developments and his own career in the service continued, he must certainly become aware that his deformities were irrelevant in his military capacity and existed only from a civilian point of view, and the knowledge should serve to further strengthen his attachment to the uniform. The fact that the likelihood of marriage is reduced for one reason or another among certain kinds of mutants should allow them to devote a peculiar and celibate fervor to the military calling, which they could regard with reason as their foster parent, their family, and the home and sense of their existence. That part of the defective's apparent solitariness which is the active awareness of an impeding difference would be given a situation where it could develop naturally; he would be among his fellows, and his uniform would declare that he was not ashamed of it. That part of the defective's secretiveness which might prove to be essential to him might also be of use. And the arbitrary selection of individuals for military service, which now gives rise to complaints of injustice, would no longer be assailable, because it would no longer be human.

I must say again that even with the most determined efforts such a system could not be expected tomorrow. There might in fact be enough defectives in the present population of this country (some two million) to supply a good part of the services by the time the services could be made ready for them, but those whose condition is probably due to weapons tests are at this writing outweighed many times over by those whose occurrence is part of the natural order. And though the ratio can be expected to change as the mutation rate slowly rises, it cannot be expected to do so in such a way as to make it apparent which mutations are due to which causes—a fact which makes it difficult for the government to assess its exact minimum responsibilities. It may be necessary for the armed forces to assume charge of all recognizable mutants as the mutations manifest themselves, in recognition of the fact that the state's responsibility for their condition, if it is not yet preponderant, is growing, and in the knowledge that the use that can be made of them is at last in sight. The public, of course, would have to be prepared for such a move, and for developments arising from it, but the military purpose should be a sufficient answer to any attempt to discredit the plan as being socialistic. Other helpful preparatory steps could be taken at once. The education of mutant children, whether or not already in uniform, surely merits attention. While favoring their induction as early as possible into the service best suited for them, I am inclined to feel that where possible they should have a certain degree of educational contact with civilian children. I would suggest, for instance, that certain nonmilitary subjects such as anti-Communism should be taught to mixed mutant and civilian children. The presence of the mutants could not fail to impress the civilian children with certain realities of the situation, while the knowledge must inevitably add to the mutants' sense of their special purpose and their feeling of confidence. Questions such as the commendability of organizing a female defectives' auxiliary, and at what age, and whether or not changes in the uniform should be contemplated with a view to mutant-adaptability—these and other related topics might benefit by early consideration, and might serve as talking points in a public relations campaign to introduce the idea.

Finally, even with the fullest use of a steadily growing source, it is difficult to visualize a future in which some military functions would not be better filled by normal individuals. I do not see that this represents a problem. What I have been suggesting is that those who would ordinarily be conscripted should be replaced by what might otherwise be an idle and inevitably discontented segment of the population. For the other military needs—as has been observed of tax collectors, policemen, and executioners—there will always be volunteers. However, as the number of mutants grows and as the military system makes more efficient use of them as a result both of automation and practice, the need for normal personnel may grow more and more limited. I suggest without levity that as a result of making the armed forces a life's work for defectives, the pride in uniform may so increase (while the attractions of civilian liberty continue to dwindle) that where in the past we have heard of cases of conscripts mutilating themselves in order to avoid military service, it may become necessary to institute means of discouraging sound individuals from deliberately stunting, deforming, or maiming themselves in order to embellish their chances of being accepted.

ON BEING LOYAL

(Merwin read the following statement before a poetry reading at the State University of New York at Buffalo on Oct. 14, 1970.)

I must ask your forbearance for not following that introduction at once with poems, as I had expected to do, and would have preferred to do. There are a few things that I feel I have to say first.

I was invited here last August, to spend the best part of three days, give a reading of my poems, and talk with students twice in some manner that might be construed as lecturing them. I did not know, when I accepted, that there was a string attached. I must say at once that the members of the faculty here who invited me were unaware of this string when they did so, that they told me about it at once, and with shame, when they discovered it a couple of weeks ago, and that they have since tried their best to disentangle it. It was not until a few hours ago that it became clear that the string was inseparable from the pocketbook.

This was the form of it. When I came here I would be asked to sign the following, pursuant to Section 3002, Education Law of the State of New York, as amended: "I do hereby pledge and declare that I will support the Constitution of the United States, and the Constitution of the State of New York, and that I will faithfully discharge the duties of the position of ——— [in my case, I understand, the wording here would be 'visiting lecturer'] according to the best of my ability."

Words have something essential to do with my having been asked here in the first place—but not this kind of language. I suppose I understand the purpose of the demand for such pledging and declaring. I mean, I cannot imagine what other purpose it can have than to serve as a trap for such teachers as might be tempted to voice political views unwelcome to those currently in positions of political power, at least while the teachers are within the walls of what are probably still the freest institutions of our society. (I mean, in case anyone wonders what institutions I am referring to, the universities—even the state universities.)

I have not asked who else may have signed this statement nor for what reasons. That is none of my business. Others perhaps stand to lose things of real value to them by refusing to sign. As for me, I was told that it could be made easy for me; that I might append to my signature my reservations, whatever they might be. But I saw no reason why I should be thus maneuvered into rendering my signature meaningless— for that is what it would have come to—for the sake of money. In my own case, if I did not sign I could not be fired. I would merely not be paid the money that I had been offered when I was invited to come here. The money is Caesar's, and those are Caesar's terms. It seemed to me that I had no choice: and I will not sign this thing. I believe I owe those who framed this condition no explanation for my refusal. I am not sure that they would understand one. I am not sure, to tell the truth, that I can fully explain my refusal to anyone, but I want to take this occasion to try to set down a few of my reasons, not for them, nor for anyone who may have been paid to sit here tonight, but for us. Well, yes, for them too; for all of us. I hope you will bear with me if my reasons, as I try to formulate them, seem to you—as Thomas Jefferson put it—self-evident.

And at the head of my own hurried and necessarily incomplete statement I would like to quote (correctly, I hope, because I'm doing it from memory) a question which I think must be described as rhetorical, from the Stoic Epictetus: "Can the soldiers' oath be compared to ours? For they have sworn to obey Caesar before everything, but we to respect ourselves first of all."

Let me deal first with a few minor quibbles. Legal language presumably has a precision of its own, perhaps even when it sounds—as it does here—to mean not, but blunder round about a meaning. What are these duties of a visiting lecturer which I am to discharge faithfully, in the opinion of heaven knows who among the politicians of this sovereign state? I asked no favor of them, and I am not grateful to them for being put in a position in which it might appear as though I had. I was asked to come here. It seems to me that I am, at the moment, faithfully discharging my duty in addressing anyone, including myself: I am trying, in a given situation, to tell the truth. As for the reading or speaking of my poems, I will not be accountable to these faceless worthies on that subject for the sake of money, even though it were more money than they can pretend to command.

Next, the signer pledges himself to "support" these two constitutions. I take the provision seriously—perhaps more seriously than the framer of the oath. And I have to confess, for one thing, that I am not at the moment deeply conversant with the constitution of the State of New York, and would scarcely have had time to study it properly between being told the conditions under which I might be paid, and this evening. I have a longer acquaintance—of an amateur sort—with the Constitution of the United States. It is one of the many subjects that we are frequently told should be left to professionals to interpret—unless it's a question of swearing to support it, despite the limitations of our private understanding.

Speaking from my own limitations, I cannot believe that the framers of the Constitution of the United States meant it to be a humiliating experience to be an American citizen. I find the existence of this oath, and the demand to sign it, here, now, for such reasons, humiliating, and I would find it still more shaming if I were to sign it, in these circumstances. It seems to me, in my position as an ordinary, relatively helpless citizen who has never sought public office, that I could not better support the Constitution of the United States—whatever about it I respect, and whatever its authors meant to protect—than by refusing to sign a statement which is clearly a small legislative outrage against individual liberty, perpetrated in its name.

I believe that what the legislators who framed and adopted this condition had in mind was not the Constitution but only the interpretation of it that suited their immediate convenience. I am far from sure that I could promise to support that, when they apparently saw no inconsistency between the Bill of Rights and the loyalty oath in question, in a situation like this.

I know that someone can usually be paid to argue more quickly, more cleverly, more deviously, probably more convincingly, than the ordinary citizen. In a society based on buying and persuading to buy, this is a phenomenon that we watch daily, and that compounds the temptation to despair. One virtue of the situation, perhaps, is that it drives us back—if we had needed to be driven back—to things that cannot be bought. I was asked to come here not because I am, in fact, a visiting lecturer (that was simply the category in which I was put, for administrative purposes) but because those who invited me thought of me as a poet. What does that have to do with buying and selling? If I am a poet—and I say that with complete seriousness—what responsibilities, what loyalties does that entail? I hope I wouldn't presume to prescribe them for anyone else. Occasionally, in my own case, I think I know. I remember Bertrand Russell saying that if a poet can't be independent, no one else can be. I'm not sure he had that the right way around. It seems to me that in so far as a man prizes some spring of independence— independence from the cant of economics and the tyranny of history—in himself, the hope of being fully human, which is integral to all poetry, remains alive.

As for me, whatever independence I can bear seems precious to me, something not to be sold for a bit of money, or a bit of security, or the approval of a few of the leaders of a corrupt and desperate society. I am not what is sometimes called "politically minded." Politics in themselves bore me profoundly, and the assumption of the final reality of the power to manipulate other men's lives merely depresses me. But injustice, official brutality, and the destruction on a vast scale of private liberties are all around me and I cannot pretend that it's not so, nor that I can accept such things, when I have a chance to say no to them. Section 3002 of the Education Law of the State of New York, as amended, seems to me, layman that I am, a deliberate degradation of all that the authors of the Bill of Rights had in mind.

It is not really surprising to me that such a situation should obtain at a time when the laws of the United States, as currently interpreted, apparently condone the continuation of an undeclared, racist war conducted against small countries—heaven knows how many of them at this moment—halfway around the world, and when the laws of the State of New York permit police entry without warning, and the holding, month after month, without trial, of the Panthers in New York City. Is it, after all, those who protest these circumstances, or those who perpetuate them, who are displaying the real contempt for the Constitution of the United States—and, for all I know, that of the State of New York? I hope there is never a better time to say that I believe that the insistence on individual liberty and poetry itself rise from the same source—what Keats called the truth of the imagination, and what others have called the human spirit. And I hope I may never hesitate in placing my loyalty to that source, as and when I can recognize it (for no one else can recognize it for me) before my loyalty to any state document or institution.

Those, at any rate, are some of the reasons why I refused to sign. I have spoken of them to no one else here, and the responsibility for what I have said cannot be laid in whole or in part upon any member of the faculty of this university. Now I am going to read anyway, and you will all know what I mean if I call it a free reading.

ON BEING AWARDED
THE PULITZER PRIZE

I've been informed that I have been awarded the Pulitzer Prize for poetry for 1971.

I am pleased to know of the judges' regard for my work, and I want to thank them for their wish to make their opinion public.

But after years of the news from Southeast Asia, and the commentary from Washington, I am too conscious of being an American to accept public congratulation with good grace, or to welcome it except as an occasion for expressing openly a shame which many Americans feel, day after day, helplessly and in silence.

I want the prize money to be equally divided between Alan Blanchard (Cinema Repertory Theater, Telegraph Avenue, Berkeley, California)—a painter who was blinded by a police weapon in California while he was watching American events from a roof, at a distance—and the Draft Resistance.

W. S. Merwin

Montana, *May, 1971*

To the Editors:

As a fellow citizen whose views on American foreign policy are, I should guess, pretty much the same as his, as a fellow poet and, let me add, an admirer, and as a onetime member of the Pulitzer Poetry Prize jury, I feel it is my duty to say that, in my opinion, Mr. W. S. Merwin's public refusal to accept the prize money, as reported in your *Review* of June 3, was an ill-judged gesture.

To begin with, it implies that the Pulitzer juries are politically official bodies, which they certainly are not. On the contrary, if there were, as, thank God, there is not, a living American poet of major importance who openly supported our intervention in Vietnam or George Wallace, as Yeats came out in favor of Macduffy's Blueshirts, I think it highly unlikely that he would be awarded the Pulitzer Prize for Poetry.

Secondly, Mr. Merwin has no right, if he does not wish to receive the money, to dictate to others how it shall be spent. I should have thought the obvious thing for him to do, feeling as he does, was to accept the money and then privately donate it to the causes he has at heart.

Lastly, the impression made on the reader by his gesture is the exact opposite of what, I am certain, he intended: it sounds like a personal publicity stunt. His position, if carried to its logical conclusion, would require him to abstain from any publication in the United States, for every time a magazine publishes a poem of his, or a member of the public buys one of his volumes, a poet receives "public congratulation."

W. H. Auden

Hinterholz, Austria

W. S. Merwin *replies:*

I'm sorry to learn of Mr. Auden's admiration for my writing from a statement that calls in question the intelligibility of a piece that I was at pains to make as clear—though as brief—as possible.

I don't see how my comment on receiving the Pulitzer Prize (June 3 issue) implies that the juries are "politically official bodies." (The organizers of concerts in Spain are not, I imagine, "politically official bodies" either, most of them, and yet the meaning of Casals's refusal to play in Spain seems plain to most people.) On the other hand the prize is one of the two or three that receive most attention in this country, and for that reason I was moved, in a way that I am sure is familiar to Mr.

Auden, to direct what public attention there might be, in my case, toward what seems to me most important in my present relation to the public of the country in which I was born.

I can't see what was "ill-judged" in that, nor why it should be any more surprising than my feeling about the war itself. On the contrary, if I had behaved, in the circumstances, as though I thought that the only permissible response to the award was silence, there would have been real grounds for questioning my respect for those connected with the giving of it. Is it, after all, dishonoring the present distinction to use it to register once again an abhorrence at being swept along, as we are, and most of the time anonymously, in this evil?

I thought I had made it clear that what I did was not intended as a comment upon or a prescription for the behavior of anyone connected with the prize. If I did not, I meant to do so by implication, and I mean to do so still more directly now.

Then, I did receive the money. I "dictated" how it was to be spent only to my bank. I imagined, rightly or not, that the purpose for which I did so would be better served by making the act public. I didn't and I don't believe that that could be construed—except willfully—as a publicity stunt. If anything of the kind had been my intention, surely I might have gone about things differently.

As for what Mr. Auden terms the "logical conclusion" of my position (i.e., not publishing at all) I've thought of that, too, logically or not— haven't we all? But the logic of many kinds of mourning would be to die. And yet we mourn, at times, and still hope to go on living. I'm sorry if he was troubled by it, but what I did was an act of mourning, and I can't regret the form of it.

IV

Poetics and the Translator's Mirror:
Essays and Statements

ON TRANSLATION

From "A Sight of the Bright Life"

(1972)

Every approach to the indigenous literature of the Americas, and in particular to those works whose forms and main or entire impulse antedate the European conquest, is troubling, and this is so in close proportion to the degree to which the reconstruction evokes the life and excitement of the original. The fact that the reconstructions are indispensable to us common readers—that our knowledge of these words out of the past of the Americas in which we were born and learned to speak depends (entirely, in most cases) on their representations in languages brought from Europe by the same conquest that overran the American natives—is and should be a part of what troubles us, as it is part of the uneasy elusive richness of our cultural lives, and of the bad conscience and sense of inherited deprivation which these works stir in us.

We come to them as to remnants salvaged from the burned-out libraries of the East, and even as our means of comprehending some of the surviving works appear to improve, they shed light as well on the surrounding void, making clearer how much has been lost. They remind us that the libraries are still burning, in Vietnam and Cambodia, in Latin America, and in our own West, under the auspices of the same unleashed rapacity and self-righteousness that engineered the destruction of our Indies from the beginning.

For unless our concern with these works is nothing but dilettantism,

Review of Munro S. Edmonson, trans., *The Book of Counsel: The Popol Vuh of the Quiche Maya of Guatemala*. Reprinted with permission from *The New York Review of Books*. Copyright © 1972 Nyrev, Inc.

vanity (amateur or professional), the collector's disguise of idleness, one thing that troubles us in their presence is the growing certainty that what has been lost was rightfully ours, a part of ourselves not only insofar as we are Americans, but insofar as we are a people—or people—at all. As for being Americans, the dead (if only in Blake's sense) who have acted in our name, the speculators, the exploiters, the Andrew Jacksons, the Nixons, seem never to have had any doubt that the designation meant simply belonging to an immense enterprise for the unlimited bloating of the members' egos, and they still call this pathetic club their dream. Whereas many of the best of the invaders and their descendants have spent much of their lives trying to determine, for their own sakes and ours, just what, in fact, it might mean to be American. The inquiry, more often than not, has bespoken a painful awareness of something missing, of a handicap inherent in the unhealing rawness of their—and our—situation.

There must be few instances in history of a population telling itself as often and as piously that it was a "people," and with as vague and ill-imagined a notion of what the term entails, as we have done, and do. Yet we have only to open the *Popol Vuh,* the sacred book of the Quiche Maya Indians—even transposed into another language—to recognize that the voice that is speaking to us is that of "a people" in a different sense, in the sense of Nietzsche's "Where there is still a people, it does not understand the state and hates it as the evil eye, and the sin against customs and rights." Whereas we, if we are a people at all, or are still, or ever were, are now perched incongruously on the base of the new idol itself, the state, as though a new flood were all around us. When it comes to being people in the sense of being our free selves, we are drawn with a peculiar insistence by these works to the recognition that what of America has been lost to us was ours like our own forgotten dreams, and that it had something to impart to us about ourselves, which we may now have to grope for in nameless bewilderment, before we can truly awaken.

It is ironic but not surprising that the very time when we realize such a loss should also produce a new attitude to the value of the works themselves, embodied in new scholarship and perhaps most of all in new translations. I am thinking, among others, of the translators in Jerome Rothenberg's collections *Technicians of the Sacred* and *Shaking the Pumpkin;* of Rothenberg's own translations and theories on the subject; of the magazine *Alcheringa,* edited by Rothenberg and Dennis

Tedlock (in which a section from Edmonson's *Popol Vuh* first appeared); of Tedlock's own Zuñi translations and his critical writing on the subject of translating "primitive" works; of such productions as the beautiful reprint, in 1969, of the Navajo ceremonial *Where the Two Came to Their Father,* with a commentary by Joseph Campbell, a work which I mention in particular because it invites thematic comparison with sections of the *Popol Vuh.* Professor Edmonson's work, both the broad and agile erudition and the ground-breaking translation, at once takes a salient place in this wave of interest and involvement.

Foreword to *Selected Translations 1968–1978*

(1979)

When Pope set out to translate Homer almost everything (as it appears to us) was known beforehand. He knew who most of his immediate readers would be: they had subscribed for the translations. They, in turn, knew—or thought they knew—who Homer was, and they knew the text, in the original. Both the subscribers and the translator took it for granted that the proper form for heroic verse, in English, must of course be the heroic couplet. Pope's work was expected to display the wit, elegance, and brilliance with which he could render a generally accepted notion of the Homeric poems into a familiar English verse form.

Since the eighteenth century, and especially since the beginning of modernism, more and more translations have been undertaken with the clear purpose of introducing readers (most of them, of course, unknown to the translators) to works they could not read in the original, by authors they might very well never have heard of, from cultures, traditions, and forms with which they had no acquaintance. The contrast with Pope's situation is completed by the phenomenon that has appeared with growing frequency in the past half-century, of poet-translators who do not, themselves, know the languages from which they are making their versions, but must rely, for their grasp of the originals, on the knowledge and work of others.

New—or different—assumptions mean different risks. New assumptions about the meaning of the word *translation,* whether or not they are defined, imply different aspects of the basic risk of all translation, however that is conceived. Which is no risk at all, in the terms of the most common cliché on the subject: that all translation is impossible. We seem to need it, just the same, insofar as we need literature at all. In our time, an individual or social literary culture without it is unthinkable. What is it that we think we need? We begin with the idea that it is the original—which means our relative conception of the original, as scholars, potential translators, or readers. At the outset, the notion is probably not consciously involved with any thought of the available means of translation. The "original" may even figure as something that might exist in more forms than one, just as it can be understood by more than one reader. But if we take a single word of any language and try to find an exact equivalent in another, even if the second language is closely akin to the first, we have to admit that it cannot be done. A single primary denotation may be shared; but the constellation of secondary meanings, the moving rings of associations, the etymological echoes, the sound and its own levels of association, do not have an equivalent because they cannot. If we put two words of a language together and repeat the attempt, the failure is still more obvious. Yet if we continue, we reach a point where some sequence of the first language conveys a dynamic unit, a rudiment of form. Some energy of the first language begins to be manifest, not only in single words but in the charge of their relationship. The surprising thing is that at this point the hope of translation does not fade altogether, but begins to emerge. Not that these rudiments of form in the original language can be matched—any more than individual words could be—with exact equivalents in another. But the imaginative force which they embody, and which single words embody in context, may suggest convocations of words in another language that will have a comparable thrust and sense.

By "rudiments of form" I mean recognizable elements of verbal order, not verse forms. I began with what I suppose was, and perhaps still is, a usual preconception about the latter: that fidelity in translating a poem should include an ambition to reproduce the original verse form. Besides, I started translating partly as a discipline, hoping that the process might help me to learn to write. Pound was one of the first to recommend the practice to me. I went to visit him at St. Elizabeth's in the '40s, when I was a student. He urged me to "get as close to the original as possible," and told me to keep the rhyme scheme of the poems I was translating, too, if I could, for the exercise as much as anything else. He was generous. And eloquent about what the practice could teach about the possibilities of English. He recommended that I should look, just then, at the Spanish *romancero,* and I did; but it was almost fifteen years before I actually made versions of many of the *romances* — and without the original rhyme schemes. I kept to his advice, at the time. When I did come, gradually, to abandon more and more often the verse forms of poems that I was translating, I did not try to formulate any precise principle for doing so. Translation is a fairly empirical practice, usually, and the "reasons" for making particular choices, however well grounded in scholarship, are seldom wholly explicable. I would have recognized, probably quite early, a simple reluctance to sacrifice imagined felicities of the potential English version, to keep a verse pattern that was, in a sense, abstract. The preference seems to me practical, at least. I think I began to consider the subject more systematically when I was trying to decide on the best form for a translation of the *Chanson de Roland.* I had before me versions in blank verse both regular and more or less free, and one which contrived to keep not only the metrical structure of the Old French but the rhyme scheme: verse paragraphs known as *laisses,* sometimes many lines in length, each line ending with the same assonance. The result, in English, struck me as nothing more than an intellectual curiosity; unreadable. The word order of the lifeless English was contorted, line by line, to get those sounds to come out right. As for any of the virtues of the original that had moved hearers for centuries and contributed to the poem's survival over a thousand years, there was scarcely an indication of what they might have been. It's easy to multiply examples of this kind of translation. And yet it must be true that in translating, as in writing, formal verse, exigencies of the form itself occasionally contribute to the tension and resonance of the language. But I realized at some point that I had come to consider the verse conventions of original poems as part of the original language, in which they had a history of associations like that of individual words— something impossible to suggest in English simply by repeating the forms. Verse conventions are to a large degree matters of effects, that depend partly on a familiarity which cannot, of course, be translated at all. The effects of the convention in the new language can never be those it produces in the former one. This is true even with forms that have already been adopted. There would be certain obvious advantages in retaining the sonnet form in English, if translating a sonnet from

Italian, but however successful the result, the sonnet form in English does not have the same associations it has in Italian; its effect is not the same; it does not mean the same thing. And sometimes an apparent similarity of form can be utterly misleading. The *Chanson de Roland*, again, for example. The original is in a ten-syllable line, and an English-speaking translator would naturally think, at first, of iambic pentameter. But if the poem is translated into any sort of blank verse in English (leaving aside the question of the relative vitality and brightness of that form in our age) the result is bound to evoke reverberations of the pentameter line in English from Marlowe through Tennyson—echoes that drown the real effect and value of the Old French verse.

I am describing a general tendency drawn from practice and not enunciating a principle. On the other side of the question, I am quite convinced of the impossibility of ever really translating the *Divine Comedy* into any other language, yet I am grateful for several English versions of it, rhymed ones included, for insights into the original, and I recognize that certain of the rhymed translations—for short passages, at least—convey glimpses of what Dante was doing with his highly functional form. But I think that is a recommendation, also, for having many versions, by different hands, of a given poem. And if I had to choose one translation of Dante, it would be "literal," and in prose.

The whole practice is based on paradox: wanting the original leads us to want a translation. And the very notion of making or using a translation implies that it will not and cannot be the original. It must be something else. The original assumes the status of an impossible ideal, and our actual demands must concern themselves with the differences from it, with the manner of standing in stead of it. When I tried to formulate practically what I wanted of a translation, whether by someone else or by me, it was something like this: without deliberately altering the overt meaning of the original poem, I wanted the translation to represent, with as much life as possible, some aspect, some quality of the poem which made the translator think it was worth translating in the first place. I know I arrived at this apparently simple criterion by a process of elimination, remembering all the translations— whatever their other virtues—that I had read, or read at, and set down, thinking, "if the original is really *like* that, what could have been the point of translating it?"

The quality that is conveyed to represent the original is bound to differ with different translators, which is both a hazard and an opportunity. In the ideal sense in which one wants only the original, one wants the translator not to exist at all. In the practical sense in which the demand takes into account the nature of translation, the gifts—such as they are—of the translator are inescapably important. A poet-translator cannot write with any authority using someone else's way of hearing.

I have not set out to make translations that distorted the meaning of the originals on pretext of some other overriding originality. For several years I tried to maintain illogical barriers between what I translated and "my own" writing, and I think the insistence on the distinction was better than indulging in a view of everything being the (presumably inspired) same. But no single thing that anyone does is wholly separate from any other, and impulses, hopes, predilections toward writings as yet unconceived certainly must have manifested themselves in the choices of poems from other languages that I preferred to read and wanted to translate, and in the ways that I went about both. And whatever is done, translation included, obviously has some effect on what is written afterwards. Except in a very few cases it would be hard for me to trace, in subsequent writings of my own, the influence of particular translations that I have made, but I know that the influences were and are there. The work of translation did teach, in the sense of forming, and making available, ways of hearing.

Reexamining and choosing the collection that was to be published as *Selected Translations 1948–1968* provided a natural occasion for reviewing what I thought I had been trying to do, and for considering what relation future translations of mine might conceivably bear to their originals. Since then I have tended, at least part of the time, toward a greater freedom from the original verse conventions, with a view to suggesting some vitality of the original in forms native to English. The tendency was not altogether new, and has not been consistent. It was more like the recognition of a curiosity than a decision. In translating several modern poets from French and Spanish—Follain, Sabines—where the forms of the originals seemed to bear affinities with what is most hopeful in contemporary American poetry, I tried to suggest the original cadences as closely as I could. I had come to feel that one function of translation was to extend what could be said and heard in the new language—as original writing would do—but I was not anxious to conclude that there was only one way of doing so. I had been reading, for instance, Budge's translations of Egyptian Pyramid texts, and had been struck by how much more life—and to my way of hearing it, poetry—there was in the transliterations, hieroglyph by hieroglyph, than in the version Budge had edited into "good English." I wanted to leave some of the habits of English prose word order in abeyance, to see just how necessary they might or might not be, and find new tensions by other means—a process as old as poetic convention itself, a displacement of old forms with the elements of new ones. In the translations in *Asian Figures* I let the sequence of the ideograms (which in most cases I had in front of me, with their transliterations) suggest the English word order, where that could be done without destroying the sense. One object in working with three sonnets of Quevedo's was to have the Spanish baroque phrasing evoke some of the same gnarled diction in English, and to echo the movement, the dramatic development of the sonnet form, but not the form itself. The series of translations from Ghalib, made from literal versions, scholarly material, and direct guidance supplied by Aijaz Ahmad, were part of the same impulse. My first drafts remained close to the original *ghazal* form, and both Aijaz and I thought them papery. As he planned to include in the eventual publication the original texts, literal versions, and his notes on vocabulary, the whole point of the enterprise was to produce something else from the material— poems in English, if possible. The rule was that they were not to conflict with Ghalib's meaning, phrase by phrase, but that they need not render everything, either. Translation was viewed as fragmentary in any case; one could choose the fragments, to some degree. Considering the inadequacy of any approach to translation, I had been thinking of Cézanne's painting the Montagne St. Victoire over and over, each painting new, each one another mountain, each one different from the one he had started to paint. I imagined that in translating a poem something might be gained by making a series of versions bringing out different possibilities. I still think so, though I realize that versions, however many, from a single poet-translator are likely to sound like variants of each other, and echo the translator's ear at least as clearly as they do the original.

The Ghalib translations are among those made without any firsthand knowledge of the original language, as I have explained. I don't know that such a procedure can either be justified or condemned altogether, any more than translation as a whole can be. Auden, for one, thought it the best possible way of going about it. I suspect it depends on the circumstances—who is doing the work, and their relations to each other and to the poetry they are translating. I have had my doubts about working this way, and have resolved several times not to do any more translation of this kind (as I have resolved not to translate any more at all) but I have succumbed repeatedly to particular material.

I should make it clear that the only languages from which I can translate directly are Romance languages, and that I am less familiar with Italian and Portuguese than with French and Spanish. All the translations from other sources, in this collection, were based on someone else's knowledge.

Foreword to *Asian Figures*

(1973)

There is an affinity which everyone must have noticed between poetry—certain kinds and moments of it—on the one hand, and such succinct forms as the proverb, the aphorism, the riddle, on the other. Poetry, on many occasions, gathers the latter under its name. But it seems to me likely that the proverb and its sisters are often poetry on their own, without the claim being made for them. In order to do more than suggest this, I would be led, no doubt, to step out onto that quicksand which is the attempt to define poetry, and I am not about to do that. It was never part of the purpose of what is in this book anyway. What I did want to do was to try to give voice and form to something that these other genres, and what I take to be poetry, share. There are qualities that they obviously have in common: an urge to finality of utterance, for example, and to be irreducible and unchangeable. The urge to brevity is not perhaps as typical of poetry as we would sometimes wish, but the urge to be self-contained, to be whole, is perhaps another form of the same thing, or can be, and it is related to the irreversibility in the words that is a mark of poetry.

A few instances, more or less at random, of family resemblance:

Art of eating

> lesson number one
> don't pick up the spoon
> with the fork.

> (Antonio Machado)

When a dog runs at you, whistle for him.

> (Thoreau, Journal for June 26, 1840)

After the house is finished, leave it.

> (George Herbert, *Jacula Prudentum*)

He whose face gives no light shall never become a star.

> (Blake, *Proverbs of Hell*)

Even the smallest of creatures carries a sun in its eyes.

> (Antonio Porchia, *Voices*)

> And the heart
> Is pleased
> By one thing
> After another.
> (Archilochos, trans. Guy Davenport)

In the *Figures* that follow, I did not set out to prove that the material I was using was "really" poetry. It's true that I was trying to embody, or at least to indicate, particular qualities of poetry which I think that kind of material often has. But what I aimed for in each case was something that seemed to me single, irreducible, and complete in a manner plainly its own. I was not concerned with whether it was complete grammatically, for example, and the occasional ellipses of language would make it clear to me, if I had not known it, that I was more concerned with the spoken idiom (my own, that is) than the written convention. It occurs to me that this has been another perennial blood-link between this kind of material and poetry. And I wanted what makes these pieces complete (if they are) and what holds the words in their order, to be the same thing.

I do not, in case anyone wondered, know the original languages.

Several years ago, Mrs. Crown, of the Asia Society in New York, gave me a number of collections of Asian proverbs, short poems, and riddles, saying that she thought I might be interested in them. They were presented, for the most part, ideogram by ideogram, with literal renderings, in the original order, and notes. It was not long before I discovered what some of my interest—the part of it that led to these *Figures*—was. I have relied throughout on those collections and translations—in other words, wholly on prior English versions, and the scholarship of others. My own adaptations of the material were not undertaken with a view to being— necessarily—literal, or to adding to anyone's knowledge of Asian literature as such. At the same time, I have not at any point deliberately altered the main sense of the original. It was important to me, for the purpose I've described above, that it should be just what it was—material, and anonymous—and I felt indebted to the original meaning, insofar as I could grasp it.

ON POETRY AND POLITICS

[Both these excerpts reflect at once the contexts in which they were written and Merwin's own struggle to write poetry which could have political impact without being rapidly dated. At the time Merwin wrote the first selection, he had himself written, but not published, a number of very topical political poems. The later piece, from a short essay on Agostinho Neto (1922–79), the poet, physician, and revolutionary leader who became president of Angola, was written to accompany Merwin's translations of Neto's poetry. At the time Merwin was writing, Neto was in prison. Eds.]

From "Four British Poets"

(1953)

Louis MacNeice's position, among the poets with whom he has been associated since he began to publish (W. H. Auden, Stephen Spender, C. Day Lewis, etc.), would seem by now evident: he and Auden, I think, remain incomparably the most interesting, rich, and alive poets of the group—not only in the extensive corpus of their poetic output to date, but in the work they are doing at the moment—and it seems possible that their poetry will extricate itself from the thicket of nonintegral commitments, causes, and so on, that the work of the "thirties poets" now connotes, and may continue to interest long after the "thirties poets" as such do not. I realize that to put it this way seems to beg the question of just which of the commitments with which these poets saddled their poetic selves were "integral"; on the other hand I should

Excerpted from a review of W. S. Rodgers, *Europa and the Bull;* Kathleen Raine, *The Year One;* Edwin Muir, *Collected Poems;* and Louis MacNeice, *The Burnt Offering* in *Kenyon Review,* 15 (Summer 1953).

suppose that poetry in itself is a means of naming and thereby discovering what is integral, essential; or one might even say that what is, in such writing, poetry, is what in the long run, when everything else has been, as it were, pared away, will be seen to be "the thing itself"—its only context the constant one of the human condition. This, of course, is to talk as though poetry could ever exist under ideal circumstances; I do not pretend to say that a poet should or should not "commit" himself to ephemeral particulars (and—precisely in proportion to how well "integrated" a man-and-artist he is—if he commits any part of himself he will commit his poetry). Obviously a poet cannot proceed without committing himself to values, which do not exist in a vacuum but in present, actual, necessarily confusing contexts—topically. Further, insofar as a poet loves, he will feel a need to commit himself to the particular world. But he may, in the case of "currents" and opinions, find it difficult beyond a point to tell when these things strike on his imagination, or on his intellect only—he may even confuse the two. It is a matter of degree, then, to what extent a poet can—not "safely," but without himself dissolving as a poet—commit himself to the topical, the actual context, the flux of his society, the world of intellection, concepts, and ideologies. The degree will depend on how much of this world the poet's sensibility can *imaginatively* grasp, how much of it he can really *make*, make new, make poetry. For the central risk of imaginative commitment should not, indeed, deter, but it should be recognized: it is the disintegration of the poetry.

One of the things which has distinguished the "thirties poets" as a school, to the point of having become a cliché in the description of them, is their poetry's reliance on a topical context—their "social consciousness," their attempt to use, to pass poetic opinion on, the events, the political and intellectual currents of their period. I am chary, first off, about the ways in which poetry may supposedly be made out of opinion; I should think that it would be precisely the unintegrated, unformed, incompletely imagined opinion still mere opinion, therefore, and never poetry, that would be pared off with time, to leave the poetry, the core, the finally created truth. Again, all these points are most risky: creation is never final though it seem so, and experience may partake of opinion, so that to eschew opinion would be in a sense to perform in the same way as to use it too loosely: and I would appear to be heading into the jaws of that modern aesthetician's "how many angels can stand on the point of . . . ," viz.: "does time, or whatever you're talking about, in

paring away, pare the form or the content; if you can pare from the whole
and yet it remain whole . . . " etc. Of course. But the "thirties poetry"
loses as the "climate of opinion" and events shift away from it, and I
wonder if it does not tend to lose, other things being equal, where it over-
committed itself and was topical at the expense of being imaginative—
this seems to me almost a truism, but it is probably only time which
will be able to distinguish just when and where the imagination was
undersold.

This sounds like discussing these poets as though they were dead
already, as though the body of their work were finished, and finished as
the work of a school, and could be summed up so. There is in fact a
tendency to talk of them in this way, which can be explained, I think,
by the strong characteristics they shared, their poetry shared, as a group,
by the fact that their poetry was peculiarly, in some senses more than
usually, of their time, which has changed. But this way of regarding
them is to say the least perilous; short of writing off their recent work as
worthless, or at least as making no new contribution, how can it take
into account, for example, the fact that at least three of these poets, Day
Lewis, Auden, and MacNeice, are still very much alive as practising
poets, that each of these three has in fact recently published a volume of
new poetry? Besides, the characteristics they shared as a group have
become less definite; whereas, with each of these three, recently, quite
new ground has been broken and their individual powers have asserted
themselves more fully than ever before. What they now share seem to be
qualities of working rather than more or less mutually held attitudes
toward a similar subject matter. In particular, Auden and MacNeice
both remain *professional* poets in the best senses of that word: they
consistently command a high competence, they exercise adaptable, sure
technical abilities, their attitude toward their work as seen in the work
itself is practical, steady, matter-of-fact, fitting itself to the job in hand
with the least possible fluster and fuss and posturing, and with an eye
primarily to getting the job done as well as possible. The dangers of this
attitude toward one's work have always been evident—and have been
quoted by those too lazy, or too unsure of themselves, or too sorry for
themselves to use it, as rationalizations for not being able to use it:
overadaptability, adaptability without discretion or for the wrong ends
in the wrong projects (one must be sure of what one's own subject really
is, and of one's honesty or the depth, effectiveness, direction of one's
guile) and a kind of facility of texture in which mere execution covers

up for lack of seed-and-slow-growth imagination. (It has often been remarked that MacNeice studied and admired Dryden—these were among Dryden's virtues and dangers.)

From "To Name the Wrong"

(1962)

It is possible for a poet to assume his gift of articulation as a responsibility not only to the fates but to his neighbors, and to feel himself obligated to try to speak for those who are in circumstances resembling his own, but who are less capable of bearing witness to them. There are many kinds of dangers involved in any such view of what he owes himself and his voice. There is, for instance, the danger that his gift itself, necessarily one of the genuinely private and integral things he lives for, may be deformed into a mere loudspeaker, losing the singularity which made it irreplaceable, the candor which made it unteachable and unpredictable. Most poets whom I have in mind would have considered this the prime danger. But the other risks have all claimed their victims. Where injustice prevails (and where does it not?) a poet endowed with the form of conscience I am speaking about has no choice but to name the wrong as truthfully as he can, and to try to indicate the claims of justice in terms of the victims he lives among. The better he does these things the more he may have to pay for doing them. He may lose his financial security, if he has any. Or his health, his comfort, the presence of those he loves, his liberty. Or his life, of course. Worst, he may lose, in the process, the faith which led him to the decision, and then have to suffer for the decision just the same.

Put at its simplest, and with its implications laid out all plain and neat, the decision to speak as clearly and truthfully and fully as possible for the other human beings a poet finds himself among is a challenge to obscurantism, silence, and extinction. And the author of such a decision, I imagine, accepts the inevitability of failure as he accepts the inevitability of death. He finds a sufficient triumph in the decision itself, in its deliberate defiance, in the effort which it makes possible, the risks it impels him to run, and in any clarity which it helps him to create out of

Excerpted from *Nation*, Feb. 24, 1962.

the murk and chaos of experience. In the long run his testimony will be partial at best. But its limits will have been those of his condition itself, rooted, as that is, in death; he will have recognized the enemy. He will not have been another priest of ornaments. He will have been contending against that which restricted his use and his virtue.

I have to talk about Agostinho Neto as though he were dead. I mean that, after I have read what poems of his have found their way into print, and what information about him has managed to evade the obscurantists who govern his country, I have to accept my remaining ignorance of him and of his situation as though it were final. He is a man whose vocation it is to articulate, to say, to make sense out of language; yet as far as the man himself is concerned I must rely to a great extent upon inference, as though he were incapable of saying anything more on his own account. I infer, to begin with, that he is a poet who, early in his life, made the decision I have been trying to describe, and adhered to it.

But that much is easy. Neto's crime was an articulate objection to Salazar's cynical and brutal use of the Angolan people—a transgression which is scarcely surprising. The plight of the people of Angola is not a school for indifference, and one of the dominant themes of Neto's poetry is the relation between his personal predicament and the experience of the people among whom he grew up. Such a preoccupation has led some poets toward propaganda; they have employed their talents in the making of public announcements. As far as I can tell, that is not Neto's temptation. Rather, in the best of his poems about Africa, he is at pains to reveal his own situation as he glimpses it in the lives of other Africans.

NOTES FOR A PREFACE

(1966)

If he starts trying to formulate statements about the undomesticated phenomenon that is poetry, the man who may have been, on occasion, a poet, is likely to realize that he is virtually as thorough a layman as anyone. He can remember a few times when he wrote what he took to be poetry, but the memory is as tragically partial as that of any particular moment of sex, and doubtless he knows that the instances, as they were real, are unrepeatable. He has learned this beyond question if he has ever been tempted, by cowardice, to repeat them, instead of trying to call the next real creatures from the ark. What gifts he can muster as a summoner do not necessarily preclude him from being able to generalize about what he is doing, but it often seems so, whether he listens to other laymen making the attempt, or makes it himself.

When statements emerge, privately he is likely to be reminded that they will help him less than his daily prayers that he may be condemned to continue. The statements usually apply to what has happened—as Aristotle would have told him—and he is concerned with something else.

Yet there is what appears to be, among all degrees of laymen, a more urgent demand for statements about poetry than for poetry itself. I am certainly no historian (though our time and its future increasingly appear to me like part of the past) and it is not a preference which I share, but I have watched it as an object for a while, and imagine that I have noticed some characteristics. Those who write or hope to write poetry (and these, for other reasons, are apparently among the few who still read it) often like to formulate, attend to, collect, and repeat statements about it by way of reliquaries toward which they can direct their hopes. The devotion is understandable; the reliquaries have an interest and often a beauty of their own; sometimes the relics are genuine and even still virtuous. It is hardly necessary to remark that when the cult of relics is exalted above the vision itself it is a sign of ultimate despair.

Of those who do not look to write poems but simply to read them, evidently even among these few there are many who would rather read about them. Some reasons for this are obvious and several have been presented many times. The fact, for instance, that reading, of the kind that poetry assumes, is a dying activity, and the capacity for it is flattered but not fed. This, coupled as it inevitably is with the fact that contemporary poetry makes, and is chiefly famous for making, greater demands on its readers than it did in days when it was sure that they existed and could read. For those who feel that they should know about modern poetry without having to submit to it themselves, the literature about it also provides the required digests for busy lives.

But these explanations are automatic and there must be others. The demand is often for a substitute, a translation, and is regularly made by those who are poorly acquainted, or uncomfortable, with the original idiom. But the original seems more and more frequently to be, not a particular mode of poetry, but the great language itself, the vernacular of the imagination, that at one time was common to men. It is a tongue that is loosed in the service of immediate recognitions, and that in itself would make it foreign in our period. For it conveys something of the unsoundable quality of experience and the hearing of it is a private matter, in an age in which the person and his senses are being lost in the consumer, who does not know what he sees, hears, wants, or is afraid of, until the voice of the institution has told him. Still, the voice of the institution has able apologists as well, some of whom go so far as to insist that it too is sometimes poetry.

At that point it is my turn to be glad not to understand. In any case, poetry, as I have been speaking of it, is found satisfying less and less often by those who still require any art at all. The search for substitutes in activities remarkable chiefly for their evocation of special wave-lengths that are seldom within earshot, or for their deliberate abandon, points to the same abdication. But there is nothing original in observing that man, if that is what he still is, has chosen to pass mutilated into the heaven of the modern world, nor in remarking that the rift between experience (which is personal, and inseparable from the whole) and activity (which may well be communal, and shared with machines) was widening, and that the species had opted for activity, activity, both as a means and, it would appear, as an end, though it meant abandoning something, and perhaps something essential, of themselves. Poetry, and the need for it, may be among what is being left behind.

Any such intimation, of course, is likely to be assailed by rotarian voices reminding in puzzlement and dudgeon that never before has the institution paid so much money toward poetry, to say nothing of attention. In our land corporations and universities give of what they have to encourage it to be itself as much as possible. And, at least partly as a result, they may truthfully claim that the production figures have never been so good. But what they are pointing to is activity, which is what the institution is capable of fostering. The encouragement of poetry itself is a labor and a privilege like that of living. It requires, I imagine, among other startlingly simple things, a love of poetry, and possibly a recurring despair of finding it again, an indelible awareness of its parentage with that biblical waif, ill at ease in time, the spirit. No one has any claims on it, no one deserves it, no one knows where it goes. It is not pain, and it is not the subconscious, though it can hail from either as though it were at home there. On the other hand, thinking of the activists I remember the bee gorging honey (for the circumstances, as it realized, contained a menace of some kind) though its abdomen had been amputated. For some minutes it continued to devour nourishment, since its motor system was rightly informed that this was lacking. As closely as could be observed it was so far from feeling pain that it had no conception of its loss. All that it ate poured through the wound and was gone, and it died of starvation. I am haunted by its other death, before or after, in a useless gland of the lost abdomen. The fact that one is haunted by it does not mean that it stayed alive.

But then, among my peculiar failings is an inability to believe that the experience of being human, that gave rise to the arts in the first place, can continue to be nourished in a world contrived and populated by nothing but humans. No doubt such a situation is biologically impossible, but it is economically desirable, and we exist in an era dedicated to the myth that the biology of the planet, as well as anything else that may be, can be forced to adapt infinitely to the appetites of one species, organized and deified under the name of economics. It would be impossible not to be familiar with the contention that experience is merely a factor of circumstances, any circumstances, and can be equally valuable whatever they are. The argument is often presented as an excuse or consolation for activities undertaken or omitted for other reasons. The tendency of the arts, in a landscape fabricated entirely of human contraptions, to seek nourishment in accident and decay—the very places where the complex and unpredictable natural world continually reinvades the machine—may indeed be no more than an atavistic nostalgia for something no longer necessary. But it may be that the arts themselves are atavistic, or man, for that matter, as he has been defined until now, with the nonhuman world entering always into the definition. One of the vexed points of modern biology is precisely the definition of a species, and the point at which adaptation to changed circumstances requires a new definition for a species that has been transformed into something essentially new. I cannot escape the notion that it is because circumstances do have an effect on experience that they are not all equally valuable, and that many of the circumstances common to contemporary existence are contributing to a general destruction of what the arts until now have helped to dignify in what they called human. For one thing, the arts and their source were fed from the senses, and the circumstances that have been conceived and are being developed in the name of economics are relegating these anarchistic voices to the bee's abdomen. Indeed they must do so, for the senses, if they were not uniformed, duped, and cowed, would constitute a continuous judgment of the world they touched on, and not only of its means but of its ends. Instead of the world of the senses, which was unprovable but you never knew what it might say, the creature that is replacing the Old Adam has substituted comfort and erotic daydreams (whether or not physically enacted) and tells you that they are not only more convenient and more fun, but cleaner.

Along with the insistence that all circumstances are equally valuable, there sometimes goes an odd and guilty assertion (and all injunctions that do not proceed from the biblical waif ventriloquize for the institution) that the artist must go along with the life of his time, as though he could do anything else. In many instances no doubt this somewhat priggish platitude bespeaks little more than a frustrated longing to escape from the salient characteristics of that life the moment occasion or courage offers. Sometimes it appears to betray, chiefly, a sense of being outside it, or just outside. But what is interesting about it is the assumption that man, the animal and artist, and the arts that have conceived him until now, are infinitely adaptable to man-made circumstances; and "adaptable," as the most unavoidable acquaintance with economics will reveal, means "simplifiable," when so used.

Going along with the life of his time in an earnest fashion may or may not benefit the attempt to give utterance to the unutterable experience of being alive, and consciously mortal, and human, in any time. It does not necessarily entail going along with all possible activities of an emergent and epidemic species which scorns all life except its own withering existence, and is busily relegating the senses its predecessors were given to apprehend their world, and the creatures with which they were privileged to share it.

Here and there a form of art has become recognizable as a feature of the era. Stemming from a more or less deliberate and exclusive immersion in the metropolitan life of our time, it resorts perforce to increasingly extreme states of consciousness as though they were the desperate retreats of truth, yet its images are frequently at a remove from any direct and integrated sensual criteria. When it provokes recognition of anything it is usually of the squalid landscapes of a world made and polluted by man alone, from which it shows that there is no escape. It is not an art which I wish to decry nor to avoid, but I would hope not to be limited by it nor identified with it, any more than I would want to do my dying in the bee's anterior part.

However that may be, absolute despair has no art, and I imagine the writing of a poem, in whatever mode, still betrays the existence of hope, which is why poetry is more and more chary of the conscious mind, in our age. And what the poem manages to find hope for may be part of what it keeps trying to say.

ON OPEN FORM

(1969)

What is called its form may be simply that part of the poem that had directly to do with time: the time of the poem, the time in which it was written, and the sense of recurrence in which the unique moment of vision is set.

Perhaps this is why in much of the poetry of the high Middle Ages the form seems transparent. Both the role of time in the poem and the role of the poem in time doubtless seemed clear and simple to the Arcipreste de Hita, Dante, Guillaume de Lorris, and Chaucer. We can be sure of neither, and we cannot even be certain whether the pretense to such certainty that characterizes some later periods of society (in particular certain phases of neoclassicism) is one of the absurd disguises that can help an art to survive, or merely one of the shrouds that are hardly more than wasted efforts to lend decency to its burial.

The invention of a new form of stanza was a matter of genuine poetic importance to the troubadours. To us it would probably seem scarcely a matter for much curiosity. For the troubadours the abstract form (which certainly they did not hear as an abstract thing) was unquestionably related to that part of the poem that was poetic. For us it is hard to remain convinced that the form, insofar as it is abstract, is not merely part of what in the poem is inescapably technical. For us, for whom everything is in question, the making keeps leading us back into the patterns of a world of artifice so intricate, so insidious, and so impressive, that often it seems indistinguishable from the whole of time.

In a world of technique *motions* tend to become methods. But the undependable life that appears on occasion as poetry would rather die, or so it seems, than follow this tendency, and when a poet himself follows it farther than the source of his gift warrants, his gains of technical facility are likely to render him the helpless master of mere confection.

And yet neither technique nor abstract form can be abandoned, finally. And no doubt neither is dangerous in itself as long as each is recognized as no more than a means, and is not made into an idol and loved for itself. (But it seems to be characteristic of a technological age that means come to dwarf and eclipse or destroy their ends.)

And certainly neither of them automatically excludes or implies the other.

In an age when time and technique encroach hourly, or appear to, on the source itself of poetry, it seems as though what is needed for any particular nebulous unwritten hope that may become a poem is not a manipulable, more or less predictably recurring pattern, but an unduplicatable resonance, something that would be like an echo except that it is repeating no sound. Something that always belonged to it: its sense and its conformation before it entered words.

At the same time I realize that I am a formalist, in the most strict and orthodox sense. For years I have had a recurring dream of finding, as it were in an attic, poems of my own that were as lyrically formal, but as limpid and essentially unliterary, as those of Villon.

Much of what appears, or appeared, as great constructive energy in the poetic revolutions of the first half of this century must have been in part energy made available by the decomposition of a vast and finally antipoetic poetic organism that had become a nuisance even to itself. The original iconoclasts have reared up other antipoetic poetic monsters that have achieved senility far more quickly since their shapes were less definite and their substance more questionable from the start.

A poetic form: the setting down of a way of hearing how poetry happens in words. The words themselves do not make it. At the same time it is testimony of a way of hearing how life happens in time. But time does not make it.

To recur in its purest forms (whether they are strict, as in Waller's "Go, Lovely Rose," or apparently untrammeled, as in the Book of Isaiah in the King James Version) poetry seems to have to keep reverting to its naked condition, where it touches on all that is unrealized.

Our age pesters us with the illusion that we have realized a great deal. The agitation serves chiefly to obscure what we have forgotten, into whose limbo poetry herself at times seems about to pass.

What are here called open forms are in some concerns the strictest. Here only the poem itself can be seen as its form. In a peculiar sense if you criticize how it happens you criticize what it is.

Obviously it is the poem that is or is not the only possible justification for any form, however theory runs. The poem is or it is not the answer to "why that form?" The consideration of the evolution of forms, strict or open, belongs largely to history and to method. The visitation that is going to be a poem finds the form it needs in spite of both.

The "freedom" that precedes strict forms and the "freedom" that follows them are not necessarily much alike. Then there is the "freedom" that accompanies poetry at a distance and occasionally joins it, often without being recognized, as in some proverbs. ("God comes to see without a bell." "He that lives on hope dances without music.")

SIDELIGHTS

(1975)

I started writing hymns for my father almost as soon as I could write at all, illustrating them. I recall some rather stern little pieces addressed, in a manner I was familiar with, to backsliders, but I can remember too wondering whether there might not be some liberating mode. In Scranton there was an anthology of *Best Loved Poems of the American People* in the house, which seemed for a time to afford some clues. But the first real writers that held me were not poets: Conrad first, and then Tolstoy, and it was not until I had received a scholarship and gone away to the university that I began to read poetry steadily and try incessantly, and with abiding desperation, to write it. I was not a satisfactory student; . . . I spent most of my time either in the university library or riding in the country: I had discovered that the polo and ROTC stables were full of horses with no one to exercise them. I believe I was not noticeably respectful either of the curriculum and its evident purposes, nor of several of its professors, and I was saved from the thoroughly justified impatience of the administration, as I later learned, by the intercessions of R. P. Blackmur, who thought I needed a few years at the place to pick up what education I might be capable of assimilating, and I did in fact gain a limited but invaluable acquaintance with a few modern languages. While I was there, John Berryman, Herman Broch, and Blackmur himself, helped me, by example as much as by design, to find out some things about writing; of course it was years before I began to realize just what I had learned, and from whom.

I am not, I believe, a teacher. I have not evolved an abstract aesthetic theory and am not aware of belonging to any particular group of writers.

Reprinted from *Contemporary Authors*, vols. 13–16, edited by Clare D. Kinsman (copyright © 1965, 1966, 1975 Gale Research Company; reprinted by permission of the publisher), revised edition, Gale Research, 1975, pp. 553–54.

301

I neither read nor write much criticism, and think of its current vast proliferation chiefly as a symptom, inseparable from other technological substitutions. I do not admire government processes nor the necessities they reveal, and I put no faith in material utopias whether socialist or capitalist; they too, like much criticism, seem to me to be projections of a poverty that is not in itself material. Not that I think them impossible. But I imagine that a society whose triumphs one after the other emerge as new symbols of death, and that feeds itself by poisoning the earth, may be expected, even while it grows in strength and statistics, to soothe its fears with trumpery hopes, refer to nihilism as progress, dismiss the private authority of the senses as it has cashiered belief, and of course find the arts exploitable but unsatisfying.

Writing is something I know little about; less at some times than at others. I think, though, that so far as it is poetry it is a matter of correspondences; one glimpses them, pieces of an order, or thinks one does, and tries to convey the sense of what one has seen to those to whom it may matter, including, if possible, one's self.

MILTON: A REVISITATION

(a talk presented at a Milton conference in 1967)

I want to start, as Milton started the first of his Cambridge prolusions, by registering a certain dismay at what I have agreed to do. Though I was asked to speak as a poet, not as a scholar, the circumstances remain awkward, for Milton is celebrated—or notorious—for being the most learned poet in English, and perhaps in several other languages besides. He was a poet who believed, with a fixity that is rather forbidding, in the importance of learning to a poet's formation. And we know how long and earnestly he addressed himself to this formative process. Oddly enough, Milton's certainty about the poetic vocation was one of the things that first drew me to him as a sort of patron (or at least alibi) during my second somewhat unorthodox year in college—though I was not a very reliable follower, if I could have been called one at all. I was unable to see how the excitement of most of the little poetry I had then read had much to do with the other excitements that occupied me at the time, and certainly any attempts I made at poetry myself did not go very far toward a revelation, though they were, as Milton said they should be, simple, sensuous, and passionate. I had bouts (sometimes quite long ones, especially when my allowance ran out earlier than usual) of being a sort of trampy *penseroso*, and while waiting on table in the dining hall I would occasionally exhort myself

> ... let my due feet never fail
> To walk the studious cloisters pale,
> And love the high-embowed roof,
> With antique pillars massey-proof,
> And storied windows richly dight,
> Casting a dim religious light.

There was quite a lot of neo-Gothic there to help. And I can remember coming out of movies when I should have been studying, and muttering in a sudden burst of guilty resolution

303

> . . . let my lamp at midnight hour
> Be seen in some high lonely tower,
> Where I may oft outwatch the Bear . . .

But the Bear was never seriously concerned. There were distractions, even there: among others a stable full of unexercised army horses a half mile away, which took up so much of my time that I am puzzled now at how I got through that year at all.

I suppose it sounds as though I was not serious about poetry, and almost certainly, in any sense that Milton would have recognized, I was not. I felt about it a kind of hovering desperation, occasionally relieved by flashes in my own erratic and obsessive reading, but seldom for long, and not at all relieved by my incessant attempts at writing. It is a feeling I can scarcely imagine in Milton at any age, though I have come to recognize it in certain of my contemporaries (and I hope none of us who suffers from it ever outgrows it, whatever may be added to it). But perhaps I am wrong about Milton in this, since his insistent certainty about the vocation of poetry with its duties, its rigors, and its privilege speaks as much for his doubts as for his assurance—justifying the ways of John Milton to John Milton. I can't see how it could be entirely otherwise; but I would not go so far as those who would require such tokens of doubt in order to find the man sufficiently "human" to deserve their regard.

I must make it plain before I get drawn in any further that I am not very familiar with the ins and outs of the Milton controversies of the last fifty years. I am acquainted as we all are with the fact that Pound and Eliot deplored Milton and his language, points which had in fact been partly suggested by Dr. Johnson, and that they did so to considerable effect in the literary world and in the world of scholarship. And I am aware that the man's character has been impugned by Middleton Murry and other watchful souls, whose high-mindedness I cannot always understand. Self-righteousness is the thing in Milton's character that I find hardest to abide, and many of his detractors seem to share it. I remember my own introduction to the disparaging of Milton. I should perhaps explain that my enthusiasms in poetry (and I was just learning how anxious I was for enthusiasms) had leapt from Milton, with only a relatively brief pause at Shelley, straight to Pound, who was both the first modern poet and the first modern critic who caught my imagination —he was almost the first of either I had read. I realized that I was learning from Pound more about some of the things I had wanted to learn from Milton than I was learning from Milton, but I could not believe that the two were *totally* incompatible, that no one should be able to learn from both. Yet I was unsure and very troubled by passages like "we have long since fallen under the blight of the Miltonic or noise tradition," "Milton is the most unpleasant of English poets, and he has certain definite and analysable defects," and "He tried to turn English into Latin." I could see that the defects that annoyed Pound were often real, though for some time I was reluctant to admit it. But some of Pound's own defects were quite as distressingly plain to me, and others were happily pointed out by *his* perennial detractors, and while I was reluctant to admit some of those too, I was convinced that they did not render the rest of *his* writing worthless and indeed pernicious. At the time I was lucky in being able to go once a week to John Berryman with whatever I had been writing in the interval, and he would tell me why it would not do. Finally I put my confusion before him. I think he already regarded my enthusiasm for Pound as somewhat overdone, though his own was considerable when I could get him onto the subject. Anyway, I remember my relief at his telling me that he thought Milton was here to stay.

But I did not then, nor have I since, read further, at least with any sequence, in the critical give-and-take over Milton, partly because I was already rather a procrastinator when it came to reading much criticism in a row, and partly because it was not very long after that that I stopped reading Milton. Except for occasional rereadings of some of the short poems, and a few passages in the others, I have not read him since — that is until the last month or so. The reasons for that are probably too devious, and possibly not interesting enough, to go into here. I had in fact gone too far in my eagerness to learn from someone. I have heard recently that Robert Lowell has credited me in my absence with having had, while I was at college, the whole of *Paradise Lost* by heart. He is sometimes too generous with his friends, and he loves Milton. But I can't think where he got the idea, though when I first knew him I could still recite a few longish passages from here and there. But the fact is that I came to realize that Milton had become deafening for me. I had to listen so hard for whatever I might be able to write myself that I could not afford to have this great angel choir opening up at my elbow whenever I tried — and in a language that was by no means mine. And, in fact, Milton was making it hard for me to hear other poets as well.

The result is that, in an age in which Milton's reputation had been savagely assailed and more quietly observed and attended, I know only that I loved him once—I suppose because I came to him with little choice and no criteria but my own excitement and the plea of my own ignorance that required poetry without any certainty of what it was—and that I have felt inclined to avoid him ever since, for my own reasons, and not for those of Pound or Eliot or Middleton Murry, even though I may have seen their force. So I have welcomed an excuse to look at him again after all this time, and some of what I may have to say about him should be regarded as a journal of a revisitation, reflections on what I wanted and found in Milton then, and what I imagine I find in him that is to my own interest now.

Because, of course, to ask someone to approach a subject like Milton as a poet is not to ask for universality of the sort to which critics and scholars are often supposed to aspire. Most poets (who do not have to do so for other reasons such as teaching) read the mighty dead chiefly because of something in the poetry that speaks directly to their own trouble, confusion, and indeed ambition—and so perhaps are closer to the general reader than to literary historians and their concern for canons. This explains both some of the otherwise exotic enthusiasms of poets in every generation and some of the abiding gaps in most poets' acquaintances. Also, I should note that, since I stopped reading Milton, I have run across indications in other modern poets I admire that his influence is not dead among all of those who have grown up since Pound and Eliot cast their bans: Berryman himself, for instance, who seems to me one of the living masters of the actual ordering of language and who uses inversions to an effect that is like nothing else in English. I remember him talking on the subject when my own ears were scarcely dry, and discussing the inversions in Milton with penetration; and I remember his impassioned admiration of "The Nativity Ode." It is worth keeping both in mind in reading

> There sat down, once, a thing on Henry's heart
> só heavy, if he had a hundred years
> & more, & weeping, sleepless, in all them time
> Henry could not make good.
> Starts again always in Henry's ears
> a little cough somewhere, an odour, a chime.

And there is another thing he has in mind
like a grave Sienese face a thousand years
would fail to blur the still profiled reproach of. Ghastly,
with open eyes, he attends, blind.
All the bells say: too late. This is not for tears;
thinking.

But never did Henry, as he thought he did,
end anyone and hacks her body up
and hide the pieces, where they may be found.
He knows: he went over everyone, & nobody's missing.
Often he reckons, in the dawn, them up.
Nobody is ever missing.

And Lowell too. It was not long after I had left off reading Milton that I read Lowell's "The Ghost," which Berryman had pointed out to me in *Poetry.*

I will not hound you, much as you have earned
It, Sextus: I shall reign in your four books—
    I swear this by the Hag who looks
    Into my heart where it was burned:
        Propertius, I kept faith;
If not, may serpents suck my ghost to death
And spit it with their forked and killing breath
Into the Styx where Agamemnon's wife
Founders in the green circles of her life.

It may be simply the hazard of the order in which I read them, but would it have been this way if Milton, with his love of names (itself partly formed, I imagine, by Marlowe and Spenser) had never written? Lowell's work was the more exciting to me because I could see that one of the other great influences on it must have been Pound, whose own writing may well have suggested Propertius as a subject, and his attitude, or some adaptation of it, as a tone. Pound's influence on Lowell was not less valuable for being indirect. This was encouraging to me because I had not then and have not since learned how to use directly any influences that I may, from time to time, have *wanted* to affect me. This is one reason I have occasionally been puzzled by some of the influences that have been discovered in poems of mine—and by learning that at times I have even been influenced by writers I have not read.

To name one more, there is the poetry of Muir, which was probably influenced by Milton as much at secondhand, through Wordsworth (a poet whom I have never been able to read for long with pleasure). It seems to me that the influence of Milton, often indirect and always deeply assimilated, is there in most of Muir, differently in his different phases. And the first poem in *One Foot in Eden* — his last book before his collected volume—is entitled "Milton"; I quote it because it brings me to another point I want to make:

> Milton, his face set fair for Paradise,
> And knowing that he and Paradise were lost
> In separate desolation, bravely crossed
> Into his second night and paid his price.
> There towards the end he to the dark tower came
> Set square in the gates, a mass of blackened stone
> Crowned with vermilion fiends like streamers blown
> From a great funnel filled with roaring flame.
>
> Shut in his darkness, these he could not see,
> But heard the steely clamour known too well
> On Saturday nights in every street in Hell.
> Where, past the devilish din, could Paradise be?
> A footstep more, and his unblinded eyes
> Saw far and near the fields of Paradise.

There is little that is obviously "Miltonic," in any of the more hackneyed senses, in Muir's language in this sonnet. What makes the poem interesting to me is the subject—which no one, I imagine, would claim was deliberately biographical. Only in a very free, removed, broad, unintimate, and undetailed fashion is Muir concerned with Milton as someone who caught colds, shaved, had a shoe size and a first name. He is concerned with Milton as a figure—not so much of literature or history as of tradition and the imagination. He is deliberately using Milton as a legend. Here I may be close to saying something "improper," because this image of Milton, which can scarcely be ascribed to his soberer biographers or explicators, is probably one of the least respectable things about his memory—at least in our century. References to it tend to be rather romantic, vague, unjustifiable. Yet even the dreamlike association that I imagine it often has with the brooding of Blake's God quite as much as the brooding of Blake's Milton does not prevent it from evoking parsonical stuffiness and joyless nightshirts as regularly as it does any particular splendor. We are not very good at the sublime; we usually find it hard to acknowledge any hankering after it, and would be still more shy of describing that evasive quality (as distinct from our suspicions of it) with the help of this ill-defined image of the legendary Milton; part of us finds his very quest for the sublime, as a writer and as a man, misguided and ridiculous. But I think the image is with us just the same (in some limbo it shares with other lofty shades) and that, for whatever reasons, it has a fairly active underground existence. Like most images of the kind that have received relatively little attention in our age but are still distantly traditional, it is a hard one to depict accurately, though if one were to hit the right details they would probably be generally and instantly recognized. I think that for most of us who have had literary educations based to a considerable extent on English literature Milton the legend remains one of the nearer, if not more seductive, forms of that vaguer, larger legendary emanation, the Poet. Perhaps more massively than any other in our language Milton presents this figure. I do not mean to imply that I think he is the greatest or in some way most poetic poet in English: the legendary figure is not necessarily more congruous with the actual man and his writing than it was in the case of Keats, say, or Byron, who exemplify the same phenomenon in other ways. And if the *figure* of Byron is more pleasing and attractive and kaleidoscopic than that of Milton, the *figure* of Milton is probably more haunting, and seems less a product of circumstances; it is simpler, more monolithic, more somber and humorless, easier to make fun of but harder to come to terms with. Here to stay. Probably the epic, rather than lyric or dramatic, nature of Milton's ambition and achievement contributes to this, helped by the fact that his blindness inevitably associates him (an association that occurred to him first of all) with that greater, still simpler and remoter image of the same presence, Homer, in a way that seems to bear the mark of imaginative destiny. Of course the image is helped by romantic frontispieces in old books of poetry we saw as children, and by other not particularly relevant evocations of the ponderous, aging, noble, misunderstood figure dreaming of Samson. It seems to me that this image, attractive, respectable or not, is something that enriches our shared imagination, and that it probably feeds some of our more personal and urgent figurations of independence, moral rectitude, and endurance, just as it continually helps to fill our composite notions of tiresomeness, ill-humor, and glum arrogance. The ambivalence we feel about it is probably salutary, too, since the very separation of the legend and the man is not clear. I imagine it is easier to fall into that peculiarly dangerous form of idolatry, hero worship, when the legend seems to be at least propped on fact, than when it is relatively pure. Personally, I think Milton, as an exemplary figure of the Poet, has some unfortunate limitations. It would make me feel happier to think that young students were trying to model themselves on Homer.

This is why I have given so much time to something finally so nebulous. There are things in the legendary figure of Milton that are quite as undesirable — as influences on those who are starting out to try to write poetry and (what is not always thought to be the same thing) to be poets — as any of the (by now heavily signposted) "defects" in his poetry. Some of the dangers of the legend for young poets, I suppose, are its particular self-justifying melancholy, of a kind that has perennial appeal to certain characters at all ages, and to many at the time when they are first thinking of writing poetry. Is this worse as an exemplar than the theatrical melancholy of some of the romantics? Maybe not, except that it often seems to sit among the plain feelings as though they were creatures from below stairs making a nuisance in the library. When students imitate the analogous melancholy among the romantics (for many want *some* image of melancholy to emulate, however secretly) they may treat what they take to be their own feelings with an opposite disrespect (but one that gives the feelings exercise, at least), exaggerating them, and calling them by the wrong names, but with luck and a bit of gumption they may find their own feelings by trying. The peculiar form of cerebral melancholy given off by the Miltonic legend may encourage a disrespect for private, emotional experience in oneself and in others, and for the ordeal of its expression.

If I had suddenly to choose one seventeenth-century English writer to commend to students, especially those who wanted to write poetry, it might well be Traherne, who could scarcely be more different from Milton:

Is not the vision of the world an amiable thing? Do not the stars shed influences to perfect the air? . . . For there is a disease in him who despiseth present mercies, which till it be cured, he can never be happy . . . He therefore that will despise them because he hath them is marvellously irrational: the way to possess them is to esteem them . . . Prize it now you have it, at that rate, and you shall be a grateful creature: nay you shall be a Divine and Heavenly

person. For they in Earth when they have them prize them not,
they in Hell prize them when they have them not.

A reputation of less literary prestige, a writer of smaller ambition, a
more attractive figure perhaps, but one deceptively difficult to follow.

Still, the effect of the figure of Milton brings me to what may be the
chief undesirable influence of Milton's poetic practice. Not that "he
wrote English as though it were Latin," as Pound said. That, and some
of the other common objections are, I think, symptoms, and not always
unpleasant ones. The tension in poetic language that makes it vibrate
comes from the feelings and the imagination, but also—need it be
said—from the ordering of the language itself, which in each writer not
only derives in some idiosyncratic way from speech, his own and what
he has heard, but also differs from the same living speech in a personal
way, distorts it and makes it move in a manner that is at once privately
his and alive in a way that is, finally, beyond him. The possible
distortions are infinite, and while those that are best and most simply
derived—most, as they say, "natural"—are perhaps often the most profoundly satisfying, yet ours is hardly the age to carp at the influences of
foreign construction on Milton's English—an artifice that sometimes,
in fact, seems to be the very thing that gives it its essential excitement,
when it has it. His tangled abuses of the process have been pointed out
often enough. My own Latin is nonexistent, so perhaps my own choice
of example, while I am venturing to defend him, will not be ideal, but
it certainly is one in which his intention, explicitly stated, was to be as
Latinate as the language would bear. It is also a poem I have always
admired, with certain reservations (including the fact that I have never
been sure I understood several phrases), and which had its influence on
me when I was beginning to write. It is Milton's translation of the fifth
ode of Horace—"Rendered," as he says, "almost word for word, without
rhyme, according to the Latin measure, as near as the language will
permit."

> What slender youth, bedowed with liquid odours,
> Courts thee on roses in some pleasant cave,
>   Pyrrha? For whom bind'st thou
>   In wreaths thy golden hair,
> Plain in thy neatness? Oh, how oft shall he
> On faith and changed gods complain, and seas

> Rough with black winds and storms
> Unwonted shall admire!
> Who now enjoys thee credulous, all gold;
> Who always vacant, always amiable,
> Hopes thee, of flattering gales
> Unmindful. Hapless they
> To whom thou untried seem'st fair! Me, in my vowed
> Picture, the sacred wall declares t'have hung
> My dank and dropping weeds
> To the stern God of Sea.

It can be objected that this is not Miltonic, but certainly it exemplifies the defect or enlivening essential distortion I have mentioned, and to me at least makes a virtue of it. It also exemplifies—though somewhat less well, for the subject was obviously in no sense his—a more critical danger of Milton as a mentor. But I think other and more typical examples, which are often reckoned among the "beauties" of Milton, would serve better. Anyone could choose them: passages displaying the ornate piling up of sounds, especially in *Paradise Lost,* or the frequently admired elaborate wedding-cake sentences. I am not simply saying that I do not now like the baroque in poetry, because in many instances I do. I am suggesting that "Lycidas" and much of *Paradise Lost,* with their gorgeously inwrought grammar, diction, and euphony, when coupled with Milton's repeated and embodied baroque belief in "elaborate composition," advocated in his peculiar moral tone, can powerfully reinforce a notion in would-be poets (perhaps not in their theoretical assertions or conscious ambitions, but in the place where their composite model keeps changing) that the language is the place in which it all happens, and that verbal proliferation and dexterity—"skill" as it is called—with the language will somehow eventually produce the miracle itself. I think there is always a tendency to feel this way when poets are starting out—though it would be the last thing most of them would admit. Their excitement with the discovery of the language—a thing in itself essential to them—helps them to it, and few critics and almost no poets would deny that this excitement is in itself a dangerous, though beloved, necessity.

Obviously I am talking about what is now called "craft" or "technique," though in a specially baroque sense and with certain peculiarly Miltonic touches. And I want to contrast, briefly, the quest for it in the emulation of Milton with another sort of activity: translation. Translation is one of the great schools of poetry, both in the obvious sense that is concerned with words themselves, and in that other that has to do with their source. But I do not mean translation undertaken primarily for the ability in handling the language that it may impart. That is the means, or part of it, and I believe it is unwise to give oneself to it at the start as though it were an end. I am thinking of translation as an intuitive exercise in trying to conjure up the intention, the essential life and value of the original, using the two languages, the original and English, as paradigms of the sort that help to channel many intuitive exercises. I cling to the belief that this kind of effort, pursued as an outcome of a real love of poetry, can reveal to a translator something that is unmistakably his own intention, his own voice, his own language—something that will not be part of his translation but an access to what is his own. This is related to my suspicion that if one must have models it may be better if they are foreign. But I know there are dangers in this practice too—and not only the contemporary ones of fad and self-indulgence that make of translation an extension of every poetic fashion. A poet's "craft," his "technique" if you will (a word I detest in the context), however it is come by, is always partly separate from what is in the full extent his poetry—least so at moments which must, even in our day, be described as inspired, which seem wholly unmerited and miraculous, and in which the poet's acquired knowledge, if it works independently at all, proves to him once again that the great sin of the intellect is to suppose that it can ever *make* anything. Its function is the ordering and judgment of what already is.

When I set out to go through Milton again after all these years I had some notion that I would raise at the same time some of the questions I have turned up, in the meantime, about the whole business of "craft" in poetry. There were two reasons why I thought this might be appropriate. First, what I had looked for in Milton at the ripe age of seventeen had been a sort of guide to how to do it, and I suppose it seemed that I might find something of the sort in Milton because of the deliberation with which he had set about preparing himself for poetry, and because the actual manner—the "artistry" if you like it, the "craft" if you think you are neutral about it, the "contrivance" if it annoys you—seem, to many of our age, to be peculiarly obvious in Milton, the Milton of "Lycidas" and the Paradise poems particularly.

I paid less attention to the fact that Milton, in a sense peculiar to him, set out to use rhetoric in the service of the spirit. Rhetoric has been a dirty word in the discussion of poetry in our language for several decades, and a great deal of necessary nonsense has been said on the subject. I am using the word not to refer to the well-known "grandeurs" of Milton's verse, the things that made Addison say, "The language sunk under him"—those, again, are simply effects. By rhetoric I mean simply the art of persuasion. It is an art which generally begins with a well-defined end in view, a purpose, and its function is not to question that but to impose it. That is one of the reasons why the discussion of it rouses such heat when it involves poetry. For (as Yeats discovered, to his disappointment, after years of trying to remove the rhetoric from his poetry) it is an art from which poetry is not and cannot ever be entirely free, any more than it can be entirely free of words and their time and decay and apparently random histories. But rhetoric itself is not poetry. It is the devil's art—the devil can always *persuade* better than anyone, if the field is open to persuasion alone. It is almost his definition. Poetry, and its startling voice, is not finally concerned with persuasion but with things I can only guess at though they concern me entirely: discovery for one. Here is something of what I mean; it is a description of an environment of persuasion in which rhetoric, including certain kinds of poetry, would seem quite at home: "France was living on a familiar wisdom which explained to the young that life was so constructed that one must learn how to make concessions, that enthusiasm was all very well for a while, and that in a world where the clever were always right, one must try not to be wrong." So Camus's description of prewar France, a passage whose persuasiveness shows the whole paradox of the question—is it the truth of Camus's vision or the artifice of his expression that seizes us? Milton himself is eloquent on the dangers of persuasion in a world in which values are undependable, but his distinctions between the rhetoric of good and that of evil, carefully pointed out though they have been by several critics, are still sometimes unclear to me, and sometimes, again, unconvincing. The devil's rhetoric is seen to work for evil within the poem itself, but Milton's rhetoric, if considered in terms of his avowed purpose, the preaching of his theological and philosophical views, and his wish "to inbreed and cherish in a great people the seeds of virtue," leaves one with no very great illusions about poetry as a didactic force, in our time at least. Conscripting the impulse of poetry to the uses of persuasiveness is a procedure that risks doing violence to that free impulse and misleading whatever in ourselves is capable of loving it and being moved, opened, and clarified by it. If that suggests that I connect poetry with the moral nature of man, I would not deny it, though I would not presume to define the connection, and am not convinced that an adequate definition is possible.

Perhaps my real misgiving about this poetic necessity—craft—is something like this. The habits, echoes, knowledge, practice, and fear that make it up become, from very tender years, an apparatus for repeating. Poetry is exceptional. In the end the exceptions of which reality is made may become shy of the whole welcoming machine that is our "technique," and instead of showing us that they make up everything, they may refuse to appear at all in their true light, and instead leave the machine to go on welcoming itself.

Whether it is a manipulation of anonymous traditional practices, or a display of one's own invented verbal resources, craft is linked with that part of the poetic practice which is moved by vanity—this is one reason why Milton may have been of the devil's party "without knowing it." I am not going to pretend that vanity, display, and pyrotechnics do not have a permanent place in poetry, but they are not what makes one go back to it as an inexhaustible resource and one of the pure reminders, when there are few others, that man is a spirit.

I am chronically beset with misgivings of this kind on the subject of poetic craft, which, as I say, no one who tries to write poetry can hope to do without, and the misgivings return in a particular way after every reading of "Lycidas," say—a poem whose beauty I would not dream of denying—and many sections of *Paradise Lost.* It is no use, I do not return to the Paradise poems with sustained pleasure, and cannot read them for long without feeling that I am running up a siding. I am talking of them as *poems,* rather than as pieces of literature to be studied while the question of their poetry or lack of it is left in abeyance. I am unlikely ever to study them again as literature if I am not drawn to them first as poetry.

I do not have the same reservations concerning *Samson Agonistes* —the reality of the pain and hope in it, the language that embodies them, keep me caught in a terrible spectacle that I believe in and recognize. And some poems of Milton I love without argument—above all the sonnet "On His Deceased Wife":

Methought I saw my late espoused saint
Brought to me like Alcestis from the grave,
Whom Jove's great son to her glad husband gave,
Rescued from Death by force, though pale and faint.
Mine, as whom washed from spot of childhood taint
Purification in the Old Law did save,
And such as yet once more I trust to have
Full sight of her in Heaven without restraint,
Came vested all in white, pure as her mind.
Her face was veiled; yet to my fancied sight
Love, sweetness, goodness, in her person shined
So clear as in no face with more delight.
But, O! as to embrace me she inclined,
I waked, she fled, and day brought back my night.

Here everything that Milton was and may have known about poetry was caught up and enslaved, as it should have been, in the grief, the unique pain, the strangely nourished hope, of his experience. Every phrase of the poem and the order in which it falls contributes to this. The classical reference in the opening lines, with the peculiarly Miltonic twist through which "Jove's great son" is made to infer Christ as well as Herakles, as if only for this one occasion, evokes the peculiar suffering of the tragedy of Euripedes; it also involves us in the desire for the return of the beloved from death, and warns us at the same time that the return is illusory, something on a stage in another world. And it is followed by the simple tender solicitude that would be appropriate for flesh and blood, that one would feel and be *glad* to feel—"though pale and faint." The next lines about purification in the Old Law have been criticized as pedantic; to me, for once, they are anything but that; they are Milton's pleading with whatever powers there are, whatever law, to admit that "this is all right." "It is all right, please see; the conditions *have* been fulfilled; the taint of death has been removed like the taint of birth; please let it be real, and let me accept it without doubt." And it is the knowledge of doubt and the habit of bleakness, deprivation, and reality as we ordinarily see it in our blind way, that makes the lines pathetically poignant. And they are followed by the lines in which (*before* he has lost her in his narrative) he reminds himself and us of his hope of seeing her "really" in Heaven "without restraint." The rest of the poem, what can one say about that? That intricately unbearable phrase about his "fancied sight" with all the levels of meaning by which it refers to his living eyes and their blindness, to his dream, to appearance itself, to his wife whom he had never seen even in her lifetime, as he had never seen the garden of Eden, to the present vision of her, and to the hope of vision and her presence in an afterlife. Then the embrace. The rest. The motion of it, the action, is absolutely central to Milton, and moments that rephrase it are scattered through all his poetry, and very often have a peculiarly authentic directness to them: I mean the circumstances of vision, the yearning toward it and then having it snatched away and having to sit in the dark and explain it, try to prove it to oneself, try to set it in the future again, having suffered its loss in the past. It is the argument of *Paradise Lost* and *Regained* and of *Samson Agonistes.* It was obviously his real theme. It is already there in "The Nativity Ode," where his vision of the golden age—the first, and one of the most touching of his statements of the vision of Eden—is suddenly caught up short with: "But wisest Fate says No—This must not be so," we cannot return to Eden until, in that poem, the child Jesus has grown up and been crucified, with all that the story of the passage implies about human behavior and life.

Milton's great theme has to do with innocence, but early in his writing a division in his approach to it was already clear; it provided for many of the pages in Milton that I am not presently drawn to, and for some of the most moving, vibrant, and pure things he wrote. It was Innocence that allowed Harmony with the Creation, and allowed us to be at one with its purpose and hear its music. But already in *Comus* Milton is concerned not with Innocence but with Virtue, and indeed most explicitly with Chastity, and there is nothing to convince us that these were to be understood as poor symbols of Innocence itself. The connection between Virtue and Innocence may have been closer in the seventeenth century, but I cannot believe that the words were ever synonymous. And it seems to me that a great deal of the Milton of the Paradise poems, while apparently concerned with the subject of Innocence, is really occupied, and deliberately so, with Virtue. There are moments, of course, and some sustained ones, when the glimpse of Innocence recurs—one of the most famous being, through a profound irony, the one evoked by the end of *Paradise Lost* and the departure from Eden. For me, the compelling poetry in Milton is as elusive as these glimpses, to which his celebrated rhetoric may well bear the same relation that Virtue does to Innocence, and poetic craft to the gifts of the ear. These are moments that would seem to have come to him apart from all his artifice: they must, as he says, have been favors of his celestial patroness

> who deignes
> Her nightly visitation unimplor'd
> And dictates to me slumb'ring, or inspires
> Easie my unpremeditated Verse.

I find them in unexpected places, including passages that I have long
known, no longer care for in the main, but in which I never saw them;
these lines, for instance, in the opening of *Paradise Lost,* which suddenly ring out with a different note:

> What in me is dark
> Illumine, what is low raise and support;

or this, to Eve:

> Whom fliest thou? Whom thou fliest, of him thou art,
> His flesh, his bone; to give thee being I lent
> Out of my side to thee, nearest my heart,
> Substantial life, to have thee by my side . . .

or this, of Satan:

> Now conscience wakes despair
> That slumbered; wakes the bitter memory
> Of what he was, what is . . .

or this:

> as when the total kind
> Of birds, in orderly array on wing,
> Came summoned over Eden to receive
> Their names of thee . . .

or the irony of the blind slave Samson, saying of himself

> Ask for this great deliverer now . . .

and

> if it be true
> That light is in the soul,
> She all in every part, why was the sight
> To such tender ball as th' eye confined.

I am not sure what Virtue has to do with poetry, even Milton's, but I
believe that Innocence is something of which poetry never entirely
despairs. The loss of Innocence, and the incapacity for it, are somewhere

behind almost all of tragedy, and they haunt much of the grief in the world's elegies.

Perhaps only fragments of Milton still speak to me; yet some of them speak more clearly than I could have hoped, and they are the passages— and I hope more may be uncovered to me—in which that part of Milton that was the poet of Innocence managed to speak like himself.

"FACT HAS TWO FACES": INTERVIEW

Ed Folsom and Cary Nelson

EF: I know you have some ambivalence about doing interviews. Why?

WSM: If the interviewers are unprepared or the questions are remote, you have to give a monologue to save the occasion. Then the risk is self-indulgence. The interviews we know well, I suppose, started with those in *Paris Review,* about twenty-five years ago. Then it became a very popular form, and I think it's been a happy hunting ground for all sorts of self-indulgence, both in the making and in the reading. It's often a substitute for really thinking about a problem and trying to say something coherent. It can be spontaneous, but sometimes it's just louder, given more seriousness and attention than it probably deserves, but I assume we're doing something different.

EF: You were telling us recently that you have been reading *Leaves of Grass* again. I'm curious about what you find there now.

WSM: I've always had mixed feelings about Whitman. They go back to reading him in my teens, having him thrust at me as the Great American Poet. At the time, coming from my own provincial and utterly unliterary background, I was overly impressed with Culture (with a capital C) so the barbaric yawp didn't particularly appeal to me when I was eighteen, which is an age when it is supposed to, nor did I feel that this was *the* great book written by an American. I've tried over the years to come to terms with Whitman, but I don't think I've ever really succeeded. I've had again and again the experience of starting to read him, reading for a page or two, then shutting the book. I find passages of incredible power and beauty. . . . Yet the positivism and the American

This interview is edited and compiled from three separate conversations with Merwin: Apr. 3, 1981, at a symposium on Merwin's poetry held at Beloit College, arranged by Mary Slowik; Oct. 11, 1981, and Oct. 11, 1984, at Cary Nelson's home in Champaign, Ill. An earlier version of this interview first appeared in *Iowa Review.*

optimism disturb me. I can respond to the romantic side of Whitman, when he presents himself as the voice of feeling, but even then it's not a poetry that develops in a musical or intellectual sense. It doesn't move on and take a growing form—it repeats and finds more and more detail. That bothers me, but in particular it's his rhetorical insistence on an optimistic stance, which can be quite wonderful as a statement of momentary emotion, but as a world view and as a program for confronting existence it bothered me when I was eighteen and bothers me now. It makes me extremely uneasy when he talks about the American expansion and the feeling of manifest destiny in a voice of wonder. I keep thinking about the buffalo, about the Indians, and about the species that are being rendered extinct. Whitman's momentary, rather sentimental view just wipes these things out as though they were of no importance. There's a cultural and what you might call a specietal chauvinism involved. The Whitmanite enthusiasm troubles me for the same reasons; it seems to partake of the very things that bother me in Whitman. I don't know how to say it better than this, which is one reason I didn't write to you about it. I'm not sure I'm very clear about it.

EF: I think you're very clear about it. We were talking this morning about the problems inherent in putting together a *Collected Poems,* especially for you, since you have developed individual books so clearly and with such integrity. People who follow your writing closely, I think, conceive of your career in terms of the various books, more so perhaps than in terms of individual poems. The books are each organic wholes, and each is a separate and clear step in your development, with growth and change in evidence. Each marks an important evolutionary shift. Whitman, on the other hand, is a poet who insisted on writing one book over a lifetime, and that's part of the reason for the uncomfortable positivism that pervades his work, isn't it? He starts out with this incredible positivism which is rampant in the mid-century, in the 1850s, which grows out of his sense of exhilaration about manifest destiny, about America as a ceaselessly growing field of unified contrarieties. As his career developed, though, the two major historical events of his adult life—the Civil War and the closing of the frontier—destroyed the persona that he had taken on with such burgeoning enthusiasm. Consequently the book—his one growing book—became a burden to him in a way. He could not contradict the book because he was not writing new ones; he was adding on to and readjusting the old one. I'm wondering if some of that positivism in Whitman is there because he refused ever to set his past aside and begin again?

WSM: Several times Whitman sees something essential about the American situation. F. O. Matthiessen describes it too: in a democracy one of the danger points is rhetoric, public rhetoric. I think now, looking back, that he is also describing his own weakness. Both Whitman's strength and his weakness is that he is basically a rhetorical poet. And he's rhetorical not only in the obvious sense that all poetry is rhetorical, but in the sense of rhetoric as public speech: you decide on a stance and then you bring in material to flesh out that stance, to give details to your position. This is one of the things that makes me uneasy about Whitman. The stance is basically *there;* and much of the poetry simply adds detail to it. So many of the moments in Whitman that I really love are exceptions to this. Yet to my mind, these exceptions occur far too infrequently. Most of the time he's making a speech. The whole *Leaves of Grass* in a sense is a speech. It's a piece of emotional propaganda about an emotional approach to a historical moment. It's almost set up in a way which makes it impossible for it to develop, to deepen, or to reflect on itself and come out with sudden new perspectives.

Certainly that urge to write propaganda is one I not only understand but sympathize with. But I think it's an urge that doesn't often make poetry. Of course poetry should never be completely devoid of the desire to make something happen—it would only be decoration then—and that desire to make something happen is the part of you that is writing propaganda: so it's always there. After all, there is a kind of desperate hope built into poetry now; one really wants, hopelessly, to save the world, and one tries to say everything that can be said for the things that one loves, while there's still time. But I don't think it can be messianic, you know; poets can't go out and preach on the street corners to save the world.

EF: What about some of the poems of the "Drum Taps" period like the "Wound Dresser"?

WSM: They're some of my favorite passages, because his theory won't support him there. He's simply paying attention to what he sees in front of him. I find those poems both sharper and more moving than many other things in Whitman.

EF: But they tend to get lost in that vast programmed structure of *Leaves of Grass . . .*

WSM: He allows himself to get lost in it, insisting on inciting the bird of freedom to soar . . .

CN: Even in those poems in which he is depressed by what he sees and admits his difficulty in dealing with it—rather than announcing it yet again as an appropriate occasion for his enthusiasm—some of the same role as the representative speaker for the country, the role of the speaker voicing the collective condition of America, continues to be foregrounded, though perhaps with less mere rhetoric, less oracular theatricality.

WSM: I'm very anxious not to be unfair to him. I'm not altogether convinced, as you must guess, by the deliberate stance, but there's obviously a wonderful and generous human being behind it, and a quite incredible and original gift, equally incredible power. But those misgivings have been quite consistent now for all these years, so I guess I'm going to have to live with them.

EF: Do you conceive of your own writing, your own career, as the creation of one large book?

WSM: Well, your whole work *is* one large book, because there is a more or less audible voice running through everything. At least I would like to think that one's work becomes a coherent project eventually, that poems are not merely disparate pieces with no place in the whole. But I don't conceive of deliberately trying to construct a single book the way Whitman was trying to do with *Leaves of Grass*. I don't think of that even in terms of the separate books. I never set out to write *The Lice*, or to write *The Carrier of Ladders*, but wrote until at a particular point something seemed to be complete. On what terms, or on the basis of what assumptions, I wouldn't be able to say, any more than I would with a single poem be able to say, "Ah, that poem is finished."

EF: You have said that when you go back to nineteenth-century American writers for a sustaining influence, it's not Whitman you turn to, but Thoreau. I think a lot of people throw Whitman and Thoreau together as part of the American transcendental and romantic tradition. What draws you to Thoreau that doesn't draw you to Whitman?

WSM: I suppose the way in which he meant "In wildness is the preservation of the world" for one thing. Or the recognition that the human cannot exist independently in a natural void; whatever the alienation is that we feel from the natural world, we are *not* in fact alienated, so we cannot base our self-righteousness on that difference. We're part of that whole thing. And the way Thoreau, very differently from Whitman, even in a paragraph takes his own perception and develops it into a deeper and deeper way of seeing something—the actual seeing in Thoreau is one of the things that draws me to him. I think that Thoreau saw in a way that nobody had quite seen before; it was American in that sense. I don't know if Williams talks about Thoreau, but I would have liked to hear what Williams had to say about Thoreau's capacity to see, even though Williams's great sympathy is more toward Whitman. Indeed I've suspected for a long time that an American poet's sympathy would tend to go either toward Whitman or toward Thoreau, not toward both. Gary Snyder at this point is rather snippy about Thoreau, says he's very uptight, WASP, and so forth. That's a way of describing Thoreau's weaknesses all right—such as his lack of any automatic spontaneous sympathy for his fellow human beings. Thoreau is not all-embracing. The kind of hawky thing in Thoreau puts off the enthusiasts of enthusiasm itself, the great Whitmanite hugs of feeling, the lovers, "I love my fellow man." Perhaps if you really are there you don't have to say it so often and so loudly. A good friend recently was reading Henry James and Thoreau and getting very impatient with James and reading a passage of Thoreau and saying, "You know, for James the natural world is scenery outside the window." There's never anything alive out there. And for Thoreau, when he sees it, it's alive, completely alive, not a detail in a piece of rhetoric. And he leaves open what its significance is. He realizes that the intensity with which he's able to see it *is* its significance. This is an immense gesture of wisdom in Thoreau that I miss in Whitman. Whitman's wonderful expansive enthusiasm isn't there in Thoreau, though he has things of equal beauty and power. The last page of *Walden* is certainly one of the most beautiful things ever written, and of a kind of elevation that Whitman himself was trying to reach all the time.

EF: Yes, Whitman does tend to dwell a bit too long on "camaraderie," as if it's something he's trying to *invoke* rather than to *describe.* I think in that sense there's a real loneliness at the heart of Whitman.

WSM: There is at the heart of both of those writers, but it's quite obvious in Thoreau, he makes no bones about it. There's that wonderful passage where he says, I don't pay enough attention to my fellow human beings, I don't feel strongly enough about them, I don't take enough interest in them, and I'm going to do something about that: these people down here working on the bridge, I'm going to walk closer to them and see if I can't think of them as though they were groundhogs.

EF: Do you read Thoreau often?

WSM: Well, I keep him in the john. He's been there for years. So I go back and read things over again. I think *Walden* is an incredible book. I feel grateful to Thoreau in a way. He's been a companion. Yet I see

Thoreau's limitations, too, including whatever it is that makes him write by tacking one sentence onto another sentence out of notebooks, and putting them together. It's a strange way of writing, though he's not the first person in history to write that way, after all.

EF: Your myriad translations suggest all kinds of affinities for you from outside America, but are there other American writers besides Thoreau that you find yourself returning to, that you would call sustaining influences?

WSM: Thoreau is really the main one that I go back to. There's nobody really before Thoreau. There was a time when I used to read Mark Twain for fun, but apart from *Huckleberry Finn,* which I love, I find that he doesn't last very well. I don't even find him very funny anymore. And then I read an early book, his book about Hawaii. It's amazing how much racism and John Wayne-ism there was in that generation.

CN: Has Thoreau been behind some of the prose that you've written recently? You're writing about your family and your past, which are very different topics from his, but there's a certain humility about phenomenal existence that I see both in Thoreau and in these pieces from your prose book, *Unframed Originals.*

WSM: I hadn't thought of that, Cary; that's interesting. Maybe so, who knows?

EF: Certainly that position you put yourself in when you buy the old abandoned house in France at the end of that one autobiographical essay, called "Hotel"—the position of moving into that house only so far, not wanting to clear the floor and put panes in the windows and paint the walls, but rather only lie there on a simple cot—is a very Thoreau-like position. It's like his bean-field: half-cultivated and half-wild.

WSM: Yes. I guess that's part of what I was talking about a minute ago. That's a wonderful way of putting it, too—his humility before the phenomenal world. If you don't accept the genuine chairness of the chair, if it's all just background, as it is for a great many people in the contemporary world—first the separation from the natural world, then from the phenomenal world—things tend to be seen only in terms of their uses, or in terms of what abstraction they can serve. If the reality of the unreal objects cannot be accepted as an infinite thing in them, you can't see anything. You only see counters in a game that is of very doubtful value.

CN: I feel in your recent pieces a real wariness about rhetorical overstatement, a wish to write in a very delicate and lucid way and not to fall into what might be a Whitmanesque mode of thinking about your own past, but to speak in simple and direct terms about it if possible.

WSM: Well, of course I don't have to tell you that you're always writing in a rhetoric of one kind or another, but I am working to avoid as much as possible a kind of rhetoric which is an emotional screen that keeps you from seeing what you're trying to look at. That's something I did want to do. And I also realized, part way through, since one of the main themes of *Unframed Originals* is what I was not able to know, what I couldn't ever find out, the people I couldn't meet, that reticence was one of the main things I was writing about. Indeed it was a very reticent family. But I felt if I could take any detail, any moment, anything I could clearly see, and pay enough attention to it, it would act like a kind of hologram. I'd be able to see the whole story in that single detail—just the way, if you could really pay attention to a dream, the dream would probably tell you everything you needed to know for that time and place. But obviously any exaggerated rhetoric you were using at that point, in the sense of waving an emotional flag in front of the thing itself, would prevent that from happening.

CN: I have been trying to distinguish between the way your poetry of the last twenty years makes me think about language and the rather different view of language that I detect in *Unframed Originals.* At least from *The Moving Target* on, it seems you felt it necessary—if you were to write as the present conditions of the world required you to write—to let language *do* to you what it would, to let language in effect have its way with you. In these recent prose pieces I sense a new wariness about that, a desire *not* to let language have its way. I'm wondering whether that rings true at all, or even whether you have some sense that the recent prose pieces are written in a significantly different mode, that they show a real change in your relationship to words?

WSM: It must be, but I wasn't aware of it when it was happening. And to connect that with what we were just saying, when you're trying to avoid that one kind of rhetoric, of course you're developing a different kind of rhetoric. I had a feeling of trying to write in what years ago I suppose I would have described as a kind of classical way, in which the form of the prose, the form of the writing, was in the service of but not swallowed up by the subject, so you were really deliberately formed through the language. The language ordered what you were seeing, unlike, to choose a very different alternative, a stream of consciousness style. Yet I'm unaware of some of the other differences. I certainly don't want to keep doing what I've done before, and if it feels as though I'm just doing something I've done before then obviously I don't want to be doing it. But I don't very often have some deliberate, conscious notion of what direction I want to move in; when I started off to write those pieces I knew that I wanted to handle that material, to put it down, to give it what would be the clearest and sharpest possible form, but I didn't know how to go about it, and having finished the book, I would still feel I didn't know how to go about it, and don't know now. I don't think I *know* how to write anything, but particularly I don't know how to write prose.

EF: Certainly there is a dramatic shift in the way your prose *feels* from *The Miner's Pale Children* to *Unframed Originals.*

WSM: How do you see the difference?

EF: I see the difference corresponding to the difference between the poems from that period and your most recent poems. The change of voice in your most recent poems is surprising, and moves further in the direction of the more colloquial language of *The Compass Flower.* Your recent poems are allowing a much more colloquial language into themselves than I've heard before. They're allowing a kind of clear narrative development that they have not had before—one of the ones you read the other night, as I told you, reminded me of Williams's "Plot of Ground." It seems to me a movement that is first evident in many of the poems of *Compass Flower.* The language seemed to grow less gnomic in tone, much more inviting. The voice became more relaxed, and I sense the same thing in the recent prose. As I'm describing this, I realize I'm not saying the same thing Cary is—Cary senses something almost opposite to this in the recent prose, a reticence and a tightening. . . . But we would both agree that *The Miner's Pale Children* is a book which goes much more with the period of *The Lice* and *The Carrier of Ladders* than these recent pieces. Do you feel that?

WSM: But I don't think there's a contradiction. You're saying different things, but I think it's possible for both of these things to be happening at the same time. I certainly wanted the prose to handle material that it never had before, and to do it as plainly and directly as possible. Plainness is the thing you are both saying is involved here.

CN: It seems that it would have been immensely dissatisfying for you to write about this subject matter in the style of *The Miner's Pale Children* or *Houses and Travellers.*

WSM: But I also think there's been an impulse in the direction of plainness for a long time. It's been growing, and it goes back quite far. I've seen some critical commentary confusing plainness and what's been called the *quietness* of the poems. I don't know if they really are quiet or not. They don't seem quiet to *me* obviously. But there are not so many decibels as there are in Whitman, though Whitman has moments of another kind of power. A line like "A woman waits for me" seems to me to have at least as much emotional power as "I hear America singing"—you know, I don't care if he hears America singing; I *do* care when he says "A woman waits for me."

CN: But there are moments, at least in *The Lice* and *The Carrier of Ladders,* when one might say you hear America dying. There is something of that role of speaking in a representative way for the culture, obviously not with Whitman's enthusiasm, but with virtually the same energy in reverse. Were there times in working, say, on the American sequence in *The Carrier of Ladders* and on some of the poems of real horror in *The Lice,* when you felt yourself in Whitman's position but with a very different message, with a very different tone?

WSM: Very much, yes. One of the things that I found happening, not deliberately, as I tried to write those American poems at different times, again and again—I don't think it's possible for me to see or to approach that subject—it never has been—without the feeling that Ed was describing as we drove across the country yesterday, this feeling of inhabiting a palimpsest. However long the culture may have left, we are *not* just sitting here on a Sunday afternoon. Insofar as there is any historical or temporal continuity at all, that continuity involves these many layers, many of them invisible, and they are not different at all from the repressed, pressed, and forgotten layers of our own experience. And if we really are so dishonest and so mutilated that we can't make any sense of the world, or come to any terms with them, then our lives are maimed and truncated accordingly—our imaginative lives and probably our physical lives too. You know I've felt various things about that over the years and very often the rage that you, Ed, said that your father felt when he saw what was happening to the soil of this country—I can imagine feeling it about the soil, too. For a while I used to think of it in terms of two myths, two Western myths, one of them the myth of Orpheus obviously—the important thing there is that Orpheus is singing with the animals all around him listening—and one can take that as a myth of arrogation or as a myth of harmony. It's both, you know, it is homocentric but it's also inclusive, and everything is there in the act of singing. And the other is the myth of Phaethon, who says "Daddy, I want to drive those horses," and ends up with a holocaust . . . and the beginning of racism. It's probably not as simple as that, but at one point I kept seeing it in terms of those two myths—harmonious interaction with the living world, or envy and exploitation of it. But the American poems. Let me approach them in another way.

F. O. Matthiessen, as I remember, years ago was talking about the attempt of a number of American writers to find an American myth of history; Richard Howard quotes that wonderful passage at the beginning of his book, from which his title comes, *Alone with America.* You know, one can begin to see differently the great phony myth of the "winning of the West"—it was the *destruction* of the West. It *was* heroic, but it was heroic in an incredibly cramped and vicious way. People did suffer and were magnificent, but they were also broken and cruel, and in the long run incredibly destructive, irreversibly destructive. What we've done to this continent is something *unbelievable* —to think that one species could have done this in a hundred years. Right where we're sitting. And this is our lives. This is not something to have an opinion about, this is what we live with, this is our bodies and our minds, this is what our words come out of, and we should know.

EF: Cary was suggesting that in *The Lice* and *The Carrier of Ladders* you sometimes take on the voice of the culture in a kind of negative way. I'm wondering if sometimes too the voice in those books is not that of the other animals, if your desire throughout your work is not in part to accomplish what is both impossible and absolutely necessary, that is, to give voice to the voiceless beings, to those creatures that cannot speak their rage. Do you at times feel your voice coming not from the human culture but instead from the silent herds being destroyed by that human culture?

WSM: It would be very presumptuous to agree to that, but insofar as I dare to suggest a formula for myself or anyone else, I think it's very important to remain open to that possibility, to welcome it, and to evoke it if possible. Otherwise, what else is there? Otherwise, one is there in an ego-bound, historical, culturally brainwashed, incredibly limited moment. One can't perceive anything because one has no perspective at all. The opposite—the nearest thing I can imagine to what I would think of as a sound or even healthy approach and attitude toward existence as a whole (as distinct from the endless separation of the human species from the rest of existence that leads to evaluating the one at the expense of the other)—would be Blake's "How do you know but ev'ry Bird that cuts the airy way, / Is an immense world of delight, clos'd to your senses five?" It works both ways, one both can be and can never be the bird.

EF: I think of "For a Coming Extinction," where the voice shifts a great deal, trying to speak to the gray whale while being aware of the fiction that the gray whale can hear us anyway, and then at the end of the poem becoming the voice of the culture: "Tell him / that it is we who are important." The most ironic lines in your poems occur when your voice shifts into that mode of speaking for the culture.

WSM: I hadn't thought of that.

EF: And when the voice seems least ironic and the most enraged, it seems to be speaking from somewhere that one cannot name, that is not within our culture. It is not a voice speaking from within, but a voice that has to dismiss itself from the culture for a time in order to speak the rage.

WSM: Like "Avoiding News by the River."

EF: Yes.

CN: It's more difficult, it seems to me, to decide what voice is speaking in the passage right before that in "For a Coming Extinction": "Consider what you will find in the black garden / And its court / The sea cows the Great Auks the gorillas / The irreplaceable hosts ranged countless / And fore-ordaining as stars / Our sacrifices." At first in that passage there's an extraordinary and, I think, powerfully unresolvable sense of anger . . .

WSM: I was going to say, even when you read it, that all I hear is the anger with which it was written. It overrides these other distinctions.

EF: But there's a clear double-voice there: "Our sacrifices" carries all of the pride of the destructive culture.

WSM: Yes.

EF: And yet it comes out sounding incredibly angry because we know that the voice that is really speaking this poem and mouthing those words is not emerging from the source that would speak those words with pride.

CN: One also hears a certain contempt even, earned.

WSM: Yes, and you know, driving in the West, I've thought and remembered afterwards, and see it in Hawaii watching these things: you drive along and you see some pile of ditched cars, or a little place where they serve trash—deep-fried food, or something like that—and you think, in order to bring this about dozens of young men were sent off to die of leprosy in the leper colonies, or hundreds of Indians and thousands of buffalo were killed and the whole place has been poisoned for years in order to bring about this little pile of shit. And it's described in terms of the triumph of civilization. What kind of impossible lie is this that we're all subscribing to?

CN: I have a poster version of "For a Coming Extinction" upstairs that I see each time I walk in that room. It's a more immediate and continuing relationship than one can easily have with a poem in a book. Every time I read the poem I enter into a cluster of remarkably divided emotions. Each stanza seems simultaneously fractured and sustained by contradiction. "The End / That great god" suggests at first our lust for extinction, for a kind of demonically hieratic narrative conclusion. Yet a sense of transcendence also enters into the reference to "The End" as a "great god." To the extent that the poem confers a static immortality on the gray whale, it too participates in that act of "sending." There is a certain beauty in these animal "hosts ranged countless," a beauty not canceled either by a sense of loss or by their status as a collective indictment of human history. If we are appalled at the numerical accumulation of slaughtered animals, we are also in awe of the "irreplaceable hosts" now ranged before us. These two impulses are inextricably linked by the poem; it becomes fascinated with that miraculously awful achievement and thus puts forward a far more radically compromised voice than anger alone would permit.

WSM: It would be very difficult and very rare to make a poem out of pure anger, or out of pure anything. Even love poems are seldom made out of pure love. Actually, they're made out of words, so all of the paradoxes that are built into any phrase come into it. Pure anger would just be a scream.

EF: And there can't help but be a fascination with those people who at the end of the poem say, "It is we who are important." You can despise those people, but there's a fascination with them, and you have to come to terms with them because they've constructed the layer of the world we're living on and dying on right now.

WSM: Yes, you *have* to come to terms with them; that doesn't mean that you have to say it's okay.

CN: No, but there are texts of more unqualified anger about this kind of subject matter, not necessarily in your work but elsewhere in contemporary poetry. I think yours is a poem that forces you, if you want to read the poem carefully, to think through your own motivations. It doesn't let you away easily. It doesn't let you off being convinced that you won't continue in this pattern. You may already be part of it.

WSM: That aspect of it is even more apparent probably—from what people have told me, whether they've responded to it with pleasure or with annoyance—in that pineapple poem that was published a couple of years ago. People obviously find that they're being got at in different points in the poem, and don't like the attack.

EF: That reminds me of another poem from *The Lice,* "A Scale in May," where this issue of a double-voice is central. The "I" in this poem seems to be able to identify the problem of human arrogance while simultaneously recognizing his own participation in that arrogance.

A Scale in May

Now all my teachers are dead except silence
I am trying to read what the five poplars are writing
On the void

Of all the beasts to man alone death brings justice
But I desire
To kneel in a doorway empty except for the song

Who made time provided also its fools
Strapped in watches and with ballots for their choices
Crossing the frontiers of invisible kingdoms

To succeed consider what is as though it were past
Deem yourself inevitable and take credit for it
If you find you no longer believe enlarge the temple

Through the day the nameless stars keep passing the door
That have come all that way out of death
Without questions

The walls of light shudder and an owl wakes in the heart
I cannot call upon words
The sun goes away to set elsewhere

Before nightfall colorless petals blow under the door
And the shadows
Recall their ancestors in the house beyond death

At the end of its procession through the stone
Falling
The water remembers to laugh

Looking back on it now, what can you tell us about the voice in this poem?

WSM: I'm trying to remember exactly when the poem was written, and I can't. Obviously it was written sometime in the '60s, in the spring. I'm not a theorist and in any case I don't want to embed it in a theory that implies it was written with the whole thing worked out intellectually in advance. But in hindsight I think I see that certain things I've been trying to say for years seem to have been converging all the way along. I see quite a number of them in that poem. But I'd better say something first about the progression; the middle part—the second, third, and fourth sections—are set up in ways which can be taken either straight or ironically, and I would like them to be taken both ways. They've been written about, in criticism, from both points of view, as though each excluded the other, and that wasn't the intention. And, as Ed has pointed out, the use of language in a particular way to possess the world is part of what I *felt,* much of my life, to be a very dangerous human arrogance, one which no one is exempt from—we're sitting here as part of that arrogance. We arrogate to ourselves things that do not belong to us, that don't belong to anybody. I don't want to develop that as a kind of ethical matter and say how I think we should solve the ecological problems, pollution, and so on. As I suggested the other night, I think that the first hope of mankind begins in simply caring about those things.

The thing that I *do* want to try to say something about, as a basis for talking about the poems of that time, and probably all of the poems I've written since, is that—to put it personally first—I used to feel that it was a terrible fault of character not to be able to come to clear resolutions and decisions about things, that I would always be seeing two sides of something, and saying "Yes, but." Of course that *is* a fault of character, but at the same time the character *does* use a left and right hand, the heart does beat both ways. And I've come to believe that existence—and by that I don't mean just human existence, I mean existence as a whole—has always got, basically, these two aspects to it, one which is relative, and the other which is not relative at all. The second, of course, is the teacher who is not dead, the world of silence. But that's also the world in which you can't call upon words. The arrogance comes from saying that that world doesn't exist or is of no importance, when of course in my view it's that world that gives words their real life. It also allows them to be luminous, transparent, and to illuminate the world, which in itself is transparent and luminous. Arrogance and an attempt to possess that world as something which is absolutely solid and can belong to somebody, completely nullifies that whole dimension of existence, and deprives existence of any kind of sense, and it deprives it of its senses. It deprives us of our own senses. The sense of smell is the first, most obvious one; we've almost lost it; it's going away from us. If you take that as a basic note to the poem, I think it will help make the poem ring clear. And I don't think that idea is a very difficult one, though it's probably a difficult *feeling* to come to terms with. And very little of our public, social, and historical experience, our experience in the time that we live in, fits us for coming to terms with it; we're being shunted away from it all the time, and it is very uncomfortable, until we accept it. Then I think it is the only comforting thing there is. That's why the water remembers to laugh.

EF: I'm curious about what you might have to say about the form that you used in this particular poem—a three-line stanza which becomes a form you return to quite often: in *Asian Figures,* in *Finding the Islands.* In this poem these varying perceptions are all captured in those three-line moments. What attracts you to that form?

WSM: Well, it goes farther back than that. There are poems in *The Moving Target* which are in that form, and I wrote a number of poems in the form at that time, but I didn't publish most of them. A little later I tried to develop and figure out what I was doing. One of the things I wanted to find ... you know, when people say "I don't understand modern poetry" or "I don't understand any poet," sometimes they mean they have difficulty in apprehending intention and subject and so on, but I think that sometimes it's a temporary inability to grasp an unfamiliar sense of completeness, a new recognition of how things can be complete. And at one point I wanted to see what it was that made a poem complete as a small, if not the smallest, unit; it was a way of discovering what was the single thing that would stand by itself. Why I gravitated to a three-line form I don't know, but that seemed to me the ideal small form. And in *Asian Figures* I really was trying to see just what was the *smallest* form, not that I wanted to stay there, but I wanted to explore this idea of completeness. And then when you start putting these complete things together, do you see them as separate or in relation to each other? It's a question, I think, that art is always suggesting: this is complete, yet at the same time, what is its relation to everything? I would like these poems to do some of the same things that haiku do in

Japanese, though they aren't haiku and I don't read Japanese, so I don't know precisely what haiku do in Japanese. But I am intrigued with Bashō's linked haiku, small units playing off each other, creating a whole.

EF: Returning for a moment to the irony, the double-voice, in this poem—to what extent does the "I" separate itself from the world of fools?

WSM: Well, you're asking a question that has a double answer: how much do I remember about my intention of the poem, and what do I feel now, which is the only place I can answer it from. I think that was deliberately left up in the air because the "I" is *not* separate from the fools; on the other hand, the "I" is judging a kind of human action, a human gesture, it wants to be separate from. Of course we're all fools; I have a watch in my pocket (I don't have it strapped on). The foolish thing is to take that world which we have made as the real, total, absolute final world, and say we have it—it's ours. You know, I doubt whether one can come to anything that resembles a moral judgment without seeming to be outside it. On the other hand, you can't altogether make one without identifying yourself with the person you're judging, whether you know it or not. You don't see it if you're totally separate from it. But deploring an action doesn't necessarily mean that one is saying "It's them"—it's us. If you see someone beating a dog, and there's nothing you can do about stopping it, you feel angry, but part of your anger probably is bound up with the fact that somewhere inside you, you're capable of beating a dog. But you may not stop to think, "Is it me? Am I being self-righteous?" You want to stop the beating of the dog. I want "them" to stop destroying the Northwest, killing the salmon, killing them both in the sense of thinking that they're unimportant, and in the physical sense of polluting the rivers; both of them are really the same thing.

But I can't really remember with any close or absolute accuracy what I was trying to do in this poem. And, you know, it would not be an authentic poem if the *intellectual* intention were the real, final guiding force in the poem. This is another way of recognizing that other dimension; I think a real poem comes out of what you don't know. You write it with what you know, but finally its source is what you don't know. There's a passage where Thoreau says, "How can someone find his ignorance if he has to use his knowledge all the time?" The arrogance would be the assumption that what you know has some kind of final value and you can depend upon it, and it will get rid of a whole world which you will never know, which really informs it. . . . Both of these worlds, in my view, are without meaning; there is absolutely no meaning in either, but the *sense* of the world of relation comes from them nonetheless.

EF: When we get to *The Compass Flower*, the ecological rage and ironies and devastations that I feel everywhere in *The Lice* seem to have changed dramatically. The ecological poems in *The Compass Flower* tend to have a tone like that of "The Trees"—a sadness at what's about to be gone and a recollection of what it is that the trees have offered. It's a very different tone from that in *The Lice*. Obviously you could not remain at the point you had arrived at in *The Lice*, where it seems to me that you were on the verge of not writing poems at all . . .

WSM: Absolutely right. In fact most of the time that I was writing *The Lice* I thought I had pretty well given up writing, because there was really no point in it. For different reasons—much the same way that I think some writers of continental Europe felt late in the Second World War and after, that there was really no point in going on writing; what they had experienced was just terrible beyond anything that language could deal with, and there was no point in even trying, and there was probably no one to write it for either, for very long. That can easily be described as despair, but I think it may not be just despair—it may be a kind of searing vision: a dumb vision, and I don't think you can stay there if you're going to go on living.

EF: Your books since *The Lice* form a clear and eloquent record of how you have come to grips with that despair, and moved beyond it. But I'm interested in your own personal version of how you came to terms with going on to write after *The Lice*. What happened to the rage and the anger and the despair?

WSM: Oh, I think they're all still there, but I suppose some lucky recognition that the anger itself could destroy the thing that one was angry in defense of, and that the important thing was to try to keep what Cary described as humility before phenomenal things: the fact that that chair may be destroyed tomorrow is no reason not to pay attention to it this afternoon, you know. The world *is* still around us, and there is that aspect of other human beings which has *not* been solely destructive, and to which one is constantly in debt, and which involves simply the pleasure of existing together, being able to look and see the trees, the cat walking in and out of the room. The answer to even one's anger is in the way one can see those things, the way that one can live with them. Not very often, perhaps for no more than a few seconds at a time. Even so, one lives second by second.

CN: I have been reading *The Compass Flower* the past few days and thinking about its relationship to the four books preceding it. From *The Moving Target* through *Writings to an Unfinished Accompaniment,* your special vocabulary—including words like silence, darkness, emptiness—is taken up by historical circumstances, permeated by a particular feeling about our culture's destiny. During that time it seemed to many of us that our culture's destiny was being played out in very visible and unarguable ways. In *The Compass Flower* you are often trying to write very different poetry, including love poetry, yet this vocabulary in a way returns to haunt you. In writing the poetry of *The Compass Flower* was it a struggle to deal again with words that were colored by a different sense of history, or at least words that seemed decisively to belong to the public world and its power to enter into and transform our private lives?

WSM: I think so. They are words that I used with increasing caution, because they can become habitual, they can become counters. They can have an emptiness which obscures their real emptiness; they can become sentimental indeed in that way. They can simply become one's own signatures that are habitual. That's really self-defeating.

CN: I would say that some of those same words become habitual in Kinnell. Indeed it's a risk for many poets—a vocabulary like that becomes so much a part of the way they write that it's merely instinctive.

WSM: Yes. Well, obviously I'm not going to try to never, never use those words, but I use them with increasing, deliberate self-consciousness. If I use them now it's with a kind of self-consciousness I wouldn't have had using them fifteen or twenty years ago.

CN: In the period of *The Lice* the self-consciousness would have gotten in the way.

WSM: That's right. The funny thing is now, when you're both talking about that, I realize that there is a small group of relatively recent poems in which the kind of magma that produced *The Lice* suddenly insisted on writing, bringing out the same vein again, just before the inauguration of Reagan.

CN: Well, we're going to have more occasions like that. The history that wrote *The Lice* or that's there in *The Lice* has hardly left us.

WSM: I think so. I didn't set out to write those poems. Several poems suddenly came out with more of that quality than I knew was going to be there. At that particular time, I felt a great deal of that: the British presence in Ireland, what Reagan was up to, and Watt, my return to Pennsylvania and seeing what the result of the new policies was there— total devastation.

EF: Those recent poems surprise me somewhat. I feel in them the same anger that was in *The Lice,* the same rage, but what is different is that the historical allusions are direct and clear. The allusions are not defamiliarized for the reader, as often happens in *The Lice.* In *The Lice,* you may be talking about an assassination, but the name of who was assassinated does not appear, and in fact there would not be a direct or clear allusion to any of the actual events of the assassination.

WSM: Actually both of the assassination poems in *The Lice* were written before the assassinations.

EF: So they really were not historical poems . . .

WSM: The one was written very shortly before the Kennedy assassination; the other one very shortly—about three days—before Martin Luther King was killed. I better not write any more of them.

CN: I think it's difficult to say the poems in *The Lice* are not historical poems. The process at work for a reader is one in which a core of precise historical referentiality becomes uncertain and unstable, even blurred, in the poem. Yet in a way the poem's historicity becomes more representative as a result. The poem presents a history potentially more possessive of us and where we are in time. The specificity begins to erode as the poem proceeds.

WSM: I have a recent poem with a reference to the IRA hunger strike, but I'm uncertain about that passage, and I'm thinking of taking the extremely specific reference out of the poem. Although I very much wanted it to be in there when I wrote the poem, I'm not sure it belongs there. I don't think it strengthens the poem, or even serves the reasons for having that specific passage there in the first place.

EF: This talk of referentiality ties in with your description of how you came to deal with writing poetry after arriving at the wordless position you were in upon completing *The Lice.* There seems to be a gradual realization that the world is still here, that you could still be attentive to the things that were around you—that's certainly the feeling that I sense growing book by book after *The Lice.* A striking example of this new feeling is "St. Vincent's" in *The Compass Flower.* This is a poem that to me marks a new kind of attentiveness, a new kind of use of language, that I find more and more, as I've said, in your autobiographical prose pieces. We have that same concern with wanting to keep the senses open—there seems to be a feeling in this poem that there's been a place there for a long time that has been part of your common experience; you see it every day, and yet you've never seen it. You've never paid attention to it, never really looked at it. "I consider that I have lived daily and with / eyes open and ears to hear / these years across from St. Vincent's Hospital." And what happens in the poem, then, is a kind of opening of the eyes and ears to the sights and sounds one has learned to dull one's senses to, so that "long / ago I learned not to hear them / even when the sirens stop / they turn to back in / few passers-by stay to look / and neither do I." So there's a sense now of *staying* to look, staying to record, staying to imagine what might be going on beyond the things that one can see and hear if one is attentive enough. And then the poem ends with a question, "who was St. Vincent": the name given to the thing that one has lived across from all the time—I take it that the question *does* ask for an answer, who *was* St. Vincent, and I think of St. Vincent who defined his life by paying attention to those elements in society that no one else paid attention to. So, too, this is a poem about learning to pay attention, it seems to me, to things that one has learned not to pay attention to, by custom, by habit, and then learning to overcome that.

CN: Before you read "The Last One" the other night, you said that you wished that the poem would become so untopical that no one would know what it was about, a comment that I found appealingly subversive. "St. Vincent's" is a poem whose referentiality is more or less inescapable: I wonder if you are comfortable with that, or do you sometimes wish that it, too, had a quality of undecidable plurality, making it impossible merely to link it with that building and that structure.

WSM: No, I don't feel that; I'm very fond of that building. The poem was written in January, I think it was 1975. I've had an apartment for many years across the street from St. Vincent's Hospital, so that's the time and place of it. And it was, I suppose, a particular attempt to do that thing we were talking about, to honor the very specific historic immediate circumstance, to make the poem directly out of that. The poem was a deliberate attempt to practice something closer to the tradition of Williams and Whitman. One of the things that I envy about that tradition sometimes is the ease of address, the immediacy of the use of historical circumstance, which sometimes I would very much like to have been able to use more familiarly myself. But obviously I can't believe that I'm ever going to be in the center of that tradition; I don't share any of the original assumptions. It has seemed to me that *fact* has two faces, too. Fact is in the world of relation—one is always looking at the outside of facts. One sees all the facts from the outside. One is never going to be on the inside until one is caught up *in* the *relation,* then of course you don't *see* the inside; there is no separation between the inside of you and the inside of what you're looking at. They're the same thing. "Who was St. Vincent" remains a question, and it's a question that one goes on asking; it's the question that asks what the relation *is* between the world of history and the world that's shared. And between them and oneself.

There's a moment in St. Vincent's biography when he gave up the life that he'd been living and went to live with the poor whom he'd been serving, because he felt that what he'd been doing was inadequate ... and after the first night of introduction to this terrible squalor, with people beating each other and misery and hunger and the lives falling apart, he woke up in the middle of the night in tears, saying, "Forgive me, God, I did not *know* that this was going on. I didn't know that suffering went this far. I didn't realize that this was in the world."

EF: In "St. Vincent's" the referentiality is very clear; it's all there —we're given the name of the hospital, we're given the context in the book of poems to let us know we're in New York, we know exactly what the building looks like. Is the original St. Vincent's still extant, by the way?

WSM: It's still there, but, you know, like everything else, it's changing. They're tearing the inside out of part of it now, and keeping the facade, which is quite beautiful, the old part of it. But they're expanding. I had a surprise when the poem was published. I met somebody who said that they'd been over there to St. Vincent's for medical reasons, and they'd found the poem pasted on the walls of the elevators. I got a letter from the nun in charge of public relations, who said, "There are a lot of questions in that poem, and if you'd really like them answered, please come by and I'll take you through the hospital," and I did, and had a whole afternoon going around St. Vincent's. . . . The questions are still unanswered.

EF: But the unanswered questions are very different from those in your earlier New York poems. I think, for example, of "Before That" from *The Moving Target,* where you have an image of "Cemeteries sifting on / the city's windows." Do you anticipate that your reader will see the referentiality that you described at your reading the other night, about the crosses being the white *X*'s on the windows of condemned buildings, or is that something that you *remove* from the realm of referentiality in the poem, and only restore at the reading?

WSM: Well, assuming there is going to be a historic future, which is an assumption that we make but we have no real reason to, one can't double-guess which of our historic circumstances are going to be known or matter to people a hundred, two hundred years, hence. I'm unsettled to realize that as the natural world recedes, and as generations of students grow up without having had any contact with it, an enormous number of really very basically simple images are becoming remote, increasingly inaccessible, in traditional poetry and in our own. There's an image in a poem of mine about flies in the middle of the room going around a statue of nothing, and a poet, Robert Bly, came to visit me one day in France and was talking about my poetry being surrealist and used this image as an example; I said, "Come on," and I took him to a room and opened the door and said, "Look," and there were flies going around and around in a circle. There's a whole lot of simple sensual experience related to the natural world which is becoming a thing of the past; I don't think this *can* continue indefinitely. I don't see how we can exist in such an attenuated and deprived context.

CN: When you introduce a poem like "Before That," a poem that seems very open and in some ways gnomic and unstably suggestive, and you gloss certain lines by identifying their object or their occasion, seeming thereby to grant the poem a source and the writing process a moment of origin, what do you feel you've done to the text?

WSM: I feel that I've obscured it. Because I think that I probably provided you and anyone who reads the poem with a distraction. The important thing is to arrive at that insight not through referentiality but through response. Now of course there would be no response without some kind of reference. But obviously I didn't feel that the poem should have more reference than it had when I wrote it. And in a sense putting more "chat" around it than it had then betrays it. Not that I want for it to be a kind of mystification, or anything like that. I want it to present a kind of experience in terms which are not those of the habitual and customary referentiality which is dulled and blunted and exterior. It *is* a cemetery, you know; it's not *like* a cemetery, it's not a lot of white things painted on a window. And its sense is the sense of cemeteries on windows. Just that.

CN: Is it just the pressure of a reading, then, wanting to break the rhythm and make things, at least for a moment, accessible?

WSM: It's a moment of weakness and friendliness.

CN: Was the title poem in *The Drunk in the Furnace* based on a real incident?

WSM: No, it's a complete fiction.

EF: This whole matter of referentiality, historical allusion, is tricky business. Specific references in your poetry can be quite explicit when they are personal or derive from a personal experience. References like that never become "topical" in the way that references to current events do. Topical things fade in a way that personal references don't.

WSM: It has to do with a consistent feeling about poetry, and probably about all of the arts, but certainly about my own poetry, which is that no deliberate program for writing a poem works. A poem begins to be a poem when a sequence of words starts giving off what you might describe as a kind of electric charge, when it begins to have a life of its own that I sense the way I would if I suddenly picked up a shorted electric wire. If it doesn't have that, even if it's got what I would very much like it to have, then it's not working as a poem. I suppose all poets work that way in one way or another, but I notice in many of my contemporaries a more deliberate approach to what they want to put in their poems, though they do it differently and in ways that I have never been able to do it. There are many things I would like to write about or to include in poems, but I've never been able to work that way. The life of the language doesn't happen when it's done that way, so I have to wait. . . .

I had a conversation with Allen Ginsberg some years ago, in New Orleans, when Allen said, "Okay, how would you write a poem about this room?" And I said, "Well, Allen, the difference is that you assume, I guess, that you could write a poem about this room just because you chose to, and I can't make any such assumption. I'm not sure I could write about this room. Perhaps at some point I might be able to, though I wouldn't start necessarily by just jotting down details." It would start with the room, obviously, but we might not agree about what "the room" was. It's a different way of approaching the whole idea of how you write a poem. I'm not sure that I can write a poem just by deliberately setting out to write a poem about, you know, the sofa, or . . . It's a nice idea, but basically there's a part of me that would think, well, you could always do it as an exercise, but if a certain extra dimension isn't there, the brilliance of the exercise won't disguise the fact for very long. This seems to me so obvious that I almost take it for a doctrine, but I realize that there are many poets who don't see it that way at all. I feel that way when I'm reading poems, too. If I can't eventually find that quality there, the poetry bores me.

I think I'm probably often deluded about what I'm doing in my own writing because I keep thinking that I'm getting nearer and nearer to an immediacy of historical detail, and yet when people talk about the poems I realize that may not be their impression. But then for years I thought that I was writing more and more simply and directly, and people kept saying the poems were getting more and more difficult, opaque, harder to read.

EF: We've discussed your relationship with Whitman and other American writers, but what poets do you feel the most natural affinity with?

WSM: My favorite poets, the two that I live with as talismans, are very remote in time and didn't write in English. I would feel even rather diffident about naming them, both out of superstition and awe: François Villon and Dante—not very far apart from each other in time, both medieval poets. And when I began I was fascinated with medieval poetry. I think some of that was due to Pound's influence; I had great admiration for Pound when I was in college. That was partly it; a rebellious stage, because almost no one else admired Pound, and I used to walk around with a beard which I grew just like Pound's. There's one thing that we all owe him, the debt to his way of hearing. That incredible ear runs through much of the *Cantos*. I find them hard to read, not because of intellectual references, which are reason enough, but I keep getting irritated with what the man is saying, the stance, and that cornball American lingo that he keeps lapsing into. But my debt to him began very early.

Whether the affinity with the medieval poets is as close as it was I don't know. I have a debt, as I think everyone does whether they know it or not, to Anonymous; to oral literature as the best one can work toward it. That's the real matrix of possibilities that's always there. I keep saying I'm going to stop translating, and then I find someone else I want to translate. There's still so much possibility that one hasn't touched, found, heard.

EF: Pound clearly had a great influence on you as a translator; how old were you when you met him?

WSM: Well, let's see, eighteen or nineteen; it was three years before

I went to Europe, so I met Pound in 1946. I was only on one visit; I went down to Washington and spent an Easter week or so; I think I went and saw him a couple of times—a couple of afternoons is an awful lot when you're eighteen years old visiting Ezra Pound. It sort of marked me for life, I guess. You know, I admired a lot of things about him, and I dismissed the whole political thing as just something I didn't have to deal with, which wasn't true. But I admired the eccentricity, too, as much as any other thing—the intransigence, the insistence on being a poet, not on following other people's paths.

EF: You have written a good deal about the art of translation, the changing assumptions about what translation is and what needs it serves. One of your translation projects that most fascinates me is your work on the project to translate Ghalib's Ghazals—you translated some of them and they were printed along with translations by several other poets.

WSM: That was an interesting project, several poets translating the same material; not enough was made of it, really. In some cases, with the ones I translated, I did several translations of the same poem: what I had in mind was Cezanne's *Mont Sainte-Victoire* paintings, where he painted the same mountain over and over. There was a book published ten years or so after Attila Jozsef, the great Hungarian poet, committed suicide—sometime in the 1950s a bunch of French poets—Cocteau and Eluard, many of the best French poets who were then alive—took a dozen poems of Jozsef's, and they all did translations of the same poems into French, so that you could read the poem in eight or nine different translations by different poets. By the time you had done it, you didn't have the Hungarian, but you had a funny, strange sense of the poem as though it had been reflected by eight or nine different mirrors. I thought there was a lot to be said for translating that way, even for myself, because there are many ways of looking at a single poem that you've been wanting to bring over; you may want to bring over different aspects of it each time. There's no final way of translating anything. And so you might as well make several mirrors of the same poem, make several poems out of it.

EF: I'm curious about how your translation work teaches and forms voices for your own poetry, or how much your own poetic voice predetermines the voice of your translations. When you read "The Last One" the other night, you mentioned that you had in mind a creation myth—is that the "Creation of the Moon," which you translated from the Amazon native original? A part of that translation reads, "So the head started to think what it would turn into / If it turned into water they would drink it . . . " and so on. It moves on with that repetitive line structure, and the feel of the poem is very much like "The Last One." Do your translations modify your own voice, or vice versa? I guess it can't help but work both ways . . .

WSM: Yes, I think it works both ways. I'm very anxious not ever to do that—and I don't mean this as a pejorative comment on Cal Lowell's work at all—but I never wanted to do what he did; I never wanted to take the work of someone else and use it simply as a springboard for providing poems of my own. And I persuaded myself, for the sake of practice, until the late '60s, and that first book of selected translations, that I did keep them separate. There were various ways of keeping them separate. On the other hand, something that you become involved with as intimately as translation, if you're working at it over a period of time, and something in which you use words as deliberately as you do in translation, is bound to affect your own writing. And besides, what you want to translate is already an indication of an affinity that you had before you found that poem to translate. So I was not ever deliberately looking around in translation for something that I could use as the starting point for poems of mine. Yet that particular kind of movement— the repetitive line structure—that you're describing is an example of something that provided a suggestion, something I wanted to echo, a deliberate allusion.

A great deal of anonymous oral literature seems to me endlessly suggestive, not as something to be imitated, crudely and directly, but as a reminder that the possibilities open to us at any moment are not as limited as we might suppose. The world is not as simple and as codified and conventional as you thought it was. There is even a convention that recurs in oral literature in which the consideration of possibilities becomes itself a kind of form. In one Spanish ballad a girl has had her dead lover for seven years in the room, and she says, "If I tell my father, this will happen; if I tell my mother, this will happen; if I tell my brother, this will happen," and so on. And you can think of many fairy tales in which that happens. I think that's something that you find much less often in written literature than you do in oral literature. Eliot talked about tradition in that way, at least once as I remember it, in a lecture on Dr. Johnson. He was comparing Marlowe and Tennyson, saying as the verse form developed, and as literature developed, in a way it refined itself at the expense of possibility. In the earlier, apparently cruder way of doing it, you have not only a different kind of energy, but you have a different sense of possibility. I think this is one of the things that happens in English—the metrical verse form that was most traditional in English begins at the time of Chaucer with an importation of the romance form of iambic pentameter into a language which is already a mixture. And of course the new meter replaced a basic parallelism in Middle English, which Middle English shared with Hebrew poetry and with a great deal of oral poetry, with a great deal of the poetry of the Americas. I think that parallelism is probably one of the deep basic forms of poetry, perhaps the basic structure of verse, and is never really lost. . . .

CN: "The Last One" is a poem that's always troubled me a bit, because I've heard you read it before and, with its energy and parallelism and repetition, it's a poem that often generates a murmur of approval and satisfaction from an audience. I tend to suspect that positive reaction, though, because my guess is that people feel the poem gives them a secure moral or ethical vantage point. It's a poem that may seem to be simply in the mode of the conventional science fiction "revenge of the despoiled earth on those who despoiled it." Yet I don't think that's what the poem does. The poem begins "Well they made up their minds to be everywhere because why not," and in a sense the poem in the end makes up *its* mind to be everywhere because why not; or at least the poem, in the voice and manner of the shadow, proceeds to carry out a rhetorical appropriation of the same totalizing, universalizing, covering motion that the possessors begin with as the poem opens. And in that sense— although I think the sense of pain and despair at the kind of ecological tragedy that the poem communicates is not undercut—what *is* undercut, it seems to me, is any secure moral position that we feel we can take in the midst of that catastrophe. Somewhat the same exaltation in power occurs again in "Now It Is Clear" from *The Carrier of Ladders,* which includes the lines "As though I were a great wind / which is what I pray for." The speaker in the poem, and the poem itself in a way, becomes the great wind, as the second half of the poem moves forward. These formal and rhetorical co-optations should force people to call their own moral certainty into question, though at the same time the poems leave that moral certainty as something that is immensely desirable to us.

WSM: I'm so glad you said that, because my chief doubt about the poem is precisely what you have suggested, that it might be understood

as simply saying, from a secure moral vantage point, that *those* people
are doing such dreadful things. That's not the poem, as I see it, and I
think the index of what I mean is in the last line—with its suggestion that the relation with what the shadow is in the poem has been
ignored, despised, thrown away; that's quite as important to me as the
science-fiction aspect of the narrative. I'm reminded of the line in the
psalm, "Yea they despised the pleasant land." The pleasant land was
themselves.

CN: There are a number of irreducible ironies in that last line, "The
lucky ones with their shadows." Are their personal shadows uniquely
their own, as they (or we) might like to believe; i.e., are their shadows
unlike the consuming, generalizing shadow of the rest of the poem? Or
do they each already carry within themselves the semblance, the vestige,
of that covering shadow they hope they have escaped?

WSM: Both. When two people stand together and their shadows run
together, whose shadow is whose? Who owns the shadow?

CN: We've talked about how translations can help initiate your own
poems, but more generally how do your poems *start?* What are the first
things that happen as you begin to write? Is it that sense of a certain
sequence of words coming alive? Does a line or two come to mind as a
first step?

WSM: There's that sort of excitement coming from somewhere. Sometimes it's not even in words yet; it's just somewhere around. But I never
got very far away from that more or less spooky feeling about poetry, you
know, that it does have something to do with the muse's presence, as
Berryman used to describe it—some really very ancient presence that is
referred to and alluded to and invoked again and again in all talk about
poetry up until very recently. It's talked about very foolishly very often,
and very embarrassingly, but without that presence what the hell are
we paying attention to. Without it we're playing an intellectual game
and there are some very brilliant intellectual games going on in the
world at the moment, but among games it's a matter of taste, not a
matter of importance.

EF: You mentioned the other day something Berryman said to you
when you were nineteen . . .

WSM: He said, "At this point I think you should get down in a corner
on your knees and pray to the muse, and I mean it literally."

CN: Once the muse has departed, do you revise a lot?

WSM: Well, I don't know quite how to answer that, Cary; in a sense, a lot—if I look over a draft of a poem, I see that things have been scratched out and scratched out and scratched out, but actually what I really do is write very slowly, and change it a lot as I'm going on. Although very often getting quite close to the final thing right at the beginning, then making minute verbal adjustments until it seems to come out right. But once it reaches a certain point I very seldom go back to it, except maybe either to throw it out or cut hunks out of it, see if I can do with less, see if I've overwritten it.

CN: Do you save chunks that didn't fit in and use them other places?

WSM: I keep thinking I'm going to, but as a matter of fact I very seldom look at them again.

CN: In the manuscript archives there are countless notebooks, pages, scraps of paper, on which there are fragments, sometimes stunning ones, that you have written: you'll write one, draw a line, write another, draw a line. And quite often they are things that never make their way into finished poems. Is that a different kind of writing for you?

WSM: Well, they always represent the hope of writing the full thing of which each is the fragment. They aren't the sort of notes from which you work up a poem, but rather the total idea out of which the poem could grow. And if you don't do it in time, the life goes out of it.

CN: I'm also interested in the published poems you don't collect in books. In *Green with Beasts,* for example, you collect only a few of the animal poems you published.

WSM: All those animal poems were at one time part of that book, but I came to feel that aspect of the book was far too heavy and unbalanced the whole collection. I felt the book was terribly overweighted with rhetoric. In fact, *Green with Beasts* was already in page proof with all those animal poems in it. I called up Rupert Hart-Davis, a wonderful man, and he agreed to make the cuts.

EF: A moment ago you described the "spooky" feeling you have in writing poetry. Do you have the same feeling when you're about to write a piece of prose? Or is writing prose a very different kind of act for you than writing poetry?

WSM: It's not a *very* different kind of act. There's something of the same thing there. I can't write anything without that, because I don't know what else holds imaginative language together. And writing anything else, I find it rather boring, wearisome, and a rather depressing process. That doesn't mean that there's not a great deal of labor involved in writing. I find writing very hard, and I find writing prose in particular very hard. It takes a long time before this mass of writing begins to generate an energy of its own that sustains it, keeps it going. But I don't mean a kind of baroque energy either—sometimes the plainer it can be the stronger it is.

EF: This might be a good time to talk a bit about your new prose project—a book about Hawaii, isn't it?

WSM: Yes; it didn't start out as a book, though—it began as an essay focusing on the island of Kaho'Olawe and on the history of the 'Ohana, the "Protect Kaho'Olawe 'Ohana": *'Ohana* is a Hawaiian word for which there are really no words in the American vocabulary—loosely, it means kin or extended family. "Protect Kaho'Olawe 'Ohana" is literally the family to protect the island—and by extension to protect all of the Hawaiian land from the desecrations it has and is suffering. It's in some ways not a very hopeful cause; maybe there aren't any hopeful causes left. But Kaho'Olawe is an island that needs protecting; it is a national historic monument and also a sacred island for the Hawaiian people, of the same significance for them as Delos is to the Greeks or Iona to the Scots. And it has been bombed by the military since 1939 and is still being used as a bombing target by the Navy. White people have always described it as of "no economic importance," but, to the great surprise of the Navy, it turned out by the late 1970s to be of enormous archaeological significance; through the ages Hawaiians had used it as an observatory and a place of religious instruction. The Kahunas had a kind of Druid college there—it's a place of the spirit. Kaho'Olawe is also the name of the God of the West, the God of the Dead. And this island *is* Kaho'Olawe—in a sense it *is* the god. And, you know, many Hawaiians go to Christian churches and sing fundamentalist hymns, but a part of their psyche is still reserved for their gods, and they don't feel that fooling around with Kaho'Olawe is such a good idea.

EF: How did the essay begin to grow into a book?

WSM: I've had a growing list of things I've wanted to write about that have to do with Hawaii. I think of this Hawaiian book as a gathering together of almost all of my interests—interest in nonliterate peoples, in their and our relation to the earth, to the primal sources of things, our relation to the natural world, our relation to and necessary opposition to the overweening authority of institutions and institutionalized greed, the destruction of the earth for abstract and greedy reasons. Originally I was going to write a series of essays, about fifteen pages each, on different subjects: the one I thought I'd write first was about what was happening to the last of the lepers, the last of the leprosy victims in Hawaii. I was a little hesitant about writing about Hawaii at all, because I thought one more *haole,* one more white person, one more white foreigner writing about the Hawaiians, who needs it? If you want to read Hawaiian history, almost all of it has been written by Americans, and the little bit at the beginning that was written by Hawaiians was written by Christian converts—you don't have anybody coming from inside the culture. And I just didn't want to add to that, because all that vicarious contact with the culture is suspect. But when the nuclear-free ordinance came about, I thought okay, now it's all coming together. I'd been talking to some of my friends who are leprosy patients, who were Hawaiians and were very eager to talk, and I started talking to Leslie Kuloloio, a Hawaiian native friend, and it all started pouring out. I turned on the tape recorder, thought I'd get one little tape from Les, and I think I've got six tapes on both sides now, maybe eight. His story, the story of his relation to the island and what it represented of the Hawaiian past, his family's involvement, the growing Hawaiian movement, and so forth, made so wonderful a narrative that the text of the book began to form, the writing began to swell and swell. And then the same thing happened with a lot of other people too. The history began to emerge in their own words, so I'm using as much of it verbatim as I possibly can.

EF: So the project is becoming something of an oral history.

WSM: Yes, at least it's branched out: you have the basic story, the Hawaiian one, which goes into the whole terrible, unjust, sad story of what's happening to the Hawaiians and their land, and the other story of the rapidly growing military presence, which has been growing over a long period, resulting in CINCPAC now, the abbreviation for probably the largest concentration of manpower in the world. There is a huge nuclear concentration there. The county of Maui, which includes the island of Kaho'Olawe, has recently adopted a nuclear-free ordinance which applies to all four islands and the surrounding waters in Maui County. The county can't enforce it, of course, and the Navy makes a rule of violating it; but it's a case of the federal military deliberately violating the local ordinance and the wishes of the local people. And this fits the pattern of the overall Hawaiian story—again and again this story which one finds in the modern world of people feeling helpless in the face of monolithic power. For me, now, the Pacific, this little uninhabited island of Kaho'Olawe, is the focus of history.

EF: You said your guiding spirits in poetry are Dante and Villon; do you have similar guiding spirits in prose?

WSM: Well, I suspect Cervantes would be one. I love Cervantes: the funny thing is that even when he's not being ironic, there's irony in the prose. I think great prose very often has got one hand on irony. Anything that depends on rational structure has got one hand on irony. If it's really rational, it realizes it. Thoreau's a hero, too, of course; I love his prose.

EF: At what point do you sense when an experience or a feeling will become a poem instead of a piece of prose? I'm curious about what draws certain experiences into prose for you and others into poetry.

WSM: I'm not sure about that at all. Years ago when I was starting to write *The Miner's Pale Children* I wondered about that quite a lot, and sometimes I would start to write something as the one and I'd realize it was the other. The differences I still don't know, yet I've come to the conclusion, thinking about this, that the more passion or intensity there is in a piece of writing, whether it is prose or poetry, the more it calls into question the writing's generic allegiance. In other words, the more charged a piece of prose is, the more it tends toward the condition of poetry. Then you begin to describe it as poetic, or you begin to ask what it was that separated it from poetry. And oddly, I think that this happens with poetry too. The more charged poetry is, then the more it's driven to the point where it does some of the things that prose does. I suppose I believe that because to me the ideal poet is Dante, and some of the most powerful passages in Dante are, as Eliot said, rather flat. At least they look rather flat, though you realize they are anything but flat, but the *plainness* of Dante leads you to think it's just like prose, except it's utterly unlike prose.

CN: Earlier in your career you were writing poems about your family and about your past, some of them never collected in books. Now you're writing prose pieces about the same things.

WSM: New poems about them, too.

EF: That's what led me to think about that corresponding nature of the prose and poetry, because some of the poems in *Opening the Hand* sound very much as if they are the corollary in poetry of the *Unframed Originals* prose pieces.

WSM: Those connections I don't know, of course, because they're not deliberate. As you notice them, or I notice them, then I can guess at what the connections are, but I don't really *know.* One doesn't really know what the connections are between so closely related but obviously distinct things. You don't in your own writing or in your own life.

CN: Is there a sense of return, circularity, completion, in coming back to those topics after so many years?

WSM: There's a sense of it happening, but it's not utterly deliberate, except it was deliberate in that I wanted to deal with that family material in *Unframed Originals.* I've been waiting for two or three years to get circumstances together where I could do it. My notes were in a warehouse and I had no desk to work on, and so forth. A lot of it was done in the house that we were trying to build, before the carpenters would show up in the morning. I'd go down when it got light and work until they arrived about ten o'clock, then stop and start hammering pieces of wood the rest of the day. I never know how to answer those questions about the connections of different writings of the past, because so few of the connections are plotted beforehand. It's like saying, what's the connection in your mind between different parts of a poem—well, you can describe them in terms of the poem, and maybe you set it out beforehand, but maybe it developed as you went along and then you saw what the connection was both as you wrote it and as you look back on it. But a great deal of it is bound to be very subjective, and finally it's not something you can articulate or describe yourself.

CN: You really began writing *Unframed Originals* many years ago, didn't you? In your manuscripts at Illinois, there's an old notebook which you entitled "A View from the Palisades." It's about your taking an old Princeton friend to Union City where you revisit scenes from your childhood, and many of the events you tell end up in *Unframed Originals* in a very different form.

WSM: Yes, I know I began some of that autobiographical writing in the early 1950s; that particular notebook was probably later. There were at least three attempts at writing a long piece of autobiographical prose, which were abandoned for various reasons. They were written in very different ways, and I wasn't satisfied with any of them.

EF: This seems to parallel a process that is evident in your poetry. In *Opening the Hand* we have a rich collection of autobiographical poems that sound very different from the poems we had gotten used to in *The Lice* through *The Compass Flower.* The new poems take us back to *The Drunk in the Furnace,* where we have a much smaller collection of autobiographical poems at the end—but there were also lots of other autobiographical poems that you published in various journals in the 1950s but that you never collected in your books.

WSM: Yes, I thought I had too many of them, and they kind of fell over each other. For all kinds of reasons, during those years in England I was becoming very discontented with being there and with the life I was leading there, and I was feeling more and more cut off from America, and was trying to figure out what it meant, trying to read about it, think about it, remember it, write about it. So some of those poems came out of that, and then they also come out of the first year or so of coming back to America, and again trying to write about it. Most of those poems about my family and about Pennsylvania come from the mid-1950s.

EF: Once we absorb the autobiographical insights of *Unframed Originals, Opening the Hand,* and *Drunk in the Furnace,* and those uncollected poems, I find that much of the rest of your work that before had seemed distant and allegorical begins to resonate with specific autobiographical incidents, sounds more personal.

WSM: Camus said, you know, that writers keep returning to a few basic images. That's probably an oversimplification, but it's more true than is generally noticed. I mean there are certain landscapes and images that one keeps trying to make clearer and clearer, and more keeps coming out of them—they are real images. A real image is a kind of fusion of all aspects of perception and being in one tiny focus. It opens out and reveals everything, doesn't it?

EF: You've mentioned your fondness for Williams. As you talk about the differences between prose and poetry, Williams is certainly one figure in American literature who has worked with that distinction—or lack of it—quite a bit.

WSM: Who calls it constantly into question. I think that's a measure of imaginative richness, calling it into question. You don't wonder about it when you're reading Sidney Lanier, but you wonder about it when you're reading Melville. You wonder about it when you're reading Thoreau, whose verse isn't very interesting, but the power of the wonderful passages in *Walden* is the power of poetry. The energy of the language is as intense as anything in nineteenth-century poetry. You have to think of Keats or Hopkins for something comparable.

EF: Do you go back to Williams?

WSM: Yes. But not as a cult figure, as some people do. I go back to him with great affection and reverence. I really do love Williams, and I read him over and over when I was about twenty; I still read him. I go back to him, how shall I say it, as an engraver. It's the visual quality of individual moments in Williams: not the magnificence of the long poem in *Paterson*, but passages in *Paterson* which I see as separate poems, or the early collected poems, *Spring and All* and that period. Or some of the very late poems.

EF: *Pictures from Brueghel?*

WSM: Yes. He's come back to that vein with a wonderful serenity by that point. And such purity of language. The element of Williams which some of his admirers like so much, the "experimental" element, sometimes seems to be just fooling around. Nothing the matter with fooling around, but I don't find myself returning to it irresistibly. But I imagine I will continue to reread parts of Williams with fondness and gratitude.

EF: Do you go back to the prose of *Spring and All,* or only the poems?

WSM: Less to the prose. I don't like his prose so much as the poems that I'm fondest of. And I read the autobiography, but the prose there is often limp.

EF: *In the American Grain?*

WSM: *In the American Grain* is a wonder—I love that.

CN: Much of that is beautifully composed prose—sentence by sentence, phrase by phrase.

WSM: Yes. Many of the Williamsites seem to ignore the element of composition in that great book, probably the most impressive and imposing single book that he wrote.

CN: I reread parts of it every year.

WSM: There's nothing in it like the really exquisite lyrics, but it's there on the shelf with the great American single volumes. It's on my shelf.

EF: When I think of Williams and his experimentation, I think of course of the poetic line. Whitman and Williams and Olson and Ginsberg— all have written so much about the poetic line, and all have theories about its origins, which they all associate with breath. The theories probably culminate in Olson's "Projective Verse." Williams talked of dividing the Whitman line into three parts, coming up with the triadic line composed of three variable feet, and so on. What are your thoughts about the origin of the line in your own work? Where does your line emerge from?

WSM: I think the line is a matter of absolutely essential importance. If the line is not that important, why is one writing verse in the first place? One of the meanings of verse after all is "a line." Yet one of the ironies of what you just said about Whitman-Williams-Ginsberg is that, though they talked a lot about the line, their tradition has been involved in the demise of the clarity of the line in a great deal of modern and contemporary American verse. It's one of the danger signs in recent verse. There's a huge amount of talent around now, including some really gifted young people coming out of colleges, but some of them have a very shaky sense of what a line is. This is obviously bad for individual poems, but it's also very bad for the possibility of their development as poets or for the development of anything resembling a tradition—even for the continuation of an Olson or a Williams tradition. You can't go anywhere if you're not fairly clear about what a line is. Yet I'm not even sure that I want to say what I think a line is, though I've thought about it. I'll describe how I've taught the topic, though that may prevent me from doing it again.

With students in certain places I've thought it was valuable to try to force them to figure out what they thought a line was. A couple of years ago I was at Oberlin, where the students were very gifted. I read a lot of manuscripts and said, "I'm not going to do the workshop thing of going over your papers and making little suggestions. I don't think that's really the most appropriate thing. What I'd like to do is go around the room and make everybody who wants to be involved in this try to figure out what a line of verse is." After two hours, we hadn't got very far. They realized that they'd never really thought about it. We left it with my saying, "I think this is what you have to think about the next time you stop a line somewhere. At the risk of losing a great deal of spontaneity for a while, you need to look closely, to figure out what in hell you think you're doing: why you stop it after three syllables, why you stop it after two beats, or why you stop it where you do—what are you doing? Are you just writing prose and saying, 'I like it better this way,' or is there really some reason for doing it?"

As far as they could get spontaneously in two hours, these young people who'd read a lot—mostly in their own contemporaries, but they were addressing themselves to poetry with some seriousness—was to realize that a line was a unit of something. What it was a unit *of* was something they couldn't agree on.

CN: Do line breaks seem to come to you naturally as you write, or is that one of the things you have to work with to change?

WSM: Both. And of course there are two things that a line is doing—

it's making a rhythm of its own by means of stopping where it does; and unless you're doing it wrong, unless it's working against you and you've lost it, lost this *line,* it's making a continuity of movement and making a rhythm within a continuity. It's doing those two things at the same time. And this is something that you don't see happening very often in these limp, unheard little bits of prose—lines just tacked one after the other. And their continuity is the continuity of prose. There's no real reason why it should stop at any particular place.

EF: Over the years you've used many different lines. Certainly your lines derive in part from your study of various traditions—I suppose this is one thing that takes you back to Pound, his experimentation with different lines. But does line have any association with breath for you?

WSM: No, I don't think so. It *can,* but I don't think there's any necessary connection. I think of stopping at a given point as a rhythmical gesture, and also as a gesture of meaning—because where you stop, if the rhythm is working, is going to have an effect on the meaning, particularly if you're not punctuating. But it's important to stop in such a way that the stop itself has something to do with impetus. It keeps the motion of the poem going, both in terms of rhythm, sound, and in terms of meaning, denotative meaning.

CN: Your control of line breaks is clearly one of the real strengths of your work over a long period of time. It always seems minutely perfect, yet I have the uncanny feeling that it simply comes to you instinctively.

WSM: I pay a lot of attention to it.

CN: You mentioned punctuation. I don't think you've ever talked about your decision not to use punctuation for such a long period of time. It has always seemed absolutely right. I can't imagine the poetry with punctuation, but have you worked out the appeal and the poetics of abandoning punctuation?

WSM: I don't know about its appeal, but there are various things that led to that decision. I had virtually stopped writing poetry at the end of the '50s, because I felt that I had come to the end of something and that if I wrote again I'd want to do it quite differently. James Wright went through very much the same process, although we never conferred with each other to know that we had both reached that point at the same time. Of course during the time when I wasn't writing, I was thinking about it. There's a passage from Milosz's *The Captive Mind* about the suddenness with which he had this moment of crisis when he was lying on his face on the cobbles with machine gun bullets going around him and friends being herded into trucks, and thinking, what do I want to remember, what poetry has been most important to me, what poetry do I want now, right *now*, this minute? And I thought, I don't ever want to forget this about poetry again: I want to write something to take with me at a bad time. Because we're going to have a bad time from now on.

One of the corollaries of that is that there's a lot you really don't need in poetry. You have to pay attention to things and see what their function is. If there's really no function, what are they doing there? Why are you writing poetry that includes things you really don't need there? This process of trying to see what was unnecessary, of strengthening by compressing and intensifying, of getting down to what was really essential, led me to write poetry that was farther and farther away from conventional stanzaic and metrical structure.

Of course none of this was quite so deliberate. It was part of practice more than theory, and discontent with what I was doing and wanting to articulate the direction in which I was going. I recognized I was moving away from stanzaic verse, but I also saw myself moving farther from prose. So I asked myself what the point was of staying with prose punctuation. Punctuation is there as a kind of manners in prose, articulating prose meaning, but it doesn't necessarily articulate the meaning of this kind of verse. I saw that if I could use the movement of the verse itself and the movement of the line—the actual weight of the language as it moved—to do the punctuation, I would both strengthen the texture of the experience of the poem and also make clear its distinction from other kinds of writing. One would be paying attention to it in those terms. I also noticed something else right away. Punctuation as I looked at it after that seemed to staple the poem to the page, but if I took those staples out the poem lifted itself right up off the page. A poem then had a sense of integrity and liberation that it did not have before. In a sense that made it a late echo of an oral tradition. All this gave the poetry new rules, a new way of being, and I haven't really changed enough to want to give that up.

Someone was asking me the other day about what they called my "broken back" line, the two-part line that I use in a lot of the poems in *Opening the Hand*. I was writing it for a couple of years, and I would still like to feel it is available. Indeed I would like to have it generally available in English. You know, meter is never something permanently absent. I think that line is related to the Middle English line of *Piers Plowman*, which to me is the basic line of English, overlaid—we talked about palimpsests—overlaid, as I said earlier, by the Italianate iambic pentameter. But the caesura in the iambic pentameter is like a ghost of the old Middle English line asserting itself all the time, saying I'm here all the time. I think it's there under what we hear in iambic pentameter. And as the iambic pentameter becomes harder and harder to hear or to stay awake through in contemporary poetry, I think the other, the deeper, older line is something one, with the slightest effort, might be able to hear again.

The difference between that line and iambic pentameter, I think, is a traditional one. Iambic pentameter, because of the long tradition, developed a flexibility which the Middle English line never did. The flow-on qualities of enjambment in iambic pentameter became incredibly varied, but eventually they played themselves out, so that there's hardly a meter there at all. By the time you get to someone like Conrad Aiken you're writing essentially a kind of vers libre. But the enjambment of the Middle English line never developed that way, didn't last long enough probably. If you take up something that is like a continuation of it, it seems a little stiff, but it can do things that iambic pentameter probably can't. And I don't even think of that line with the heavy caesura as a strict meter in the way Pope would have thought of iambic pentameter, but as a different kind of pattern or paradigm.

EF: The caesura obviously controls breath—when you read a line, the line controls your breathing. Maybe this has to do with what you were saying the other day—that one problem with "projective verse" as a theory is not that it assigns too much importance to breath, but not enough.

WSM: But the pauses in verse are not necessarily the pauses of breath, breathing. If the pauses of verse are exactly the pauses of anything else, it becomes boring. It has to have its own pauses.

I like some of Olson's poems very much, but I never cottoned onto that "projective verse." As I remember it, he talks about projective verse and its relation to breath, but it seems to me truistic: the relation of poetry to breath is absolute. And you can come at it from any angle you want to. He talks about it in a rather limited way—that outbreathing and inbreathing in themselves are a kind of metric. I think it's far more complicated, so I doubt that there's much to be gained in pursuing that particular argument.

CN: Different poetry teaches you to breathe in different ways. As you read it there's a learning process; you adjust to it. But I've never seen any way of treating Olson's line as the equivalent of a single breath.

EF: Ginsberg is probably the one who has come closest to trying to suggest that that's absolutely true, that he breathes a line and when his breath is out he moves to the next line.

CN: But it takes a tremendous effort to pull that off, and when he reads in public it's by no means easy to establish that relationship in any literal way.

WSM: Yes, and that also rules out something which is inseparable from it and in a sense more interior or inward—the whole role of hearing, listening, both in writing and in reading or listening. The Ear—the fact that the body is the ear. Breathing also is a way of hearing; they're not separate. But if it's just physical breathing, what role do the ear and listening play?

EF: What's Olson's physiological formula—the Head, by way of the Ear, to the Syllable; the Heart, by way of the Breath, to the Line. Part of his idea, at any rate, is that the *syllable* is what the ear has to do with, not the line. The line has to do with the breathing.

WSM: I don't see that at all, because I think one of the things that happens with all units in verse, in poetry, is tension. There's always one element playing against another one, whether or not it's metrical. In conventional verse the line is made of variations on the iambic pentameter pattern, so you have the pattern and the variation playing against each other, and the tension resulting—and that's one way of seeing the vigor and the energy in the line. And I think this is true in every kind of metric, whether it's conventional and regular or whether it's what you could call organic. There are always going to be two sorts of forces playing against each other: an expectation and either an answering, a refusing, or a variant on the expectation. The expectation sets up a sense of repetition. You either fulfill the repetition or you don't. That tension runs through the making of lines or the making of stanzaic paragraphs, for the whole poem.

EF: That same pattern of expectation and variation is also apparent in the overall rhythm of each of your books as well. Has there been any single one of your books that has affirmed itself to you as *a* book, as a complete thing, more than the others, or do they all have a similar sense of completion?

WSM: They all do, particularly since *The Drunk in the Furnace.*

EF: Including *The Drunk in the Furnace?*

WSM: Including *The Drunk in the Furnace.* The first three seem to be much more gatherings, but they too each finish with the end of a phase. Of course I don't feel that close to them now.

CN: Still, the idea of putting them all together in a collected volume seems inappropriate. I like them as separate objects, even the first four books. But I certainly don't want *The Lice* in the same volume as *The Compass Flower*. They're separate books to me.

WSM: I don't really either. What do you think about a *Selected Poems?*

CN: I can't think of any reason to do it.

WSM: Well, I've resisted it, because I would not like to undercut the separate books.

CN: It may be that if you grow with the poetry and live through the period of time when the poet is actually writing you have a strong feeling of loyalty toward the individual books. Fifty years from now most readers would probably just as well have a *Collected Merwin*. With Yeats, although I am conscious of the huge differences among the books, I'm perfectly happy to have the *Collected Poems*. People who collected the separate volumes, however, often prefer to read them in that form.

WSM: Yes, but Yeats has been collected in the only way that it would make any sense to me. If I were ever collected I would want it done that way, where you're very much aware of the books as divisions. And you'd have to do that with Lowell too, you know, although all of Cal's fooling around with *History* and *Notebooks* presents problems. Nonetheless, you'd want his books very distinct—you wouldn't want *Lord Weary's Castle* and *Life Studies* combined into something like a *Collected Browning*.

EF: One thing that gives your books each a very separate identity are the titles. You tend not to title your books after the name of a poem that is in the book, although you did with *The Drunk in the Furnace*.

WSM: "The Drunk in the Furnace" is really the kind of poem that is about everything the book is about. Generally, though, I don't do that. I guess I made up my mind about it in a conversation with Bill Arrowsmith a long time ago. I'm not proposing this for everybody, but for me a title should contribute something important. So that if you took a poem's title away, it would be missing something. The title should not just be a redundancy. Of course the relation between a poem and its title is far more specific and intimate than the relation between a book and its title, but the title of a book should still make a significant contribution.

EF: Because of the nature of your book titles, the reader is forced to carry the title through each poem, and to allow the juxtaposition of the title of the book and any particular poem to play itself out. The titles of your books force the reader to come to grips with the book as an interrelated whole. At what point do titles for your books come to you?

WSM: I think it's been different. Sometimes I've hung around for a while, listening for one to come, waiting for it. I had a superstition, in the days when I was writing plays, that if I got my title too soon, especially if I got the title before I started to write, that I'd never get the play finished. In any case, there's no point in rushing it. I suppose one reason I know the new collection isn't finished is that I don't have a title for it yet.

The title for *The Lice* came fairly early. It jumped out of that passage in Heraclitus while I was working on the poems. *The Moving Target,* on the other hand, came late. I know that I've got several pages of false attempts at that title. I was also a time waiting for the title to *Writings to an Unfinished Accompaniment,* trying to figure out what on earth is the title of this collection. With *The Compass Flower,* however, I had the title before the book was finished.

CN: Do you save notes for titles and all drafts of poems?

WSM: I keep all the drafts now. I still have some of the old things I wrote in college, but for a while after that I destroyed things. Then Graves told me to save everything and since then I have.

EF: Can you reconstruct the process you go through to come up with a retrospective title like *Writings to an Unfinished Accompaniment?* Do you think through the poems in some way?

WSM: I wasn't thinking at all; I was sitting and waiting for the title. I can remember the chair and the room in Mexico. Of course I was doing other things as well, but ten days went by before the title came. When I got back to New York, Adrienne Rich said, "What are you going to call the new book," and I told her, and she said, "That's it, that's what we all want to write." Those were happier days.

W. S. MERWIN was born in New York City in 1927 and grew up in Union City, New Jersey, and in Scranton, Pennsylvania. From 1949 to 1951 he worked as a tutor in France, Portugal, and Majorca. After that, for several years he made the greater part of his living by translating from French, Spanish, Latin, and Portuguese. Since 1954 several fellowships have been of great assistance. In addition to poetry, he has written articles, chiefly for *The Nation,* and radio scripts for the BBC. He has lived in Spain, England, France, Mexico, and Hawaii, as well as New York City. His books of poetry are *A Mask for Janus* (1952), *The Dancing Bears* (1954), *Green with Beasts* (1956), *The Drunk in the Furnace* (1960), *The Moving Target* (1963), *The Lice* (1967), *The Carrier of Ladders* (1970), for which he was awarded the Pulitzer Prize, *Writings to an Unfinished Accompaniment* (1973), *The Compass Flower* (1977), and *Opening the Hand* (1983). His translations include *The Poem of the Cid* (1959), *Spanish Ballads* (1960), *The Satires of Persius* (1961), *Lazarillo de Tormes* (1962), *The Song of Roland* (1963), *Selected Translations 1948–1968* (1968), for which he won the P.E.N. Translation Prize for 1968, *Transparence of the World,* a translation of his selection of poems by Jean Follain (1969), *Osip Mandelstam, Selected Poems* (with Clarence Brown) (1974), *Selected Translations, 1968–1978* (1979), *From the Spanish Morning* (1985), and *Four French Plays* (1985). He has also published three books of prose, *The Miner's Pale Children* (1970), *Houses and Travellers* (1977), and *Unframed Originals* (1982). In 1974 he was awarded the Fellowship of the Academy of American Poets. In 1979 he was awarded the Bollingen Prize for Poetry.

ED FOLSOM teaches English at the University of Iowa, where he also edits the *Walt Whitman Quarterly Review* and coedits *The Iowa Review.* He is coeditor of *Walt Whitman: The Measure of His Song* and *W. S. Merwin: Essays on the Poetry.* He has published numerous essays on American literature and is presently completing *Talking Back to Walt Whitman.*

CARY NELSON teaches English and criticism and interpretive theory at the University of Illinois, where he was also the founding director of the Unit for Criticism and Interpretive Theory. He is the author of *The Incarnate Word: Literature as Verbal Space* and *Our Last First Poets: Vision and History in Contemporary American Poetry,* the editor of *Theory in the Classroom,* and the coeditor of *W. S. Merwin: Essays on the Poetry* and *Marxism and the Interpretation of Culture.* He is presently completing *Reading Criticism: The Literary Status of Critical Discourse.*